THE ANNOTATED BIBLE

Volume 4

THE ANNOTATED BIBLE

Volume 1

Genesis to Deuteronomy (I)
Joshua to Second Chronicles (II)

Volume 2

Ezra to Psalms (III)
Proverbs to Ezekiel (IV)
Daniel to Malachi (V)

Volume 3

Matthew to The Acts (VI)
Romans to Ephesians (VII)

Volume 4

Philippians to Hebrews (VIII)
James to Revelation (IX)

(Originally published by "Our Hope Press" in nine volumes)

The Holy Scriptures Analyzed and Annotated

The Annotated Bible

by

ARNO C. GAEBELEIN

VOLUME 4

Philippians to Revelation

MOODY PRESS

LOIZEAUX BROTHERS

A Nonprofit Organization, Devoted to the Lord's Work
and to the Spread of His Truth

ISBN 0–87213–210–2 (complete set)
ISBN 0–87213–214–5 (this volume)

Library of Congress Catalog Card Number: 78–119745

Printed in the United States of America

CONTENTS

The Epistle to the Philippians 1
The Epistle to the Colossians 37
The First Epistle to the Thessalonians 87
The Second Epistle to the Thessalonians 123
The First Epistle to Timothy 143
The Second Epistle to Timothy 177
The Epistle to Titus 203
The Epistle to Philemon 219
The Epistle to the Hebrews 227

Second Section

The Epistle of James 1
The First Epistle of Peter 47
The Second Epistle of Peter 89
The First Epistle of John 123
The Second and Third Epistles of John 163
The Epistle of Jude 173
The Revelation 185

PHILIPPIANS

CONTENTS

PAGE

Introduction **1**
Division of the Book of Philippians **4**
Analysis and Annotations **6**

The Epistle to the Philippians.

Introduction.

The city of Philippi was built as a military position by Philip the Great of Macedon to keep the wild Thracians in check, which were the neighbors of the Macedonians. Later it became a Roman colony by Augustus, as a memorial of his victory over Brutus and Cassius. It was not a very important city. The Jews had not settled there at all, so that the city did not contain a synagogue. In Acts xvi:12 Philippi is called "the chief city of that part of Macedonia." This does not mean that Philippi was the chief city of all Macedonia, which Thessalonica was; but Philippi was the chief city of that district and the first city to which Paul and his companions came. The historical record of the Apostle's visit to Philippi and how the Gospel was preached there, for the first time on European ground, is found in the book of Acts (Chap. xvi). The conversion of Lydia, her hospitality to the servants of Christ, the demon possessed girl and her deliverance, the suffering of Paul and Silas on account of it, their prayer and praise in the prison, the earthquake, the conversion of the jailer and of his house, are the interesting and blessed incidents connected with the beginning of the church in Philippi. The Apostle probably visited this city twice after this (Acts xx:1 and 6), though the details of these visits are not reported in the book of Acts.

The church in Philippi was greatly attached to the Apostle Paul. He had no need to defend his apostleship and authority, for the Philippians had not been affected by the false Judaizing teachers, who had wrought such havoc in Galatia and Corinth. This must have been due to the fact that there were few Jews in that city. But the Apostle evidently feared the invasion of the Philippian assembly by these false teachers. This we learn from the warning given in chapter iii:2. The church itself was poor and had much trial and affliction; yet did they minister out of their deep poverty to other needy saints (2 Cor. viii:1–2; Phil. i:28–30). They had also ministered liberally to the Apostle twice shortly after he had left them (Phil. iv:15–16); he received their fellowship in Thessalonica. The third time they had remembered him. Epaphroditus was their messenger who brought the love-gift to the prisoner of the Lord. In return the Apostle sent to the beloved Philippians another gift, this beautiful epistle, dictated by the Spirit of God.

Written From Rome.

That this epistle to the Philippians was written by Paul seems almost impossible to doubt. "Indeed, considering its peculiarly Pauline psychological character, the total absence from it of all assignable motive for falsification, the spontaneity and fervor of its effusions of feeling—he must be a bold man who would call its authorship in question" (Alford). Yet the critics are bold and leave nothing unquestioned and some have questioned the genuineness of this document. Needless to say the epistle has not suffered by this foolish criticism. The ancient testimony of Polycarp, Irenaeus, Clement of Alexandria and others mentions this epistle as being Pauline and written by him in Rome, during his imprisonment, of which we read in Acts xxviii:30–31. The question arises at what time of his prison life he wrote this letter. It was not in the very beginning, but must have been towards the end. The Philippians had heard of his imprisonment and had made up a sum of money which Epaphroditus carried in person to Rome. And Epaphroditus had fallen sick and the Philippians had heard of his severe illness "nigh unto death" (Phil. ii:30). This sickness of their beloved Epaphroditus had been in turn reported to them (Phil. ii:26) and the Apostle heard how they had been grieved on account of it. All this necessitated a number of journeys from Rome to Philippi and back. This took a good many months. And furthermore, in the beginning of his stay in Rome he dwelt for two years in his own hired house and seemed to have perfect liberty (Acts xxviii:30). In his epistle to the Philippians he writes that he is in the praetorium and no longer in his own house. "But I would have you know, brethren, that the circumstances in which I am here turned out rather to the furtherance of the Gospel, so that my bonds have become manifest as being in Christ in all the praetorium and to all others" (Phil. i:12–13, revised translation). The praetorium was the place where the praetorium guards were kept, next to the palace of the Emperor Nero. He had now been put in stricter confinement and felt his bonds more severely (see Phil. i:18). The epistle must therefore have been written by him after the epistles to the Ephesians, Colossians and Philemon, that is, about the middle of the year 63 A.D.

The Epistle of Christian Experience.

Philippians is put in our Bibles between Ephesians and Colossians. A better arrangement is to put this epistle after Colossians. The epistle to the Ephesians shows the believer's position in Christ and what he possesses in Him; Colossians reveals the glory of Christ as the Head of the body in whom all the fullness of the Godhead dwells bodily. Philippians also speaks of Christ, but not in a doctrinal way. It is an epistle which describes the walk and the life of one who has apprehended his position in Christ and walks therefore in the power of the Spirit of God. It shows what manner of lives those should live on earth who are saved by grace and who are waiting for glory. The epistle assumes the knowledge of what the salvation of God is. We therefore find nothing said about justification, peace with God or assurance of salvation. The word "salvation" as used in Philippians has nowhere the meaning of salvation by grace in the sense of deliverance from guilt and condemnation. Philippians shows us what true Christian experience is in the power of the Spirit of God. The words "sins" and "sin" are not found in this epistle. The true believer knows that his sins are put away and that the old man was crucified with Christ. The question of deliverance from the guilt of sin and from the power of sin, as so blessedly revealed in Romans, does not enter into true Christian experience. True Christian experience is to walk in the power of the Holy Spirit and to manifest Christ in that walk. This the epistle to the Philippians reveals from beginning to end. The name of our Lord is used over fifty times in the four chapters. He is the believer's life; Christ must be always before the heart and He must be made known by the believer in his life, following Him as the pattern and looking to Him as the goal.

The words "joy" and "rejoicing" are used eighteen times in Philippians. It is the epistle of rejoicing. "He went on his way rejoicing" is the description of the experience of the Eunuch after he had believed on the Lord. The true believer's way should be one of constant rejoicing. The whole atmosphere of this epistle is that of joy, and so the believer in whatever earthly circumstances he may be placed should manifest the joy of the Lord. Paul, the great Apostle, and now the prisoner of the Lord, as years before in the Philippian prison, sends forth from the Roman prison the triumphant song of faith and holy joy. There is not a word of murmur or complaint. It is "counting it all joy" and "glorying in tribulation." He had Christ; He knew Christ; Christ was his all; he knew himself in His hands and the glorious goal was ever before him and the Holy Spirit filled him therefore with joy. And such should be the experience of every believer. The word Philippians means "those who love horses." The race-horse in fullest energy stretches its neck to reach the goal. This epistle describes also the Christian race. This is especially seen in the third chapter where the energy and holy ambition of the new life to win Christ, to attain and to reach the goal is given. The epistle likewise reveals the real affection and fellowship which exists between the servant of the Lord and those who have received blessing through his ministry. The annotations of this precious little epistle contain many hints on the true Christian experience and walk.

The Division of Philippians.

The division into four chapters is the correct one. As stated in the introduction it is true Christian experience which this little epistle unfolds, showing the motives which should govern the believer in his life, the energy he should manifest, the resources which are at his disposal and the victory over all circumstances through Christ. The Christian in a normal, spiritual condition as seen in this epistle has been aptly described as on a journey with an object before him, which is Christ. The Lord Jesus Christ is therefore the theme of each chapter. Hence we have four aspects of the true Christian life and experience.

In the *first* chapter Christ is made known as the all-controlling principle of the life of the believer. Christ is our life; He indwells the believer, and true Christian life and experience is to live for Him and be fully controlled by the Lord. "For to me to live is Christ and to die is gain" (i:21). In the *second* chapter Christ is seen in His humiliation and obedience as the believer's pattern. The One who passed through this life, who left the glory to humble Himself, who was obedient unto death, the death of the cross; He who endured the cross and despised the shame, who is now exalted at the right hand of God and has a name which is above every name, is to be constantly before the believer's heart. "Let this mind be in you, which was also in Christ Jesus" (ii:5). In the *third* chapter Christ is the bright object and the final goal before the believer. In the energy of the new life the believer reaches out after that goal, never satisfied with anything else. It is the desire to win actually Christ, to lay hold of that for which he has been laid hold of by Christ. "That I may know Him, and the power of His resurrection, and the fellowship of His sufferings, being made conformable unto His death; if by any means I might attain unto the out-resurrection from the dead" (iii:10–11). In the *fourth* chapter we learn that Christ is enough for all circumstances. The believer, who, like the great Apostle, can say, "for me to live is Christ"; who ever follows His path of self-humiliation and obedience, constantly reaching out for the goal, will find that Christ is sufficient for all earthly circumstances. "I can do all things through Christ who strengtheneth me" (iv:13). This then is the division of this brief but most important and practical epistle:

I. **CHRIST, THE CONTROLLING PRINCIPLE OF THE BELIEVER'S LIFE.** Chapter i.

II. **CHRIST, THE BELIEVER'S PATTERN.** Chapter ii.

III. **CHRIST, THE OBJECT AND THE GOAL.** Chapter iii.

IV. **CHRIST, THE BELIEVER'S STRENGTH, SUFFICIENT FOR ALL CIRCUMSTANCES.** Chapter iv.

Analysis and Annotations.

I. CHRIST, THE CONTROLLING PRINCIPLE OF THE BELIEVER'S LIFE.

CHAPTER I.

1. The Introduction. 1–2.
2. The Fellowship in the Gospel. 3–8.
3. The Apostle's Prayer. 9–11.
4. Paul's Victory. 12–20.
5. Paul's Life and Confidence. 21–26.
6. Exhortation to Walk Worthy of the Gospel. 27–30.

Verses 1–2. The introductory words to this epistle differ from those of the preceding epistles in that he does not mention his apostleship. The reason for this omission is because his letter to the Philippians does not unfold the great doctrines of the Gospel, nor does it correct evil teachings. In writing to them about his own experience as illustrating Christian experience, he does so as a member of the body of Christ. Associating Timotheus, his son in the gospel, with himself as servant of Christ Jesus, he addresses all the saints in Philippi with the bishops and deacons. Notice the way the name of our Lord is used in this opening verse of the epistle: "Servants of Christ Jesus" (not Jesus Christ as in the authorized version) and "saints in Christ Jesus." Christ is His name as the risen One, as Peter declared on the day of Pentecost, "God has made Him both Lord and Christ." The attention is directed at once to Him as the risen, glorified One by putting His title "Christ" first. Believers are saints, that is, separated ones, and servants in the risen, exalted Lord; He must ever be before the heart in life and walk down here and all service must come from Himself. All the saints are mentioned first and then the bishops and deacons. The bishops are the overseers, who are also called elders; the deacons were ministers. The custom of ritualistic Christendom in electing a man a bishop, who has charge over a diocese, the oversight of so many churches, with certain functions of authority, is not according to Scripture. They had a number of bishops, overseers, in the small assembly in Philippi as well as in Ephesus. Acts xx:28 gives their work and responsibility. "Take heed therefore unto yourselves, and to all the flock, over which the Holy Spirit hath made you overseers (bishops), to feed the church of God, which He hath purchased with His own blood." And these chosen ones who labor for the flock are to be recognized and esteemed. "And we beseech you, brethren, to know them which labor among you, and are over you in the Lord, and admonish you. And to esteem them very highly in love for their work's sake" (1 Thess. v:12–13). The deacons probably ministered more in temporal affairs. Of bishops and deacons and their qualifications the Apostle writes more fully in 1 Tim. iii.

Verses 3-8. And as he remembered them all and thought of their love and devotion he thanked God for them. "I thank my God upon every remembrance of you, always in every prayer of mine making request for you all with joy, because of your fellowship in the gospel from the first day until now." He remembers with praise to God their fellowship in the gospel, how they took part in the trials, labors, conflicts occasioned by the preaching of that gospel. They had taken a zealous part in the gospel Paul preached and manifested a loving interest by ministering to the needs of the Lord's servant. The remembrance of all which had happened when he was in Philippi and their combined fellowship and steadfastness filled the prisoner of the Lord with gratitude and joy. Therefore he prayed for them continually; he carried them upon his heart and in the prayer of intercession mentioned their names before the throne of Grace. How Christ-like this was. He ever carries His dear people upon His heart and intercedes for them. If we love the saints of God we also will pray for them. This gives joy, courage and confidence. Being confident of this very thing, that He who hath begun a good work in you will perform it until the day of Jesus Christ. Even as it is meet for me to think of you all because ye have me in your hearts,* and that, both in my bonds and in the defence and confirmation of the gospel, ye all are partakers of my grace." The grace of God had wrought this loving spirit in the Philippians; the Lord had produced all this interest in the gospel and their whole-hearted devotion. And so the Apostle is confident that He who had done all this in them, who had begun the good work, would surely complete it until the day of Jesus Christ, when all His Saints meet Him face to face. They had him in their hearts, not merely as a fellow-saint, but they had loving sympathy for him in his sufferings and as the one who suffered for the defence and confirmation of the gospel. And Paul, knowing their love and heart-fellowship, in return longed after them. The response to their affection was his affectionate desire. What a blessed illustration of the command of our Lord, "A new commandment I give unto you, that ye love one another, as I have loved you, that ye also love one another" (John xiii:34). How little of this real affection there is among the children of God! How much fault-finding, sectarian exclusion from fellowship, especially among those who claim deliverance from sectarianism, and how little real manifestation of love towards all the Saints! It is one of the leading characteristics of the Laodicean condition.

Verses 9–11. The Apostle now utters his inspired prayer for them. It is still the prayer of the Holy Spirit for God's people. They had love, but he prays that their love may abound yet more and more. But this abounding love is to be "in knowledge and all intelligence." Love must not and will not tolerate evil. If the heart is fixed on the Lord Jesus Christ, then the Christian will manifest this love in knowledge and all intelligence, having discernment of good and evil. As Christ is before the heart the believer will abound yet more and more in love and also "judge of and approve the things that are excellent." Walking after this rule means to be "pure and without offence till the day of

*The authorized version has it "because I have you in my heart"; the correct translation is "Ye have me in your hearts."

Christ." That day is not the Old Testament day of the Lord, when He is revealed on earth in power and glory to judge and to establish His kingdom, but it is the day for the Saints when they meet Him in the air and then appear before His judgment seat. And such a walk produces the fruits of righteousness which are by Jesus Christ, unto the glory and praise of God. Thus it is seen that love is the source of everything in the life of the believer.

Verses 12–20. After the words of love and prayer Paul speaks of himself and his circumstances. But how does he speak of that which had happened unto him? There is not a word of murmur or complaint. Not a word of uncertainty or doubt. Not even a thought of self-pity or discontent. He might have accused himself about having gone to Jerusalem; to create sympathy he might have complained and described his bonds and the sufferings. But he rises above all. Christ is in his life the controlling principle. His own self is out of sight and he bears joyful testimony how all turned out for good, for the furtherance of the gospel. He had written to the Romans years before that all things work together for good to them that love God. In Rome, a prisoner, he shows practically the truth of that statement. The overruling hand of the Lord was manifested in the furtherance of the gospel, even in the praetorium, adjoining Nero's palace. It was enough for him who was so devoted to Christ and the gospel of grace. And his bonds encouraged many in becoming more bold to speak the word without fear. Who were they who preached Christ out of envy and strife, who tried to add still more affliction to his bonds? They were such who were selfish, envying the great apostle for his gifts and power. They were jealous of him. And now when he was in prison, his widespread activities completely arrested, they began to speak against his person and perhaps used his imprisonment as an evidence against him, that claiming too much authority, the Lord had set him aside. By their envy and strife, they would add affliction to the apostle. And yet they preached Christ. The prisoner of the

Lord rises above it all. He is not self-controlled, but Christ controls him. And so he writes, "What then? notwithstanding every way, whether in pretence or in truth, Christ is preached; and I therein do rejoice, yea, and will rejoice." "God was with His servant; and instead of the self-seeking which instigated these sorry preachers of the truth, there was found in Paul the pure desire for the proclamation of the gospel of Christ, the whole value of which he deeply felt, and which he desired above all, be it in what way it might." His own self was completely out of sight. Christ was his all; in Him he rejoiced and though he was in prison he was filled with joy that the worthy Name was being proclaimed.

He speaks next of his confidence that this will turn out to his salvation through their prayer and the supply of the Spirit of Jesus Christ. What salvation is it he means? It is not salvation in the sense of deliverance from guilt and condemnation. Of this the Apostle Paul was not in doubt; for this he did not need the prayers of others. Deliverance from the guilt of sins and from condemnation is the gift of God in Christ Jesus. We are saved once for all by the finished work of the cross. To this salvation nothing can be added. Believers are saved and forever safe in Christ. "There is therefore now no condemnation to them that are in Christ Jesus" (Rom. viii:1). Salvation in the New Testament has two more meanings. There is a salvation for the believer when the Lord Jesus comes again. "We are saved in hope" (Rom. viii:27). And there is a present salvation which the believer needs day by day as he journeys towards the blessed goal. In the midst of trials, temptations, hardships and other perils, victory over all these things is to be gained and Christ's name to be exalted and glorified. The salvation we have in Christ through Christ is to be practically manifested. For this the Apostle desired the prayers of the Philippians; for this he needed, and we also, the supply of the Spirit. The latter certainly not in the sense, as some teach, of a new baptism of the Spirit. The Holy Spirit indwells the believer and if the heart is set upon Christ and controlled by Him, the supply of the Spirit will not be lacking. Therefore the Apostle's earnest expectation and hope was that he would be ashamed in nothing, that he would be victor in all these circumstances. Christ would be magnified in his body whether by life or by death.

Verses 21–26. The great principle of his life, the all governing principle, was Christ. He was all in Paul's life. "For me to live is Christ" means that Christ lived in him (Gal. ii:20); he lived by Him and for Him. If death should come it would be gain, for it would bring him to Christ. But he finds himself in a strait betwixt two things. He has a desire to depart and to be with Christ, which would be far better and yet, if he was to live still down here, it was worth his while. Far better for him personally to depart and be delivered from all the conflicts, trials and sufferings; but, on the other hand, the needs down here, the Saints who needed him and his labors, induce him to decide to choose "to abide in the flesh," for it was more needful for them. So he decides to remain, no matter what sufferings were still in store for him, so that he might minister unto their spiritual needs. How unselfish! How very much like Christ! Self again is all out of sight. And there is no mention made of Nero and his power. Through faith Paul knew himself not in the hands of Rome but in the hands of Christ.

We must not overlook the argument against the false doctrine of soul-sleep, which is contained in the words of the Apostle—"to depart and be with Christ, which is far better." This false doctrine claims that when the believer dies he passeth into a state of unconsciousness. If this were true it would certainly not be "far better" to depart, or as the original states, "much more better." Enjoying the fellowship with the Lord is a good and blessed thing. To pass out of the body and to be with Him is "much more better," for in the disembodied state, the Saints of God enjoy and know the Lord in a degree that is impossible down here. And the best of all is when the Lord comes and all the redeemed receive their glorified bodies.

Verses 27–30. And now he desires that their life should be worthy of the gospel he loved so well. He wants them to stand fast in one spirit and with one mind striving together for the gospel; this was to be their attitude whether he was present with them or absent. Only the Holy Spirit could accomplish this; He only can give to believers oneness in all things and power to strive together for the gospel. Walking thus believers need not to be terrified by the adversaries, those who oppose and reject the gospel. These adversaries always try to inspire fear, like the enemies of Israel in the land. But looking to the Lord, letting Him govern all things, walking in the Spirit, it was an evident testimony of their own promised salvation (which here means the final deliverance) and to their enemies an evident token of perdition. And suffering through which they passed in Philippi, as well as the Apostle in the prison of Rome, is viewed as a gift of God, just as much as believing on Christ. It is then a gracious, God-given privilege to suffer for His sake. Murmuring and complaining will be completely silenced when suffering for Christ's sake is looked upon as a gift of grace. "Blessed are ye when men shall revile you and persecute you and shall say all manner of evil against you falsely for my sake. Rejoice and be exceeding glad, for great is your reward in heaven, for so persecuted they the prophets, which were before you."

II. CHRIST, THE BELIEVER'S PATTERN.

CHAPTER II.

1. Oneness of Mind through Self-Effacement. 1–4.
2. The Humiliation and Exaltation of Christ. 5–11.
3. Work Out your Own Salvation. 12–13.
4. As Lights in the World. 14–16.
5. The Example of Paul. 17–18.
6. The Example of Timotheus. 19–24.
7. The Example of Epaphroditus. 25–30.

Verses 1–4. This chapter puts before us Christ as our pattern. The path He went is to be the believer's path. He trod the way, and the many sons He brings ere long with Himself to glory are called upon to follow Him in the same way. And what honor, what glory, to be called to follow in the same path! The chapter begins with a loving appeal of the prisoner of the Lord. He reminds them of the comfort in Christ which was their blessed portion, of the comfort of love and the fellowship of the Spirit and the bowels of mercies, the results of these precious possessions of the gospel. And now while they had manifested all this in a practical way among themselves and towards the Apostle, he tells them that they would fulfill his joy by being of the same mind, having the same love, united in soul and thinking one thing. That they had difficulties among themselves may be learned from the fourth chapter. And so he desired that all might be one. It is a precious echo of our Lord's prayer in John xvii. Nothing is to be done among His people in the self-seeking spirit of strife or vain-glory. This is the spirit of the natural man and of the world. The true way which becomes the followers of the Lord Jesus Christ, who live by Him and for Him, is to esteem the other better than himself in lowliness of mind, regarding not each his own things (or qualities) but each the things of others also. To walk in such a manner is only possible with those who have received, by being born again, a new nature and walk in the power of the Spirit of God. To be utterly forgetful of self, complete self-effacement and self-denial and thus the absence of strife and vain-glory and the manifestation of true humility, is the manifestation of the mind of Christ. But is it possible at all times to esteem each other better than himself?

We let another answer: "There will be no difficulty in this if we are really walking before God; we shall be occupied with each other's good, and the one will esteem the other better than himself, because when the Soul is really before the Lord, it will see its own short-comings and imperfections, and will be in self-judgment; and according to the love and spirit of Christ see all the good that is from Him in a brother and one dear to Him, and will therefore look upon his fellow-Christian as better than himself, and so all would be in beautiful harmony; and we should be looking after each other's interests too."* How true it is, love likes to be a servant; selfishness likes to be served.

Verses 5–11. With the fifth verse begins that portion of the chapter which reveals Christ as our pattern. Christ in His humiliation and His exaltation; Christ who did not please Himself, who was obedient unto death, the death of the cross; Christ, who is now exalted and has a name which is above every other name, is blessedly before us in these verses. There are seven steps which lead down deeper and deeper, even to the death of the cross. And there are seven steps which lead up higher and higher.

His Humiliation.

1. He thought it not robbery to be equal with God.
2. He humbled Himself.
3. He became a servant.
4. He was made in the likeness of man.
5. He was found in fashion as a man.
6. He became obedient.
7. Obedient to the death of the Cross.

His Exaltation.

1. God highly exalted Him.
2. Gave Him the Name above every name.
3. Every knee is to bow at His name.

*On Philippians, by J. N. Darby.

4. Things in heaven must acknowledge Him.
5. Things on earth.
6. Things under the earth.
7. Every tongue must confess Him as Lord.

"Let this mind be in you which was also in Christ Jesus." The Spirit of Christ is in the believer for this very purpose, not that we should be imitators of Christ, but that His own life may be reproduced in us. We have this mind of Christ in the divine nature. What wonderful grace that we are called with such a calling, to be in His fellowship and follow His own path! Having delivered us from guilt and condemnation we are called to walk even as He walked down here, the author and finisher of the faith.

We trace briefly His path. We behold Him first in His absolute Deity, "subsisting in the form of God." He ever was and is God; as we know from the opening of the gospel of John, "In the beginning was the Word, and the Word was with God and the Word was God." Who can describe what glory was His? And the equality with God which is His He did not esteem an object to be grasped at, but He emptied* Himself. He gave up something which was His; He laid aside His outward glory. Some teach that He laid aside His Deity. This is positively an unscriptural and evil doctrine. It is widely known in theological circles as the Kenosis-theory, which is so dishonoring to our adorable Lord. He could never be anything else but the true God and the eternal life. He came down from the heights of eternal and unfathomable glory and took on a body prepared for Him, yet in that body He was very God. John xvii:5 shows of what He emptied Himself.

The next step tells us that He who gave up, came down. "He took upon Him the form of a servant, taking His place in the likeness of men." Had He taken upon Himself the form of an angel, it would have been an humiliation, for He created the angels. But He was made a little lower than the angels. He took on the servant's form in

*This is the correct translation and better than the St. James version, "He made of Himself no reputation."

the likeness of men. But in Him was no sin, so that it was impossible for Him to sin, for He knew no sin and was in all points tempted as we are, apart from sin.

But the path did not end with this. He who gave up the glory, He who came down and became a servant also became obedient. It was an obedience unto death, the death of the cross. Wonderful condescension and love. It was all for our sake. And redeemed by His precious blood, called into His own fellowship, His way must become ours; we are to follow Him. If we then consider Him and let this mind be in us which was also in Christ Jesus, self will have nothing more to say; all strife and vain-glory will be at an end. And this path of giving up, coming down, true humility, self-denial and true obedience is the only one in which there is perfect peace and rest for the child of God. "Learn of Me, for I am meek and lowly in heart and you shall find rest for your souls."

The description of His exaltation follows. God has highly exalted Him and given Him a name which is above every name. God raised Him from the dead and gave Him glory. What glory it is! In the first chapter of Hebrews we read that the risen man Christ Jesus is the heir of all things, "made so much better than the angels, as He hath by inheritance obtained a more excellent name than they" (Heb. i:4). In Him we have also obtained an inheritance. Before He ever received that glory He prayed to the Father "the glory Thou hast given me I have given to them" (John xvii:22). In His glorious exaltation He is likewise our pattern. We shall see Him as He is and shall be like Him, His fellow-heirs. And while we follow in His steps down here we can look upon Him seated in the highest heaven and rejoice that we shall some day be with Him and share His glory. Every knee must ultimately bow at the name of Jesus, even beings under the earth, infernal beings. They must own His title in glory. Yet this does not make them saved beings. Nor does this passage teach that ultimately all the lost will be saved, as claimed by restitutionists and others. The fact that every tongue will have to confess that Jesus Christ is Lord does not mean the salvation of the lost. In Col. i:20 things, or beings in heaven and on earth are also mentioned in connection with reconciliation, but then the things under the earth are omitted. See our annotations on that passage.

Verses 12–13. Words of exhortation come after this blessed paragraph in which the Lord Jesus is put before us as our pattern. "Work out your own salvation with fear and trembling, for it is God who worketh in you both to will and to do according to His good pleasure." These words are misunderstood by many Christians. It is being taught that Christians should work for their own salvation. This is the grossest perversion of this exhortation. Every true believer has salvation which is given to Him by grace. It is his own salvation; he does not need to work for it. Others say that one who is really saved by grace must work in order to stay saved, and work with fear and trembling. They tell us, if a believer does not keep on working, if he fails and sins, he will fall from grace and is in danger to be unsaved and lost again. This also is unscriptural; the Word of God teaches the eternal security of all who have received eternal life, the gift of God in Christ Jesus our Lord. The exhortation does not mean that we must work to keep ourselves saved, but it means that our *own* salvation which we *have* in Christ is to be worked out into result. Salvation is to be practically manifested in the life and walk by glorifying Christ. We are to work it out after the blessed pattern of Christ with fear and trembling, not the fear of being lost, but the fear of failure in not walking in lowliness of mind, in true humility and in obedience. This will ever be the chiefest concern of the believer who walks in the Spirit. "It is this, therefore, which is to induce the fear and trembling; not in selfish dread, but the sense of our responsibility to Him to whom we owe our all and whose our life is. Plenty there is to make us serious in such work as this, but nothing to dishearten us. If God has taken in hand to work in us after this fashion, that is ample security for our success. The fact that the apostle was now absent from them, whose presence had been so great a comfort and blessing to their souls, was only to make them more completely realize this divine power which was carrying them on to the full blessing beyond."*

Verses 14–16. If we thus work out our own salvation, with Christ ever before us as our pattern, following after Him in the same path, we shall do all things without murmurings and reasonings. These are the fruits of the old self. But following Him as our pattern there will be no more strife and vain-glory; we shall esteem the other better than ourselves and consequently there will be no murmurings. Furthermore, like our Lord was "harmless and sincere," we shall be harmless and sincere, irreproachable children of God in the midst of a crooked and perverted generation, without any self-assertion whatever. And as He was the light down here, so are believers now to shine as lights. As He on earth was the Word of life, holding it forth is what the apostle writes believers should also do, "holding forth the Word of life, that I may rejoice in the day of Christ, that I have not run in vain, neither labored in vain" (See 1 Thess. ii:19–20).

Verses 17-18. Three witnesses follow whose experiences tell us that the grace of God can produce such a character after the pattern of Christ in the believer. First, the Apostle speaks of himself. "Yea and if I am poured out as a libation on the sacrifice and ministration of your faith I rejoice, and rejoice in common with you all. For the same cause also do ye joy and rejoice with me." With death threatening, the prisoner of the Lord expresses His joy. Paul speaks of what the Philippians did, their ministrations of faith as the greater thing; he looks upon it all as a sacrifice and himself and his service only as a libation; that is, he views his own life poured out upon it. Thus he manifested lowliness of mind in regarding the devotion of the Philippians as the sacrifice, and the devotion of his

---

*Numerical Bible.

own life he regards only as poured out as a drink offering (the symbol of joy) upon their sacrifice.

Verses 19–24. Timotheus is the next witness. Of him Paul writes, "For I have no one like minded who will care naturally for your state (or, who will care with genuine feeling how ye get on). For all seek their own things and not the things of Christ." Many already there lived selfishly, seeking in service their own things and not serving and walking, glorifying Christ. So it is today in the Laodicean condition into which Christendom is fast sinking. But Timotheus, Paul's spiritual son (1 Tim. i:2) was a blessed exception. He was in fullest fellowship with the Apostle, like-minded, who forgot himself completely and cared genuinely for the Philippians. They knew the proof of him, for as a son with the father, he served with the Apostle in the gospel. The two, Paul and Timothy, illustrate what it means "to be like-minded, having the same love, being of one accord, of one mind" (verse 2). And thus it ought to be among all the members of the body of Christ. What a comfort Timotheus must have been to Paul in the Roman prison! What cheer and joy to have such a one with him! What refreshment to his soul! But he is willing to give him up. "But I trust in the Lord Jesus to send Timotheus shortly unto you, that I also may be of good comfort, when I know your state." Not seeking his own, in self-denying devotion, he is willing to part with him, so that the Philippians might enjoy his fellowship.

Verses 25–30. Another gracious witness is Epaphroditus. He also manifests the mind of Christ. Epaphroditus was the messenger of the Philippians. He brought to Rome the collection, expressing the fellowship of the church in Philippi. But he had been taken violently ill in the exercise of his service, "for the work of Christ he was nigh unto death." He did not regard his own life and in this he exemplified the Lord Jesus Christ. "Greater love can no one show than that he lays down his life for his friends." His was a service in entire forgetfulness of self. And when he was sick nigh unto death "God had mercy on him." The

Philippians also heard of the dangerous illness of their beloved messenger. They must have been deeply grieved. Then unselfish Epaphroditus was greatly distressed because the Philippians had heard of his illness. In his suffering, nigh unto death, his thoughts were with the Saints in Philippi, and he was grieved that they had anxiety for him. It all shows the mind of Christ.

III. CHRIST, THE OBJECT AND THE GOAL.

CHAPTER III.

1. The True Circumcision. 1–3.
2. Paul's Past Experience. 4–7.
3. The One Passion. 8–11.
4. Pressing Towards the Mark. 12–16.
5. The Goal of Glory. 17–21.

Verses 1–3. Finally (or, for the rest), my brethren, rejoice in the "Lord." Rejoicing in the Lord, not merely in the salvation which is ours, nor in His mercies, in His gifts or in our service, but in Him, is what gives strength and victory down here. He rejoiced in Him because He knew the Lord was controlling all and that he was in His hands; he followed the same path in humiliation, which he knew would lead him to the glory where He is. And the prisoner of the Lord enjoying the blessedness of fellowship with Christ, following Christ, looking to Him and not to earthly circumstances, exhorts the beloved Philippians to find their joy in nothing less than the Person Christ. It was not a grievous thing for him to write them the same things, but it was safe for them. They needed the exhortation in the midst of spiritual dangers, for nothing else keeps from evil as heart occupation with the Lord Jesus Christ. He warns "beware of dogs, beware of evil workers, beware of the concision." By these terms the same false teachers are meant which disturbed the Galatian churches, which did such evil work also among the Corinthians. He speaks of these perverters of the gospel in severe terms, but not too severe. They boasted of religiousness, of righteousness by the observance of ordinances and the keeping of the law; they trusted in the flesh and set aside Christ. They, with their religion of the flesh, are branded by the apostle as dogs, unclean and outside, therefore unworthy of fellowship. They called the Gentiles dogs, but now the Spirit of God shows that they are not better than the Gentiles (See Gal. iv:8–10). They were evil workmen who led souls away, as the havoc they had wrought shows. They gloried in ceremonies, the circumcision of the flesh; in reality they were the concision, the mutilators of the flesh, who knew nothing of the true separation through the cross of Christ and union with a risen Christ in whom the believer is complete.

Dogs, evil workers and the concision, are terms which fit the many cults today, including "Christian Science," the "new thought,"— "the new religion and modern theology," all of which deny the gospel of Jesus Christ. True believers are the circumcision, not a circumcision made by hands, but a spiritual circumcision, the putting off of the body of the flesh by the death of Christ (Col. ii:11). The cross of Christ separates the believer from the flesh, the religious forms, and self-improvement, and separates him unto God. And knowing that Christ is all, glorying in Him with no more confidence in the flesh, the believer worships by the Spirit of God, and no longer in ordinances. The indwelling Spirit fills the heart with Christ, glorifies Him, and true worship by the Spirit is the result. To have no more confidence in the flesh, to expect nothing whatever from ourselves, to glory only in Christ Jesus is true Christian attainment and experience.

Verses 4–7. And this blessed servant of the Lord Jesus speaks of his experience as a Hebrew. He might have had abundant reason to place confidence in the flesh. He had something as a natural, religious man to glory in. What fleshly advantages were his! He was circumcised the eighth day, of the stock of Israel, of the tribe of Benjamin, an Hebrew of the Hebrews; as touching the law a Pharisee; concerning zeal persecuting the church; touching the righteousness which is in the law blameless. He had indeed, as he testified before, "profited in the Jews' religion above many my equals in mine own nation, being more exceedingly zealous of the traditions of my father" (Gal. i:14). He was a very religious man, for he belonged to the most religious sect of his day, with a blind zeal which led him to persecute the church, yet touching the righteousness in the law, he knew himself blameless.

And all this religiousness and zeal for God, his law keeping and blamelessness he looked upon as being of value and gain for him, though they did not give him peace or fellowship with God. A change came. The things which were religious gain to him he now counted loss for Christ. On the road to Damascus he had seen the glorified Christ and that vision had laid him in the dust so that he saw himself as the chief of sinners.

Verses 8–11. From that moment when it pleased God to reveal His Son to him the self-righteous Pharisee could say, "I count all things* loss on account of the excellency of the knowledge of Christ Jesus my Lord, for whom I suffered the loss of all things, and do count them refuse that I may win Christ and be found in Him." What had been gain to him he cast aside. He had seen Christ and that was enough, he would have nothing else after that. Christ had become his all. The excellency of the knowledge of Christ Jesus, whom the erstwhile persecutor now blessedly calls "my Lord," made it a joy to suffer the loss of all things, yea, to count them refuse. How he suffered the loss of all things, things needful in life, suffering, hunger, stripes; giving up all earthly distinction and advantage, we know from his own testimony (2 Cor. xi:22–31). He suffered the loss of all things and counted them refuse. "This is the marvellous estimate of one who had all advantages in the world; and then had known all sufferings from it in behalf of Christ, looking upon the former as worse than nothing, as a detriment, and the latter to be nothing, because the knowledge he had already gained of Christ outweighed them all." All earthly things, all human attainments, everything which

*"He does not say: When I was converted I counted all things loss When a person is truly converted, Christ becomes and is everything; the world then appears as nothing. It has passed from the mind and the unseen things fill the heart. Afterwards as the convert goes on with his duties and with his friends, though Christ is still precious, he does generally not continue to count all things loss. But Paul could say, 'I count all things loss' not I did. It is a great thing to be able to say that."

exalts man was counted as loathsome things in comparison with Him whom He had beheld in the glory light.

But what does he mean when he expresses the desire "that I may win (or gain) Christ and be found in Him"? Did he not possess Christ already? Was he not in Him and Christ in him? He possessed Christ. He was in Him. Nor does the apostle mean that he reaches out, as some teach, after a "deeper life" experience or some such thing. He had perfect assurance of his standing before God in Christ; no doubt whatever as to that could be in the apostle's heart. Nor did he need some kind of an experience, as some claim, a holiness-perfection experience, to give him greater assurance. His wish to win Christ, to gain Christ, is his longing desire for the actual possession of Christ in glory. Christ in glory is the great object and goal for the believer down here. This object and goal must ever be before the heart in the Christian's race. Like the racer who has no eyes for his surroundings, but whose eye is steadily fixed upon the goal, so the believer is to look to the glorified Christ and press forward toward the mark. This is the truth unfolded in this chapter. Paul knew that Christ belonged to him, that his destiny was to be forever with Him, and then his passion was to be worthy of all this. And when Christ is gained in glory and the goal is reached then he would be "found in Him, not having mine own righteousness which is of the law (the righteousness which is nothing but filthy rags), but that which is through faith of Christ, the righteousness which is of God by faith." How he emphasizes this righteousness in which he delighted! And this great servant of the Lord, who knew Him so well, wants to know Him and the power of His resurrection and the fellowship of His suffering "being made conformable unto His death, if by any means I might arrive at the resurrection from among the dead." The power of His resurrection he desires to know is more than a spiritual power, for he knew that power in practical experience. Of this he had written to the Ephesians (chap. i:15–ii:10). It is again the goal of the Christian's life towards which he reaches out.

He wants to arrive at the resurrection from among the dead by any means and to get there though it means fellowship with His suffering being made conformable to His death. And this was before him in the Roman prison. He wanted to be with Christ, and to arrive there he desired to be like Christ in participating in His suffering even to be made conformable to His death.

It is important to note here the difference between "resurrection *of* the dead" and "the resurrection *from among* the dead." The latter is the correct translation of verse 11. There is a resurrection of the dead, of all the dead. But there is a resurrection from among the dead, which elsewhere in the Word is called the first resurrection. The Lord Jesus was raised *from* the dead. When the Lord spoke to His disciples of His resurrection from among the dead they were astonished and spoke among themselves "what the rising of the dead should mean." They did not know what it meant. When the Lord was raised He became the first fruits of them that slept, that is, the righteous dead. And God raised Him from the dead, because His delight was in Him, for He had glorified Him and finished the Work the Father gave Him to do.

The first resurrection, the resurrection from the dead, is the expression of God's delight and satisfaction in those raised; it is His seal on Christ's work. Because He finished that great work which glorified God, all who are in Christ will be raised from among the dead, while those who live when the Lord comes, will not die, but be changed in a moment, in the twinkling of an eye (1 Cor. xv:51–52). But it is not on account of the believer's attainment, but because of Christ that the power of God will take His own out. The rest of the dead will be left until the second resurrection.

The Apostle knew that through grace he belonged to this out-resurrection from among the dead. He had an absolute certainty of it. But in divine energy he presses on towards it. All in him wants to get there where the grace of God in Christ had put him. He reaches out for this blessed goal and when he speaks of attaining "by any means" he gives us to understand that nothing shall hinder him in the race. May the cost be what it will, I want it; I want it because I have it in Christ and through Christ and I want to be worthy of it. And therefore he despised the loss of all things and was ready to suffer and die the martyr's death.

Verses 12–16. The words which follow show that this is the true meaning of the desire he expressed. "Not as though I had already attained (obtained), or am already made perfect, but I press on if so be that I may apprehend that for which also I am apprehended of Christ Jesus. Brethren, I do not count myself yet to have apprehended; but one thing I do, forgetting the things which are behind, and stretching forward to the things which are before. I press towards the goal for the prize of the calling on high of God in Christ Jesus." The goal had not yet been reached, he was still on the way and had not yet obtained nor was he made perfect. He constantly presses on towards the goal, Christ in glory. He knew that he had been apprehended, taken possession of, by Christ Jesus and for Christ and therefore he also wants to take possession, to apprehend it. He forgets what is behind and even stretches forward to the things which are before, the blessed goal. This was his constant attitude, ever occupied with the Lord Jesus Christ to be like Him and with Him in glory. "The whole of Paul's life was founded on that and completely formed by that. The Son of God was forming his soul day by day, and he was always running towards Him and never doing anything else. It was not merely as an apostle that he entered into the fellowship of His sufferings, and conformity to His death, but every Christian should do the same. A person may say he has forgiveness of sins. But I say, What is governing your heart now? Is your eye resting on Christ in glory? Is the excellency of knowledge of Christ Jesus so before your soul as to govern everything else, and make you count everything loss? Is that where you are? Has this excellent knowledge put out all other things? Not only an outwardly blameless walk, but has the thought of Christ in glory put out all other things? If it were so, we would not be governed by everyday nothings."* Some teach that these words of Paul, speaking of attaining and not yet perfect, mean that he was still in doubt as to having a share in the first resurrection. We quote the words of a leading advocate of this interpretation:

"But what was the goal towards which Paul was thus directing his efforts? 'If by any means,' he continues, 'I may attain to the select(?) resurrection out from among the dead.' In other words, his aim was to be numbered with those blessed and holy ones who shall have part in the first resurrection. But we must notice that he had, at the time, *no certain assurance* (italics ours) that he would compass the desire of his heart. . . . Just before his death, however, it was graciously revealed unto him that he was one of the approved."—Pember in "The Church, the Churches and the Mysteries," page 40.

Think of it! The prisoner of the Lord who suffered joyfully the loss of all things, who counted all but dung, who walked in such separation and devotion, still uncertain about his share in the first resurrection! This interpretation is not only wrong, but it denies the grace of God in the Lord Jesus Christ, by making the first resurrection a question of attainment when it is purely the matter of divine grace. This teaching aims at the very vitals of the Gospel of grace and glory.

An exhortation follows. He exhorts all who are perfect to be thus minded. What does the word perfect mean and who are the perfect? Above, when he said he was not yet made perfect, it applies to Christ-likeness in glory by being conformed to His image. True Christian perfection will be reached when the Lord comes and we shall see Him as He is and be like Him. Now those are the perfect down here who have no confidence in the flesh, who glory in Christ and who know He is all in all, that by one offering He has perfected forever them that are sanctified, that they are accepted in the Beloved and complete in Him in whom the fullness of the Godhead dwells bodily. And they are all to be "thus minded" like he was, ever occupied with

---

*J. N. Darby.

Christ in glory, doing this one thing—pressing on towards the goal for the prize of the calling on high of God in Christ Jesus.

Verses 17–21. "Brethren, be followers (imitators) together of me, and mark them which walk so as ye have us for an ensample." What a blessed thing that Paul could write this! Grace had enabled him to follow Christ fully. But even then there were those over whom Paul wept because their walk showed that they were the enemies of the cross. "For many walk, of whom I have told you often, and now tell you even weeping, that they are the enemies of the cross of Christ, whose end is destruction, whose God is their belly, and whose glory is in their shame, who mind earthly things." Were these real believers? The statement "whose end is destruction" answers this question. They could not be true children of God, but were such who had professed Christianity, having the form of godliness, but denying the power thereof (2 Tim. iii:5). They turned the grace of God into lasciviousness. "Their god was really their belly; that is to say, the fleshly craving in them had never been set aside by any satisfaction that they had found for themselves in Christ. The craving of the old nature led and governed them." Instead of minding heavenly things, seeking the things which are above where Christ sitteth, they minded earthly things, showing thereby that they had never really known Christ. If there were "many" then among God's people who were enemies of the cross, who had with all their profession no desire for the heavenly calling, how much larger is their number now at the end of the age. They are religious, yet they cling to the world, love the world and thus deny the cross of Christ, which makes them the enemies of the cross.*

*"There is nothing like the cross. It is both the righteousness of God against sin, and the righteousness of God in pardoning sin. It is the end of the world of judgment, and the beginning of the world of life. It is the work that put away sin, and yet it is the greatest sin that ever was committed. The more we think of it, the more we see it is the turning point of everything. So, if a person follows the world, he is an enemy of the cross of Christ. If I take the glory of the world that crucified Christ, I am glorying in my shame." **J. N. D.**

"They walked according to the flesh, minding earthly things instead of the heavenly, the heavens being the proper and only sphere of spiritual life, demonstrated that they knew nothing of the matter as to the heart, and for the truth of resurrection and life in a risen Christ, were walking according to their own religious feelings, making this their god. And surely there is enough of this everywhere, a bringing down revelation of the truth to the standard of human feelings and experiences, making these the umpire instead of God. It is a religious appetite ruling and hungry, and satisfied with its own sensations when filled. Israel was charged to take heed lest when they had eaten and were full, they should forget Jehovah (Deut. viii:14) and the prayer of Agur in Prov. xxx:9 is, 'lest I be full and deny Thee.' The Grand Object, Christ Himself, is ignored, and religious excitement, like any other intoxication, displaces Him and occupies the soul to its damage and peril. It is the belly, not Christ. It is religious emotions, it is not Christ. It is perfection in and of the flesh; it is having no confidence in the flesh. The flesh may find its satisfaction and growth as much in religion as in the lower passions and the more secular world. The cross came in to put all this to death. Hence these are enemies to the cross of Christ, even though much mention may be made of the cross, and even continual prostrations before it practiced."†

In the last two verses the blessed goal itself is fully revealed. "For our conversation is in heaven (or commonwealth-citizenship)‡ from whence also we look for the Saviour, the Lord Jesus Christ, who shall transform our body of humiliation into conformity to His body of glory, according to the working whereby He is able even to subdue all things unto himself." This is the blessed hope and the blessed goal. All we have as Christians, our relationships, rights and possessions are in heaven. Some blessed day He, for whom we wait, will come and take us to the

†M. Taylor

‡The Greek word is "*politeuma*," from which we have our English "politics." Hence one might say "our politics are in heaven."

place where He is transforming our body of humiliation into conformity to His body of glory. Then we shall have attained that for which down here we hope and pray (see 1 Thess. iv).

IV. CHRIST, THE BELIEVER'S STRENGTH, SUFFICIENT FOR ALL CIRCUMSTANCES.

CHAPTER IV.

1. Stand Fast. Rejoice. 1–4.
2. Dependence on God and True Heart Occupation. 5–9.
3. I Can Do All Things through Christ. 10–13.
4. The Fellowship of the Philippians. 14–20.
5. The Greetings. 21–23.

Verses 1–4. And now the final testimony of the prisoner of the Lord, telling us from his own experience that Christ is sufficient for all circumstances down here. The first verse is filled with the precious fragrance of the great apostle's affection. What refreshment there is for all His dear saints in these opening words of this chapter! "Therefore my brethren dearly beloved and longed for, my joy and crown, so stand fast in the Lord, dearly beloved." How he loved the saints and longed for them. He looked upon them as his joy and crown; his joy down here and his crown in the day of Christ. So the aged John testified, "I have no greater joy than to hear that my children walk in truth" (3 John, verse 4). They were to stand fast in the Lord, for this gives strength and the Lord constantly before the heart and mind gives victory.* Eudoias and Syntyche, two sisters in the Lord, are exhorted to be of the same mind in the Lord. They had difficulties and had become separated. How graciously and tenderly they are exhorted to overcome their differences. The true yokefellow is probably Epaphroditus, who was now fully restored and carried this letter to the Philippians. Paul requests him to assist those women who had contended with him in the gospel, of course in the sphere which belongs to woman. And there were Clement and other fellow laborers, whose names are

*"Were a light at the end of a long straight alley, I would not have the light itself till I get to it; but I have ever increasing light in proportion as I go forward; I know it better. I am more in the light myself. Thus it is with a glorified Christ, and such is the Christian life."

in the book of life. These names are known to Him and in His day their labors will come to light and they will receive their reward. It is enough for the laborer to know that his name, though unknown to the world, is in the book of life, and his service, though unapplauded by the world, has His approval. Once more he exhorts to rejoice in the Lord alway, under all circumstances, at all times. And again I say, Rejoice. He did not write such words when he was taken up into the third heaven, but these blessed words come from the prison in Rome. When the Lord is before the heart, if He is the controlling principle of our life, the pattern and the goal, never lost sight of, then He giveth songs in the night.

Verses 5–9. And this walk in Christ and with Christ must be characterized by dependence on God. "Let your moderation be known to all men. The Lord is at hand." Walking thus means to walk in meekness, not reaching out after the things which are but for a moment, content with such things as we have, never asserting one's right. Moderation means to put a check upon our own will. How easy all this becomes if we just have it as a present reality that the Lord is nigh and that when He comes all will be made right. A little while longer and all will be changed. And while we walk here in His fellowship, His command to us is, "Be anxious for nothing." All rests in His loving hands. His people have tribulation down here. He told us so. "In the world ye shall have tribulation; be of good cheer, I have overcome the world" (John xvi:33). And prayer is our refuge. Most blessed words! How the child of God loves, appreciates and makes use of them! "Be anxious for nothing, but in everything by prayer and supplication with thanksgiving let your requests be made known to God. And the peace of God, which passeth all understanding, shall keep your hearts and minds through Christ Jesus." We can cast all our cares upon Him, for we know He careth for us. He is our burden bearer. We may look upon all our burdens as being permitted by Him so that we may give them back to Him and find out His love and power.

"We are in relationship with God; in all things He is our refuge; and events do not disturb Him. He knows the end from the beginning. He knows everything, He knows it beforehand; events shake neither His throne, nor His heart; they always accomplish His purposes. But to us He is love; we are through grace the objects of His tender care. He listens to us and bows down His ear to hear us. In all things therefore, instead of disquieting ourselves and weighing everything in our own hearts, we ought to present our requests to God with prayer, with supplication, with a heart that makes itself known (for we are human beings) but with the knowledge of the heart of God (for He loves us perfectly); so that, even while making our petition to Him, we can already give thanks, because we are sure of the answer of His grace, be it what it may; and it is *our* requests that we are to present to Him. Nor is it a cold commandment to find out His will and then come: we are to go with our requests. Hence it does not say, you will have what you ask; but God's peace will keep your hearts. This is trust; and His peace, the peace of God Himself, shall keep our hearts. It does not say that our hearts shall keep the peace of God; but, having cast our burden on Him whose peace nothing can disturb, His peace keeps our hearts. Our trouble is before Him, and the constant peace of the God of love, who takes charge of everything and knows all beforehand, quiets our disburdened hearts, and imparts to us the peace which is in Himself and which is above all understanding (or at least keeps our hearts by it), even as He Himself is above all the circumstances that can disquiet us, and above the poor human heart that is troubled by them. Oh, what grace! that even our anxieties are a means of our being filled with this marvellous peace, if we know how to bring them to God, and true He is. May we learn indeed how to maintain this intercourse with God and its reality, in order that we may converse with Him and understand His ways with believers!"*

---

*Synopsis.

Our prayers may not always be answered as we want to have them answered, for He alone knows what is best. We speak to Him about our cares and put them thus into His heart and He puts His own peace into our hearts.

> What are thy wants to-day? Whate'er they be
> Lift up thy heart and pray: God heareth thee,
> Then trustfully rely that all thy need
> He surely will supply in every deed.
> But every prayer of thine, and every want
> Of either thine or mine, He may not grant,
> Yet all our prayers God hears, and He will show,
> Some day, in coming years, He best did know.†

And in the life down here, surrounded by every form of evil, we are to be occupied with only that which is good, things true, things noble, just, pure, lovely, things of good report; if there be any virtue or any praise, think on these things. This is the way how peace of mind and blessing, happiness and joy may be maintained, not being occupied with the evil which surrounds us, or the evil in others, but with the very opposite. The Word of God is given to us for this purpose. As we read it prayerfully and meditate on it we are kept in that which is good, true, noble, just and lovely. Walking according to these exhortations they would find that the God of peace is with them. And so shall we.

Verses 10–13. Paul also rejoiced in the Lord greatly because their care for him had flourished again, and added "wherein ye were also careful, but ye lacked opportunity." They had ministered to him as the Lord's servant, in temporal things. The words, "now at last your care of me hath flourished again," indicates that they had delayed their ministration, but he puts another meaning upon it. He does not insinuate that it was a failure and neglect on their side, "but ye lacked opportunity." He did not mention this in respect of want. "For I have learned in whatsoever state I am, therewith to be content." He had learned it all practically and knew about being abased and

†C. Murray.

abounding—"everywhere and in all things I have learned the secret, both to be full and to be hungry, both to abound and to suffer want. I can do all things through Christ who strengtheneth me." The secret of this victory over all circumstances, whether good or evil was, Christ. It was "not I but Christ." In himself he had no strength, but all His strength to be abased and to abound, to be full or hungry, in abounding and in suffering want, was the Lord Jesus Christ. And this strength continually flows from and is supplied by our relationship with Christ as it is maintained by faith in a close walk with Him. He had learnt to trust Him fully; he trusted Him and walked in fellowship with Him in adversity, and, also, which is more difficult, in prosperity. His faith always reckoned on Christ. He kept him from being careless and indifferent, when he was full and abounded in all things* and He kept him from being discouraged and dissatisfied when he suffered privations. He had found Christ sufficient in every circumstance. This is the happy life, which, too, we may live if Christ is our object and our all.

Verses 14–20. He reminds them of their faithfulness to himself; he had not forgotten their love and what they had done in the past. He delighted in the remembrance of it, nor does God forget the ministries to His servants. "But to do good and communicate forget not, for with such sacrifices God is well pleased" (Heb. xiii:16). "For God is not unrighteous to forget your work and labor of love, which you have showed toward His name, in that ye have ministered to the saints, and do minister" (Heb. vi:10). Yet he does not want them to misunderstand him, as if he was anxious to receive further fellowship from them for his personal need. Therefore he adds, "Not because I desire a gift, but I desire fruit that may abound to your account.

---

*Prosperity in earthly things is for many children of God a snare. The person who requested prayer for a brother who was getting rich made a good request. We need more prayer and need more watching when all goes well and when we abound. Then the danger to become unspiritual and indifferent is great.

But I have all, and abound; I am full, having received of Epaphroditus the things which were sent from you, an odor of a sweet smell, a sacrifice acceptable, well pleasing to God." In reminding them and himself of their love he did not desire more gifts for the sake of having it, but he desired the fruit which would result from their faithfulness and liberality, which would abound to their account in the day of Christ. All ministry to God's servants and to the Saints should be done from this viewpoint.

"But my God shall supply all your need according to His riches in glory in Christ Jesus. Now unto God and our Father be glory for ever and ever. Amen." The God whom He had learnt to know so well in all circumstances—my God, as he called Him—would supply all their need. It is not a wish that He may do so, nor a prayer that he prays, but it is an assured fact. He knows his God so well that he counts on Him for the supply of all the need of the beloved saints according to His riches in glory in Christ Jesus.

Verses 21–23. The greetings close this blessed little epistle of love and joy, so full of the realities of true Christian experience, made possible for every child of God through the indwelling Spirit. He sends his greetings to every saint and conveys the greetings of the saints with him, chiefly they that are of Caesar's household. Blessed hint that even there the Gospel had manifested its power in the salvation of some.

COLOSSIANS

CONTENTS

Page
Introduction.................................... 39
Division of the Book of Colossians............ 43
Analysis and Annotations...................... 44

The Epistle to the Colossians.

Introduction.

Colossae was a city of Phrygia, a district in Asia Minor. It was pleasantly located in the valley of the Lycus, a branch of the Meander. Two other cities are also mentioned in this Epistle to the Colossians, the cities of Laodicea and Hierapolis (chapter iv:13). Laodicea was only nine miles and Hierapolis, thirteen miles from Colossae. Laodicea was a very rich and influential city. Hierapolis was famous for its hot springs. Colossae was the smallest of these three cities. Christian believers lived in all three cities and later the Lord selected the church of the Laodiceans and addressed to it the final message of the seven churches (Rev. iii). The region of Phrygia was well settled by Jews, some of whom were in Jerusalem on the day of Pentecost (Acts ii:10). We shall find through the study of this Epistle that a Jewish sect which held evil doctrines flourished in the whole region; this sect was known as the Essenes, and the Spirit of God warns against their false teachings in the Epistle. Phrygia also was known as the seat of other heresies, especially an oriental-philosophical mysticism.

The Church in Colossae.

It seems that the church in Colossae was pre-eminently a Gentile church (ii:13). How did it come into existence? Paul evidently did not visit the city, though he passed through Phrygia (Acts xvi:6; xviii:23), for he writes in this Epistle, "For I would that ye know what great conflict I have for you, and for them in Laodicea, and for as many as have not seen my face in the flesh" (ii:1). It seems also clear that the church in Colossae came into existence after Paul had passed through that region the second time as stated in Acts xviii:23, for if a church had existed then in that city, he would probably have visited Colossae. If we turn to the nineteenth chapter of the Book of Acts, which records the long sojourn of the Apostle Paul in Ephesus, we find a hint on how the gospel was made known to the Colossians. First we read that Paul continued for two years, "so that all they which dwelt in Asia heard the word of the Lord Jesus, both Jews and Greeks" (Acts xix:10). And then Demetrius the silversmith witnessed to the extension work of Paul while being in Ephesus. "Moreover ye see and hear, that not only in Ephesus, but almost throughout Asia, this Paul hath persuaded and turned away much people . . ." (Acts xix:26). Asia does not mean the continent, but a province of Asia Minor, of which Phrygia was a part. The whole region heard the gospel during his stay in the prominent city of Ephesus; among the visitors who listened to the messages of Paul were people from Colossae, Laodicea and Hierapolis. These carried the gospel back to their homes and thus churches were formed. Philemon and Epaphras of Colossae must in this way have heard the gospel from the Apostle and became the instruments through whom the church in their home-city was founded. That Epaphras was the more prominent one becomes certain from chapter i:7 and iv:12-13.

The Occasion and Object of the Epistle.

Paul in Rome had received, probably through Epaphras, the information that the Colossian Christians were facing great dangers as to their faith. What the danger was the text of the Epistle will show us more fully. A number of false doctrines emanating from philosophical speculations, oriental mysticism, asceticism and Judaism, were being advocated amongst them and threatened the complete corruption of the church. Later a system known by the name of Gnosticism (from the Greek word "*Gnosis*"—knowledge) wrought great havoc in the church; the beginning of it was troubling the Colossians, who seemed to have been an intellectual class to whom the philosophical, mystical and ascetic teachings appealed in a special way. Gnosticism attempted to explain creation, the origin of evil, God., etc., apart from the revelation God has given in His Word. Besides speaking of a certain class of beings, half-gods of different rank, they denied that God had created the world, but that an inferior being had called it into existence. This system taught that matter is evil and that the only way to escape from evil would be to repudiate matter completely. The worst feature of these Gnostic teachings was a denial of the Deity of the Lord Jesus Christ and His work of redemption. It was a philosophical, theosophical speculation, anti-christian throughout. Well did Polycarp say to the Gnostic Marcion, "I know thee, thou first-born of Satan." While this evil system had not yet fully developed in the Colossian church, the foundation for it had been laid and the Holy Spirit anticipated its coming, and in sending this document to the Colossians answers the false teachings of Gnosticism. This is of equal interest and importance to the church in the twentieth century. "Christian Science," so called, that philosophical-theosophical-mystical cult, is a satanic revival of ancient Gnosticism. The Epistle to the Colossians must, therefore, be an effectual weapon against this cult, which denies the two pillars of Christianity, the Son of God and the finished work of the Cross. The Colossians were also being misled, as the second chapter shows us, by other false teachers. Judaizers were at work among them. We are not left to infer respecting the class of religionists to which these teachers belonged, for the mention of "new moon and Sabbath" in chapter ii:16, at once characterizes them as Judaizers, and leads us to the then prevalent forms of Jewish philosophy to trace them. Not that these teachers were merely Jews; they were Christians (by profession), but they attempted to mix with the Gospel of Christ the theosophy and angelology of the Jews of their times. They became infected with theosophic and ascetic principles and were gradually being drawn away from the simple doctrine of Christ. This false system of philosophy and ascetic mysticism, attempting to intrude into unseen things, with which was linked angel-worship, limited the superiority and greatness of the Lord Jesus Christ and more so the sufficiency of His work of redemption.

The occasion of the Epistle was the existence of these evil things among them. The object in writing was more than counteracting the false doctrines. The Holy Spirit unfolds the truth of the Gospel, showing in this Epistle the majesty and glory of Christ, that He has the pre-eminence in all things, head of creation and head of the church; it unfolds the completeness of His redemption and the believer's completeness in Christ as risen with Christ and in living union with Him, in whom the fullness of the Godhead dwells bodily. Like all the great Pauline Epistles, containing the revelation of God to man, the Colossian Epistle with its vital and glorious truths, is meat in due season for God's people, especially in these days when we are confronted by the same errors in modern movements and energized by the power of Satan to destroy the very foundations of the faith.

Colossians in Contrast with Ephesians.

Colossians was written by Paul about the year 62 A. D., from the Roman prison, and, as stated in the introduction to the Epistle to the Ephesians (Annot. Bible Vol. II, N. T., page 233), was carried by the same messenger who also received the Ephesian Epistle from the hands of the Apostle. Tychicus was this messenger (Ephes. vi:21; Col. iv:7–9). There is a striking resemblance between these two Epistles, which have been called "twins." Dean Alford speaks of it as follows: "In writing both, the Apostle's mind was in the same frame—full of the glories of Christ and the consequent glorious privileges of His church, which is built on Him, and vitally knit to Him. This mighty subject, as he looked with indignation on the beggarly system of meats and drinks and hallowed days and angelic mediations to which his Colossians were being drawn down, rose before him in all its length and breadth and height, but as writing to *them*, he was confined to one portion of it, and to setting forth that one portion pointedly and controversially. He could not, consistently with the effect which he would produce on them, dive into the depths of the divine counsels in Christ with regard to them." Ephesians and Colossians embody the highest revelations God has given to man. Colossians is the counterpart of the Ephesian Epistle; each may be viewed as a supplement to the other. In Ephesians the revelation concerns mostly the body of

Christ (the church), the fullness of that body, its rich privileges and heavenly destiny; in Colossians the head of that body in His fullness and glory is blessedly revealed. In Ephesians we find repeatedly the blessed position of the believer stated "in Christ Jesus"; in Colossians we read of Christ in the believer, "Christ in you." Ephesians reveals the calling of God and exhorts believers "to walk worthy of the vocation wherewith we are called"; Colossians making known the Lord and His glory, exhorts "to walk worthy of the Lord." Controversy concerning evil doctrines and errors is absent in Ephesians, it is prominent in Colossians. In Ephesians the Holy Spirit and His work in the believer is fully brought out. Then we read of the quickening, the sealing, the filling of the Spirit and are warned against quenching and grieving the Spirit; in Colossians nothing is said about the Holy Spirit, the doctrine concerning the Spirit is absent. The annotations will point out the reason for this. At the same time the redemption truths of Ephesians as well as Romans and Galatians are all touched upon in Colossians. The great truths contained in these wonderful Epistles must ever be kept in freshness and in power by the Spirit of God before the heart and mind of God's people, so that they can live and walk as those who are redeemed and be kept in the enjoyment of salvation. The more these deep and precious documents are studied the greater the blessedness for God's people. May God the Holy Spirit, the author of this Epistle, fill, through His message, our eyes and hearts with Him who is our Lord and the Head of His body.

The Divisions of Colossians.

Chapter ii:9–10 is the centre of the Epistle. "For in Him dwelleth all the fullness of the Godhead bodily. And ye are complete in Him who is the head of all principality and power." It is the very heart of the Epistle, the key which unlocks its heavenly treasures. We get in this verse the scope of the Epistle. The apostle does not begin by warning the Colossians of the danger and by exposing the fatal errors which were creeping in among them. He writes first of Him and His glory. The Spirit of God wants the Colossians to get the right estimate of the Person and glory of the Lord Jesus Christ, of His dignity and pre-eminence in all things, of the great work of reconcilation, the peace which was made in the blood of the cross and the present and future results of this work. Then He shows that the believer is in Christ, that He who is bodily in glory, in whom all the fullness of the Godhead dwells is the fullness of the believer. Each is complete in Him. And therefore ordinances, philosophy, traditions of men, intruding in mysterious things, angel-worship, cannot add anything to the believer's knowledge or perfection. His perfection is Christ. Then follow exhortations, how a believer who is risen with Christ and one with Him should walk down here. We divide, therefore, this Epistle into three parts.

I. **THE PERSON OF CHRIST. HIS GLORY AND HIS WORK.** Chapter i.

II. **COMPLETE IN HIM, IN WHOM ALL THE FULLNESS DWELLS.** Chapter ii.

III. **THE PRACTICAL RESULTS. LIVING AS RISEN WITH CHRIST.** Chapter iii:4–iv:18.

Analysis and Annotations.

I. THE PERSON OF CHRIST. HIS GLORY AND HIS WORK.

CHAPTER I.

1. The Introduction. 1–8.
2. The Prayer. 9–14.
3. The Person and Glory of Christ, Head of Creation and Head of the Church. 15–18.
4. The Work of Reconciliation and the Double Ministry. 19–29.

Verse 1–8. This Epistle unfolds the doctrine of Christ and therefore Paul speaks of himself as an Apostle of Christ Jesus by the will of God; Timotheus is spoken of as a brother. In addressing the Philippians, the apostle spoke of himself and of Timotheus as servants and did not mention his apostleship at all. In addressing the Colossians, when error is to be refuted and truth to be revealed, he uses his title as apostle. He addresses them as saints and faithful brethren in Christ and the precious greeting to such whom God has separated from evil and unto Himself follows: "Grace be unto you and peace, from God our Father and the Lord Jesus Christ." Grace and peace belonged to them, as it belongs to all who are in Christ. Their state could not affect what God had bestowed upon them in His Son. Then he gives thanks "to God and the Father of our Lord Jesus Christ, praying always for you." He had heard of their faith in Christ Jesus; of the love which they had towards all the Saints and then mentions the hope which is laid up for them in heaven. Faith, love and hope are the blessed marks of all true believers, produced in them by the Spirit of God. Their faith in Christ Jesus was manifested in love for all the saints. "This is His commandment, that we should believe on the name of His Son Jesus Christ, and love one another, as He gave us commandment" (1 John iii:23). "We know that we have passed from death unto life, because we love the brethren" (1 John iii:12). And they also know the blessed hope which they had heard and learned in the word of the truth of the gospel. The gospel then had produced these blessings among the Colossians, who were once heathen; and the same gospel was also going out in all the world bringing forth fruit wherever it was received in faith. Could this be said of the various philosophical systems which were being introduced among the Colossians? Or could mysticism and law-keeping show such results? Only those who hear and believe the Gospel know the grace of God in truth. Then he mentions Epaphras, the beloved fellow servant, who was for them a faithful minister. Through his ministry they had learned these things, while Epaphras had declared unto Paul their love in the Spirit. This is the only time the Spirit of God is mentioned in this Epistle. It is different in the Epistle to the Ephesians. There the fullest teachings concerning the Holy Spirit are given. Every chapter in Ephesians speaks of the Holy Spirit. We read there that He is the seal and the earnest; He is the Spirit of wisdom and revelation; access is through Him unto the Father; the church is described as the habitation of God through the Spirit, who has also made known the mystery hid in former ages. Furthermore He strengthens the inner man that Christ may dwell in the heart by faith. Then the unity of the Spirit is spoken of in Ephesians; believers are not to grieve the Spirit by whom they are sealed unto the day of redemption; the filling with the Spirit, spiritual songs as the result, the sword of the Spirit and prayer in the Spirit are likewise mentioned in the Epistle to the Ephesians. Why is all this omitted in Colossians? Why is this Epistle silent about the work of the Spirit in the believer? The reason is of much interest. Our Lord said concerning the coming of the Spirit of truth, "He shall not speak of Himself," and again He said, "He shall glorify Me" (John xvi:13, 14). While the Ephesians knew Christ, owned Him and His glory, the Colossian Christians, through false teachers, were being turned away from Christ; they began to lose sight of the glory of Christ by listening to philosophy (ii:8); their eyes were no longer only on Christ. He therefore aims in this Epistle to glorify Christ, to lead the Colossians back to a full realization of the Person and Glory of Christ and their completeness in Him. He directs their hearts to the Lord Jesus Christ and thus fulfills His mission, speaking not of Himself and glorifying Christ.*

Verses 9 14. Next follows a prayer, Paul being only the instrument of the utterance of the Spirit of God. And it is a prayer fully adapted to the conditions of the Colossian Christians. It is still the prayer of the Holy Spirit for all the people of God. The leading petition in this prayer is for the knowledge of the will of God—"that ye might be filled with the knowledge of His will in all wisdom and spiritual understanding." All the other requests may be looked upon as the results of a spiritual understanding of the will of God. What is the meaning of the will of God? It is that will of God of which we read so much in the first chapter of Ephesians and concerns those who are in Christ. What we possess in Christ, what God has made us in Him and given to us with Him, according to the good pleasure of His will, is that which believers need to know. What God has willed for those who are redeemed by the blood of His Son, how they are constituted in Him holy, put into the place of sons, accepted in the Beloved, heirs of God, sealed and indwelt by His Spirit, is the knowledge with which Christians should be filled. This the Colossians lacked. The full knowledge of that will would have kept them from listening to the enticing words of false teachers, who promised them wisdom, knowledge and other benefits, which are only found in Christ and which the believer possesses in

---

*Certain sects which claim a restoration of Pentecostal power and gifts are constantly occupied with the Holy Spirit, His work in the believer; they speak much of the Spirit, the feelings He produces, the energy He gives, etc. Nowhere in the Word are believers told to be occupied with the Spirit. The one object given to the believer to have ever before the heart is the Lord Jesus Christ and His Glory. One finds among these people who claim a restoration of Apostolic gifts (notably the smallest, speaking in tongues) those who are quite ignorant of the Work of Christ, and the Glory of Christ.

Him. And this knowledge of His will is a growing knowledge and must govern the walk of the believer. It is needed "to walk worthy of the Lord unto all pleasing." Such a walk is only possible by enjoying constantly the relationship into which the gracious will of God has brought the believer; the more we enter into all grace has done for us and lay hold of it, the more we shall walk worthy of the Lord. And this walk is "unto all pleasing," With a true Christian, God may be displeased, though He condemn not; and there is a lack of felt fellowship. Only as walking worthily of Christ can we abound in obedience to God, and be as children intimate with their father. Every Christian's habitual question should be, not, "What must I do to escape censure, or win wages?" But "What will please God?" It produces also fruit bearing in every good work and growth by the true knowledge of God. And this gives strength in the way down here.

"Strengthened with all power, according to the might of His glory, unto all patience and long suffering with joy." In the midst of tribulation and suffering strength is supplied through the might of His glory. It is the glory of Christ and Christ in glory which strengthens the believer, gives power to endure and to pass through every trial and hardship with joy. To know this will of God in Christ and Christ and His glory constantly before the soul, this is what leads to Christlikeness and what gives victory as we walk through a world to which the believer no longer belongs. "For, with our feet outside of the land, our way must be a toilsome and afflicting one, dreary enough and a perpetual outrage to the soul strung to heavenly purity and peace and worship. But He who was from heaven and is now its attractiveness went through it all with a glow of gladness that broke out in a rapture at times of greatest neglect and misapprehension and hatred from without (Matt. xi:25–27). He was as a weaned child, desiring nothing here. There has been no promise of making things smooth here, but the opposite, and if we nestle we must have made the nest by gathering worldly materials, by accepting a friendship where He would get hate. God brings nothing before us to hold the heart in comfort, peace, and joy, but the glory to be revealed. And is it not enough for that and enough to wait for?"*

Being filled with the knowledge of His will produces likewise worship. "Giving thanks unto the Father who hath made us meet to be partakers of the inheritance of the Saints in light; who hath delivered us from the power of darkness and translated us into the kingdom of the Son of His love; in whom we have redemption, the forgiveness of sins." It is a part of the prayer that Christians might give thanks to the Father in spiritual worship. And these things mentioned are known to the believer if he is filled with the knowledge of His will, for they tell us what God *hath done* for the sinner who believes on His Son. Here are the most assuring statements, the things forever settled for those who have accepted the Lord Jesus Christ. There is an inheritance of the Saints in light and the Father hath made us meet to be partakers of it through the work of His Son. From the Father we receive this inheritance. The title to that inheritance, which every true child of God fully owns, is the blood of the Lord Jesus Christ, and the fitness to be there is the new nature bestowed upon the believer. It is therefore not, as so often stated, that we try to fit ourselves for heaven; this is impossible. The moment a sinner accepts the Lord Jesus Christ, he is made meet to be a partaker of that inheritance. All the glory of that inheritance is at once put on the side of him who trusts on Christ. All was done for us once for all when Christ died; in Him we are sons and if sons, heirs of God, the fellow heirs of Christ.

"There can be no greater acceptance of us in heaven than God gives us now in Christ, for even there we shall stand accepted in Him alone. Our Father will not more fully rejoice over us there than He does here; for then, as now, He will see us only as in Christ. Our meetness, then, for the one part of the inheritance is just our meetness for

---

*M. Taylor on Colossians.

the other part. And so, when some eminent saint comes to his death-bed, what is it that gives him his comfort, his serene triumph, in that critical hour? Is it his progressive practical sanctification? Indeed, no. He is too conscious of many failures, that he should rely on that as his passport through the gates into the city. Thankful he is to God, that He has enabled him to serve Him with whatever degree of faithfulness, and he may speak of it to the praise of the glory of His grace; but he rests not his destination on so imperfect a prop as that. What is it then? Just this: the infinite value of the blood which sprinkled him. On that he rests, as on the Rock of Ages. Yes, Christ Himself is our only meetness for the inheritance, and our believing on Christ is our having the meetness."*

And more than that, "He *hath* delivered us (not a gradual deliverance, but a deliverance accomplished) from the power of darkness and hath translated us into the Kingdom of the Son of His love." And the deliverance takes place as well as the translation into His Kingdom, when we believe on Christ. There is a power of darkness. Satan is the ruler of darkness and to this power of darkness the unsaved sinner belongs. We are by nature the complete subjects of this power and also the children of wrath (Eph. ii:1–3). As such we are in a helpless condition and if deliverance is to take place it must come from the side of God. And it has come for all believers. All who are in Christ are no longer under the authority of Satan, the prince of the power of the air, they are taken from his domain and rule and are translated into another Kingdom, the Kingdom of the Son of his Love.

"My chains are snapped, the bonds of sin are broken,
And I am free.
Oh! let the triumphs of His grace be spoken
Who died for me."

The expression "Kingdom of the Son of His Love" has been identified with the church, while others make it to

*Bishop W. Nicholson.

mean the coming kingdom, which will be set up when the Lord Jesus Christ comes again. But it does not mean the body of Christ and much less the kingdom on earth, which is termed the kingdom of the Son of man. We quote from the Synopsis by Darby, who gives the correct meaning of this term.

"Here alone, I believe, is the kingdom called the kingdom of the Son; and, I think, it is only as introducing His Person as the centre of everything and giving us the measure of the greatness of the blessing. It is the kingdom of One who has this place, the Son of His love, into which we are introduced. It is indeed His kingdom; and in order that we may apprehend the character of this kingdom as it is now for us, and our nearness to God as having part in it, it is called the kingdom of the Son of His love. It is this which is the present foundation and characteristic of the relationship with God of those who are truly in and of it. As the kingdom of the Son of man, it is His manifestation hereafter in glory and in government. Here it is characterized by the relationship of the Son Himself to the Father, in His Person, with the addition of that which gives us a full title to share it—redemption through His blood, the forgiveness of sins."

Blessed possessions! Blessed assurance! In Christ, fit for glory; in Christ, delivered from the power of darkness and near to God now as He, the Son of His love, is near, belonging to same realm of glory; in Christ redemption, the forgiveness of sins. There are no "ifs" and no questionings. All is positive. For all this we should give thanks to the Father and praise Him for what He has done for us. Such worshippers the Father seeketh (John iv) for they delight in His Son, in whom all His delight is. Yet how little such true worship is rendered! And why? Because Christians are so little filled with the knowledge of His will, with that which grace has accomplished in Christ.*

---

*The spiritual condition of a Christian may be learned by his prayer.

Verses 15–18. With these verses we reach the heart of this chapter. Christ, the Son of His love, having been named in the prayer, the Holy Spirit reveals Him now in His Person and glory as well as the work of redemption accomplished by Him. It is a remarkable portion of this Epistle in which all the errors about the Person of Christ are refuted and silenced. Arianism, Socianism, Unitarianism, Russellism, Christian Science and other "isms" which rob the Lord Jesus Christ of His full glory and deny His Deity, are completely answered in the brief words which unfold His glory. It was Arius of Alexandria who taught in the beginning of the fourth century that the Lord Jesus was a creature, the first of all created beings, though super-angelic, yet not eternal in His being nor a partaker of the divine essence. The council of Nice (325 A. D.) condemned the wicked theory of Arius. Socinus in the Reformation period revived this error, as did Priestly and Martineau in England and Channing and others in America. It remained for one Charles T. Russell, whose system is known by different names, to popularize these false and corrupt views and spread them throughout Christendom. Russell with Arius asserts that in His pre-existent state Jesus was a pure spirit, higher than the angels, yet only a creature. When born of the Virgin Mary, He dropped His spirit nature while on earth. He teaches that the atonement offered by our Lord was only human, having nothing divine about it. Russellism also denies that the human body of our Lord was raised from the dead. The whole system is a conglomerate of Arianism, Ebioniteism and Rationalism. Christian Science equally denies the Deity of Christ and

---

One who knows what God has done, who has looked deep into the Gospel of God, whose heart knows and enjoys Christ will praise much and thank the Father for all these blessed realities. But how many ask God constantly to give to them that, which they already possess; and there is no real worship possible unless we know and enjoy His grace. Bye and bye all our prayers will cease and it will be all praise and worship—when we are with Him in glory and know what grace has done for us forever.

contains in itself all the fatal errors of Gnosticism, which the Colossians were facing in their day.

1. The first statement concerns His absolute Deity—"*Who is the image of the invisible God.*" He is the image of God in all His fulness and perfection. As the image of God, the invisible God, He therefore is God. "He is the effulgence of His glory and the expression of His substance" (Heb. i:3). He has made known God to man; in Him we see what God is. "No man hath seen God at any time; the only begotten Son, who is in the bosom of the Father, hath declared Him" (John i:18). Were He not the essential image of God in His own person, one with God in eternity and glory, He could not be the representative image of God in incarnation.

2. "*Firstborn of all Creation*"—not as the authorized version has it "the firstborn of every creature." It is here where the false teaching originates, which claims that our Lord was after all only a creature, called into existence by God, and not very God. This passage teaches no such thing. The title "Firstborn" denotes His priority to creation, for He is creation's Head; the Headship of all creation belongs to Him. When He who is the image of the invisible God takes His place in creation, as He did in incarnation, it can only be as the Firstborn, as the Beginning of the Creation of God, the Head of all. He, who became man, under whose feet as the second Man all things will be put in subjection (Ps. viii; Heb. ii), is the Lord from Heaven, the Creator of all things.

3. That He is not a creature, though He took on the creature's form, is at once demonstrated by the words which follow. The Holy Spirit anticipated the errors which would deny His glory and therefore we read of Him as the Creator. "*For by Him were all things created, in the heavens and upon the earth, things visible and invisible, whether they be thrones or dominions, or principalities, or powers, all things were created by Him and for Him.*" It is therefore absolutely certain that the "Firstborn" does not mean that our Lord is a creature, but the Creator. These

words which were written by the Apostle are revelation. Nor is Paul the only instrument through whom the Spirit of God makes known His glory. John wrote in the beginning of his gospel the same truth. "All things were made by Him; and without Him was not anything made that was made" (John i:2).

The Son of God is therefore the Creator, yet not to the exclusion of the power of the Father, nor the operation of the Spirit. The three are one, in character and in their work; in creation and in redemption the three persons of the Godhead are active. What a dignity and glory is His! All things visible were created by Him and for Him; all life, vegetable and animal, all matter and all physical forces, the small things and the big things, everything was called into existence by Him. The heavens are the work of His fingers (Ps. viii:3); the firmament showeth His handiwork (Ps. xix:1). The millions of stars with their suns, the planets and comets, the whole universe, unfathomable and incomprehensible for the creature, were all called forth by His omnipotent word. Not by science, nor by searching do we know of this, but "through faith we understand that the worlds were framed by the Word of God, so that things which are seen were not made of things which do appear" (Heb. xi:3). And then things invisible—how little we know of these! The innumerable company of angels, this vast and wonderful world of the unseen, are also created by Him. It is all "by Him" and "for Him"; He is the primal cause of it, as well as the final cause. In the presence of such deep and blessed revelations, which man's mind could never discover, in the presence of the infinite, the reasonings of Unitarianism and Darwinianism and all other reasonings crumble into dust. The evolutionary hypothesis of the creation of a cell or of "primordial germs" from which, through millions of years, all things were developed is an invention of man and completely silenced by this passage and other portions of the Word. "And what a wonderful light do these words throw upon creation itself and upon its destiny! Christ is not only the One under whom it is; He is not only the One who will bring it all into blessing, but He, the One who has become the man Christ Jesus, is the One for whom it all exists!" And such a One, the Lord of creation, by whom and for whom are all things is our Lord, with whom all who have accepted Him are one. How blessed, how safe we are in Him and with Him, sheltered and kept by His mighty arms! And when all things are put under His feet, when in the dispensation of the fullness of times, all things in heaven and on earth are headed up in Christ, when the glories of the new creation are manifested, what glory will be ours in Him and with Him!

4. "*And He is before all things and by Him all things consist.*" Everything depends upon Him; all things are held together by Him. Without Him all would cease to be. Four times in these two verses we read of "all things." All things created by Him; all things for Him; He is before all things; all things consist by Him.

Verse 18 reveals another headship and glory. "*And He is the head of the body, the church, who is the beginning, the firstborn from among the dead, that in all things He might have the pre-eminence.*"

From creation the Holy Spirit now leads us to another sphere, that of Redemption. Creation became marred and ruined by sin and He who is the head of all things in Creation had to come to earth in the form of man to redeem. He died, and, raised from among the dead, He is the Firstborn, the head of the body, the church, and as such the Beginning, that is, a new Beginning. The church was not in existence before His death and resurrection from the dead. He could not be the Head of the church till He had become the Firstborn by resurrection. And now He has a body, composed of all who have believed on Him as Saviour and Lord, born again and one Spirit with Him. This body is one with Him in life, in position and in glory. This body is the new creation, completely identified with Him, who is the Head, the fullness of Him who filleth all in all (Eph. i:23).

"He is the First-born of creation, He is the First-born according to the power of resurrection, in this new order of things in which man is predestined to an entirely new position, gained by redemption, and in which he participates in the glory of God (as far as that which is created can do so), and that by participating in divine life in Jesus Christ, the Son of God and everlasting life; and, as regards the church, as members of His body. He is the First-born of creation, the First-born from among the dead; the Creator, and the conqueror of death and the enemy's power. These are the two spheres of the display of the glory of God. The special position of the church, the body of Christ, forms a part of the latter. He must have this resurrection-glory, this universal pre-eminence and superiority also, as being man, for all the fulness was pleased to dwell in Him."*

Thus in all things He has the pre-eminence. And we also must give Him in all things the first place. As we lay hold on the glory of Christ, the Head of Creation, the risen One now, the Head of the body in glory, and look forward to the day of consummation and glory to come, when we shall see Him as He is and participate in the glory, which His grace has bestowed upon us, we shall indeed walk worthily of the Lord and be strengthened according to the power of His glory.

Verses 19–29. His great work of redemption and the ministry connected with it is the theme of the remaining verses of this chapter. "For it pleased the Father that in Him should all fullness dwell." It is to be noticed that the words "the Father" are supplied. If a word is to be used it must be the word "Godhead." (See chapter ii:9). But there is no need to do that. The correct rendering of the verse is "In Him all the fullness was pleased to dwell," and that is the fullness of the Godhead. It is a blessed and deep truth that the whole Godhead manifested itself in Him for the great purpose of redemption. The Father, the Son and the Holy Spirit dwelled in all fullness in the blessed One who walked among men. He could say of Himself that the Father dwelleth in Him (John xiv:10);

---

*Synopsis.

he that hath seen me hath seen the Father (John xiv:9) and again, "I am in the Father and the Father in me. And He who spoke thus was and is the Son of God. And the third person of the trinity, the Holy Spirit, was not given to Him by measure (John iii:34) but He was in Him in all His fullness. The fullness of the Godhead was pleased to dwell in the incarnate One. The Gnostic teachers, which began then to sow their evil seed in the early church, used the word "fullness" (pleroma) very much, and meant by it the absolute perfection of Deity. But they taught that portions of this fullness was given to various Divine incarnations and angels, who were generated by a supreme Being. Christ, according to their philosophy, was an inferior being, who did not possess the pleroma of the Godhead. In answer to this perversion the Holy Spirit witnesses to the truth that in Him all the fullness, the pleroma, was pleased to dwell. The fullness of the Godhead dwelt in Him and was manifested through Him, yet man, His creation, would not have Him. Man gave Him a cross which showed that man was irreconcilable as far as he was concerned. "He in whom all fullness dwelt, who was the one altogether lovely, who manifested the very character of God and brought among men unimagined goodness and power, who dealt with every need, going about doing good, who never refused a single soul, He was despised and rejected by man, hated without a cause. They crucified the Lord of Glory, the Creator of all things.

"And what was to be done? Ah! this was the serious question, and this it was which God was waiting to solve. He meant to reconcile man spite of himself; He would prove His own love to be the conqueror of his hatred. Let man be unmendable, let his enmity be beyond all thought, God, in the calmness of His own wisdom, and in the strength of His unwearied grace, accomplishes His purpose of redeeming love at the very moment when man consummates his wickedness. It was at the cross of Christ. And so it was that, when all seemed to fail, all was won. The fulness of the Godhead dwelt in Jesus; but man would have none of it, and proved it above all in the cross. Yet the cross was the precise and only place where the foundation that cannot be moved was laid. As he says, 'having made peace through the blood of his cross, by him to reconcile all things unto Himself; by him, I say, whether it be things on earth or things in heaven.' "*

He made peace in the blood of His cross. Then the great work of redemption was accomplished. And through the blood of the cross, all things are to be reconciled by Him to the Godhead, whether things on earth or things in heaven. What reconciliation is this? It is a reconciliation which is not yet accomplished. It includes all creation and the universe. The heavens and the earth will be completely delivered from the power of evil. This reconciliation of all things in virtue of the blood of His cross will take place when He comes again, when all things are put in subjection under His feet. All is in disorder in creation; it is a groaning creation. Satan with his wicked spirit is in the heavenlies and defilment is there. Yet the purchase price has been paid in the blood of His cross. The reconciliation of all things yet to come is the same which Peter preached as "the restitution of all things of which God has spoken by the mouth of His holy prophets since time began" (Acts iii:19-21). Therefore the prophets in the Old Testament give us the meaning of this coming reconciliation. We find it predicted in portions of the prophetic Word, concerning the coming age, when righteousness reigns, peace is established, the knowledge of the glory of the Lord covers the earth and the earth is full of His glory, when Israel has received the promised blessing and glory, and groaning creation no longer groans under the curse (Isaiah xi:6–9; Rom. viii:19–22). It will all be accomplished when He returns, whose right it is to reign and who paid for all in the blood of His cross. Then all present disorder will cease, the curse will be removed, Satan will be bound.

---

*W. Kelly.

This dispensation of the fullness of times will have come and Christ will reign and His Saints with Him.

Does this reconciliation include the unsaved, the unregenerated, who reject Christ and remain in their sins? Does it include Satan and the fallen angels? Some, who call themselves "Reconciliationists" or "Restitutionists" teach this; and so does Russellism and other cults. But it is not so. The Scriptures do not teach such a universal reconciliation which reaches the wicked dead and wicked spirits. The best proof is when we compare the statement here with a similar one in Phil. ii:10. In this passage Paul speaks of the things under the earth, which are the lost. It is there the question of acknowledging the supreme authority of the Lord. But here in Colossians where it is the question of reconciliation, things on earth and things in heaven are mentioned, but the things under the earth are omitted, because there is not reconciliation for such. "These shall go away into everlasting punishment"; no future reconciliation is anywhere promised in the Word of God for the lost. There is no new birth, no repentance, no faith in hell. Not a drop of the living water will ever reach there to quench the spiritual thirst of the damned.

But while the reconciliation of all things awaits the return of our Lord to put all things in order, there is another reconciliation which is already effected. "And you being in time past alienated and enemies in mind by wicked works, yet now hath He reconciled in the body of His flesh, through death, to present you holy and unblamable and irreproachable before Him; if indeed ye abide in the faith, grounded and firm, and not moved away from the gospel which ye heard, which hath been preached in the whole creation which is under heaven, whereof I Paul was made a minister" (verses 21–23). This is spoken of those who have believed on the Son of God. All were once estranged from God and enemies in mind by wicked works, but having believed His work, His sacrificial death on the cross hath reconciled them. In virtue of this reconciliation believers are no longer enemies but made nigh, accepted in the

Beloved and presented holy, unblamable, and irreproachable before God. What a change! And it is not of man, by his work, or having become a believer by living a fully separated life, but it is all through His death. In Him we are constituted holy, unblamable and irreproachable; this is the believer's standing before God. The words "if ye continue in the faith," etc., are words of caution. They do not touch the election and perserverance of the Saints who are members of the body of which He is the head. A believer thus reconciled will continue in the faith and will not be moved away from the hope of the gospel; this is one of the tests of salvation. There was danger for the Colossians to abandon the great fundamentals of Christianity; if they did so they rejected the grace which presented them to God and in doing this they showed that they had never received the reconciliation, for one who is reconciled continues in the faith and remains upon the sure foundation.

"All the blessedness that Christ has procured is for those that believe; but this of course supposes that they hold Him fast. The language does not in the smallest degree insinuate that there is any uncertainty for a believer. We must never allow one truth to be either shut out or enfeebled by another; but then we need also to remember that there are, and have always been, those that, having begun seemingly well, have ended by becoming the enemies of Christ and the church. Even antichrists are not from without in their origin. "They went out *from* us, because they were not *of* us." There are no enemies so deadly as those who, having received enough truth to overbalance them and to abuse to their own self-exaltation, turn again, and would rend the church of God, wherein they learnt all that gives them power to be specially mischievous. The apostle could not but dread the slide on which the Colossians found themselves; and the more so as they themselves had no fears, but on the contrary thought highly of that which had attracted their minds. If there was danger, certainly it was love to admonish them; and in this spirit he therefore says, 'If ye continue in the faith, grounded and settled.' "*

Then Paul speaks of himself as being the minister of that gospel which hath been preached in the whole creation. How he termed this gospel "my gospel" and received it by revelation, and the meaning of all this we learned from Romans and Galatians. And the sound of this gospel goes forth into all creation.

We must notice here that up to this point in this Epistle we have learned of the *two headships* of Christ. He is *head of creation* and *head of the church.* Then followed a twofold reconciliation. *The reconciliation of all things* which includes all creation over which He is the head, and *the reconciliation of believers,* who are in that body over which He is the head. All these wonderful revelations fully answered the teachers who brought among the Colossians the most deadly errors, denying the Deity of Christ, as if some Demiurge had created the world, etc. And these great statements of verses 15–23 also answer all heresies of to-day.

To the two headships of Christ and the two reconciliations there is now added a twofold ministry. The *ministry of the Gospel* and the *ministry of the church.* Twice Paul writes he was made a minister, the minister of the Gospel (verse 23) and the church, whereof he was also made a minister (verse 25). It means that to him was given the revelation concerning the gospel of grace and glory and through him was also made known the truth concerning the church, the body of Christ. There is then a blessed harmony in these statements.

---

*If thousands and tens of thousands of members of the professing church turn to "Christian Science" or accept the teachings of the "New Theology" and in doing so abandon the Gospel and deny the doctrine of Christ, they show thereby that all their profession was only a sham, that they never received the love of the truth, were never real believers who have been reconciled. They were at least the enemies of the cross who more openly deny Christ.

I. The twofold Headship of Christ: *Head of Creation. Head of the Church.*

II. The twofold Reconciliation: *Reconciliation of all things.* (Creation). *Our Reconciliation.* (The church).

III. The twofold Ministry: *The Gospel.* (Preached in all Creation). *The Church* (To present every man perfect in Christ).

Paul, to whom the Spirit of God revealed these great truths, fulfilled in this way the Word of God, for the truth about the church, the body of Christ, is the highest revelation. He was shut up in a prison and was suffering "for His body's sake," which sufferings he looks upon as filling up that which remained of the sufferings of Christ in them. He rejoiced in these sufferings for he knew they were "for His body's sake." He knew and declared "the mystery which hath been hid from ages and generations, but now hath been made manifested to His saints, to whom God would make known what are the riches of the glory of this mystery among the Gentiles, which is Christ in you the hope of glory." The mystery of which he writes is not the coming of Christ to this earth, His incarnation, death, resurrection, ascension and coming again. All this was not a mystery, for it was revealed in the Old Testament. The mystery made known through him and of which he writes is a glorified Christ who unites all in His person, the Head in glory, who has a body composed of saved Jews and Gentiles, who are one in Him, and "Christ in (or among) you the hope of glory"—which looks forward to the consummation, when this body which is now forming, through the preaching of the Gospel, is to be with the Head in glory. This is the mystery which was hid in former ages. It is unrevealed in the Old Testament and therefore exclusively a New Testament revelation. With such a revelation and ministry he preached, "warning every man, and teaching every man in all wisdom that we may present every man perfect in Christ Jesus; where unto I also labor, striving according to His working which worketh in me in power." Every man "perfect" means full-grown. (See Phil. iii:15 and Heb. v:14.) It is the believing apprehension of what Christ is for us and what we are in Him. Through this knowledge and heart occupation with the Lord of glory the believer becomes full grown and true Christian character is formed. And what toil and energy the great Apostle manifested that this might be accomplished!

II. COMPLETE IN HIM, IN WHOM ALL THE FULLNESS DWELLS.

CHAPTER II.

1. The Mystery of God. 1–8.
2. Complete in Christ. 9–15.
3. Exhortations and Warnings. 16–23.

Verses 1–8. In view of the last verses of the preceding chapter we can understand his anxiety and the great conflict he had for the Colossians and for those living in nearby Laodicea, and for as many who had not seen his face in the flesh. He was deeply concerned about them after he heard of their danger of going into error. It was a spiritual conflict. He was greatly exercised in his thoughts and feelings. He knew the powers of evil so well; hence the burden for the Colossians, for the Laodiceans and for all others. In writing to them about his great conflict for them, and therefore his prayerful interest in them, he did so that their hearts might be comforted thereby and then, being knit together in love for this purpose: "unto all riches of the full assurance of understanding to the full knowledge of the mystery of God* in which are hid all the treasures of wisdom and knowledge." And what is this mystery of God in which the treasures, yea all the treasures of wisdom and knowledge are hidden? The mystery of God is *Christ.* But it is not Christ in incarnation, in His life on earth, His death on the cross and His resurrection. Nor is it Christ at the right hand of God, or Christ coming again to rule over the nations on earth and establish His Kingdom of glory. All these things are the subjects of divine revelation in the Old Testament. They are not a mystery. It is Christ, the Head of the body and believers in union with the glorious Head, joined to Him by His Spirit, possessing His life, one with Him, destined to share His glory. This is the

---

*The translation in the authorized version is not correct. The words "of the Father and of Christ" must be omitted. It is "The mystery of God, in which are hid all the treasures of wisdom and knowledge."

mystery of God in which are hid all the treasures of wisdom and knowledge. And what treasures these are! How little His people know of all this mystery of God contains! It will take eternity to know and enjoy these treasures, the unsearchable riches.

The Greek word for knowledge is "gnosis"; the false teachers called themselves, after this word, "gnostics," boasting of superior knowledge and as if they possessed mysteries unknown to those who believed on Christ. We understand in this light the brief exhortation which follows: "And this I say, lest any man should delude you with enticing words." Being in Christ they had all in Him and no human philosophy or science, falsely so called, could give a greater wisdom or knowledge, than that which God had made known by revelation. The enemy's work is to keep God's people back from fully enjoying their union with Christ and increasing in the knowledge of it. Satan does this work in the garb of an angel of light, through all kinds of theories and inventions.

Before the Apostle sounds a more definite warning, he expressed his joy in seeing their order and steadfastness of their faith in Christ. No doubt a part of the Colossian church stood unwavering for the faith, while others had given ear to the delusive teachings. "As ye have therefore received Christ Jesus the Lord, so walk ye in Him, rooted and built up in Him and stablished in the faith, as ye have been taught, abounding therein with thanksgiving." This was their danger, as it is still more in these days of declension and delusion, our danger, not to walk in Him, rooted and built up in Him. They were not satisfied with Christ only. They did not realize that the secret of blessing and all a Christian needs, is to go on and know more and more of Christ. This they did not do but turned instead to other sources and listened to that which was not after Christ.

"When we have received Christ, all the rest is but a development of that which He is, and of the glory which the counsels of God have connected with His Person. Knowledge, or pretended knowledge, outside this, does but turn us away from Him, withdraw our hearts from the influence of His glory, throw us into that which is false, and lead our souls into connection with the creation apart from God, and without possessing the key to His purposes. Thus, since man is incapable of fathoming that which exists, and of explaining it to himself, his efforts to do so cause him to invent a mass of ideas that have no foundation, and to endeavor to fill up the void that is found in his knowledge through his ignorance of God by speculations, in which (because he is at a distance from God) Satan plays the chief part without man's suspecting it."*

Then follows a stronger and important warning. "Beware lest any man spoil you through philosophy and vain deceit, after the tradition of men, after the rudiments of the world, and not after Christ." It is a warning against the natural man's philosophy, and the religious man's traditions; both are not after Christ, but aim at the Person, the work and the glory of Christ. Rationalism and Ritualism are still the pronounced enemies of the Lord Jesus Christ, as they were when He walked on the earth.† Both may use His name, but deny His glory and reject the great truth of His Headship. Philosophy is the wisdom of this world. Well has it been said: "Philosophy is an idol of man, a blind substitute for the knowledge of God." It is false and ruinous whether it leaves Him out or tries to bring Him in, whether it denies the true God, or sets up a sham god. Atheism and Pantheism are the ultimate goal and results of Philosophy, and both set God and His revelation aside. This is especially true of the present day destructive Bible criticism, which claims to be "scientific" and "philosophical." It is the most subtle deception the father of lies has produced. This destructive criticism, which denies with a show of learning the Word of God, denies with it God and His blessed Son;

---

*Synopsis.

†The Sadducees were the Philosophers, the Rationalists. The Pharisees, the most religious sect, the Ritualists. Both combined in hatred of Christ

it is an anti-christ, preparing the way for the final great delusion, the full manifestation of the mystery of iniquity, the man of sin. The evolution theory is another philosophy. Though proven to be untenable, preachers, and especially the teachers of the young, still adhere to it and thereby deny God's revelation. The evolution-philosophy has no explanation for the sin and misery of the world, but makes it all a part of the nature of things which God could not avoid when He started the world evolving. It makes God the author of sin. And evolution offers no remedy for sin and its results. Evolutionists as found in all the prominent sects or denominations of Christendom teach that sin is only animalism left in man; and then they substitute for true conversion, regeneration, for reconciliation by the death of Christ and salvation by grace—they substitute for it a development for the better by civilization and culure.* Evolution-philosophies are the enemies of revelation and the cross of Christ.

"Christian Science" also comes under the garb of a philosophy. This wicked system with its outrageous deceptions may be termed the Masterpiece of Satan. Against its blasphemous inventions the Spirit of God bears a perfect witness in the first chapter of this Epistle. Christianity is not Science. Science is knowledge gained by experience, by searching. Christianity is a revelation from God. It is a faith.

The traditions of men and rudiments of the world are

---

*"But obviously this evolutionary 'salvation' is largely or wholly a salvation of the race through the prospective future perfectibility of mankind as a whole; and it is childishly inadequate in dealing with the poor individual here and now who, under this hideous handicap, fails in the sad conflict with his inherited animalism; and it has no gospel for these present moral failures (or those of the past), unless they can be reincarnated at a higher stage of the racial development, or have 'another chance' under some less hard conditions in the future; while it goes without saying that, in the view of these theistic evolutionists, this racial culture or development can be accomplished without the intervention of a divine Mediator and the help of a divine Sacrifice."—Prof. Price.

terms which apply to the religion of the flesh, by which we mean a religion which the natural man can lay hold of and which suits perfectly the natural, unregenerated man. This is Ritualism, the Galatianized gospel which has the curse of God resting upon it. It brings in man's works, law-keeping, ceremonies, holy days, saints days, the mass and other things. But it is not after Christ. Against these two currents, Rationalism and Ritualism, the Spirit of God warns. Any one who follows either one must deny Christ and becomes spoiled and ruined. The ninth and tenth verses introduce us to the heart of this great document. "*For in Him dwelleth all the fullness of the Godhead bodily, and in Him ye are filled full, who is the head of all principality and power.*" How this blessed statement recalls our attention to the great truths of the first chapter we do not need to point out. While in the first chapter He is displayed as the incarnate One, who walked on earth, in whom all the fullness was pleased to dwell; in this statement of the second chapter we see Him as the risen One, who is in glory as the glorified Man and in Him dwelleth all the fullness of the Godhead bodily. Glorious truth that there is the Man, in glory, in a real human body, the Man, who made peace in the blood of His cross. The fullness of the Godhead dwelleth in Him and out of this fullness we receive grace upon grace, and that we might also be filled with all the fullness of God (Eph. iii:19). In Him believers are filled full. In Him we possess perfection and completeness before God and are not wanting anything whatever as to our position before God. Believers are in Him before God, not in what they do or according to their service, or anything else, but in perfection of what He is. Who could add to His fullness and who can add to the fullness and completeness the believer possesseth forever in Him! The child of God has no need of philosophy, ceremonies, asceticism, advanced thought, or any other thing. No need of the traditions of men as embodied in ritualism, a man-made priesthood (which He hates; Rev. ii:15); or the mass with its terrible blasphemy, or the worship of angels! We have and are all in Christ. Our only concern must be to lay hold in a practical way of this fullness, to take more and more of Him and walk in the power of it.

This is viewed next. The literal rendering of verses 11 and 12 is as follows:

"*In whom also ye have been circumcised with circumcision not done by hand, in the putting off of the body of the flesh in the circumcisim of Christ; buried with Him in baptism, in whom ye have been also raised together through faith in the operation of God, who raised Him from among the dead.* Circumcism done by hand is for the Jew, the sign of separation from the Gentiles. Believers are circumsized in the circumcision of Christ, that is, "the putting off of the body of flesh,"* separated from it, by being made partakers of the efficacy of His death. In the death of Christ the old man is put to death as more fully demonstrated in Romans vi; we are dead to sin, because we are in Christ, who is our life. And having now no more confidence in ourselves we are the true circumcision, who worship God in the Spirit, and rejoice in Christ Jesus (Phil. iii:3). Baptism is the symbol of this "buried with Him in baptism." And we are raised up with Him through faith in the operation of God who raised Him from among the dead. It is "through faith" this is accomplished and not in an ordinance; we are risen with Christ in possession of life.

"It is thus that we are set free from the thought of deliverance by an ordinance, which so many hold to-day. We are 'raised up through the faith of the operation of God who raised Him from among the dead.' Here we see distinctly what is meant. Resurrection is the opposite of burial. In burial a dead man is put among the dead. In resurrection a now living man is given his place among the living; and it is seen that Christ identified with us through grace in His death has been raised up of God, that we might find, therefore, our own title and ability to take our place amongst those truly alive. But then all depends upon this identifi-

---

*Not "putting off the body of the sins of the flesh."

cation of ourselves with Him. Our eyes are now, therefore, to be upon Christ. He is in this character our true self; and our confidence, therefore, is to be in Him. As we have had it in Galatians, we live, yet no more we, but Christ liveth in us. It is the One who is before God for us who is before us now in faith and whom we accept as now our true self, a self in whom we can have confidence, a self that we can contemplate with joy and satisfaction, and without the least tendency to such pride of heart as results naturally from what we call self-occupation. Here is One who will draw us away from self, who will, as a heavenly Object draw us completely out of the world, and accomplish our deliverance in both senses at the same time."*

The truth unfolded in the Ephesian epistle (chapter ii) is also mentioned here by the Apostle. "*And you being dead in offences and the uncircumcism of your flesh hath He quickened together with Him, having forgiven you all trespasses.*" Blessed truth again! What follows has a meaning for both Jewish and Gentile believers. "*Having blotted out the handwriting in ordinances that was against us, which was contrary to us, He has taken it out of the way, having nailed it to the cross.*" The Colossians were Gentiles, they had not been under the law and its ordinances, therefore he writes not which were "against you" but "against us." All the ordinances were against them, for they were as Jews under obligation to keep them, as they had, so to speak, put their handwriting, their signature to it, when they said with one voice, "All the words which the Lord hath said will we do" (Ex. xxiv:3). And inasmuch as they did not keep these ordinances, they were against them. The work of Christ has taken it out of the way; all was nailed to the cross. Then the signature was erased and the debt paid. The ordinances are removed. This applies to Gentiles as well and also in another sense. The law and the ordinances was the middle wall of partition, which excluded the Gentiles. Christ "has broken down the middle wall of partition,

---

*Numerical Bible.

having abolished in His flesh the enmity, the law of commandments in ordinances, for to make in Himself of twain one new man, so making peace" (Ephes. ii:14–15). At the same time He spoiled principalities and powers, made a show of them openly, leading them in triumph by it. This means the principalities and powers of Satan and the wicked Spirits. They were against us, but He has vanquished them in His death on the cross and in it has triumphed over them. Trespasses are forgiven; ordinances blotted out, completely gone; principalities and powers triumphed over.

Verses 16–23. The chapter closes with warnings and exhortations. The first warning exhortation is against Ritualistic legalism. "*Let none therefore judge you in meat or in drink, or in matter of an holy day, or new moon, or of the Sabbath, which are a shadow of things to come; but the body is of Christ.*" All the ceremonies of the law were shadows; the substance has come and the shadows have ceased. Ritualistic Christendom has aped the shadows and by doing so practically denies by it the truth of the gospel. It is a turning away from the substance and moving after the shadow. A religion in ordinances, so-called sacraments with mysterious powers, with an imposing ritual for the eye and the ear, which gives the flesh something to do and to boast in, is an invention of Satan. True Christianity has no holy days and feast days, saints days, lenten days, etc.; nor does it need these "beggarly elements."

The Sabbath is also mentioned. Some keep the seventh day, Saturday, and claim that this is the day to be kept. But the church has no Sabbath to keep in the legal sense. The first day of the week, the Lord's day, is the day of worship.

The next warning is against the worship of angels and occultism. "*Let no one fraudulently deprive you of your prize, doing his own will in humility and worship of angels, entering into things which he has not seen vainly puffed up by the mind of his flesh, and not holding fast to the head, from whom all the body ministered to and united together by the joints and bands, increases with the increase of God.*" Here the Romish idolatry comes into view. It began early in the church. Angels are ministering spirits who minister to the heirs of glory. Their presence with and ministry to God's people may be believed, but never must they be worshipped. Putting them between Christians and Christ as a mediatorial agency is idolatrous, sinful and a denial of the Headship of Christ. The worship of angels denies the union of the believer with the head. The Head, Christ in glory, ministers to the body in spiritual things. All looked like humility when it was in reality self-will and pride. Intruding into unseen things points to such evil systems as Spiritism, Theosophy, psychical research and other cults. Whoever follows these things proves thereby that Christ as the Head over all is not recognized but denied. He who knows Christ and is in conscious union with Him will never crave after any of these things.

Asceticism is the concluding thing against which the Holy Spirit warns. "If ye have died with Christ from the elements of the world, why as if alive in the world do ye subject yourselves to ordinances?" Then he gives an illustration of these "Do not handle, do not taste, do not touch."* This and the concluding words reprove asceticism "the harsh treatment of the body" not keeping the body in a certain honor and all to the satisfaction of the flesh, as he writes: "According to the injunctions and teachings of men (which have indeed an appearance of wisdom in voluntary worship, and humility, and harsh treatment of the body, not in a certain honor), to the satisfaction of the flesh." These errorists taught that matter is evil and the body is the source of sin and therefore they treated the body harshly. They denied honor to the body but it was for their own satisfaction of the flesh.

"Asceticism is utterly powerless to effect the object aimed at: it does not, it cannot sanctify the flesh. It has a show of wisdom. It is extravagant in its preten-

*Strange it is that these words are generally misapplied, wrested from the context, twisted and contorted to furnish a text for the drink-evil and to advocate prohibition. It has nothing to do with that.

sions and loud in its promises. But it never fulfills them. The apostle here declares that it has no value against the indulgence of the flesh (v. 23). It, rather, stimulates the appetites and passions it is meant to extirpate. Asceticism has often proved to be a hot-bed of vice. Some of the vilest men have been found among those who advocated the strictest austerities. They denounced the holiest of human associations, and branded as sensual the purest relations. Marriage was degraded, celibacy glorified, the family disparaged, domestic life despised. And some of these foes of truth have been canonized!

Asceticism does not touch the seat of sin. All its strength is exerted against the body. Sin is of the soul, has its seat in the soul. So long as the heart is corrupt, no bodily restraints will make the life holy. There is one remedy alone for human sin, one that reaches to its roots, that ultimately will totally destroy it, viz., the blood of Christ (1 John i:7)."*

And all these warnings are for our own times, for we live in the day when the tares the devil sowed in the field in the beginning of the age are ripening for the harvest. They are full grown. Legalism, Ritualism, Evolution, Higher Criticism, Christian Science, Russellism, Demonism, Spiritism, New Thought, New Religion, New Theology, Theosophy, Unitarianism, Romanism, Mormonism, Seventh Dayism and other still more dangerous theories, because more subtle, are about us. Only a constant realization of our position in Christ and holding fast the head will keep His people in the days of Apostasy. May God's people to-day, the faithful remnant, never lose sight of the two vital truths of these two chapters: In Him dwelleth the fullness of the Godhead bodily and we are complete in Him.

---

*Prof. W. A. Moorhead.

III. THE PRACTICAL RESULTS. LIVING AS RISEN WITH CHRIST. Chapters iii–iv.

CHAPTER III.

1. The Life Hid With Christ in God. 1–4.
2. The Contrast: The Old Man and the New Man. 5–11.
3. Manifesting Christ. 12–17.
4. Relationships. 18–iv:1.

Verses 1–4. Risen with Christ; such is the believer's position. "Ye are dead and your life is hid with Christ in God." These are the great truths of Christianity: The believer dead with Christ; risen with Christ and in possession of a life which is hid with Christ in God and therefore safe and secure. And these facts constitute the controlling motive of the believer's life on earth. If apprehended in faith they will lead the soul to seek the things which are above, where Christ sitteth at the right hand of God. The mind will then be constantly set on the things above and not on things which are on the earth. The more a believer enters into those blessed truths, making them his own by reckoning himself dead with Christ and risen with Him, with his life hid with Christ in God, the more will the things above be for him the great attraction and the things on earth will lose their charm. The things above are Christ and His glory. The things on earth include all the deceiving things mentioned in the previous chapter, such as the rudiments of the world, philosophy and words of vain deceit, legalism, ritualism, ordinances, as well as worldly ambitions, honors, pleasures and achievements. All these will fade away when the believer's heart is occupied with Him who fills the throne in glory. This is the true and only way of sanctification—heart occupation with the risen Christ. When the eyes of the heart see the risen and glorified Christ and faith lays hold of the wonderful meaning for us who believe, then we learn to walk in that separation into which God has called His people. What the Christian therefore needs is an ever increasing realization in faith of his position in Christ, and then to be energized by the indwelling Spirit to seek those things which are above and not the things on earth. Such a life means joy and peace. It is a life of obedience and quietness, victorious over all earthly circumstances. And because it is a life which is hid with Christ in God, it is hidden from the world. "Therefore the world knoweth us not, because it knew Him not" (1 John iii:1). The world, which lieth in the wicked one, cannot understand nor estimate such a life of separation through faith in an unseen person, a life which reaches out after an unseen goal and which spurns worldly honors and the things which are the boast of the natural man.* But it will not be always thus. A day is coming when this life, hidden now, will be fully manifested. "When Christ is manifested who is our life, then shall ye also be manifested with Him in glory." It will be a manifestation in glory. It comes when He comes again. "When He shall come to be glorified in His Saints, and to be admired in all them that believe in that day" (2 Thess. i:10). It is not the day when He comes for His Saints; it is the day of His visible manifestation, when all His own share His glory and come with Him, when He brings His many sons unto glory. To look constantly in holy anticipation to this promised glory-event, is inseparably connected with the statements of the preceding verses. What blessed links these are:—Dead with Christ—Risen with Christ—a life hid with Christ in God—a life to be manifested when He comes again! May God's people know the reality of all this in power and be kept from a mere profession, lifeless and powerless, of these fundamental facts of the Gospel.

Verses 5–11. An exhortation follows to mortify the members which are upon the earth. And what shameful and shameless things are mentioned here! "Fornication, uncleanness, inordinate affection, evil concupiscence, and

---

*Phil. iii:18–19 tells us that those who mind earthly things, though Christians in profession, are the enemies of the cross of Christ and that their end will be destruction. Such is the state of the masses of Christendom to-day—minding earthly things; filled with the love of the world and dead to the spiritual heavenly things.

coveteousness, which is idolatry." From this exhortation addressed to those who are believers, dead and risen with Christ, we learn that the old nature is not eradicated in the child of God. The believer knows that the old man is crucified with Christ (Rom. vi:6), that being in Christ he is now no longer seen by God as in the flesh; but the believer also knows that the old nature is still in him. He finds this out daily "for the flesh lusteth against the Spirit." The spiritually minded believer acknowledges freely that in his flesh there dwelleth no good thing, and that in his fallen nature are all these shameful things and that this old nature is capable of all of which the apostle writes. On account of these things the wrath of God cometh on the children of disobedience. "In the which ye also walked some time, when ye lived in them." The natural man lives in these things; but not so the believer. A child of God may commit these horrible things of the flesh, but he no longer lives in them And what is to be done to these members? The translation, "mortify you members which are on the earth," does not fully express the original meaning. It does not mean that we are to be doing it as it is so often attempted by resolutions, fasting and other exercises, ever trying to fight the flesh and conquer the evil things of the old nature. We are never told to fight the flesh, but to flee and abstain from fleshly lusts. Fighting the flesh, trying to put it to death ourselves leads to defeat. We cannot do it, but it has been done for us. The old man was put to death in the cross of Christ; we are now dead to sin—sin is not to have dominion over us. "Likewise reckon ye also yourselves to be dead unto sin, but alive unto God through Jesus Christ our Lord. Let not sin therefore reign in your mortal body, that ye should obey it in the lusts thereof" (Rom. vi:11–12). "Mortify your members" means keep them in the place of death where they have been put by the death of Christ. "Let it be as done"—exercise the power which redemption gives by holding in the place of death the members which are upon earth. This, however, is not possible unless the believer walks in the Spirit, is occupied with Christ and seeks those things which are above. For this reason the exhortations of verses 5–11 are the result of doing what the opening verses of this chapter put before us.

And there are other things besides the gross things of the flesh. "Anger, wrath, malice, blasphemy, filthy communications, lying one to another" are likewise the works of the flesh. They are to be put off. The same Greek tense* is here also employed—"let it be as done"—have it put off, because grace in redemption has made it possible. No need, therefore, to tolerate these things any longer in your lives, "seeing that ye have put off the old man with his deeds and have put on the new man which is being renewed in knowledge after the image of Him that created him, where there is neither Greek nor Jew, circumcision nor uncircumcision, Barbarian, Scythian, bond nor free; but Christ is all, and in all." Born again, believers have received a new nature, the nature from above; and this new man is being renewed in knowledge, not after the pattern of the first man, Adam, but after the image of Him, who created him. Christ Himself is the type of the new man; Christ is the object of the faith and the ambitions of the new nature in the believer. And in this new man all differences have ceased, all human distinctions disappear forever. Greek, Jew, circumcision, uncircumcision, Barbarian, and the worst type of the Barbarian, the Scythian, bond and free, are completely obliterated and gone. Having believed in Christ the new man is formed in each, and Christ is all as well as in all. He Himself is everything and all things are found in Him. The new man is independent of all earthly things and conditions and blessedly dependent upon Him, who created the new man.

It is a great truth that Christ is all and also "in all." The believer must look upon all fellow-believers as being indwelt by Christ, that He is *in all.* This brings deliverance from self; all jealousy, pride and fleshly ambitions

*Aorist Imperative.

will end among the Saints of God if they look upon each other after this manner, that Christ is in all. Here is comfort and power.

Verses 12–17. Therefore, as the elect of God, who are the new man indwelt by Christ and one with Him, holy and beloved, are exhorted to put on (have it done) the things which manifest Christ. Bowels of mercy, kindness, humbleness of mind, meekness, long-suffering. It is the fruit of knowing Christ risen and seated in glory. His own character is reproduced and Christ is manifested in the believer's walk.

"As the elect of God, those who owe everything to His will, His choice as those set apart to Him, and those upon whom He has set His love, we are to put on the things which properly accompany this: "bowels of compassion, kindness, lowliness, meekness, long-suffering, forbearing one another and forgiving one another." It is striking how, in all these, there is found some form of self-denial. Power is shown by competence for stooping; God turning also the very things that are against us into the means of educating us in this. Things evil in themselves may, nevertheless, furnish us with a wholesome discipline for the way and enable us, in answer, to bring forth fruit which is according to God. We are to forbear as God has forborne. We are to forgive as Christ has forgiven us; to all which is to be added love as that which is the "bond of perfectness," which keeps everything in its place and perfects every detail of life. Think how the world, even, has to put on the appearance of love, the more if it has not the reality; but love itself has no need to put on an appearance. It will manifest itself in harmony in every tone and gesture. The manifestation of the divine nature has a unity in it which makes everything to be in harmony. If there is love in the heart, the words will not be hard or unseemly; their very tone will be affected."*

"And let the peace of Christ† preside in your hearts, to

*Numerical Bible.

†Not "peace of God" as in the authorized version.

which also ye have been called in one body, and be thankful." All God's true children have peace with God and their calling in one body is also to have the peace of Christ presiding in their hearts. This blessed heritage (John xiv:27) will be enjoyed by all who walk in the Spirit, who walk in love, obedient to His will and in unbroken fellowship with Him. The crown and glory of such a walk is the peace of Christ, the very peace which He possessed while down here. Blessed, unspeakable privilege! Yet how few know this peace of Christ and enjoy it daily! If Christ is all for the believer and seen as being "in all," in every member of the body of Christ, then that peace will rule in the heart and we shall know the comfort and joy of it. Furthermore the word of Christ is to dwell richly in the believer's heart in all wisdom. And this word ever directs us to Himself. It does not teach us self-occupation but occupation with Himself, His own Person and Glory. It is through His word that we learn to know Him better and by which we are kept in His fellowship. And this again bears the blessed fruits of joy and praise, as well as spiritual fellowship with the Saints. "Teaching, and admonishing one another; with psalms and hymns and spiritual songs, singing with grace in your hearts to God." And all the believer does in word or in deed is all to be done in His own worthy name, "giving thanks to God the Father by Him." The Lord Jesus is to be in all our thoughts; in every word and in every deed must be given Him the pre-eminence.

"This consciousness of relationship with Christ, in the life which is of Him in us, applies to everything. Nothing is done without Him. If He is the life, all which that life does has Him for its end and object, as far as the heart is concerned. He is present as that which is the governing motive, and gives its character to our actions, and which preoccupies our heart in performing them. Everything relates to Him: we do not eat without Him (how can we when He is our very life?); we do not drink without Him; what we say, what we do, is said and done in the name of the Lord Jesus. There is the sense of His presence; the consciousness that everything relates to Him, that we can do nothing—unless carnally—without Him, because the life which we have of Him acts with Him and in Him, does not separate from Him, and has Him for its aim in all things, even as water rises to the height from which it descended. This is what characterises the life of the Christian. And what a life! Through Him, dwelling in the consciousness of divine love, we give thanks to our God and Father."

Verse 18—iv:1. Wives, husbands, children, fathers, servants and masters are exhorted how to walk in the different relationships while still in the body. The more complete exhortations as to husband and wife are found in the Epistle to the Ephesians (chapter v:22–23); and as to children, fathers, servants and masters in chapter vi:1–9. The same loving submission of the wives to their husbands "as is fitting in the Lord" is here stated once more. And husbands are to love their wives and be not bitter against them.* God has established and sanctioned the marriage relation; sin has come in and brought its corruption, never so much in evidence as in our own days. Believers in this relationship are exhorted to give in it a lovely display of the union which exists between Christ and the church. Children in the believer's family are to be brought up in the nurture and admonition of the Lord (Eph. vi:4), and seeing the truth that "Christ is all" exemplified in the family life they are exhorted to obey their parents in all things. The disintegration of the family life is one of the evil things of the closing days of this age.

Among the characteristics of "the perilous times" with which our age closes we find "disobedience to parents" and "without natural affection" (2 Tim. iii:1–5). And fathers must take heed so as not to provoke their children to anger by any unjust treatment, so that the children be not discouraged to obey in all things. How often a spirit of rebellion is fostered in children by the treatment of parents, which does not manifest the love of Christ. But if "Christ

---

*See Annotations Ephesians v:22–26.

is all" in the family life, if the peace of Christ presides in the hearts, if the Word of Christ dwells there richly, then love will govern all.

The servants exhorted were slaves, who had believed and become in Christ true freedmen. Not a word is said about the wrong of slavery. Sin is responsible for it. But these Christian slaves are exhorted to obey their masters according to the flesh in all things. In serving them, not with eye-service, as men-pleasers, but in faithfulness, meekness and devotedness they do it as unto the Lord. The place of honor belonged to these slaves in Christ, for they could manifest in their low place the life of Christ, who was here on earth the servant who came not to be ministered to but to minister; the servant of all. In the coming day of Christ many of the slaves who believed on Christ and served in meekness and lowliness will receive a great reward.

"Two principles act in the heart of the Christian slave: his conscience in all his conduct is before God; the fear of God governs him, and not his master's eye. And he is conscious of his relationship to Christ, of the presence of Christ, which sustains and lifts him above everything. It is a secret which nothing can take from him, and which has power over everything, because it is within and on high—Christ in him, the hope of glory. Yes, how admirably does the knowledge of Christ exalt everything that it pervades; and with what consoling power does it descend into all that is desolate and cast down, all that groans, all that is humbled in this world of sin!

Three times in these two verses, while holding their conscience in the presence of God, the apostle brings in the Lord, the Lord Christ, to fill the hearts of these poor slaves, and make them feel who it was to whom they rendered service. Such is Christianity."*

And Masters are exhorted to render unto the slaves that which is just and equal. "Knowing that ye also have a Master who is in heaven." Before that Master, all will have to appear and there will be no respect of persons.

*Synopsis.

CHAPTER IV.

1. Prayer and Ministry. 2-4.
2. Walking in Wisdom. 5-6.
3. The Fellowship of the Saints in their Service. 7-17.
4. The Conclusion. 18.

Verses 2–4. The first verse of this chapter belongs to the preceding one. Prayer is the most needed thing for those who are risen with Christ and know that they are complete in Him. Without continued prayer the full realization of the great truths unfolded in this epistle is impossible. Communion with God makes it all real. "Continue steadfastly in prayer, and watch therein with thanksgiving." The knowledge of our position in Christ, that we are in Him and have all in Him teaches us our dependence on Him. The more we enter into all these things the greater will be our sense of the need of prayer and real communion with God. The new man yearns for this. All the exhortations to seek the things which are above, to set the mind on those things and not on earthly things, to keep in the place of death the members which are on the earth, to put on the new man and manifest Christ, are impossible without prayer.* Without continued prayer the reality and power of our position and blessing in Christ is on the wane and soon lost. It is through prayer that we lay hold of all; it is the means by which we enter deeper into His knowledge. Prayer is, therefore, the greatest need for those who are risen with Christ. And while we express in this way our utter dependence on Him, conscious of Himself and our union with Him, He also delights in our fellowship. We can bring all to Him, "nothing is too small to enlist His love; nothing too great for His strength, and nothing too difficult for His wisdom." And there must be perseverance in it; a broken and interrupted communion soon tells in the life of the believer. No other way to know and enjoy our portion in Christ, to advance in it and be

*Those who boast of being complete in Christ and treat prayer slightingly show thereby how little they know of the real spiritual meaning of being dead with Christ and risen with Him.

victorious in the conflict which is ours in a world of evil, than continued, steadfast prayer, communion with God.

In prayer we are "to watch therein and be thankful"—"Watch and pray" our Lord said to His disciples in the garden, and while He prayed more earnestly they slept (Matt. xxvi:41). And again it is written, "Be ye therefore sober and watch unto prayer" (1 Peter iv:7). Our thoughts wander and our infirmities often become very evident in the exercise of this blessed privilege. We must watch before we pray, watch while we pray and watch after we have prayed, and watch for the answer, not impatiently, but in child-like faith. The spirit of praise and thanksgiving is needed for this watching.

The Apostle next requests prayer for himself and the ministry of the mystery of Christ. "At the same time praying also for us, that God may open unto us a door of the word, to speak the mystery of Christ, for which I am also in bonds, that I may make it manifest as I ought to speak." This blessed man of God was in the prison. From the Epistle to the Philippians we learned how unselfish he was. And here is another evidence. He might have requested united prayer for his deliverance, for divine interference in his behalf as it happened to Peter when he was imprisoned; he might have asked the prayers of the Saints that his needs might all be supplied. As risen with Christ he is above these earthly circumstances. His request is for prayer for the Gospel, the mystery of Christ, so preciously told out in the first part of this Epistle. God must open the door for this. How humble and dependent he was! What a contrast with present day professional evangelism! And for the open door to preach the Gospel; to speak the mystery of Christ effectively, the Saints of God must continue to pray and watch confidently for the answer. In praying for the Word that it may have free course and be glorified (2 Thess. iii:1), we can have all boldness and expectation. Such prayers has God's approval and answer.

Verses 5–6. Towards those who are without, the unsaved, believers with the profession of being risen with

Christ, for whom Christ is all, must walk in wisdom. What we are in Christ, the grace which has saved us, the love of God which is shed abroad in our hearts must be made known in our intercourse with those who know not Christ. How great is our failure! And why? Because we are not constantly occupied with our Lord and our heavenly position in Him. Lack of real communion with God and prayer for the Gospel, in behalf of the unsaved about us, strips us of the power to walk in wisdom. "Redeeming the opportunity." It means to bear witness to those without when the proper time for it presents itself. And when the opportunity comes the word spoken is to be "always with grace, seasoned with salt, that ye may know how ye ought to answer each one."

Verses 7–11. The words which follow these exhortations bring out the fellowship of Saints and their different services. Tychicus is mentioned first. We find his name also in Acts xx:4; Ephes. vi:21; 2 Tim. iv:12 and Titus iii:12. With Onesimus he was the bearer of this epistle, as well as the epistle to the Ephesians, while Onesimus carried also the letter to Philemon. Three things has Paul to say of Tychicus. He calls him the beloved brother, well known because he was a faithful minister, who preached faithfully the Gospel and as such he was for the apostle a fellow-servant in the Lord. He sent him to the Colossians to tell them about his own state, and that he might know their state and comfort their hearts.

"We see how Christian love delights to communicate and to hear. It was his confidence in their love; and this is shown not merely in his desire to hear about *them*, but in the conviction that they would like to hear about *him*. Can anything be sweeter than this genuine simplicity of affection and mutual interest? In a man it would be vain and curious; it is blessed in a Christian. No right-minded man, as such, could take for granted that others would care to know about his affairs any more than he theirs, unless indeed in case of a relation, or a friend, or a public and extraordinary personage. But here writes the lowly-minded apostle, in the full assurance that, though he had never seen them, or they him, it would be real and mutual gratification to know about one another from him who went between them. What a spring of power is the love of Christ! Truly charity is 'the bond of perfectness.' 'And my state shall Tychicus declare unto you, who is a beloved brother, and a faithful minister and fellow-servant in the Lord; whom I have sent unto you for the same purpose, that he might know your state, and comfort your hearts; with Onesimus, a faithful and beloved brother, who is one of you. They shall make known unto you all things which are done here.' "*

Onesimus, the once good for nothing slave, the runaway, also is called a faithful and beloved brother. The Epistle to Philemon will tell us more of this.

Then there was Aristarchus (Acts xix:29; xx:4) who was a fellow-prisoner of Paul and also a fellow-worker (Phil. verse 23). And how delightful to find Mark here, the sister's son to Barnabas. Twelve years before, he left the work (Acts xiii:13) and was the occasion of the deplorable separation between Paul and Barnabas (Acts xv:26–40). But now he is seen restored. (See also 2 Tim. iv:11). The third fellow-worker for the Kingdom of God, who was a comfort to the prisoner of the Lord, was Jesus Justus. These sent their greetings, as also did Epaphras. Him the Colossians knew well for this servant of Christ was one of them. He is an example of a praying saint. He continued steadfastly in prayer for them. He prayed, yea, he agonized (such is the Greek word) in prayer for the Colossians, that they might stand perfect and complete in all the will of God. He knew their danger; he had as a faithful minister communicated some of these things to the apostle. Knowing the Colossian condition, he prayed fervently. His ministry was the ministry of prayer. Paul adds his own word of commendation and approval.

"For I bear him record, that he hath a great zeal for you,

---

*W. Kelly.

and them that are in Laodicea, and them in Hierapolis." Though the Laodiceans were probably even then drifting into the lukewarm condition which the Lord from heaven so fully uncovered later (Rev. iii), this servant of Christ did not stand aside, but had a prayerful and loving interest in them.

Luke and Demas sent their greetings. Luke, the beloved physician, is the inspired author of the Gospel which bears his name. He also was with Paul in Rome as he was for some time his travelling companion. What a comfort the beloved physician must have been to the prisoner of the Lord! Demas is mentioned, but not a word is said about him. Was even then the evil working in his heart, which later broke out? No doubt it was. A short time afterward we read his sad story. "Demas hath forsaken me, having loved this present age" (2 Tim. iv:10).

Salute the brethren which are in Laodicea, and Nyruphas and "the church which is in his house. And when this Epistle is read among you, cause that it be also read in the church of the Laodiceans; and that ye likewise read the epistle from Laodicea."*

One more message is given. "And say to Archippus, take heed to the ministry which thou hast received in the Lord, that thou fulfill it." He probably had become in one of these cities the instrument for ministry. This he had received from the Lord. He alone can call into the ministry and bestow gifts. Whatever our ministry is, faithfulness in the exercise of it is the important thing.

Verse 18. "The salutation by the hand of me, Paul. Remember my bonds. Grace be with you." Like other epistles, except Galatians (Gal. vi:11) and Philemon (verse 19), this letter was dictated to an amanuensis. But this closing verse was written with his own hand (see also 1 Cor. xvi:21; 2 Thess. iii:17). And when he added these words the chain was upon his hand. "Remember my bonds."

---

*This must have been the Epistle to the Ephesians. See our introduction to Ephesians.

We may look upon it as a delicate excuse for not having written the whole letter to the Colossians, whom he knew not personally. At the same time the mentioning of his bonds were to remind them that he is the prisoner of the Lord for the Gentiles. (Ephes. iii:1). Grace be with you. Blessed be God that His Grace will always be with His people.

FIRST THESSALONIANS

CONTENTS

PAGE

Introduction 89

The Division of First Thessalonians 93

Analysis and Annotations 94

The First Epistle to the Thessalonians.

Introduction.

The City of Thessalonica was situated on the northern part of the Aegean Sea, on the Thermaic Gulf. It was a prominent city of the Roman province, Macedonia. Its inhabitants were mostly Thracians. Thessalonica was a wealthy and large city and for a time, the most influential centre in the northeastern part of the Roman empire. On account of its great commerce many Jews had settled there and a flourishing synagogue existed in the city.

The visit of the Apostle Paul to Thessalonica is recorded in the seventeenth chapter of the Book of Acts. It took place after his ministry in Philippi. It seems that the persecution there hastened his departure. Paul had said to the magistrates, "They have beaten us openly uncondemned, being Romans, and have cast us into prison; and now would they thrust us out privily? Nay, verily; but let them come themselves and fetch us out." When this came to the ears of the authorities, they became frightened for it was illegal to scourge a Roman citizen. "And they came and besought them, and brought them out, and desired them to depart out of the city. And they went out of the prison and entered into the house of Lydia; and when they had seen the brethren, they comforted them and departed" (Acts xvi:37–40). Of his experience Paul writes in his first letter to the Thessalonians. "For yourselves, brethren, know our entrance in unto you, that it was not in vain. But even after that we had suffered before, and were shamefully entreated, as ye know, at Philippi, we were bold in our God to speak unto you the Gospel of God with much contention" (1 Thess. ii:1–2). Leaving then Philippi with Silas (Silvanus) and Timothy they went along the famous highway, the *Via Egnatia* and reached the city of Thessalonica. On the way they passed through Amphipolis and Apollonia. On their arrival Paul followed his usual custom and visited the synagogue.

For three sabbaths, the record in Acts tells us, he reasoned with them out of the Scriptures. The Scriptures, of course, were the Old Testament Scriptures, for the New Testament was then not in existence. The way he dealt with his Jewish brethren is the pattern still for reaching the Jews with the Gospel. He opened the Scriptures, and without mentioning the name of the Lord Jesus at all, he showed that the Old Testament teaches that the Messiah (Christ) promised to them must suffer and rise from the dead. This great truth that the sufferings of Messiah comes first and the glory follows, had been forgotten by the Jews. A crucified Christ was their stumbling block (1 Cor. i:23). They looked only to the glory-side and the accomplishment, through Him, of the national promises. And after Paul had demonstrated from the Scriptures "that Christ must needs have suffered, and risen again from the dead," then he boldly declared that "this Jesus, whom I preach unto you, is Christ." The predictions of the suffering and the resurrection of Christ were fulfilled in the Lord Jesus. But he must have preached more than that. He also taught that Christ would come again. This we learn from the fact that the unbelieving Jews, in bringing Jason, who had believed, with other brethren before the rulers, accused them of "turning the world upside down," and "that there is another King, one Jesus" (Acts xvii:5–7). His second epistle also shows that he had given them instructions in dispensational and prophetic truths (2 Thess. ii:5).

The Church in Thessalonica.

As a result of his testimony a church was at once gathered out. "And some of them believed and consorted with Paul and Silas; and of the devout Greeks a great multitude, and of the chief women not a few" (Acts xvii:4). From this we learn that a number of Jews were persuaded that the Lord Jesus is the Christ and accepted Him as their Saviour and Lord. But the church was mostly composed of devout Greeks. These were not heathen, but Greeks who had given up idolatry and had become Jewish proselytes. They were convinced that paganism was wrong and seeking for light attended the synagogical services. Of this class a great multitude believed. The third class mentioned are women who occupied positions of distinction. Not a few of them believed. The epistles Paul wrote to the church of the Thessalonians also shows the character of those gathered. That the majority of them were Gentiles is learned from the statement that they had turned to God from idols (1 Thess. i:9). The evils against which he warns (1 Thess. iv:1–8) were mostly practised by the Greeks; and they belonged mostly to the poorer, the working class (1 Thess. iv:11).

Paul's First Epistle. When and for What it was Written.

The Epistle to the Thessalonians is the first epistle Paul wrote. Even the most outspoken critics acknowledge that it is a genuine document. Irenaeus (about 140 A. D.) bears witness to this Epistle. There are many other historical evidences, besides the contents of the Epistle, which prove conclusively that Paul is the author of it. All this is not necessary to follow in this brief introduction. The authorized version has a postscript "written from Athens." This claim is made on account of the Apostle's statement in chapter iii:1–2. "Wherefore, when we could no longer forbear, we thought it good to be left alone at Athens. And sent Timotheus, our brother, and minister of God, and our fellow laborer in the gospel of Christ, to establish you, and to comfort you concerning your faith." It is surmised that Timotheus carried this letter to the Thessalonians. This is incorrect. The epistle was written after Timotheus had returned from his visit to Thessalonica. The sixth verse of the third chapter furnishes this evidence. "But now when Timotheus came from you unto us, and brought us good tidings of your faith and love, and that ye have good remembrance of us always, desiring greatly to see us." Timothy came from Thessalonica with the good news of the happy state of the Thessalonian church and joined the apostle in Corinth (Acts xviii:5). From Corinth Paul wrote this first epistle about the year 52 or possibly a few months later.

The apostle had been compelled to break off suddenly his ministry in Thessalonica on account of the persecutions which had arisen in that city. "The brethren immediately sent away Paul and Silas by night unto Berea" (Acts xvii:10). He must have felt that the new converts needed more instructions. Of this he writes in the epistle. "But we, brethren, being taken from you for a short time in preference, not in heart, endeavoured the more abundantly to see your face with great desire. Wherefore we would have come unto you, even I Paul, once and again; but Satan hindered us" (ii:17, 18). To comfort them in the midst of the persecution and in their sorrow, to encourage them in their conflicts, he was moved by the Holy Spirit to write this first epistle. Timothy had brought to him the information of the tribulations they were undergoing. And they were especially distressed by the death of a number of believers. They sorrowed almost like those who had no hope, because they feared that these departed ones would have no share in the glory and in the kingdom of the returning Christ. To relieve them of their anxiety, to give them further light on the coming of the Lord in relation to those who are asleep and the reunion with them who have gone before, what will happen when the Lord comes for His saints, so that they could comfort each other, is one of the chief reasons why this letter was written.

The Coming of the Lord.

The blessed hope of the coming of the Lord occupies a very prominent place in this epistle. In our days we often hear the statement that the coming of our Lord is an unessential doctrine. Those who make such an assertion are ignorant of the fact that the blessed hope is a part of the gospel itself. Christian preaching and teaching which ignores the blessed hope, the coming of the Lord, is incomplete; it omits one of the most vital truths which the Spirit of God has linked with the gospel and with the life and service of the believer. The first epistle the great apostle wrote is an evidence of this. In this epistle one of the greatest revelations in the Word of God about His Coming, is made known (iv:13–18). It is the epistle in which the doctrine of the coming of Christ is unfolded and shown to be practically connected with the Christian's life. Each chapter bears witness to it (chapter i:9–10; ii:19–20; iii:13; iv:13–18; v:1–11). Christians wait for Him; serve in anticipation of His coming when all service will be rewarded and the servant crowned; His coming is the incentive to a holy life, it is the comfort and consolation and when He comes and takes His own in clouds to meet Him in the air, it will bring the unexpected judgment for the world The second epistle gives additional light on the visible manifestation of the Lord, what will precede that day and what is connected with it, when He comes with His holy angels. The fate of those who obey not the Gospel and who received not the love of the truth is made known in the second epistle.

The Divisions of First Thessalonians.

Simplicity and deep affection are the marks of this epistle. We find nothing about Judaizers, these perverters of the gospel of Jesus Christ against whom Paul had to warn in his later epistles. Warnings such as we have in Colossians and other epistles are absent. The loving apostle is not grieved in any way, but happy on account of the gracious work going on in the midst of the Thessalonians, and rejoicing in them as his beloved children. In the study of this epistle we maintain the division in five chapters.

I. **THE CHURCH OF THE THESSALONIANS AND ITS BLESSED CONDITION.** Chapter i.

II. **TRUE SERVICE, AS MANIFESTED IN APOSTOLIC MINISTRY.** Chapter ii.

III. **AFFLICTIONS AND COMFORT.** Chapter iii.

IV. **THE SEPARATED WALK AND THE BLESSED HOPE.** Chapter iv.

V. **THE DAY OF THE LORD. EXHORTATIONS.** Chapter v.

Analysis and Annotations.

I. THE CHURCH OF THE THESSALONIANS AND ITS BLESSED CONDITION.

CHAPTER I.

1. Greetings and Thanksgiving. 1–4.
2. The Gospel and its Blessed Fruits. 5–7.
3. The Blessed Condition of the Church. 8–10.

Verses 1-4. Paul, Silvanus and Timotheus were known to the Thessalonians, for they had been with them, and were the instruments of God used in bringing the gospel to them. He does not speak of himself as an apostle. In nine of his epistles, Paul uses his title as apostle. In Romans and Titus, he calls himself also "a servant of Jesus Christ and of God." In Philippians, he speaks of himself and of Timothy as "servants of Christ Jesus." In the epistle to Philemon, he also omits his apostleship, because this epistle was a private letter. He asserts his apostolic title and authority in the strongest way, when he addresses the Galatians and the Corinthians, because these churches were troubled with false teachers who impeached his apostolic calling. As this trouble did not exist in Thessalonica, he does not call to their remembrance that he is an apostle. He did not parade his title, and only mentions it when the truth he preached and which he had received from the Lord was questioned.

He addressed the church in Thessalonica as "the church of the Thessalonians, in God the Father, and the Lord Jesus Christ." The church in Thessalonica is the only one addressed in this manner. The church is looked upon as the family of God, as the children of God, and God their Father through the Lord Jesus Christ. They were the happy children of God and in simplicity of faith knew Him as their Father. What a transformation had taken place in these Thessalonians! They were idolators, worshipping idols; through believing the Gospel, they were born again and now enjoyed the blessed relationship to God as Father. There is no other way into the family of God than the way by which these heathen had been brought there. We are sons of God by faith in Jesus Christ (Gal. iii:26). And John, in addressing the family of God wrote "I write unto you, little children (those born again), because ye have known the Father" (1 John ii:13). The apostle, who had declared the gospel unto them, thanked God always for them, and with his fellow laborers made mention of them in prayer. The life which they possessed manifested itself in faith, love and hope. These are the principles which form our character as Christians. Theirs was a work of faith in the Lord Jesus Christ, in the sight of God and the Father, labor undertaken by love; all their labor in service flowed from love, and they endured because they possessed hope, waiting for Him. The objects of faith, love and hope are the Lord Jesus Christ and God the Father.

Verses 5-7. The Apostle mentions next the gospel and what it had wrought among them. "Our gospel came not unto you in word only, but in power and in the Holy Spirit and in much assurance." Paul, Silvanus and Timothy had preached to them the good news of a free and full salvation by faith in the Lord Jesus Christ and the gospel message came to them in power. He made the word effective in their souls and quickened them so that the great change took place by which they passed from death unto life; thus believing, the Holy Spirit was received by them, giving them full assurance. Here we have the divine order of salvation; the message of the Gospel heard and believed; the Spirit of God manifesting His power in the conversion and the sealing of those who believed, and the consequence: the full assurance of the truth in all its blessed power and reality. But the gospel was not only preached by these messengers among the Thessalonians; the chosen instruments also witnessed to that gospel by their life and walk—"As ye know what manner of men we were among you for your sakes." They were living and blessed witnesses of the power of the gospel which they proclaimed. Their holy walk, their self-denial, their peace and quietness had its blessed effect on the Thessalonian believers, for they became imitators of the apostles. Inasmuch as the messengers followed closely the Lord Jesus Christ, the Thessalonians, being imitators of them, became thus imitators of the Lord, having received the Word in much affliction with joy of the Holy Spirit. And then in turn they became patterns to all that believed in Macedonia and Achaia. In these simple statements, we have a blessed manifestation of the real power of the Gospel.

Verses 8-10. There was no need for Paul, Silvanus and Timothy to say anything about these Thessalonian Christians. It was not necessary to speak to others of what God had wrought in Thessalonica or to declare the genuineness of these new converts. The Thessalonian believers gave such a strong and full testimony that it was wholly unnecessary for the laborers to say anything about them. The word of the Lord was sounded forth by them with no uncertain sound. They were true lights in the world-darkness and were holding forth the word of life. Their faith toward God became widely known in every place. Throughout that region it became known through their witness of what the gospel is and what the gospel produces in the hearts and lives of those who believe.

And what was their testimony? It is stated in the last two verses of this chapter. "For they, themselves, report concerning us what manner of entrance we had unto you, and how ye turned to God from idols, to serve the living and true God, and to wait for His Son from heaven, whom He raised from among the dead, Jesus, who delivereth us from the wrath to come." In these words we have the great essentials of true Christianity. The first is true conversion. They had turned to God from idols, not, as it is sometimes quoted, from idols to God; the power of God, in believing the gospel had turned them away from idolatry. They were now serving no longer dumb idols, but the true and living God. In this service they manifested the genuineness of their conversion. And there was another prominent characteristic: they waited for His Son from heaven, Jesus, whom God had raised from among the dead. They looked earnestly for Him, in whom they had believed, who had died for them and of whom they knew He had been raised from among the dead, being now, at the right hand of God. According to His own promise to come again, they were patiently waiting for His coming from heaven, though they were ignorant of the manner of His coming. How He will come again, and what is connected with this great event, they learned fully from the two epistles they received from the inspired pen of the apostle. To wait for the coming of the Lord is a vital characteristic of true Christianity; it is a part of the gospel. A sad testimony it is to the superficial knowledge of the gospel when men say and teach that the belief in the second coming of Christ is unessential and of no practical value. It is most essential and of the greatest value to the true believer. It presents the glory-side of the gospel of Jesus Christ. He who died for our sins, who is the glorified Man, the firstborn among many brethren, has promised to have all His own with Him to be like Him and to share His glory. This is the true object of the believer's expectation and hope. He has delivered us from the wrath to come. Therefore the Thessalonians, and all true believers as well, can wait without fear for that blessed event, for they know they are sheltered by Him from the wrath to come. Before this wrath comes He will take His own into His presence. He is our deliverer from the wrath to come.

II. TRUE SERVICE, AS MANIFESTED IN APOSTOLIC MINISTRY.

CHAPTER II.

1. Apostolic Conduct and Service. 1–12.
2. Thanksgiving for the Reception of the Message. The Opposition. 13–16.
3. Looking Forward to His Coming. 17–19.

Verses 1–12. The Apostle now enlarges upon the brief statement in the previous chapter "Ye know what manner of men we were among you for your sakes." His conduct and character, as well as that of his fellow laborers, corresponded fully with the holy character of the truth they preached. They walked worthy of the gospel and worthy of the Lord. First he makes mention of the sufferings he and Silas endured in Philippi. They had been shamefully entreated. They had been stripped and scourged cruelly with the lictor's rods and cast into prison with their feet secured to the stocks. The physical discomfort resulting from such a punishment must have lasted for many days, but it did not hinder their going to Thessalonica with confidence in God to speak the gospel there, where they also had much conflict. And what a witness he bore of their unselfish conduct while they were among them! This exhortation was not a deceit, that is, out of error; nor was it in uncleanness, emanating from any low motives of self-interest; nor in guile. God had approved them; their ministry was God-given and they were fully conscious of this fact. Being intrusted with the Gospel (and what a trust it is!) so they spoke. They had no need to employ different schemes to be successful; they had full confidence in God and in the message He had given to them to proclaim. Therefore their whole aim was to please God who trieth the hearts and not men. Nor had they used flattery to win them; nor did they resort to flattering words as a cloak of covetousness, using sweet phrases to get money out of them; not alone were they witnesses of all this, but he could say, "God is witness." They had sought nothing of men, neither money nor glory. They might have been burdensome to them as the apostles of Christ. They did not use their authority, which they might have used, asserting their dignity and demanding something from them. Their whole conduct was in true humility and in great self-denial.*

This is the negative side. On the other hand they were full of tenderness and kindness. A boisterous, unkind, impatient spirit was completely absent in their ministry. "But we were gentle among you, even as a nurse cherisheth her children. So being affectionately desirous of you, we were willing to have imparted unto you, not the gospel of God only, but also our own souls, because ye were dear unto us." What blessed fragrance is, and will ever be, in these precious words! How little of this gracious, loving interest in souls is manifested today among the Lord's servants! Then he reminds them what he had done so as not to be a burden to any one when he preached the gospel of God unto them. He and his companion had worked day and night with their own hands. Paul was a tent-maker and worked with his own hands in Thessalonica and elsewhere (Acts xviii:2; 1 Cor. iv:12). And again he appeals to them as witnesses as well as to God, "how holily and justly and unblamably we behaved ourselves among you that believe; as ye know we exhorted and charged every one of you, as a father his children, that ye would walk worthy of God, who hath called you unto His own Kingdom and glory." Having such a portion in the coming kingdom and being an heir of glory, the walk of every believer should indeed be worthy of God.

Verses 13–16. He thanked God without ceasing for the reception of the message which they heard from his lips. It was the Word of God, which Paul had preached, and hearing the message, they had received it not as the word of

---

*Many a "leading" evangelist of our day stands condemned by this beautiful example of a true servant of God. What God and gospel dishonoring schemes are used! What flatteries as a cloak of covetousness! How much man-pleasing!

men, but as it is in truth, the Word of God. This Word received in faith saved them and also effectually worked in them that believed. It is still the same. Faith cometh by hearing and hearing by the Word of God. The believer is constantly dependent upon the Word of God; it worketh in him effectually through the power of the Holy Spirit. The believer's practical sanctification in the daily life is by the Word. (John xvii:17).

They also knew what suffering meant. They became followers (imitators) of the churches of God in Judea in Christ Jesus. Those churches suffered persecutions from the Jews, but the Thessalonians suffered from their own countrymen. And what a solemn charge is brought here through Paul against his kinsmen, the Jews! They had killed the Lord Jesus and their own prophets; they persecuted the apostles. And not satisfied with this, they tried to keep the Gospel they hated from reaching the Gentiles that they might be saved. The measure of sins was now filled up "and wrath is come upon them to the uttermost." The great Apostle of the Gentiles, called to go far hence to the Gentiles, in this his first epistle is used to pronounce sentence upon his own nation, which has been set aside until the fulness of the Gentiles is come in (Rom. xi:25-26).

Verses 17–19. He had an affectionate desire for them. Separated and bereaved of them* for a little season in person, but not in heart, he had great longing to see their face. Once and again he wanted to visit them, but Satan had hindered him. How the enemy hindered him in carrying out his desire, whether by attacks upon his body (2 Cor. xii:7) or by wicked men, we do not know. He then speaks of that blessed time when all hindrances will cease, when God's people are no longer separated, when those who ministered the Word and the fruits of their labors are gathered in the presence of the Lord Jesus Christ at His coming. "For what is our hope, or joy, or crown of glorying? Are not even ye before our Lord Jesus Christ at His coming?

---

*This is the more correct rendering.

for ye are our glory and joy." Here again the apostle mentions the coming of the Lord. The gathered Saints before the Lord Jesus Christ will be the crown of glorying and the joy for the faithful servant, who then finds in the presence of the Lord, in the day of Christ, the fruit of his labors. To this consummation in glory Paul directed the attention of the Thessalonians and he speaks of them as his glory and joy, "for ye are our glory and our joy."

"It should be observed here, that the special fruits of our labors are not lost; they are found again at the coming of Christ. Our chief personal joy is to see the Lord Himself and to be like Him. This is the portion of all saints; but there are particular fruits in connection with the work of the Spirit in us and by us. At Thessalonica the spiritual energy of the apostle had brought a number of souls to God and to wait for His Son, and into a close union in the truth with Himself. This energy would be crowned at the coming of Christ by the presence of these believers in the glory as the fruit of his labors. God would thus crown the apostle's work by bearing a striking testimony to its faithfulness in the presence of all these saints in glory; and the love which had wrought in Paul's heart would be satisfied by seeing its object in glory and in the presence of the Lord Jesus. They would be his glory and joy. This thought drew yet closer the bonds that united them, and comforted the apostle in the midst of his toils and sufferings."*

*Synopsis.

III. AFFLICTIONS AND COMFORT.

CHAPTER III.

1. Timotheus, Paul's Messenger. 1–5.
2. His Return with Good Tidings. The Apostle's Comfort and Joy. 6–10.
4. This Earnest Desire. 11–13.

Verses 1–5. His longing for the beloved Thessalonians and his solicitude for them became so great that he could no longer forbear and he decided to be left alone in Athens and send Timotheus to Thessalonica. He knew they had great afflictions and that there was danger that they might not endure and then his labors among them would have been in vain. He therefore sent Timotheus whom he calls "our brother, minister of God and our fellow laborer in the gospel of Christ." The purpose of his mission was to establish the believers still more and to bring them comfort concerning their faith. This would result, under the blessing of God, in their steadfastness. "That no man should be moved by these afflictions, for yourselves know that we are appointed thereunto"—it is the lot of all true believers. In fact he had forewarned them of all this when he was in their midst. "For verily, when we were with you, we told you before that we should suffer tribulation, even as it came to pass, and ye knew." This was part of the apostolic message, as we learn from Acts xiv:22. "Confirming the souls of the disciples, and exhorting them to continue in the faith, and that we must through much tribulation enter into the Kingdom of God." Tribulations had now come upon the Thessalonians and they were severely tested. He knew they were in the Lord's hands, that His watchful eye was upon them and that His power was sufficient to keep them. Yet he had deep concern and anxiety for them, for he also knew Satan's power. "For this cause, when I could no longer forbear, I sent to know your faith, lest by some means the tempter have tempted you, and our labor be in vain." The day of Christ, when the servant receives the reward and the saints are "the crown of glorying" is in his thoughts. If the tempter succeeded he would not have that crown of glorying in the presence of the Lord.* While Timotheus was away Paul left Athens from where he had sent him to visit Thessalonica. Paul went to Corinth; it was there he received the good tidings from Thessalonica, and, as we state in the introduction, after Timotheus' return he wrote this epistle (Acts xviii:5).

Verses 6–10. "But now when Timotheus came from you unto us, and brought good tidings of your faith and love, and that ye have good remembrance of us always, desiring greatly to see us, as we also to see you." It was good tidings Timotheus brought to Paul. They were standing fast in faith; they continued in love, nor had they forgotten Paul. Their hearts longed for him as his own soul desired to see them. In the midst of tribulations which had come upon them they were blessedly sustained.

And how all this cheered the apostle. He is comforted. "Therefore, brethren, we were comforted over you in all our affliction and distress by your faith; for now we live if ye stand fast in the Lord." He had also his sorrows, his afflictions and much distress. But the good tidings from the Thessalonians refreshed his spirit and filled him with new energy. As a servant of God he is so fully identified with those for whom he labored and whom he loved that he could say, "for now we live, if ye stand fast in the Lord." He feels as if he could not render sufficient thanks to God for them and for all the joy wherewith he now rejoiced, on their account before God. He also prayed night and day exceedingly that he might see their face and help them still more, so that which was lacking in their faith might be perfected. Then, knowing himself dependent upon God and the Lord Jesus Christ, He looks to Him to direct his way to them.

"What a bond is the bond of the Spirit! How selfishness is forgotten, and disappears in the joy of such affections!

---

*See 1 John ii:28. "And now little children, abide in Him: that when He shall appear, we (the laborers) may have confidence and not be ashamed before Him at His coming."

The apostle, animated by this affection, which increased instead of growing weary by its exercise, and by the satisfaction it received in the happiness of others, desires so much the more, from the Thessalonians being thus sustained, to see them again; not now for the purpose of strengthening them, but to build upon that which was already so established, and to complete their spiritual instruction by imparting that which was yet lacking to their faith. But he is a laborer and not a master (God makes us feel this), and he depends entirely on God for his work, and for the edification of others. In fact years passed away before he saw the Thessalonians again. He remained a long time at Corinth, where the Lord had much people; he revisited Jerusalem, then all Asia Minor where he had labored earlier; thence he went to Ephesus, where he abode nearly three years; and after that he saw the Thessalonians again, when he left that city to go to Corinth, taking his journey by the way of Macedonia."*

Verses 11–13. We must not overlook the testimony to the Deity of our Lord of the eleventh verse. "Now God and our Father Himself, and our Lord Jesus Christ, direct our way to you! The verb "direct" in the Greek is in the singular. God the Father and the Lord Jesus Christ are in the thought of the apostle one, though, personally, clearly distinguished. It is a striking proof of the unity of the Father and Son.

He prayed "the Lord make you to increase and abound in love, one toward another and toward all, even as we also towards you." Love is the bond of perfectness and as such the true means of holiness "in order to establish your hearts unblamable in holiness before our God and Father at the coming of our Lord Jesus Christ with all His saints." This is the third time the coming of our Lord is mentioned by Paul in this epistle. First he spoke of waiting for His Son from heaven as the characteristic of a true believer (i:9-10); then we read of the gatherings of the saints in the presence

---

*J. N. Darby.

of the Lord, the time of glory and joy, when the faithful servant will receive the reward (ii:19-20), and now another phase is added. The Lord is coming with all His saints; it is now not the coming *for* His saints, but *with* them, in the day of His manifestation as well as the manifestation of all the saints with Him. It is the same of which we read in Col. iii:4,"When Christ is manifested who is our life then shall ye also be manifested with Him in glory." He also speaks of this in his second epistle: "When He shall come to be glorified in His saints and wondered at in all that have believed (for our testimony unto you has been believed) in that day" (2 Thess. i:10). In view of this coming manifestation in glory the Holy Spirit urges a walk in practical holiness, so as to be unblamable in holiness before our God and Father. It is an incentive to holy living.

"In reading this passage one cannot but observe the immediate and living way in which the Lord's coming is linked with daily practical life, so that the perfect light of that day is thrown upon the hourly path of the present time. By the exercise of love they were to be established in holiness before God at the coming of Christ. From one day to another, that day was looked for as the consummation and the only term they contemplated to the ordinary life of each day here below. How this brought the soul into the presence of God! Moreover, they lived in a known relationship with God which gave room for this confidence. He was their Father; He is ours. The relationship of the saints to Jesus was equally known. The saints were "*His* saints." They were all to come with Him. They were associated with His glory. There is nothing equivocal in the expression. Jesus, the Lord, coming with all His saints, allows us to think of no other event than His return in glory. Then also will He be glorified in His saints, who will already have rejoined Him to be for ever with Him. It will be the day of their *manifestation* as of His."

IV. THE SEPARATED WALK AND THE BLESSED HOPE.

CHAPTER IV.

1. The Separated Walk. 1–12.
2. The Coming of the Lord for His Saints. 13–18.

Verses 1–12. "Furthermore, then, brethren, we beg you and exhort you in the Lord Jesus, even as ye received from us, how ye ought to walk and please God, even as ye also do walk, that ye would abound still more. For ye know what charges we gave you through the Lord Jesus. For this is the will of God, even your sanctification, that ye should abstain from fornication; that each of you know how to possess his own vessel in sanctification and honor (not in passionate desire, even as the Gentiles who know not God), not overstepping the rights of and wronging his brother in the matter, because the Lord is the avenger of all these things, even as we also told you before, and have fully testified. For God has not called us to uncleanness, but in sanctification. He therefore that (in this) disregards (his brother), disregards, not man, but God, who has also given His Holy Spirit to you."*

Having spoken of being unblamable in holiness at the coming of the Lord he exhorts them to live now in sanctification. The motive is to please God. The believer should constantly in his daily life ask himself this question, "Do I please God?" Exhortation to purity in abstaining from fleshly lusts follows. Fornication, licentiousness in various forms were closely connected with the idolatrous worship from which these Thessalonians had been saved. The lust of the flesh was a part of this former religion, as it is still today among different heathen religions. But why these exhortations? Because they were surrounded by these things on all sides, and because the old nature with its tendencies towards these evils was still present with them, as it is with

---

*Corrected translation.

all true believers. No circumstances or position can make the believer secure against these things, without exercise of conscience and self-judgment, and hence these solemn admonitions from the Lord. Each was to possess his own vessel (his own wife) in sanctification and honor, this would be a safeguard against the numerous immoralities practised among the heathen. If in this matter any one overstepped the rights of another and thus wronged his brother by committing adultery, the Lord would be the avenger; it would be a complete disregard of God who has not called His people to uncleanness, but unto sanctification, to be separated from all these things. Needful were these exhortations for the Thessalonians as they are still to all of us.

And the best remedy against these evil things is brotherly love. He had no need to say much about it, for they themselves were taught of God to love one another. But he exhorts them to be quiet and to mind their own affairs, working with their own hands, as he their leader had exemplified it when he was among them.

Verses 13–18. "But we do not wish you to be ignorant, brethren, concerning them that are fallen asleep, to the end that ye sorrow not, even as others who have no hope. For if we believe that Jesus died and rose again, so also God will bring with Him those who have fallen asleep through Jesus. For this we say to you in the Word of the Lord, that we, the living, who remain to the coming of the Lord, are in no way to anticipate these who have fallen asleep; for the Lord Himself will descend from heaven with an assembling shout, with the voice of the archangel and with the trump of God; and the dead in Christ shall rise first; then we, the living who remain, shall be caught up together with them in clouds, to meet the Lord in the air; and so shall we ever be with the Lord. Wherefore comfort one another with these words."

These words contain one of the great revelations of the Bible and require therefore closer attention. It is a special and unique revelation which he gives to the sorrowing Thessalonians, occasioned by the mistake they had made when some of their fellow believers had died, and they feared that these departed ones had lost their share in the coming glorious meeting between the Lord and His saints. They sorrowed on their account like those who have no hope*. We must remember that the New Testament was not yet in existence; only one of the gospels, was written; and not one of the epistles. And so the Lord gave to the apostle the special revelation which would quiet their fears and put before them the details of the coming of the Lord for all His Saints, those who had fallen asleep and those alive when He comes. Our Lord spoke that blessed word to His eleven disciples, "I will come again and receive you unto myself, that where I am ye may be also" (John xiv:3). It is the only time He mentioned His coming for His own, and in speaking of it He did not tell them of signs to precede that coming, such as wars, false Christs and the great tribulation. It was the simple announcement that He would come again and receive those who are His to Himself. He did not say a word about the manner of that coming and how He would receive His own into glory to be with Him. Nor did the Thessalonians hear definite teaching on this from the lips of Paul. They knew He would come again; they waited for Him. But as to the manner of His coming and concerning those who had already fallen asleep and their relation to that event they were in ignorance. Beautiful it is to see how graciously the Lord answered the question of these sorrowing ones and how much more He adds for the comfort of all His people.

The first statement is in verse 14. "For if we believe that Jesus died and rose again, so also God will bring with Him those who have fallen asleep through Jesus." Let us first notice that blessed statement that "Jesus died." Of the saints it is said that they have fallen asleep; but never is it said that Jesus slept. He tasted death, the death in all its unfathomable meaning as the judgment upon sin. For the

---

*Their pagan neighbors had no hope of meeting loved ones again after death. Classic Greek and Roman writers abound with dreary expressions of the hopelessness of death.

saints the physical death is but sleep.* And He who died also rose again; as certainly as He died and rose again, so surely shall all believers rise. God will bring all those who have fallen asleep through Jesus with Him, that is with the Lord when He comes in the day of His glorious manifestation. It does not mean the receiving of them by the Lord, nor does it mean that He brings their disembodied spirits with Him to be united to their bodies from the graves, but it means that those who have fallen asleep will God bring with His Son when He comes with all His saints; they will all be in that glorified company. When the Lord comes back from glory all the departed saints will be with Him. This is what the Thessalonians needed to know first of all. Before we follow this blessed revelation in its unfolding we call attention to the phrase "fallen asleep through (not in) Jesus;" it may also be rendered by "those who were put to sleep by Jesus." His saints in life and death are in His hands. When saints put their bodies aside, it is because their Lord has willed it so. "Precious in the sight of the Lord is the death of His saints" (Ps. cxvi:15). When our loved ones leave us, may we think of their departure as being "put to sleep by Jesus."

But blessed as this answer to their question is, it produced another difficulty. Hearing that the saints who had fallen asleep would come with the Lord on the day of His glorious manifestation, they would ask, "How is it possible that they can come with Him?" Are they coming as disembodied spirits? What about their bodies in the graves? How shall they come with Him? To answer these questions the special revelation "by the Word of the Lord" is given, by which they learned, and we also, how they would all be with Him so as to come with Him at His appearing. "For this we say to you by the Word of the Lord, that we, the living, who

---

*Some have perverted the meaning of "sleep," and instead of applying it, as Scripture does, to the body, they apply it to the soul. Soul-sleep is nowhere taught in the Bible and is therefore an invention by those who handle the word deceitfully.

remain unto the coming of the Lord, are in no wise to anticipate those who have fallen asleep." He tells them that when the Lord comes for His saints, those who have fallen asleep will not have an inferior place and that, we, the living, who remain to the coming of the Lord, will not precede those who have fallen asleep. When Paul wrote these words and said, "We, the living, who remain," he certainly considered himself as included in that class. The two companies who will meet the Lord when He comes, those who have fallen asleep and those who are living, are mentioned here for the first time. How the living saints will not precede those who have departed and the order in which the coming of the Lord for His saints will be executed is next made known in this wonderful revelation.

"For the Lord Himself will descend from heaven with an assembling shout, with the voice of the archangel and with the trump of God; and the dead in Christ shall rise first, then, we, the living, who remain, shall be caught up together with them in clouds, to meet the Lord in the air, and so shall we ever be with the Lord. Wherefore comfort one another with these words." This is an altogether new revelation. Nothing like it is found anywhere in the Old Testament Scriptures. In writing later to the Corinthians Paul mentioned it again. "Behold I show you a mystery; we shall not all sleep, but we shall all be changed. In a moment, in the twinkling of an eye, at the last trump; for the trumpet shall sound, and the dead shall be raised incorruptible, and we shall be changed" (1 Cor. xv:51-52).

The Lord *Himself* will descend from heaven. He is now at the right hand of God in glory, crowned with honor and glory. There He exercises His Priesthood and Advocacy in behalf of His people, by which He keeps, sustains and restores them. When the last member has been added to the church, which is His body, and that body is to be with Him, who is the head, He will leave the place at the right hand and descend from heaven. He will not descend to the earth, for, as we read later, the meeting-place for Him and His saints is the air and not the earth. When He comes with His saints in His visible manifestation, He will descend to the earth.* He descends with a shout. It denotes His supreme authority. The Greek word is "Kelusma," which means literally "a shout of command," used in classical Greek for the hero's shout to his followers in battle, the commanding voice to gather together. He ascended with a shout (Ps. lxvii:5), and with the victor's shout He returns. The shout may be the single word "Come!" "Come and see" He spoke to the disciples who followed Him and inquired for His dwelling place. Before Lazarus' tomb He spoke with a loud voice, "Come forth." John, in the isle of Patmos, after the throne messages to the churches had been given, saw a door opened in heaven and the voice said "Come up hither" (Rev. iv:1). "Come" is the royal word of grace, and grace will do its supreme work when He comes for His own. But there will also be the voice of the archangel (Michael) and the trump of God. The archangel is the leader of the angelic hosts. As He was seen of angels (1 Tim. iii:16) when He ascended into the highest heaven, so will the archangel be connected with His descent out of heaven. All heaven will be in commotion when the heirs of glory, sinners saved by grace, are about to be brought with glorified bodies into the Father's house. Some teach that the voice of the archangel may be employed to summon the heavenly hosts and marshal the innumerable company of the redeemed, for "They shall gather His elect together from the four winds, from one end of heaven to the other" (Matthew xxiv:30-31).† But this is incorrect. The elect in Matthew xxiv are not the church, but Israel. Dispersed Israel will be regathered and angels will be used in this work. Furthermore the angels will do this gathering after the great tribulation and after the visible manifestation of the Lord with His saints. The

---

*Even careful expositors, like the late Prof. Moorehead, made the mistake in speaking of a descent to the earth when He comes for His saints. "No phantom or apparition it will be, but an actual and visible descent to the earth" (Prof. M. on 1 Thessalonians, iv:16, page 105).

†Prof. W. G. Moorehead. Outline Studies, page 107.

coming of the Lord for His saints takes place before the great tribulation.

The trump of God is also mentioned. This trumpet has nothing to do with the judgment trumpets of Revelation, nor with the Jewish feast of trumpets, It is a symbolical term and like the shout stands for the gathering together. In Numbers x:4 we read, "And if they blow with one trumpet, then the princes, the heads of the thousands of Israel, shall gather themselves unto thee." The shout and the trump of God will gather the fellow-heirs of Christ. "The dead in Christ shall rise first." This is the resurrection from among all the dead of those who believed on Christ, the righteous dead. All saints of all ages, Old and New Testament saints, are included. This statement of the resurrection of the dead in Christ first disposes completely oft he unscriptural view of a general resurrection. As we know from Rev. xx:5 the rest of the dead (the wicked dead) will be raised up later. He comes in person to open the graves of all who belong to Him and manifests His authority over death which He has conquered. The dead in Christ will hear the shout first and experience His quickening power; they shall be raised incorruptible. What power will then be manifested! "Then we, the living, who remain, shall be caught up together with them in clouds to meet the Lord in the air; and so shall we even be with the Lord." All believers who live on earth when the Lord comes will hear that commanding, gathering shout. It does not include those who only profess to be Christians and are nominal church-members, nor are any excluded who really are the Lord's.* The question, "Who will be caught up into glory?" is answered in 1 Cor. xv:23—"All who are Christ's." The change will be "in a moment, in the twinkling of an eye" (1 Cor. xv:52). Then this mortal will put on immortality. It will be the

*The so-called first-fruit rapture, which teaches that only the most spiritual of all true believers, who have made a deeper experience, etc., will be caught up, and the other believers, though they are true children of God, will be left behind to pass "through the great tribulation, has no scriptural foundation and is wrong."

blessed "clothed upon" of which the apostle wrote to the Corinthians: "For in this tabernacle we groan, being burdened; not for that we would be unclothed (death) but clothed upon, that mortality might be swallowed up of life" (2 Cor. v:4). Then our body of humiliation will be fashioned like unto His own glorious body. It is the blessed, glorious hope, not death and the grave, but the coming of the Lord, when we shall be changed. And it is our imminent hope; believers must wait daily for it and some blessed day the shout will surely come.

When He descends from heaven with the shout and the dead in Christ are raised and we are changed, then "we shall be caught up together with them in clouds to meet the Lord in the air." It will be the blessed time of reunion with the loved ones who have gone before. What joy and comfort it must have brought to the sorrowing Thessalonians when they read these blessed words for the first time! And they are still the words of comfort and hope to all His people, when they stand at the open graves of loved ones who fell asleep as believers. Often the question is asked, "Shall we not alone meet our loved ones but also recognize them?" Here is the answer: "Together with them" implies both reunion and recognition. These words would indeed mean *nothing* did they not mean recognition. We shall surely see the faces of our loved ones again and all the saints of God on that blessed day when this great event takes place. The clouds will be heaven's chariots to take the heirs of God and the joint-heirs of the Lord Jesus Christ into His own presence. As He ascended so His redeemed ones will be taken up. Caught up in clouds to meet the Lord in the air; all laws of gravitation are set aside, for it is the power of God, the same power which raised up the Lord Jesus from the dead and seated Him in glory, which will be displayed in behalf of His saints (Eph. i:19-23). Surely this is a divine revelation. "How foolish it must sound to our learned scientists. But, beloved, I would want nothing but that one sentence, 'caught up in clouds to meet the Lord in the air,' to prove the divinity of Christianity. Its very boldness is assurance of its truth. No speculation, no argument, no reasoning; but a bare authoritative statement startling in its boldness. Not a syllable of Scripture on which to build, and yet when spoken, in perfect harmony with all Scripture. How absolutely impossible for any man to have conceived that the Lord's saints should be caught up to meet Him in the air. Were it not true its very boldness and apparent foolishness would be its refutation. And what would be the character of mind that could invent such a thought? What depths of wickedness! What cruelty! What callousness! The spring from which such a statement, if false, could rise must be corrupt indeed. But how different in fact! What severe righteousness! What depths of holiness! What elevated morality! What warmth of tender affection! What clear reasoning! Every word that he has written testifies that he has *not* attempted to deceive. Paul was no deceiver, and it is equally impossible for him to have been deceived."*

And the blessedness "to meet the Lord in the air"! We shall see Him then as He is and gaze for the first time upon the face of the Beloved, that face of glory, which was once marred and smitten on account of our sins. And seeing Him as He is we shall be like Him. How long will be the meeting in the air? It has been said that the stay in that meeting place will be but momentary and that the Lord will at once resume His descent to the earth. We know from other Scriptures that this cannot be. Between the coming of the Lord for His saints and with His saints there is an interval of at least seven years before the visible coming of the Lord and His saints with Him. The judgment of the saints, by which their works and labors become manifest must take place. There is also to be the presentation of the church in glory (Ephes. v:27; Jude verse 24). Furthermore the marriage of the Lamb takes place not in the meeting place in the air, but in heaven (Rev. xix:1-10). He will take His saints into the Father's house that they may behold His

*"Our Hope" February, 1902.

glory (John xvii:22). But what will it mean,"So shall we be forever with the Lord!"

"In this part of the passage, where he explains the details of our ascension to the Lord in the air, nothing is said of His coming down down to the earth; it is our going up (as He went up) to be with Him. Neither, as far as concerns us, does the apostle go farther than our gathering together to be for ever with Him. Nothing is said either of judgment or of manifestation; but only the fact of our heavenly association with Him in that we leave the earth precisely as He left it. This is very precious. There is this difference: He went up in His own full right, He ascended; as to us, His voice calls the dead, and they come forth from the grave, and, the living being changed, all are caught up together. It is a solemn act of God's power, which seals the Christians' life and the work of God, and brings the former into the glory of Christ as His heavenly companions. Glorious privilege! Precious grace! To lose sight of it destroys the proper character of our joy and of our hope."*

---

*Synopsis.

V. THE DAY OF THE LORD. EXHORTATIONS.

CHAPTER V.

1. The Day of the Lord. 1–11.
2. Exhortations. 12–22.
3. Conclusions. 23–28.

Verses 1–11. "But concerning the times and seasons, brethren, ye have no need that I write unto you. For yourselves know perfectly that the day of the Lord so cometh as a thief in the night. For when they shall say, Peace and safety, then sudden destruction cometh upon them, as travail upon a woman with child, and they shall not escape." The Apostle next mentions the day of the Lord. This is the day when the Lord is revealed from heaven, the day of His visible manifestation. It is the day when judgment will be executed upon the world. While the coming of the Lord for His saints, as made known in the previous chapter, is unrevealed in the Old Testament, the day of the Lord of which the apostle now writes, is fully revealed by the prophets. (See Isaiah ii:12–22; Joel ii–iii; Zeph. i:14–18; Zech. xiv:1–9, etc.) Our Lord spoke often of that day as the day "when the Son of Man cometh," that is His own visible, glorious manifestation. What precedes this day is also made known in the Old Testament prophetic Word; and our Lord gives us likewise the same information. "And there shall be signs in the sun and in the moon, and in the stars; and upon earth distress of nations, with perplexity; the sea and the waves roaring; men's hearts failing them for fear, and for looking after those things which are coming on the earth, for the powers of heaven shall be shaken. And then shall they see the Son of Man coming in a cloud with power and great glory" (Luke xxi:25–27). See Matthew xxiv:21–31. Judgment is in store for the world when that day comes, as judgments and tribulation are the forerunners which usher in that day. The world does not believe in such a day, but dreams of peace and safety, in a continuance of prosperity, of expansion, universal peace and a constant improvement of earthly conditions. "There shall come in the last days scoffers, walking after their own lusts, and saying, Where is the promise of His coming? for since the fathers fell asleep, all things continue as they were from the beginning of the creation" (2 Peter iii:3–4). But while the world saith, Peace and safety, their hearts are failing them for fear and they tremble in anticipation of the future. Much of all this we see clearly in our times, so ominous and so solemn. There is a false hope, a false optimism; we hear of what this world-war will accomplish, how peace and safety will come to the whole world; yet underneath it all there are hearts failing for fear. And when that day has come, when He has been "revealed from heaven with His mighty angels, in flaming fire taking vengeance on them that know not God, and that obey not the gospel of our Lord Jesus Christ," the Lord Jesus Christ will reign over the earth with His saints for a thousand years (Rev. xx). That will be the day of the Lord, as the present age is "man's day."

Before that day comes with its preceding judgments and the great tribulation, the coming of the Lord, for His saints, the fulfilment of chapter iv:16–18 must take place. Of this we shall find much more in the second epistle. When the Lord comes for His saints, the world and those who were Christians only in name, will face that coming day. It is the beginning of it. After God's true children, the praying people of God, have been removed, the age will take its final plunge into apostasy and iniquity; judgment upon judgment from above will then be poured out, as we learn from the book of Revelation.

Because these judgments, the forerunners of the day of His visible manifestation, the times and seasons connected with these events, do not concern those who are the Lord's, the apostle states that there was no need to write to them about it. The Lord had told His disciples before He ascended into heaven that it was not for them to know the times and the seasons. It shows that we are not to be occupied with the times and seasons, when the times of the Gentiles end, etc., but to wait and watch for Him, who will surely come suddenly for His own, as a thief in the night.

"Had it been possible in the apostle's days to predict the centuries of delay that have, in fact, elapsed, disciples might indeed still have waited for their Lord, but *watched* they could not, and no 'thief in the night' could have troubled their slumbers. But for the heart expectancy was needed; and they were to watch *because* they knew not. Thus for these watchers the times could not speak; and in fact when they do it will be for another people than the present Christian Church, and when this is already removed to be with the Lord in the manner which we have just had before us.

"For mere formal and worldly Christendom, the coming of the thief will then in a sense have taken place. Shut out in the outside darkness, when others have entered the chambers of light, no place of repentance will be left for the despisers of God's present grace. In a world which, having rejected the true King, will be left for that awful time to experience fully what Satan's rule is, they will fall under the power of his deception. Not having received the love of the truth that they might be saved, they will believe a lie; and comforting themselves with the cry of "Peace and safety," sudden destruction will come upon them as upon a woman with child, and they shall not escape!*

The words "they" and "you" make it still more clear that the day of the Lord is for the world. He does not say "When you shall say, Peace and safety" but when "they shall say." The apostle excludes the believer completely from that day when sudden destruction falls, for he says, "Ye, brethren, are not in darkness, that that day overtake you as a thief." And why? Ye are all the children of light, and the children of the day; we are not of the night, nor of darkness. Therefore let us not sleep, as do others; but let us watch and be sober. For they that sleep in the night; and they that be drunken are drunken in the night. This is the character of true

*Numerical Bible.

Christians, no longer in darkness, but children of light and of the day, and therefore belonging to that coming day to be with the Lord when He comes to judge, it cannot overtake them as a thief. Being the children of the day we must watch and be sober; it is that which distinguishes true Christians from the mass of professing church-members and the world. The world and those who have a form of godliness, but deny the power thereof, do not watch, nor are they sober: and being sober, walking in separation from the world, its lusts and pleasures, the believer, having on the breastplate of faith and love, can advance against the enemy. He has also for an helmet, to protect him, this promised glorious salvation. Thus we can look always up, without fear, in the midst of danger when the judgment clouds are gathering over this present evil age. "For God hath not appointed us to wrath, but to the obtaining of salvation through our Lord Jesus Christ." Blessed knowledge and twice blessed assurance! that we might be delivered from the wrath to come and share with Him eternal glory, He died for us. "Who died for us, that, whether we wake or sleep (as to the body) we should live together with Him."

Verses 12–22. Exhortations follow. He wishes that those who labored among them should be acknowledged by them and very highly esteemed in love for their work's sake. If the apostle and his co-laborers looked upon them as their crown of rejoicing, their glory and joy (ii:19-20,) they should very highly esteem them as the instruments of the Spirit of God for their edification. Be in peace among yourselves. All self-will is put aside when the heart looks forward to that coming day, when laborers and the fruits of their labors are in His presence. Then peace among His own will not be disturbed. The disorderly are to be admonished; the fainthearted comforted; the weak sustained, and patience to be manifested towards all. Then we have joy, prayer and thanksgiving as the characteristics of those who wait for His Son from heaven and look for that blessed hope. "Rejoice evermore"—our joy is in Him. The joy of the Lord is our strength. And what joy will indeed be ours when we remember that we shall see Him as He is! "Pray without ceasing." Prayer is constantly needed, including the forgotten prayer, "Even so, Come, Lord Jesus." If this petition is never wanting, His coming for us will never lack reality. "In everything give thanks, for this is the will of God in Christ Jesus concerning you." As we pray and ever take afresh from His own fulness grace upon grace, and remember all the abundant provision made for us in Him, and that the glorious future which awaits His own may burst at any moment upon us, then shall we give thanks in everything. "Quench not the Spirit." The Holy Spirit is not to be hindered in His action in the midst of His people. What sad consequences when He is quenched and how great the responsibility! Do not despise prophesyings*—the forth-telling of the truth of God, speaking out of the fulness of the Spirit. "Prove all things; hold fast that which is good. Abstain from all appearance of evil," or, as it is better rendered, "Keep aloof from every form of wickedness."

Verses 23–28. The conclusion of the Epistle begins with a prayer. "Now the God of peace Himself sanctify you wholly; and I pray God your whole spirit and soul and body be preserved blameless at the coming of our Lord Jesus Christ. He is faithful that calls you, who will also do it." God is for all who have believed in Christ the God of peace. Peace was made in the blood of the cross; believers are both reconciled and sanctified through the peace that God has made for us in the work of His Son. We stand therefore in a blessed relationship with the God of peace, have communion with Him, and from this flows practical devotedness of life and walk to God. Believers are sanctified by the three persons of the Godhead: by God the Father, by the blood of Jesus Christ, the offering of His body, and by the Holy Spirit.

We are in Christ completely set apart for God, bought with

*See Annotations 1 Corinthians xiv on the meaning of a prophecy in the New Testament.

a price and no longer our own. We possess a new nature and are indwelt by the Holy Spirit. This demands of us that we be wholly set apart to God in every faculty, whether of mind or body. This is our practical sanctification, which springs from our increasing knowledge of God. This practical sanctification is wrought in the believer by the power of the Holy Spirit, who attaches the heart to God, revealing God more and more, as well as unfolding the glory of Christ. This devotedness to God in spirit, soul and body, depends upon the believer's apprehension of his relationship to the God of peace and his communion with Him. And this is progressive. Entire sanctification will be the blessed and eternal portion of all who are Christ's, when He comes, and we shall be like Him, "conformed to the image of His Son." The perfection comes with the coming of the Lord; in the power of this blessed Hope shall we be preserved blameless even down here in this evil age.* He is faithful who calls you, who will also perform it. Blessed assurance! He has called us to this life of blessed separation with Himself. He is faithful and will accomplish it. May we trust Him daily and stay close to Him.

The Apostle closes this first epistle by requesting the brethren to pray for him and his co-laborers. With all the deep knowledge of the truth and the great revelations from the Lord, he felt his dependence and knew the blessing which

---

*"Observe again here, how the coming of Christ is introduced, and the expectation of this coming, as an integral part of Christian life. "Blameless," it says, "at the coming of our Lord Jesus Christ." The life which had developed itself in obedience and holiness meets the Lord at His coming. Death is not in question. The life which we have found is to be such when He appears. The man, in every part of his being, moved by this life, is found there blameless when He comes. This life, and the man living this life, are found, with their Head and Source, in the glory. Then will the weakness disappear which is connected with his present condition. That which is mortal shall be swallowed up of life: that is all. We are Christ's: He is our life. We wait for Him, that we may be with Him, and that He may perfect all things in the glory." Synopsis.

comes from the prayers of fellow saints. He asks for the expression of affection among themselves and adjures them to have this letter read to all the holy brethren. And the final word "The grace of our Lord Jesus Christ be with you."

SECOND THESSALONIANS

CONTENTS

PAGE

Introduction 125

The Division of Second Thessalonians 127

Analysis and Annotations 128

The Second Epistle to the Thessalonians.

Introduction.

This second epistle to the Thessalonians was written at Corinth by the Apostle Paul and in the joint names of Silvanus and Timotheus. How long after the first epistle cannot be correctly ascertained. It was probably a year after they had received the first document.

What Occasioned This Epistle.

From the second chapter we learn that they were greatly troubled about something else. The first epistle was written to comfort them on account of those who had fallen asleep and to make known the great revelation concerning the coming of the Lord for His saints. And now the Apostle writes: "Now we beseech ye, brethren, by the coming of our Lord Jesus Christ and by our gathering together unto Him, that ye be not soon shaken in mind, or troubled, neither by spirit, nor by word, nor by letter, as if it were by us, as that the day of the Lord is present" (ii:1-2). Evidently some one had troubled them and tried to convince them that the day of the Lord, with its threatened judgments, was actually present. When they had received the comforting first epistle, we can imagine how their waiting for the Lord was stimulated. With what simple, child-like faith they must have taken hold of the words, "We who are alive and remain shall be caught up in clouds to meet the Lord in the air, and so shall we ever be with the Lord." Daily, no doubt, they expected this blessed promise to be fulfilled. Certain false teachers then appeared on the scene, telling them that their hope was vain and that the day of the Lord was actually upon them, that the threatened tribulation and judgment had begun and that they had to pass through all the horrors of the times preceding the visible manifestation of the Lord. They were passing through fearful persecutions and tribulations that these teachers probably told them that these sufferings were the indication of the beginning of the day of the Lord. It was this which greatly agitated them and robbed them of the blessed hope. If they were to pass through the tribulation and judgment which is in store for the world and be on the earth when wrath is poured out, then the blessed hope ceases to be that. And it seems these false teachers had gone so far as to produce a document, which they pretended was a letter from Paul, in which he confirmed their false teaching. For this reason, that they might know that the letter they received now was really his, he added, "The salutation of Paul with mine own hand, which is the token in every epistle, so I write" (iii:17).

But who were these teachers who aimed at the joy and hope of these earnest believers and troubled them with their false message that the day of the Lord was present? They belonged unquestionably to the same class of Judaizers who had sneaked among the Galatian churches. They attacked the blessed hope given to the Church and put in its place the judgment and tribulation of the day of the Lord. They swept aside the comforting revelation of the coming of the Lord and the gathering of the saints unto Him and put the Church on earthly, Jewish ground. What is in store for the ungodly nations and for the Jews, they taught would also be shared by true Christians; it would all come before the Lord comes for His own. To correct this error the Spirit of God moved the Apostle to write this second epistle.

A Fundamental Prophecy.

Chapter ii:1-12 contains the words of instruction to show that the day of the Lord was then not present. It furthermore tells us what must precede that day, which is nowhere related to the Church of God. It is a great unfolding of prophecy, fundamental and most important. It is needed for the correct understanding of what will take place when the Lord has taken away His true Church. Here is the prediction of the apostasy, which will have for its head and climax the man of sin, the final, personal Anti-Christ, the same person of whom Daniel speaks (Dan. xi:36, etc.), who is described in Rev. xiii:11-18 and in other portions of the prophetic Word. Here we read of the necessary condition before this apostasy can come and that lawless one is revealed, and what will be the fate of all who received not the love of the truth. The strong delusion of him, whose coming is, according to the working of Satan, with all power and signs and lying wonders, will be believed and accepted by the apostates of Christendom. We have given to this portion of the epistle in our annotations the attention it deserves, and we trust it will be, under God, a help and comfort to His people.

The Divisions of Second Thessalonians.

The scope and divisions of this epistle are very simple. In the first chapter the Apostle shows that while the Thessalonians had tribulation, they suffered not in a punitive sense, but for the Kingdom of God, and that God would recompense tribulation to those who troubled them. The punishment for the world comes when the Lord Jesus is revealed from heaven. While that day brings this for the world, it will bring glory for those who have believed. As already stated in the second chapter, the day of the Lord, what must take place before that day comes is made known. Words of comfort, prayer and exhortations conclude the epistle. This gives us three divisions.

I. **THE REVELATION OF THE LORD JESUS FROM HEAVEN.** Chapter i.

II. **WHAT PRECEDES THE MANIFESTATION OF THE LORD.** Chapter ii:1-12.

III. **THANKSGIVING, PRAYER, EXHORTATIONS AND CONCLUSION.** Chapter ii:13–iii:18.

Analysis and Annotations.

I. THE REVELATION OF THE LORD JESUS FROM HEAVEN.

CHAPTER I.

1. Salutation and Thanksgiving. 1–4.
2. The Revelation of the Lord Jesus from Heaven. 5–10.
3. The Prayer.

Verses 1–4. The opening words of salutation are the same as in the first epistle. Once more he gives thanks to God for them, because their faith increased exceedingly and love abounded, the result of an increasing faith. On account of this progress and spiritual condition he wrote, "So that we ourselves glory in you in the churches for your patience and faith in all your persecutions and tribulations that ye endure." The patience of hope, which was mentioned in the first epistle, is omitted by him. Their hope had been dimmed through the false teachers and alarmists, who would have them believe that they were heading for all the tribulations of the day of the Lord. They endured persecutions and tribulations on account of which they were greatly disturbed, because of the insinuation that these were the judgments of the day of the Lord. They looked more to what was happening to them than to the Lord. They were more occupied with these conditions than with the blessed hope.

Verses 5–10. He quiets these fears. Satan was pressing upon them, terrifying their minds, and they were fearing everything, the enemy taking advantage of the persecutions and sufferings he had instigated to distress them. The Apostle tells them that all their persecutions and tribulations, far from having a punitive character, were "a manifest token of the righteous judgment of God" with this purpose, "to the end that ye should be counted worthy of the Kingdom of God, for the sake of which ye also suffer."

They were children of God, heirs of God and joint heirs with Christ, and their path was to suffer with Him, that they also might be glorified together (Rom. viii:17). A similar word he wrote later to the Philippians. "In nothing terrified by your adversaries, which is to them an evident token of perdition, but to you of salvation, and that of God" (Phil. i:28). What was happening to them was a seal upon them of their being worthy of the coming Kingdom. The persecutions they endured showed they were identified with the Lord, who was "despised and rejected of men." Their sufferings were the sufferings of Christ.

And then the contrast. When the day of the Lord comes with the revelation of the Lord Jesus from heaven, it will bring the punishment of the wicked. Their persecutions were from the ungodly, who inflicted suffering on them because they believed on the Lord. But when the day of the Lord comes God will change all by recompensing those that troubled them. "Seeing it is a righteous thing with God to recompense tribulation to them that trouble you, and to you who are troubled rest with us, when the Lord Jesus shall be revealed from heaven with His mighty angels." In other words, in His day they would have rest and peace, while their wicked enemies will suffer the well deserved judgment. From this inspired declaration they learned that the day of the Lord had not come. The day of the Lord brings the revelation of the Lord from heaven with His mighty angels, "in flaming fire taking vengeance on them that know not God, and that obey not the gospel of our Lord Jesus Christ, who shall suffer the penalty of everlasting destruction from the presence of the Lord and from the glory of His might, when He shall come to be glorified in His saints, and to be wondered at in all who have believed (because our testimony among you was believed) in that day." "In that day" is a phrase which we find many times in the Old Testament prophetic Word. In most cases it means the day of the visible manifestation of Jehovah to deal in judgment with His enemies and to deliver those of His earthly people Israel who wait for Him. "And it shall come to pass in that day, that the Lord shall punish the host of the high ones that are as high and the kings of the earth upon the earth" (Is. xxiv:21). "And it shall be said in that day, Lo, this is our God, we have waited for Him, and He will save us" (Is. xxv:9). Judgment for the world is always connected with that coming day. Our Lord, in His earthly ministry, also spoke of that day, the day of the coming of the Son of man. "For the Son of man shall come in the glory of His Father with His angels, and then shall He reward every man according to His works" (Matt. xvi:27). His visible coming out of heaven and bringing judgment is still more fully described in Rev. xix:11-21. It will be the day of vengeance after the acceptable year of the Lord is ended (Isaiah lxi:1-2). The Apostle's testimony tells us the same. Two classes are mentioned by him. Those that know not God, which means the idolatrous Gentiles and sinners in general, "and those that obey not the gospel of our Lord Jesus Christ."* These are the Jews and also nominal and apostate Christians. The latter class will suffer the greater punishment. The destruction mentioned has been explained as meaning annihilation. But that is not true. It is banishment from the presence of that glory upon which man has turned his back and which he despised—hardening himself into a final, awful incapacity for it and for communion with Him. What else is it but the destruction "of one who was made at the first in the image of God?" They will live on in eternal separation from God.

The Apostle mentions something else which is not found in the Old Testament prophetic Word. When the Lord comes in that day He will be glorified in His saints and then wondered at in all who have believed. When He comes thus in judgment upon the world the true Church is no longer on earth, but the saints, having been previously caught up to meet him in the air, come with Him in glory. It is the time of the manifestation of the sons of God, trans-

---

*The text of the authorized version having omitted the word "those" makes it appear as if it were only one class; but that is incorrect.

formed into His image, each reflecting His glory, who is the leader and the first begotten. And so these poor, persecuted, despised Thessalonians would then be the marvels for the inhabitants of the earth when they appear with Him. Blessed future for all the redeemed to come with the Lord in glory and to be like Him!

These explanations concerning the day of the manifestation of the Lord bringing judgment upon their enemies and glory to them, delivered them from the confusion into which the false teachers were leading them, and they were now ready, after being put at rest in their mind, to receive the needed additional instruction about that coming day. A prayer concludes this chapter that, called with such a calling, God may count them worthy of it, that their walk may be of such a nature as to correspond with that calling and that the Lord might be glorified in them by the power of faith, and that afterwards they might be glorified in Him, "according to the grace of our God and the Lord Jesus Christ."

II. WHAT PRECEDES THE MANIFESTATION OF THE LORD.

CHAPTER II.

1. The Gathering of the Saints Preceding that Day. 1–2.
2. The Apostasy and the Man of Sin. 3–4.
3. The Revelation of the Man of Sin and His Fate. 5–8.
4. His Deceptions and the Fate of Christendom. 9–12.

As this section of the epistle is one of the most important of the New Testament, we give it first of all in a corrected translation.

"Now we beg you, brethren, by the coming of our Lord Jesus Christ and our gathering together unto Him, that ye be not soon shaken in mind, nor troubled, neither by spirit, not by word, nor by letter, as (if it were) by us, as that the day of the Lord is present. Let not any one deceive you in any manner, because it will not be unless the apostasy have come first and the man of sin have been revealed, the son of perdition, who opposes and exalts himself on high against all called God or object of worship; so that he himself sits down in the temple of God, showing himself that he is God. Do ye not remember that, being yet with you, I said these things to you? And now ye know that which restrains, that he should be revealed in his own time. For the mystery of lawlessness already works; only there is He who restrains it until He be gone, and then the lawless one shall be revealed, whom the Lord Jesus shall consume with the breath of his mouth, and shall annul by the brightness of His coming; whose coming is according to the working of Satan in all power and signs and wonders of falsehood, and in all deceit of unrighteouness to them that perish, because they have not received the love of the truth that they might be saved. And for this reason God sendeth them an energy of error, that they may believe the lie; that they all might be judged who believed not the truth, but had pleasure in unrighteousness."

Verses 1–2. He begs them "by the coming of the Lord and our gathering together unto Him" not to be disturbed by the rumours these false teachers were circulating, as if the day of the Lord is present. The authorized version has the misleading translation, "the day of Christ."* There is

*Equally incorrect is the translation, "the day of the Lord is *at hand*." The meaning is "present", that it had actually come. The same Greek word is also used in Rom. viii:37, "things present."

an important difference between the day of Christ and the day of the Lord. The day of Christ concerns the Church, the saints of God. The day of the Lord concerns the earth—Israel and the nations. The day of Christ begins when He takes His saints in glory and they are with Him. The day of the Lord will bring, as stated before, the visible manifestation of the Lord from heaven. The day of Christ comes first and the day of the Lord follows at least seven years later. The following passages speak of the day of Christ, and it will be seen that that day is for God's people only 1 Cor. i:8; 2 Cor. i:14; Phil. i:6-10, ii:16. The day of the Lord does not concern the saints at all; it falls on the world. Before the day of the Lord can come, His saints have to be gathered together unto Him. The promise of 1 Thess. iv:16-18 needs first to be fulfilled. He uses this hope of being gathered to Christ, when He comes for His saints, as a motive why they should not listen to those who said the day of the Lord is present. He reminds them of the fact that their gathering unto Him had not yet taken place. How, then, could the day of the Lord be present? And this opens the way for still more important teaching.

Verses 3–4. The false teachers were deceiving them. Before the day of the Lord can come there must be the falling away first and the man of sin, the son of perdition, must be revealed. No such conditions need to be fulfilled before the Lord comes for His saints. But before the age closes with the visible manifestation of the Lord from heaven these two solemn things must be on the earth. A falling away from the God-given faith has been going on throughout this Christian age. But that is not *the* apostasy of which the Apostle speaks. The complete apostasy means that the entire faith will be abandoned by Christendom, even as our Lord indicated when He said, "Nevertheless, when the Son of man cometh, shall He find the faith on the earth?" That this present age closes in apostasy is more than once mentioned by the Spirit of God. See 1 Tim. iv:1-3; 2 Tim. iii:1-5; 2 Peter ii; Jude. Evidences to that effect are abundant in our own days. The destructive Bible criticism rejecting inspiration and revelation, the denial of the Person and Work of Christ and of every other article, denials which are rapidly increasing, make the way for this final apostasy. The many cults in which Satanic powers are manifested, under the garb of angels of light, such as Christian Science, Spiritism, Theosophy, etc., are also harbingers of the time of which the Apostle writes. Satan is surely actively at work to bring about this apostasy, and his ministers are transformed as the ministers of righteousness (2 Cor. xi:15), advocating reform, better living, but denying and antagonizing the doctrines of Christ. We shall hear later that this final apostasy is held back from its full manifestation by One who restraineth; only when He is taken out of the way can this predicted apostasy and renunciation of Christianity come with its leader, the man of sin.

Who is the person whom Paul mentions as the man of sin? It would take many pages to give the views and opinions of expositors as to who is meant. The Roman Empire, the Roman Emperors, Mohammed, the Pope and the Romish Hierarchy have been given as being the man of sin. During the French revolution many thought it was Napoleon, as some to-day say the German Emperor is the man of sin. Inasmuch as the great apostasy is not yet here, the person whom Paul describes has also not yet come. First there must be the apostasy before there can be the leader and head of that apostasy. And before the revelation of Christ comes from heaven the world, which rejected Christ, will get its Anti-Christ. John mentions the man of sin. "Who is the liar but he that denieth that Jesus is the Christ? He is Anti-Christ that denieth the Father and the Son" (1 John ii:22). It may be learned from this description that he will be the leader of Jewish unbelief and the unbelief of Christendom. Denying that Jesus is the Christ—that is Jewish; denying the Father and the Son, that is rejection of the Christian revelation. He will therefore take the leadership of Jewish and Christian apostasy. The most common interpretation that the Pope and the Papal system is this man of sin is incorrect, for the Pope does not deny that Jesus is the

Christ, nor does the Pope claim to be the Christ. That the Pope has certain marks of the Anti-Christ abouthim no one can deny; but that he is *the* Anti-Christ is not true.*

The final Anti-Christ, the man of sin, the son of perdition, is the heading up of the apostasy. He fills up the measure of the apostasy of humanity. He opposeth and exalteth himself against all that is called God or object of worship. He takes the place of God on earth. He will be the superman who is expected by the world to make his appearance in the near future. In the book of Revelation his number is given as 666. "For it is a man's number; and the number is six hundred and sixty-six" (Rev. xiii:18). There is no need to speculate on this number. The meaning is very simple. Seven, in Scripture, is the complete number, used in connection with what is divine and perfect. Six is incomplete, and is man's number. The number 666 signifies man's day and man's defiance of God under Satan's power reaching its climax. This "superman" takes a seat in the temple of God and sets himself forth that he is God. From this we learn that he claims a religious character. He must therefore not be identified with the little horn in Daniel's prophecy (chapter vii). This little horn is another Satan-possessed person who takes the leadership politically of the coming federation of nations, the revived Roman Empire. He is "the prince that shall come" of Daniel ix:26. The Beast out of the sea in Rev. xiii:1-10 is the revived Roman Empire; the ten horns on that beastly empire correspond to the ten horns on Nebuchadnezzar's prophetic dream image and the ten horns on the fourth beast of Daniel's vision. The little horn, the domineering head of the revived Roman Empire, comes first into prominence and is soon followed by the second beast out of the earth, having two horns like a lamb, but speaking as a dragon. Rev. xiii:11-18 describes this second beast and the work he does, in which he is helped by

---

*Certain Roman Catholic writers have charged Protestantism with being Babylon and Anti-Christian. A so-called Protestant who denies the Virgin birth, the Deity of Christ, surely is an Anti-Christ.

the first beast. This second beast is the man of sin, the son of perdition. Read now Daniel xi:36-39.* This is another description of the same person. He is called a king because, as the false Christ, he will claim kingship among the Jews. He is also called in Revelation "the false prophet." He is the one of whom our Lord spoke in John v:43, "I am come in my Father's name and ye received me not; if another shall come in his own name, him ye will receive."

But what is the meaning of "he sitteth in the temple of God, setting himself forth that he is God"? The temple of God does not mean the Church. It is a Jewish temple. When the true Church is gone the Jewish people, restored once more to their own land, established there as a nation, though still in unbelief, will erect another temple and institute once more the temple worship (See Isaiah lxvi:1-4). God will despise their worship. The man of sin will sit in that temple, demanding worship for the image he will set up and for himself. This will be during the time of Jacob's trouble, the great tribulation.† The man of sin, the Anti-Christ, will be undoubtedly a Jew. He will be filled with the energy and power of Satan. The nearness of the re-establishment of the Jewish people in Palestine in unbelief is an indication that all these prophecies are about to be fulfilled.

Verses 5–8. When the Apostle was with them he had spoken to them about those things. "The mystery of lawlessness (not iniquity) already worketh," he informed the Thessalonians. Sin is lawlessness, and that has been at work from the beginning, man having forsaken God and exalted himself in self-will. This works on till it works out into open lawlessness in an out-and-out opposition to God and His Son, culminating in the man of sin, the false Christ, "to give the world its long-sought liberty from divine re-

---

*For a complete exposition of this passage see "The Prophet Daniel," by A. C. G.

†For a closer study of the interesting details we refer our readers to "Exposition of Matthew," "Daniel," and "Exposition of Revelation," all by the author of the "Annotated Bible."

straint and bring its vaunted progress to perfection, which under Christianity it has found impossible to attain." The mystery of lawlessness will cease to be a mystery when *the* lawless one, *the* man of sin, is manifested. But what keeps back the manifestation of this lawless one? Who or what is it that restrains it? Who is to be taken out of the way before the lawless one can be revealed? Many answers have been given to this question which we do not need to investigate. It is self-evident that that which restraineth must be a power superior to man and Satan and of a nature totally different to the man of sin. The restraining one is a power and a person. It is the Holy Spirit of God.* When the Church leaves the earth then this restraining power and person, who dwells in the Church and therefore is here on earth, will be taken out of the way. As the result, in due time, the lawless one will be revealed. The Holy Spirit, who came down from heaven on the day of Pentecost to form the Church, the body of Christ, will be withdrawn when that body is complete and taken to glory to be joined to the Head, the Lord Jesus Christ. The light being gone, gross darkness will settle upon the nations, the apostasy will be here, the enemy comes in like a flood and the lawless one appears. Here we have the best evidence that the true Church cannot be on the earth during the final years with which this age closes. No true believer will be in the

*The Holy Ghost was here below; the Church, be its condition what it might, was still on earth, and God maintained the barrier. And as the porter had opened the door to Jesus in spite of all obstacles, so He sustains everything, however great the energy and progress of evil. The evil is bridled: God is the source of authority on earth. There is one who hinders until he be taken out of the way. Now, when the Church (the Church, that is, as composed of the true members of Christ) is gone, and consequently the Holy Ghost as the Comforter is no longer dwelling here below, then the apostasy takes place, the time to remove the hindrance is come, the evil is unbridled, and at length (without saying how much time it will take) the evil assumes a definite shape in him who is its head. The beast comes up from the abyss. Satan—not God—gives him his authority; and in the second beast all the energy of Satan is present. The man of sin is there.—Synopsis.

final apostasy under the lawless one, nor will the Church pass through the great tribulation. How this should fill our hearts with holy joy and our lips with praises!

Before he speaks of the lawless one with his lying wonders, he tells us at once of his fate. The Lord Jesus, in His visible manifestation, will consume him with the breath of His mouth and annul him with the brightness of His coming (see Isaiah xi:1-5 and Rev. xix:11-21).

Verses 9–12. This lawless one, the Anti-Christ, will come in the energy of Satan with all power and signs and wonders of falsehood and in all deceit of unrighteousness to them that perish, because they have not received the love of the truth that they might be saved. And for this reason God sendeth them an energy of error, that they may believe the lie, that they all might be judged who believed not the truth, but had pleasure in unrighteousness. This shows us what is coming upon the so-called "Christian nations," with their boast of progress and civilization. This is the future of the destructive critics, the Bible-rejecting, Gospel-neglecting masses of Christendom, as well as of apostate Judaism.

"Scientific infidelity now avouches with a sneer that we never see a miracle, and Hume's argument against all evidence in favor of such is its contradiction of universal experience. But it is soon to be matter of extensive experience that miracles there are; only in a very opposite interest to that of Christianity. These things are even now showing themselves in a more or less tentative and doubtful way; they are yet to throw off all reserve and challenge the faith of the world. 'Powers and signs and wonders' are the threefold designation of miracles in Scripture: 'wonders,' which excite attention and admiration; 'signs,' or things that have meaning and doctrine; 'powers,' that are evidently beyond human. These have borne witness in past time to the truth—never proved it, apart from the truth itself with which they were connected; and this is the mistake of so many at all times that a real miracle—something that could be rightly spoken of as all these—is an absolute guarantee of the message that it brings. Thus they are ready at any time to follow what is thus supported. Yet, if there are heavenly beings—'angels that excel in strength'—it is evident that, if permitted, and if evil enough to attempt it, they could at any time lead us thus according to their mind. Now that is the very thing which God has declared He will permit, when the time shall have arrived. When men have shown that they desire the truth no longer and the patient, long-suffering God has at last no justification further, that will have come to pass for the professing Christian world which we recognize as coming to pass in the history of individuals: God will say again, 'Ephraim is joined to his idols; let him alone.' And then will rise up one 'whose coming is according to the energy of Satan, with all power and signs and wonders of falsehood'—no longer in the interests of truth, but of a lie—and in all deceit of unrighteousness for those that perish; because they received not the love of the truth, that they might be saved.'

"Dangerous would it be, as well as foolish, to assert that this is of the past, and not the future; that it has been fulfilled in Romanism, or in any like way. Has the power of Rome, whatever its pretension to fabulous miracle may be, exhibited itself after this fashion? No doubt, there is a class at all times ready to be duped in this way, as we see in the rapid progress of such transparent absurdities, as, for instance, 'Christian Science'; but in all this there is only the feeble anticipation of a delusion which will yet carry away the multitudes of unbelieving profession. The arch deceiver is not in the Vatican, nor elsewhere at the present time; he is to be revealed in his time. And yet we may indeed discern the foreshadows of this tremendous iniquity and realize that his way is being prepared in many events and movements that are taking place under our eyes."*

Then the rejectors of the truth will receive their judgment. No one can even imagine what will be the fate of the millions who received not the love of the truth, but had pleasure in

---

*Numerical Bible.

unrighteousness. Horrible as the events are to-day, that coming time of Anti-Christ, the time when the lawless one reigns, energized by Satan, will be far worse. As it has been said, "Sin will be allowed to be its own terrible witness against itself, a witness at which eternity will shudder."

III. THANKSGIVING, PRAYER, EXHORTATIONS AND CONCLUSIONS.

CHAPTER II:13; III:18.

1. Thanksgiving and Prayer. 13–17.
2. Prayer for the Word and for Deliverance. iii:1–5.
3. Exhortations. 6–15
4. Conclusions. 16–18.

Verses 13–17. What blessed reasons are stated here to give thanks to God for what He has done for us and for all who believe! Brethren, beloved of the Lord, this is what believers are. Chosen we are to salvation through sanctification of the Spirit and belief of the truth. And glory is before all who have believed "the obtaining of the glory of our Lord Jesus Christ." And that glory may burst upon us at any time. For this God's people wait. Therefore we are "to stand fast and to hold fast." The word "traditions" means the instructions they had received from the Apostle; that is, the truth of God. To stand fast and to hold fast the truth are the two necessary things for God's people. He also prays for them that their hearts might be comforted and that they might be established in every good word and work.

Chap. iii:1-5. As in other epistles, so here the Apostle requests prayer for himself, "that the Word of the Lord may run and be glorified." His great ambition was to spread the Gospel and the Word of God everywhere. When sinners are saved by grace, are added as members to the body of Christ and walk in the Spirit, then the Word is glorified. Enemies were on all sides then, as they are now, obstructing and hindering the word, "for faith is not the portion of all." He counted on the faithfulness of God to establish and keep them. It is the comfort for His people to know that their keeping rests in His hands. If God be for us, who can be against us? "And the Lord direct your hearts into the love of God and into the patience of Christ." Christ, in infinite patience, waits in heaven, and His people on earth wait for Him and with Him until the appointed time comes when His waiting and their waiting ends.

Verses 6–15. Exhortations follow. It seems there was considerable disorder among them. "For we hear that there are some which walk among you disorderly, working not at all, but are busybodies." This was no doubt the result of their unsettled condition brought about by the false teachers. He therefore exhorts them to withdraw from any brother who does not hearken to the instructions he had given and who continued in a disorderly walk. Once more he cites his own exemplary life among them (1 Thess. ii:9-10). "For we behaved not ourselves disorderly among you; neither did we eat any man's bread for nought (as charity); but wrought with labor and travail night and day, that we might not be chargeable to any of you. Not because we have not authority, but that we might give you an example to imitate us." He exhorts such who were disorderly, doing nothing but living in idleness, that with quietness they should work and no longer live from the labors of others, but each their own bread. If there is refusal from the side of such, no obedience to this rule, he is to be noted and no company kept with him. Yet he is not to be treated as an enemy, but to be admonished as a brother. How well it would be if this course would always be followed.

Verses 16–18. "And the Lord of peace Himself give you peace continually in every way." This is the final prayer in these two epistles. It must be noticed how prominent prayer is in both of these epistles. And the Lord, who is with His people, will give peace continually in every way, if they walk in obedience, subject to Himself.

FIRST TIMOTHY

CONTENTS

Page
Introduction.................................... 145
Division of the First Book of Timothy.......... 148
Analysis and Annotations...................... 149

The First Epistle to Timothy.

Introduction.

The two Epistles to Timothy and the one to Titus are generally called the pastoral epistles, because they were addressed to these servants of the Lord who had been put in charge of important churches. Timothy ministered in Ephesus (1 Tim. i:3) and Titus in Crete (Tit. i:5). There never was a doubt expressed in the early church that these epistles were written by the Apostle Paul. Quotations from them are found in the writings of Clement of Rome (96 A.D.); Polycarp of Smyrna (110 A.D.); Ignatius of Antioch (110 A.D.); Irenaeus (175 A.D.); Theophilus of Antioch (168 A.D.); Justin Martyr and others. The Syriac version, known by the name Peshito, made about 135 A.D., contains these epistles, as well as other ancient versions. The greatest scholars of the early church attested them as genuine. Some of the heretics, like the Gnostic Marcion, and Tatian, rejected them, and so do the destructive critics of the nineteenth and twentieth centuries. It is hardly necessary to say that the style and internal evidences establish fully the Pauline authorship.

The Personal History of Timothy.

The name of Timothy is first mentioned in Acts xvi:1. His mother's name was Eunice (2 Tim. i:5); she was a Jewess, but his father was a Gentile (Acts xvi:1, 3). Paul called him his son, my own son in the faith (1 Tim. i:2), from which we conclude that he was converted by the Apostle's ministry. His mother and grandmother, Lois (2 Tim. i:5), were both Christians. They must have been, before their conversion, God-fearing Jewesses. This seems to be implied by 2 Tim. iii:14–15. Young Timothy had an excellent reputation among the brethren in Lystra and Iconium. After having him circumcised "because of the Jews," Paul took him as a fellow-laborer in the Gospel (Acts xvi:1–3). He must have accompanied the Apostle on his journey through Macedonia, for the Apostle left him at Berea with Silas (Acts xviii:14). He had been in Thessalonica and Paul sent him back to ascertain the state of the Thessalonian church. After that he remained with the Apostle in Corinth. He then traveled with Paul from Corinth to Ephesus. From Ephesus he was sent by the Apostle with Erastus to Macedonia and Corinth (Acts xix:22: 1 Cor. iv:17). Later we find that he was with Paul, the prisoner, in Rome (Col. i:1, Phil. i:1, Philemon, verse 1).

When Was First Timothy Written?

Much has been written on the date of the First Epistle to Timothy. The question of one or two imprisonments of the Apostle becomes important in connection with the date of the First Epistle to Timothy and the Epistle to Titus. Paul was no doubt imprisoned twice, and between the two imprisonments, when he was a free man, the First Epistle to Timothy and the Epistle to Titus were written. If only one imprisonment is maintained, the date of the writing of these epistles is hopelessly obscure, besides other unexplainable difficulties. Paul reached Rome as a prisoner in the year 61 A.D. and remained there for two years (Acts xxvii:30). During this time he wrote the Epistles to the Ephesians, Colossians, Philippians, and to Philemon. In each he speaks of the fact that he was a prisoner. He does not mention himself as a prisoner when he writes the first letter to Timothy. He tells Timothy that he hoped to come unto him shortly. In writing Titus he speaks of spending the winter in Nicopolis (Tit. iii:12). This is sufficient evidence that he was no longer a prisoner. His trusting confidence to be released had been realized (Phil. i:25; ii:24; Philemon, verse 22). The prayers in his behalf had been answered. For several years he was again at liberty, and Eusebius, a reliable source, states that it was known that Paul went forth preaching again. Another ancient source (the Muratori fragment, 170 A.D.) gives the information that Paul after leaving Rome went to Spain. The interval between the first and second imprisonment explains fully the statement in 2 Tim. iv:20, "Trophimus have I left at Miletum sick." When Paul was at Miletus before he came to Rome (Acts xx:17), he did not leave him there sick, but Trophimus accompanied him (Acts xxi: 29). Therefore Paul visited Miletus and Ephesus again; this must have been between his first and final imprisonment. Nor could the statement in 1 Tim. i:3 be explained if Paul had written this Epistle before his arrest in Jerusalem. He wrote Timothy that he had besought him to abide still at Ephesus. The Book of Acts records two visits of Paul to Ephesus. In Acts xviii:19–22 we read of his brief visit, and in Acts xix:31 we have the record of his longer stay which lasted three years. At that time he did not request Timothy to stay in Ephesus, but he sent him into Macedonia (Acts xix:22). In his farewell address to the elders of Ephesus (Acts xx:29, 30) he predicted the coming danger for that church, grievous wolves coming from the outside and false teachers from the inside. Some eight years later this prediction came true. He visited Ephesus again, and left Timothy there facing the different heresies which had sprung up, and bearing witness against them. A short time after he wrote this first epistle to his beloved Timothy, beseeching him to abide still in Ephesus. The second epistle was written from Rome after he had been thrown into prison the second time, and immediately before he suffered the martyr's death.

The Purpose of the Epistle.

It is a confidential communication which Paul sent to Timothy concerning the church as the house of God. In chapter iii:14, 15 we find the words which state clearly the purpose of this epistle, "These things write I unto thee, hoping to come unto thee shortly; but if I tarry long, that thou mayest know how thou oughtest to behave thyself in the house of God, which is the church of the living God, the pillar and ground of truth." The epistle therefore contains practical and important instructions on the order which is to be maintained in the church, as the house of God. The suitable conduct befitting to the house of God is given by the Apostle. Pure doctrine, pure worship and a faithful ministry are the leading thoughts of this pastoral letter, but he also enters into the godly conduct of the individuals which are in the church of the living God. Blessed instructions! There is failure on all sides, showing, that departure from the faith, when men no longer endure sound doctrine, is upon us, according to the warning given in both epistles. Yet individuals can always walk and live in the truth, for there is grace sufficient to lead and to maintain the members of the Body of Christ in the divinely marked out path, even in the last days, the perilous times.

The Divisions of First Timothy.

In the beginning of this epistle unsound doctrine and all that is connected with it is rebuked, and the Apostle puts a strong emphasis on true doctrine, without which no godliness is possible. This true doctrine is the Gospel of Grace of which Paul testifies, when he writes, "according to the glorious gospel of the blessed God which was committed to my trust" (i:11). Of this grace he was himself a witness. Prayer is the leading topic of the second chapter. In the third chapter the house of God and the holiness which becomes that house is the theme, what manner of persons overseers and deacons must be. Then in the fourth chapter we find a warning of the departure from the faith in the latter times. The last two chapters give different instructions and exhortations concerning the elder and younger women, widows, the support of elders, or overseers, as well as personal instructions to Timothy. This gives us a fivefold division.

I. **CONCERNING SOUND DOCTRINE.** Chapter i.

II. **CONCERNING PRAYER.** Chapter ii.

III. **CONCERNING THE HOUSE OF GOD.** Chapter iii.

IV. **CONCERNING THE LATTER-DAY APOSTASY.** Chapter iv.

V. **INSTRUCTIONS AND EXHORTATIONS.** Chapters v–vi.

Analysis and Annotations.

I. CONCERNING DOCTRINE.

CHAPTER I.

1. The Salutation (verses 1–2).
2. The Charge concerning false doctrine (verses 3–4).
3. The Law, its use, and in contrast with Grace (verses 5–11).
4. Exceeding abundant Grace (verses 12–17).
5. The Charge to Timothy, and the danger of shipwreck (verses 18–20).

Verses 1–2. Paul writes as an Apostle and mentions the fact that it is "by the commandment of God our Saviour." Necessity was laid upon him to act and write as an Apostle through the energy of the Spirit of God, and therefore all he writes is of great importance, for it is not merely loving advice to his son Timothy, but by commandment of God. The expression "God our Saviour" is peculiar to the First Epistle to Timothy and to the Epistle addressed to Titus. (See ii:3; iv:10; Tit. i:3; ii:10; iii:4.) It shows that God's character towards the world is that of a Saviour through the work of His Son. His grace, bringing salvation, has appeared unto all men, a different thing from what was under the law-dispensation. All men are now the objects of God's dealing in grace, and therefore we read in the second chapter that supplications, prayers and intercessions be made for all men (not believers only), "for this is good and acceptable in the sight of God our Saviour, who will have all men to be saved, and to come unto the knowledge of the truth." We learn from this the meaning of "God our Saviour;" it expresses His love towards the world. This sovereign mercy of God was the true starting point of all the Apostle had to declare. He then salutes his child Timothy, "grace, mercy and peace from God our Father and Jesus Christ our Lord." Here we find another interesting distinction in the use of the word "mercy." When greetings are sent by the Holy

Spirit to churches, He never mentions mercy, but only "grace and peace," but when an individual is addressed "mercy" is added. It supposes the need, the constant wants, the difficulties, the trials and the dangers of individual believers. Timothy, in Ephesus, when the grievous wolves came from the outside, and false teachers from the inside, needed mercy, so that he would be kept. As the days grow darker, the departure from the faith becomes more pronounced, individual believers need mercy upon mercy to stand and to withstand.*

Verses 3-4. The Apostle had besought Timothy to abide still in Ephesus when he left that city and went to Macedonia. He was to remain behind to charge some that they teach no other doctrine. When Paul had met the elders of Ephesus at Miletus he had made this prediction, "For I know this, that after my departure shall grievous wolves enter in among you, not sparing the flock. Also of your own selves shall men arise, speaking perverse things, to draw away disciples after them" (Acts xx:29-30). Then he went to Jerusalem, where he was taken prisoner and sent to Rome. After his release he must have visited Ephesus once more and found the very things in the assembly of Ephesus against which the Holy Spirit had sounded the warning. Timothy was with him at that visit between his first and second imprisonment. He left him behind to deal with false teachers and false doctrines.† The better rendering of verse 4 is, "neither turn their minds to fables and interminable genealogies, which bring questionings rather than God's dispensation which is in faith." The special warning is against fables and interminable genealogies. From the Greek word "muthos," translated fables, we have our English word "myths." The warning is undoubtedly aimed at the Gnostic emanations, the invention

*"Mercy unto you, and peace, and love, be multiplied" is written in the beginning of the Epistle of Jude. This Epistle pictures the darkest days of departure from the faith with the church still on earth.

†The word "doctrine" (teaching) is used eight times in this Epistle.

of "aeons" and the list of their successions. Like the church in Colosse, the church of Ephesus was also invaded by the false teachers of Gnosticism.* It was not yet fully developed. That came during the post-apostolic days in the second century. These speculations were not according to sound doctrine and the truth of God. Neither are the present-day myths of evolution, the derivation of one thing from another in an interminable chain, the myths of destructive criticism, of spiritism, theosophy, Christian Science, and other vagaries. Jewish teachings on the perpetual obligation of the Mosaic law, genealogies, and other matters, are likewise included in this warning. They all lead not upon the sure foundation of the dispensation of God,† which is in faith, but to questionings in which there is no profit, but which open the way to a complete rejection of God's truth and God's grace made known in the Gospel.

Verses 5–11. When the Apostle uses the word "commandment" he does not mean the ten commandments. It is the charge the Apostle is putting upon his son and fellow-laborer Timothy. What he enjoins is, love out of a pure heart, and a good conscience, and unfeigned faith. And this is produced not by the law, nor by human imaginations and questionings, but solely by the Gospel of Grace. Speculative questions or anything else do not act upon the conscience nor bring into the presence of God. An unfeigned faith in Christ clears the conscience from guilt and produces love out of a pure heart. Some had swerved from this, by turning aside from the dispensation of the grace of God unto the vain talk about the law, fables and genealogies. They gave heed to Jewish fables and commandments of men (Tit. i:14) and were consequently turned from the truth of the Gospel. They aimed at being law-teachers, but they did not understand what they said and what they so strenuously affirmed. They were evidently the same Judaizers, ever insisting upon law-keeping and

---

*See our introduction to Colossians and annotations on chapter ii.

†The dispensation of the grace of God (Eph. iii:2).

its ordinances, the false teachers who perverted the Gospel, who continually dogged the steps of the Apostle and tried to injure the work he was doing.

Then follows a parenthetical statement on the use and purpose of the law. The law is good (Rom. vii:12) if a man uses it lawfully. Its lawful application is to the lawless and disobedient, to the ungodly and sinners, who are condemned by the law. It has no application to a righteous person. A believer with unfeigned faith and love out of a pure heart and a good conscience is righteous, and has nothing to do with the law. In possession of the righteousness which is apart from the law, having the righteousness of God in Christ, the law has no power over the believer. He is dead to the law; the law can have no possible meaning or use for him. The law was never designed to be the rule for the life of the Christian. He is saved by grace, and that alone can produce godliness. It is grace which teaches to live soberly, righteously and godly in this present age, and also gives the power for it. To use the law is for the believer a denial of grace. He continues: "And if any other thing that is contrary to sound doctrine, according to the gospel of the glory of the blessed God, which was committed to my trust." Here we see the contrast between law and gospel. The law is for condemnation, but the Gospel proclaims the glory of the blessed God; and this Gospel, committed to the Apostle, unfolding God's counsels of glory for us in Christ, tolerates no evil. Sound doctrine is therefore not only a correct belief in the Gospel of the glory of the blessed God, what is accomplished in that Gospel to the glory of God, and the glory it puts on our side; but sound doctrine means also practical godliness.* A holy life is produced by sound doctrine, and sound doctrine must lead to a holy life. Unsound doctrines, profane and vain babblings, all the unscriptural teachings, the destructive criticism, and the cults "will increase unto more ungodliness" (2 Tim. ii:17) and eat like a canker.

---

*See vi: 3—"The doctrine which is according to godliness."

Verses 12–17. And now he speaks of himself, thanking Christ Jesus, Who gave him power and counted him faithful, appointing him to the ministry. And who was he? A blasphemer and persecutor, and injurious. "But I obtained mercy, because I did it in unbelief. And the grace of our Lord was exceeding abundant with faith and love which is in Christ Jesus." The grace which he preached, which he defended against the attacks of Judaizing teachers, was pre-eminently witnessed to by his own case. The grace of the Lord was towards him exceeding abundant, or more literally rendered, "the grace of our Lord surpassingly overabounded." He had the most marvellous experience of this grace which saves so freely and fully. "This is a faithful saying, and worthy of all acceptation, that Christ Jesus came into the world to save sinners; of whom I am chief." He knows what he says and of what he speaks. No fables, imaginations, vain speculations, or questionings here, but the fullest assurance, that Christ Jesus the Son of God came into the world to save sinners. And He had saved him, the chief of sinners, so that no man need to consider himself too great a sinner for this grace. He obtained mercy so that he might be a pattern of the grace that Christ would display towards all "who should hereafter believe on Him to life everlasting." In a special manner this is applicable to the nation to which Paul belonged; the Jews hereafter, at the time of our Lord's second coming, will obtain mercy. Paul in his experience is the pattern of the sovereignty of grace which in due time will save "all Israel." The chief, the most active, the most inveterate of enemies, was the best and most powerful of all witnesses that the grace of God abounded over sin, and that the work of Christ was perfect to put it away. It was the best refutation of the "other doctrines" against which Paul warns in these epistles to Timothy. He then gives utterance to the praise which filled his heart. Such praise the law could never teach the human heart. It knows no song of joy and blessing; its melody is the curse.

"Such was the foundation of Paul's ministry in contrast

with the law. It was founded on the revelation of grace; but it was a revelation connected with the experience of its application to his own case. Peter, guilty of denying a living Saviour, could speak to the Jews of grace that met their case, which was his own; Paul, formerly the enemy of a glorified Saviour and the resister of the Holy Ghost, could proclaim grace that rose above even that state of sinfulness, above all that could flow from human nature—grace that opened the door to the Gentiles according to God's own counsels, when the Jews had rejected everything, substituting the heavenly assembly for them—grace that sufficed for the future admission of that guilty nation to better privileges than those which they had forfeited."*

Verses 18–20. He then commits a very solemn charge to Timothy. The charge is "holding faith, and a good conscience." Some put it away, that is the good conscience, and then concerning faith make shipwreck. The faith is sound doctrine, the Gospel of Grace, the truth of Christianity. A good conscience must be maintained in order to hold that faith in sincerity and truth. Daily self-judgment, even as to the smallest things, is absolutely necessary to keep the believer from the dangerous rocks on which his faith may be wrecked. It may be a very little sin that is allowed and not confessed and put away; but this unjudged sin becomes the starting point of something worse and may lead to terrible results. If a good conscience is put away the believer begins to drift.

"To be in communion with God, the conscience must be good, must be pure; and if we are not in communion with God, we cannot have the strength that would maintain us in the faith, that would enable us to persevere in the profession of the truth, as God gives it to us. Satan has then a hold upon us, and if the intellect of one in this state is active, he falls into heresy. The loss of a good conscience opens the door to Satan, because it deprives

*Synopsis.

us of communion with God; and the active mind, under Satan's influence, invents ideas instead of confessing the truth of God. The apostle treats the fruit of this state as "blasphemies;" the will of man is at work, and the higher the subject, the more an unbridled will, possessed by the enemy, goes astray, and exalts itself against God, and against the subjection of the whole mind to the obedience of Christ, to the *authority* of the revelation of God."*

We have here an explanation why men who used to hold the faith delivered unto the saints have given up that faith. Error does not begin with the head but with the heart. Some sin was cherished; some secret sin had control. Self-judgment was not exercised; no confession made. Having no good conscience, there was no longer real communion with God and the shipwreck of faith followed in due time. Hymenaeus and Alexander, who denied resurrection, were examples of this fatal road. He delivered them over to Satan, not to be lost, but for discipline. They were to find out by sad and sorrowful experience what Satan's power is, so that broken and humbled they might be brought back. "Better surely not to need such discipline; but if we do need it, how precious to know that God turns it to account in His grace, that we might be thoroughly dealt with and exercised in the conscience."†

*J. N. Darby.

†Wm. Kelly.

II. CONCERNING PRAYER.

CHAPTER II.

1. Prayer for all men and for those in Authority (verses 1–7).
2. The place for the Man and the Woman (verses 8–15).

Verses 1–7. Instructions are now given by the Apostle. The first concerns prayer. "I exhort, therefore, that, first of all, supplications, prayers, intercessions, and giving of thanks be made for all men; for kings, and for all that are in authority; that we may lead a quiet and peaceable life in all godliness and honesty (literally, gravity). For this is good and acceptable in the sight of God our Saviour, who will have all men to be saved and come to the knowledge of the truth." The God who is our Father is also the Saviour-God, who acts in the Gospel of His Grace with love and compassion towards all men. As such He manifests a gracious willingness to have all men come to the knowledge of the truth and be saved. We must, therefore, knowing Him and the exceeding abundant grace towards us, act in love towards those who are without. God acts in grace and the household of faith must do likewise. As the Gospel of Grace goeth forth to all men, and God wants all men to be saved, so are we to pray for all men. Especially are kings and all who are in authority to be mentioned in the prayers of intercession. This is the true grace-spirit; the Jewish law-spirit knew nothing of love towards all men. Gentiles and Gentile kings were looked upon as outside, and not considered to be the objects of Divine love. The dispensation of the Grace of God having come, salvation by grace is offered to the whole world. And how this exhortation has been neglected! How little true prayer for the salvation of all men is made!* We must also remember that cruel Nero was on the throne of the Roman Empire when this exhortation was written. The house of God is to be a house of prayer for all nations, and to exercise the

*Verse 4 disposes completely of the unscriptural idea that God has predestinated a part of the human race to be lost.

priestly function of intercession. Well has it been said, "Nothing but the strong sense of the infinite blessing of the place that grace has given us could lead to, or keep up, such prayer." But often we are apt to settle down in the enjoyment of grace, without reflecting on our responsibility towards those who are unreached by that grace, which is also at their disposal. Through preoccupation within, how often we forget those without! How needful to-day when thrones totter, when democracies arise, when all forms of government break down and the shadow of the coming lawless one lengthens, to be obedient to this divinely given instruction, so that even in these days of confusion God's people may lead "a quiet and peaceable life"!

"For there is one God and one Mediator between God and men, the man Christ Jesus; who gave Himself a ransom for all, the testimony to be rendered in due time." Judaism was the revelation and testimony of the one God. Christianity reveals also the true God, but brings forth the equally great truth that there is but one mediator, as there is but one God. And this one Mediator is the Man Christ Jesus, who came into the world and who gave Himself a ransom for all.

"Precious truth! We are in weakness, we are guilty, we could not bring ourselves near to God. We needed a Mediator, who, while maintaining the glory of God, should put us into such a position that He could present us to God in righteousness according to that glory. Christ gave Himself as a ransom. But He must be a man in order to suffer for men, and to represent men. And this He was. But this is not all. We are weak—here, where we are to receive the revelation of God; and weak, with regard to the use of our resources in God and our communion with Him —even when our guilt is blotted out. And, in our weakness to receive the revelation of God, Christ has revealed God, and all that He is in His own Person, in all the circumstances wherein man could have need either in body or in soul. He came down into the lowest depths in order that there should be none, even of the most wretched, who could not feel that God in His goodness was near him and was entirely accessible to him—come down to Him—His love finding its occasion in misery; and that there was no need to which He was not present, which He could not meet."

"He came down, took part in all the sorrows of humanity, and entered into all the circumstances in which the human heart could be, and was wounded, oppressed, and discouraged, bowing down under the evil. No tenderness, no power, of sympathy, no humanity, like His; no human heart that can so understand, so feel with us, whatever the burden may be that oppresses the heart of man. It is the Man, the Christ Jesus, who is our Mediator; none so near, none who has come down so low, and entered with divine power into the need, and all the need, of man. The conscience is purified by His work, the heart relieved by that which He was, and which He is for ever.

"There is but One: to think of another would be to snatch from Him His glory, and from us our perfect consolation. His coming from on high, His divine nature, His death, His life as man in heaven, all point Him out as the one and only Mediator."*

"A ransom for all, the testimony to be rendered in due time." This statement has been perverted by some, who handle the Word of God deceitfully, to mean that the whole human race will ultimately be saved including all the wicked dead. And more than that, some of these teachers have made the astonishing statement that the testimony of their unscriptural invention was to be reserved for a certain time, and that "due time" came when they preached their "larger hope" and universal salvation.† He has given Himself a ransom for all, which means that provision is made by His propitiatory sacrifice for the salvation of

---

*Synopsis.

†Among these we mention the late "Pastor" C. T. Russell, who claimed to be a specially chosen instrument (surely not of God) to propagate this lie.

the whole race, but faith is necessary for the appropriation of this salvation. All who do not accept Christ by personal faith are not covered by His substitutionary sacrifice. If they die in their sins the great ransom cannot deliver them (Job xxxvi:18). The due time, or, its own time, when that testimony of all this was to be rendered came when the work was finished on the cross. Ever since the one Mediator between God and man gave Himself a ransom for all, the message of God's love and grace has been preached. And Paul to whom the Gospel of the glory of the blessed God was specially committed could therefore say, "Whereunto I was appointed a preacher* and an apostle (I speak the truth, I lie not) a teacher of the Gentiles in faith and truth."

Verses 8-15. "I will therefore that men pray everywhere, lifting up holy hands, without wrath and doubting." This refers to praying in public. Audible prayer in the congregation is to be made by men, and not by women. This is apostolic teaching.† The hands which are lifted up in public prayer must be holy hands (James iv:8). True piety and a separated walk are to characterize the man who lifts up his hands in public prayer. And it must be "without wrath," angry feeling against a brother, and without disputing or "reasoning," To harbor an ill feeling against another while praying or to introduce a dispute, a reasoning argument (as done quite often) makes prayer noneffective.

And now in regard to women he gives the charge that they "adorn themselves in modest apparel, with shamefacedness and sobriety, not with braided hair, or gold, or pearls, or costly array." She is to give her testimony in this way and show that she is not following the world, but is above these things. Immodest dress, bordering

---

*Literally "herald." Also used in 2 Tim. i:11; and of Noah in 2 Peter ii:5.

†There are sects in existence today which claim to have returned to apostolic doctrines and practices, yet they ignore the apostolic commandment as to the place of women in the church. In fact in many of these sects women are the leaders.

on indecency, to gratify the lust of the flesh and of the eyes, is a noticeable thing among the women of the world. The Christian woman must bear a testimony in an outward manner that she is separated from these things. Then he gives the charge about the teaching authority of women. "Let the woman learn in silence with all subjection. But I suffer not a woman to teach, nor to usurp authority over the man, but to be in silence." This is and belongs to the wholesome, sound doctrine. Woman has her sphere of service, of laboring in the Gospel and also teaching the Truth, among her own sex and children. But the place of authority does not belong to her; she is not to usurp authority, nor to exercise it. This is the Divine order, that the authority to teach is vested in the man. (See 1 Corinthians xi and xiv). "For Adam was first formed, then Eve." This is creation's order, which must be maintained on the ground of redemption. And the fall teaches another lesson. "And Adam was not deceived, but the woman being deceived was in the transgression." The able expositor Bengel wrote on this: "More easily deceived, she more easily deceives." When she leaves the place given her according to this apostolic charge, she is easily deceived, and then in turn easily deceives others. The second epistle speaks of "silly women laden with sins, led away with divers lusts." Women rejecting sound doctrine, usurping authority, have become instruments of the enemy, by inventing Satanic doctrines and perverting the Truth of God.*

Verse 15 refers to Genesis iii:16. She shall be preserved in child-bearing, delivered in the hour of trial and labor, if they continue in faith and love, and holiness with sobriety.

---

*Seventh Day Adventism had Mrs. White as prophetess; Theosophy—Mrs. Blavatsky and Annie Besant; Spiritism—the Fox sisters and the thousands of wicked and often immoral women—mediums; Christian Science—Mrs. Mary Baker Eddy and the thousands of women healers, the Irvingite movement—demon-possessed prophetess, who spoke in strange tongues; New Thoughtism has its women leaders, etc. How this bears out the Divine truth stated here.

III. CONCERNING THE HOUSE OF GOD.

CHAPTER III.

1. The Overseer (verses 1–7).
2. The Deacon (verses 8–13)
3. The House of God and the Mystery of Godliness (verses 14–16).

Verses 1–7. As stated before, the church is viewed in these pastoral Epistles as the House of God. The holiness which becomes this house is to be maintained and expressed in a practical way. The different directions given as to overseers and deacons demonstrate what God esteems highly, and what He expects of those who are saved by grace, and who constitute His House. Paul wrote these instructions to his son Timothy, so that he might know how to behave himself in the House of God (verses 14–15).

Bishops (overseers) are identical with elders (presbyters). For conclusive proof see Acts xx:17 and 28; Titus i:5 and 7. In both passages the same persons are called both bishops and elders. It is nowhere taught in the Word of God that a bishop has a place of superior authority in the body of Christ, as head of a diocese, etc. These things as practised in the Romish, Episcopal and other ritualistic churches are according to human ordinances. The work of the overseer is learned from Paul's statement in Acts xx:28: "Take heed therefore unto yourselves, and to all the flock, over the which the Holy Spirit hath made you overseers, to feed the church of God, which He hath purchased with His own blood." The Holy Spirit called them into this work, for He is the great administrator in the church. Each local church had not one overseer or bishop, but a number of them, showing that the authority was not vested in one person only (Phil. i:1). If anyone desired the office of an overseer, he desired a good work. It is a good work to exercise loving and patient care over souls which are beloved of God, and so dear to Him, who purchased them by His own blood. Such a desire would be the result of the Spirit of God, who laid the work of a overseer upon the heart.* Paul then gives Timothy the qualities which a bishop or overseer must have. He must be blameless, that is as to his moral character irreproachable, with nothing whatever against him. "He must be the husband of one wife." This has been explained as excluding all who had been married twice. This is incorrect. It may refer to those who were as pagans married to more than one woman, for polygamy was practised among the heathen in that day, as it is still. Converted to Christianity these pagans were in an unhappy condition, and on account of it could not exercise oversight in a local church. On the other hand this inspired qualification of an overseer or bishop is a complete and crushing refutation of the celibacy of the Romish priesthood. He also must be vigilant, sober, of a good behavior (modest), given to hospitality and apt to teach† (2 Tim. ii:24). Among the other qualifications we point out especially the one "not greedy of filthy lucre," that is, he must not be a lover of money. This is mentioned several times in the epistles to Timothy and to Titus. And Peter in exhorting the elders also writes, "Feed the flock of God, which is among you, taking the oversight thereof, not by constraint, but willingly, not for filthy lucre, but of a ready mind" (1 Peter v:2). The Holy Spirit anticipated the corruption of church office and ministry through the love of money. He is also to rule well his own house and have his children in subjection, "For if a man know not how to rule his own house, how shall he take care of the church of God?" We see all these are moral qualifications. They are to be men of mature age, who had shown in the government of their own household their fitness for the more blessed work of having oversight in a local assembly. A new convert may begin to give a testimony for the Gospel as soon as he has believed, but fitness for oversight, to be an elder, required

*What is not all done by those in ritualistic churches by those who desire to become bishops—because, besides the honor which is connected with it, there is a good and life-long income connected with it.

†"Apt to teach" has also been translated "ready to learn."

time and a practical walk in the Truth. Therefore Paul writes, "not a novice, lest being lifted up with pride he fall into the condemnation of the devil." How often this has been true, that in some assembly a young convert with natural gifts was made much of, and then became lifted up and aspired, like Diotrephes (3 John) to have the pre-eminence.

Verses 8-13. "Deacon" means "a servant," one who ministers. The seven chosen in Acts vi to serve tables were deacons. They were to be occupied with the external affairs of a local church, to serve the bodily need. Without entering into the different qualifications, which need hardly any further comment, we point out only one. "Even so must their wives be grave, not slanderers—sober, faithful in all things." As the deacons had their work in external things, in connection with the family and family life of a local church, there was danger of their wives making mischief and becoming busybodies and tale-bearers; hence the instruction to the wives of the deacons. Nothing was said to the wives of the overseers; theirs was a different sphere.

Verses 14–16. Paul expected to come shortly to be with Timothy, from which we gather that he was not then a prisoner. In the words which follow we have a threefold mention of the church on earth.

1. It is the **House of God.** God dwells in it on earth. Its leading characteristic on earth must be holiness. "Holiness becometh thine house, O Lord, forever" (Ps. xciii:5). All Paul had written, his solemn charge concerning sound doctrine, a good conscience, prayer for all men, about overseers and deacons, was to teach Timothy and to teach us also, how to behave in the House of God, as on earth. God dwells in the church on earth. And He who dwelt among Israel and said, "I am holy, be ye also holy," makes the same demand of the house in which He dwells now.

2. The second name is the **Church of the living God.** The Holy Spirit, the Spirit of the living God, dwells in the church. She is the habitation of God by the Spirit (Eph. ii:22). She is therefore set apart for Himself; not of the

world, as He, who is the blessed Head of the Body, is not of the world.

3. The **pillar and support* of the Truth.** While our Lord was on earth He said, "I am the Truth." He is so still; and His Word is the Truth. The church is here to maintain this Truth on earth, to contend earnestly for the faith delivered unto the saints. She is the witness for Christ on earth, Christ who is hidden now with God. Therefore the true church is the pillar of the Truth, in proclaiming it. Woe! to the men who meddle with the Truth of God, and by their wicked criticism try to undermine the support of the pillar and the house of God. God shall destroy them for their evil work (1 Cor. iii:17). When the church leaves, the earth, then the Truth will be abandoned, and complete apostasy has come. As long as the true Church (though it only may be a feeble remnant) the pillar and support of the Truth, is on the earth, the complete apostasy cannot come (2 Thess. ii). From all this we learn that the presence of the living God and the maintenance of the Truth are the foremost characteristics of the House of God.

Verse 16 brings before us the mystery of godliness (piety). It is that which the church on earth is to witness to. This mystery is the Lord Jesus Christ (see Col. ii). The first fact of the mystery is, **"God was manifested in the flesh."**† It is the incarnation. God Himself has been manifested in the form of man. The Creator God came to be the Saviour God. He appeared on earth as man. **"Justified in the Spirit."** Upon Him, the second Man, the Spirit of God descended. He lived the holy life on earth. The power of the Holy Spirit was manifested throughout His life on earth. And having offered Himself by the eternal

*Not "ground," but "stay" or "support."

†The Revised Version on account of textual criticism changed this to "He who hath been manifested in the flesh." Some would therefore rule out this text as one which speaks of the Deity of our Lord. But even if it were positive that the correct reading is "He" instead of "God," it does not affect the argument. The "He" could not be any one else but the Son of God.

Spirit without spot to God, the power of the Holy Spirit marked Him out as Son of God in resurrection. "Declared the Son of God with power, according to the Spirit of holiness, by the resurrection from the dead" (Rom. i:4). His resurrection, by God the Father and through the operation of His Spirit (Rom. viii:11) justified Him as Son of God.

"Seen of angels." Not only did man see Him as John testifies, "that which was from the beginning which we have heard, which we have seen with our eyes, which we have looked upon and our hands have handled, of the Word of Life"—but angels saw Him. The host of angels witnessed His entrance into the world, surrounded Him and were present with Him in His life on earth. He was seen of angels in His resurrection, and seen of angels when He ascended on high to take His place at the right hand of God, far above all principalities and powers, becoming the head over all things, the Head of the Church. And to these heavenly principalities and powers there is now made known by the church the manifold wisdom of God (Eph. iii:10). **"Preached unto the Gentiles."** The good news is preached in the whole world. Jews and Gentiles hear the message, and especially is He preached to the Gentiles. **"Believed on in the world."** As a result of the preaching, the hearing of the Word of God, He is believed on, and those who believe on Him constitute the house, the church of the living God. **"Received up in glory."** He ascended to the glory from which he had descended. He glorified God on earth, and now as the Risen One God has glorified Him in Heaven. And some day all who believed on Him in the world will also be received up in glory, to be with Him where He is. And all this is the truth which is to be maintained and preached in the house of God.

IV. CONCERNING THE LATTER-DAY APOSTASY.

CHAPTER IV.

1. What the Spirit has predicted (verses 1–5).
2. The Remedies against Apostasy (verses 6–16).

Verses 1–5. The mystery of godliness having been mentioned, the Apostle speaks of Satan's power in opposition to the faith and Truth of God.* "But the Spirit speaketh expressly that in the latter times some shall depart from the faith, giving heed to seducing spirits and doctrines of demons." It is a prophetic warning. Paul had given a similar warning to the Ephesian elders gathered at Miletus a number of years before, and elsewhere in the New Testament the Holy Spirit gives the same warning concerning an apostasy in the future days. Inasmuch as the faith is the foundation upon which everything rests, Satan aims to destroy this first, knowing if faith is given up and the Truth of God denied, that he, the master-mind, can easily introduce his seducing spirits and substitute for the faith, demon doctrines. All this is fully evidenced in our days, the latter times which are the perilous times (2 Tim. iii:1). The mystery of godliness, the doctrine of Christ, is being increasingly denied and rejected by seducing spirits, active in systems like the destructive Criticism, Unitarianism, the New Theology and others. And in "Christian Science," Spiritism, Mormonism and other "cults" we find the very doctrines of demons. Anyone who rejects the mystery of godliness, no matter what else he may put in its place, has departed from the faith and becomes the prey of seducing spirits who lead him on to destruction and eternal ruin. And these seducers and seducing spirits, Satan's ministers, appear as ministers of righteousness (2 Cor. xi:15). They feign sanctity, "speaking lies in hypocrisy." They teach the most deadly error under the cloak of piety,

*The mystery of godliness here, and the mystery of iniquity in 2 Thessalonians. See annotations of 2 Thessalonians.

devotion and of deeper religious knowledge. Evil and error put on the form of truth and godliness. All this fits the different systems which claim to be "Christian," but which are "anti-Christian." They have seared, that is branded, consciences; claiming to lead others into righteousness and holiness while their consciences are defiled.

Two things are especially mentioned, "forbidding to marry" and "commanding to abstain from meats."* This austere asceticism was a pretension to superior piety. Men began to teach these heresies even in apostolic days. They developed later into systems like Gnosticism; and to-day we see the same principles advocated in theosophical and other occult movements. They forbid what God has established in creation, for marriage is an institution which God has sanctified, and to use that which God has created to be received with thanksgiving by them which believe and know the Truth. They claimed that their superior holy character would not be consistent with marriage and eating meats.

"Forsaking the real and practical holiness of communion with God, and of His commandments by Christ, they created a false sanctity for themselves, which denied that which God had ordained from the beginning, and thus exalted themselves against the authority of Him who had ordained it, as though He was an imperfect or perhaps evil being."†

The Spirit of God through Paul assures us that any creature of God is good, and nothing to be rejected, if it be received with thanksgiving; for it is sanctified by the Word of God and prayer. If that which God has made for the creature for its use is refused and rejected, it is sin. But all that the Creator has provided must be received from Him with thanksgiving, and the acknowledgment of a

---

*The Roman Catholic Church forbids her priests to marry, and also commands her members to abstain from certain meats on certain days.

†Synopsis.

dependence upon Him. Prayer is needed for that, to sanctify to our use what He has so graciously given.

Verses 6–13. The rest of the chapter consists of exhortations in view of the threatening apostasy, how these evils may be combated and remedied. If Timothy put the Saints of God in remembrance of these things, he would be a good minister (deacon) of Jesus Christ, and be continually nourished up in the words of faith and good doctrine. To remember the apostolic instructions and to maintain by them faith and good doctrine effectually counteracts error and the doctrines of demons. Then profane and old wives' fables must be avoided and refused. We have an all-sufficient revelation of God; speculative things of the human mind intruding into things unseen (Col. ii:18), following the theories, imaginations and traditions of men, only lead away from godliness, and lead from foolish questionings into that which is profane.*

The true exercise must be unto godliness, pious, consecrated living; and the true exercise is self-judgment, maintaining a good conscience and communion with God. Bodily exercise by erratic living, abstaining from meats and other things, profits but little. It is far different with true godliness. It is profitable for everything, both in this life and that to come. This is another faithful word and worthy of all acceptation (i:15). And for this doctrine the Apostle labored and suffered reproach; but he had faith in the living God, who as Saviour-God, by His power and providence, sustains all men. He is the preserver of all men, but especially of those who believe. As Creator He is the preserver and benefactor of all men; but for those who believe He is much more than that. In this God as Creator and Saviour, preserver and keeper, the believer trusts. "These things command and teach." It is another remedy against the

*A believer has no business to investigate Spiritism, Theosophy, or occupy his mind with things not made known in the Word of God. We must avoid these things, refuse to have anything to do with them, else we step upon the territory of the enemy, and lay ourselves open to his attacks.

seducing spirits and doctrines of demons. None should despise his youth. He was very young when he joined Paul (Acts xvi:1–3), and now after some eleven years he was still youthful, especially in comparison with Paul the aged. He urges him to be in his life and walk a model of the believers—in word, in conduct, in faith and in purity. These are the evidences of true piety and holding sound doctrine. Then as to himself and his service, till Paul came, he was to give himself to reading, which of course must mean the Holy Scriptures, to exhortation and to teaching. He was not to neglect the gift that had been bestowed upon him. In his case this gift was a direct bestowal of prophecy, the voice of the Spirit making it known (as in Acts xiii:1). The laying on of hands by the elders had not communicated the gift. It was the outward expression of fellowship with the gift imparted unto Timothy. This gift had to be used and developed like every other gift of the Spirit. A gift may be idle and neglected, but if rightly used it will grow and be used in blessing. To do all this and meditate in these things, be whole-hearted in them, progressing constantly in godliness, is a safeguard against all error. "Take heed to thyself and the doctrine; continue in them; for in doing this thou shalt both save thyself and them that hear thee." Some have perverted this instruction as if it meant the salvation of the soul, for eternal salvation. It has nothing to do with eternal life and salvation. This the believer has in Christ through grace. "Save" has here the same meaning as in Philippians, a present salvation from the dangers in the way, being saved from error.

V. INSTRUCTIONS AND EXHORTATIONS.

CHAPTER V.

1. Concerning Widows (verses 1–16).
2. Concerning Elders (verses 17–21).
3. Responsibility and personal instructions (verses 22–25).

Verses 1–16. It is not necessary to follow all these instructions in detail and explain their meaning. An elder was not to be rebuked sharply, but to be entreated as a father, and younger men as brethren. Then he speaks of widows. Those who are widows indeed are to be held in honor. Piety was to be shown at home, if they had children. "She that is a widow indeed, and desolate (left alone) trusteth in God, and continueth in supplications and prayers day and night." Happy privilege of such, with special claims upon the Saviour-God. Thus exercising trust in God and in His promises, her special ministry is the ministry of prayer and intercession (Luke ii:36–37). God hath chosen that which is weak, widows, those who are on sick-beds, "shut-ins," to use especially in the ministry of intercession. The Day of Christ will reveal the great things which were accomplished in secret prayer. But if other widows lived in pleasure, in self-indulgence—she is dead while she liveth—that is dead to the spiritual things. For such there could be no honor, but dishonor. And if anyone did not provide for his own house, he denied the faith and was worse than an infidel, for an unbeliever generally recognizes this duty. Then we have divinely given regulations as to those who should be given relief by the church, and those who should be refused. Practical godliness is thus to be maintained in the house of God, and manifested in every way so as "to give none occasion to the adversary to speak reproachfully."

Verses 17–21. Elders that ruled well were counted worthy of double honor, and especially those who had the gift of expounding the Word of God, and teaching the Truth, "who labor in the Word and teaching." And as elsewhere in his former epistles, the Apostle here once more states the responsibility that "the laborer is worthy of his hire." The ox that treadeth out the corn is not to be muzzled. The Creator-God careth for the oxen, and made a merciful provision for them in His law. How much more then should those be ministered to in temporal things that labored in the Word, and with much self-sacrifice taught the Truth. But the laborer must remain in dependence on the Saviour-God, for he is God's laborer.* Instruction is given how an elder is to be treated if charged with wrong. Before God, the Lord Jesus Christ, and the elect angels (from which we learn that angels are silent onlookers in all these things—1 Cor. xi:10), Paul charges Timothy to observe these things, to be firm in them, without showing partiality.

Verses 22–25. He was not to lay on hands hastily on any man, the outward sign of fellowship, to acknowledge them as co-laborers and become identified with them. It might result in becoming partakers of other men's sins. How little conscience there is to-day in this matter! How often believers are in fellowship with those who are not teaching the Truth. "Drink no longer water, but use a little wine for thy stomach's sake and thine often infirmities." A small matter, yet not too small for the Holy Spirit. No doubt Timothy had a very scrupulous conscience, but the Apostle in this God-inspired letter, sets aside his scruples and tells him to use a little wine. Much criticism has been made of this divinely given instruction. Extreme faith-healers, who reject all means in a way that is not faith, but presumption, and on the other hand extreme prohibitionists, have made the astounding statement that Paul made a mistake when he wrote these words. But if Paul made a mistake here who can convince us that he did not make

---

*The almost universal custom of promising a laborer in the Word, an evangelist, pastor and teacher a salary, and the laborer depending on his bargain, is nowhere sanctioned by the Word of God. It is contrary to faith which should mark the path of the servant of Christ.

a mistake when he wrote the eighth chapter of Romans? Others state that it was not wine, but "grape-juice." We give the helpful comment of another:

"Timothy's habitual temperance is here seen: weak in body, the apostle recommends him to use his liberty by taking a little wine—a pleasing instance of grace. We have here a proof of the habits of this faithful servant. The Spirit shows us how carefully he kept himself from exciting or satisfying his passions in the least thing (at the same time that there is perfect liberty to use everything that is good when there is a true reason for it), and also the Apostle's tender interest in his fellow-laborer in the gospel. It is a little parenthesis attached to the expression, 'be not a partaker of other men's sins,' but it has great beauty. This affectionate watchfulness became the apostle; he desired holiness in his representative, but he well knew how to respect Timothy, and to maintain the decorum which he had enjoined, and to exhibit his heartfelt tenderness."*

"Some men's sins," the Apostle continues, "are open beforehand, going before to judgment"—they are manifested in the present life. "And some men they follow after"—unknown now, hidden away, but to be made manifest at the judgment seat of Christ.

CHAPTER VI.

1. Concerning Servants (verses 1–2).
2. Concerning those who oppose (verses 3–5).
3. Concerning Contentment and Temptation (verses 6–10).
4. The Final Exhortations (verses 11–21).

Verses 1–2. Servants (slaves) who had pagan masters were to count them worthy of all honor, and thus bear a good testimony for the Truth, that the Name of God and the teaching be not blasphemed. Theirs was a blessed opportunity to show forth the excellencies of Him whom they served, and who once served in obedience and submission on earth. If their masters were believers, and

---

*Synopsis.

master and slave worshipped together, there was danger that a slave might forget his place and become insolent. The apostolic exhortation guards against this.

Verses 3–5. These things Timothy was to teach and exhort. If anyone opposed these instructions, if he did not give his consent to wholesome words, the words of the Lord Jesus Christ and to the teaching which is according to godliness, he showed thereby that he knew not the real power of godliness. He gives evidence of pride of heart, that he is destitute of the Truth, knowing nothing, but doting about questions and strife of words. And from such a state of soul cometh as a result envy, strife, railings, evil surmisings, perverse disputings of men of depraved minds, and destitute of the Truth, supposing that gain is godliness. This is a good description of a good portion of professing Christendom.

Verses 6–10. While the class of people who have the form of godliness and deny its power, make piety a means of gain in earthly things, which is condemned, the Apostle speaks of true piety, or as it is called in the Authorized Version, godliness, with contentment as a great gain. True piety, in walking with God, having a good conscience, gives contentment, no matter what earthly circumstances are. A believer who seeks the things above should no longer cling to earthly things, knowing that we brought nothing into the world nor carry anything out. If the eternal things, that promised glory, are ever real before the soul, then each will be content with having the necessary things, food and raiment. And how very true are the words which follow, as not a few have found out. "But they that desire to be rich fall into a temptation and a snare, and many foolish and hurtful lusts, which plunge men into destruction and ruin. For the love of money is the root of every evil; which, while some coveted after, they have wandered from the faith and pierced themselves with many sorrows." Money itself is not evil, but the love of it is the fearful thing. No further comment is needed on these words. Examples of this evil are all about us in the professing church, and "lovers of money" and "lovers of pleasure more than lovers of God" are constantly increasing. Surely they heap treasure together for the last days. Weeping and wailing will follow (James v:3).

Verses 11–21. The man of God is to flee these things. If he does not it will rob him of his good conscience, his true piety and contentment. The thing to be coveted for the child of God, who belongs to the house of God, is not money, but righteousness, godliness, faith, love, patience, meekness. To covet this is to be the daily business of a Christian. While the believer has to turn his back upon the world and its filthy lucre, he is also to fight the good fight of the faith, and to lay hold on eternal life. This life is, as we have seen from the Gospel of John, a personal possession. It does therefore not mean the obtaining of eternal life; that is the gift of God. It must be laid hold on in faith, entered into and enjoyed. Many possess eternal life, but a practical laying hold on all that it implies and that is connected with it, is what they need. Timothy, in this respect, had confessed a good confession before many witnesses. Once more the charge before God, the Creator-God, who preserveth all things, and before Christ Jesus, the great and faithful Witness, to keep all spotless and irreproachable until His appearing. The Lord Jesus is coming again. Note what is said of that coming, "which (His appearing) in its own time the blessed and only Ruler shall show, the King of those that reign, and Lord of those that exercise lordship; who only has immortality, dwelling in unapproachable light; whom no man has seen, nor is able to see; to whom be honor and eternal might. Amen."* Those who deny the immortality of the human soul and who teach that man has no longer endless being, but dies like the beast, use the words that God "only has immortality" as their star-text, to affirm their error. God only hath immortality **in Himself;** it is His essential possession. He is the Source of it. The statement does not teach

*J. N. Darby's Translation.

that man has not immortality, but that God only hath immortality in His Being; man has received it from Him.

We but quote the final exhortations. "Charge those that are rich in this present age not to be high-minded, nor trust in uncertain riches, but in the living God (the Creator and Preserver of all) who giveth us richly all things to enjoy; that they do good, that they be rich in good works, ready to distribute, willing to communicate; laying up in store for themselves a good foundation against the time to come, that they may lay hold on eternal life." And then another warning against the errors: "O Timothy, keep that which is committed unto thy trust, avoiding profane and vain babblings, and opposition of science falsely so-called, which some professing have erred concerning the faith."*

---

*Gnosticism—and its Satanic offspring, "Christian Science" so-called.

SECOND TIMOTHY

CONTENTS

Page

Introduction.................................... 179

Division of the Second Book of Timothy....... 181

Analysis and Annotations...................... 182

The Second Epistle to Timothy.

Introduction.

This is the last Epistle the Apostle Paul wrote. He was once more imprisoned in Rome, and shortly before his martyrdom he wrote this second letter to Timothy. His movements between his first and second imprisonment may be traced as follows: After having written his first Epistle to Timothy he returned to Ephesus, as he intended, by way of Troas. Then he left the books he mentions (iv:13) with Carpus. From Ephesus he went to Crete, and after his return wrote the Epistle to Titus. Next he went by Miletus to Corinth (iv:20), and from there to Nicopolis (Titus iii:13) and then on to Rome. If he visited Spain, as tradition claims, it must have been immediatly after his release.

Timothy was evidently still in Ephesus, obedient to the charge of the Apostle delivered to him in the first Epistle. That Timothy must have been in Ephesus when he received this second letter may be learned from the persons mentioned in this Epistle. Onesiphorus is mentioned in chapter i:16–18 as having sought out the Apostle in Rome, and also having ministered to him at Ephesus. In chapter iv:19 Paul sends greetings to the household of Onesiphorus, and they lived in Ephesus. Priscilla and Aquila are also saluted, and they lived generally in that city. Hymenaeus is stigmatized as a teacher of false doctrine (ii:17). There can be no doubt that he is the same person mentioned in 1 Timothy i:20. And so is Alexander the coppersmith another evil teacher whose residence was also in that city.

The Object of the Epistle.

The Apostle knew that the martyr's death was soon to be his lot. He has a great and deep desire to see his beloved Timothy once more. He therefore wrote him to that effect, "greatly desiring to see thee, being mindful of thy tears, that I may be filled with joy" (i:4). "Do thy diligence and come before winter" (iv:9, 11, 21). Being uncertain how it might be with himself, whether he should live or be offered up before his arrival, he wrote this letter with his final warnings, exhortations and instructions.

The Contrast.

There is a marked difference between this second Epistle and the first. In the first Epistle the house of God, the church, is seen in order, and the fullest instructions are given how this order in all godliness is to be maintained. The house as such is no longer mentioned in the second Epistle, though we read of "a great house" in which are vessels to honor and some to dishonor; the believer is urged to purge himself from the vessels of dishonor. The professing church is foreshadowed as becoming now a great house; as the little mustard seed became a big tree, sheltering in its branches the fowls under heaven. And this great house no longer manifests the order as laid down in the first Epistle. It has become dilapidated and is in disorder. What has happened in the history of the church is foreseen in this Epistle, in fact the beginning of it was even then noticeable when Paul wrote this last Epistle. Paul had to see before his departure the beginning of the ruin of that which as a master workman he had been used to build, and over which he watched so faithfully. He had labored more than all the other apostles, and now he had to be a witness of the decline of that which he had loved so much; departure from the faith he had preached, and with it corruption set in. The power of God had been at work and he was the channel of that power, but man fails in it.

Because the professing church, the house of God, is anticipated in its failure and disorder, not a word is said of elders and deacons. Nor is there a promise made, nor instruction given, about a recovery from these conditions. They continue to the end of the age. It is true revivals, partial recoveries there have been, but only to show that man fails again after each renewed action of the Holy Spirit. It goes from bad to worse in the professing church, till the hour strikes when the Lord takes His faithful remnant, the true church, out of the great house (1 Thess. iv:13–18). What happens then to the great Babylon-house is written in Revelation xviii:2. The house completely abandoned by the restraining Spirit becomes "the habitation of demons and the hold of every foul spirit, and a cage of every unclean and hateful bird."

Paul before his departure is alone. It is a mournful record—"all they in Asia are turned away from me"; "Demas has forsaken me, having loved this present age"; "only Luke is with me." It also foreshadows the position of the individual believer in the midst of disorder and confusion. The sure foundation of the Lord abides forever, and as we shall learn from our brief annotations, the individual believer under these conditions is to be faithful and maintain the true testimony for the Lord.

The Divisions of Second Timothy.

The opening chapter contains the loving greeting of the Apostle, and exhortations to faithfulness, especially to hold fast the form of sound words which Timothy had heard from Paul. Then follow other exhortations to be strong, to endure hardness, to strive lawfully, to labor, to consider and to remember. It is the conflict which the true servant has in the world, in which he is to be as a good soldier of Jesus. This is followed by a description of the departure from the faith, and the path the believer is to follow. In the third chapter the last days are prominently brought into view by the Spirit of God, and all that these days mean in the manifestation of evil. The fourth chapter contains the final words of the Apostle; faithful to the end, and the Lord's faithfulness to him.

I. **PAUL'S PERSONAL WORD TO TIMOTHY.** Chapter i.

II. **FAITH'S CONFLICT. AND THE BELIEVER'S PATH.** Chapter ii.

III. **THE LAST DAYS AND THEIR PERILS.** Chapter iii.

IV. **THE LAST WORDS OF THE APOSTLE.** Chapter iv.

Analysis and Annotations.

I. PAUL'S PERSONAL WORD TO TIMOTHY.

CHAPTER I.

1. Paul's affectionate words and confidence (verses 1–5).
2. Difficulties and Assurance (verses 6–12).
3. Holding the form of sound words (verses 13–14).
4. Turning away and faithfulness in contrast (verses 15–18).

Verses 1–5. Paul speaks in this last Epistle as an apostle of Christ Jesus, by the will of God "according to the promise of life which is in Christ Jesus." It is a blessed word and shows how the prisoner in Rome, facing now the martyr's death, had full assurance that all was well. He knew that he was in the hands of God. The promise of life in Christ Jesus was his portion; he possessed that life in Him who ever liveth. Again he addressed Timothy as his beloved son (1 Tim. i:2) with the greeting of grace, from which all blessings flow, mercy, so constantly needed by all His own, and peace, which his people know and enjoy, who look to Him alone for grace and mercy. The Apostle speaks of the past; he had served God, so had his forefathers, with a pure conscience (Acts xxiii:1); they had been pious, God-fearing Jews. This also had been the case with Timothy. There was unfeigned faith in him, which dwelt first in his grandmother, Lois, and in his mother, Eunice. Both Lois, the grandmother, and his own mother, who had a Greek for a husband (Acts xvi:1) had trained the child Timothy in the Holy Scriptures (the Old Testament) and he had known them from the earliest childhood (iii:15). Therefore when the Gospel of Christ was presented to them this unfeigned faith laid hold upon it at once. It was good ground which had been prepared to receive the Gospel-seed. Thus it should be in the Christian household. The promise is "Believe on the Lord Jesus Christ and thou shalt be saved and thy house." (Acts xvi:31). Unfeigned faith will be produced in the young by instructing them out of the Word of God, for "faith cometh by hearing and hearing by the Word of God" (Rom. x:17). Without ceasing Paul remembered Timothy in his prayers night and day. He remembered his tears, occasioned no doubt by the second imprisonment. How he desired to see his beloved son to be filled with joy!

Verses 6–12. "Wherefore I put thee in remembrance that thou stir up* the gift of God, which is in thee by the laying on of my hands." God had used Paul as the instrument in bestowing a gift upon Timothy. This gift needed rekindling. The danger of decline, which began even then to be manifested, is evident by this exhortation. The rekindling of a gift needs constant use of the Word of God and fellowship with the Lord, as well as a prayerful exercise of the gift itself. And the Spirit given of God to minister is not a spirit of fear, or cowardice, fearing men and conditions, but a spirit of power, and of love, and of a sound mind. Therefore he was not to be ashamed of the testimony of our Lord, which men began to reject, nor of him, who was now the prisoner of the Lord. It was Timothy's blessed calling and privilege to be a partaker of the afflictions of the Gospel according to the power of God. He was not to shrink from the reproach and difficulties which then set in, but to endure it all, enabled by His gracious power. The Gospel may be rejected and despised, so that the enemy seemingly is victorious, but finally the Lord and His truth will have the complete victory. The believer knows this amidst all present difficulties and discouragements, for God "hath saved us, and called us with an holy calling, not according to our works, but according to His own purpose and grace, which was given us in Christ Jesus, before the world began."† "Before the world began" does not mean eternity, but the time before the dispensations "the age-times" began. And

---

*Stir up in a "flame" or "rekindle."

†More correctly translated: before the age-times, that is, before the dispensations began. It refers to the first promise in Genesis iii:15, the promise of life, salvation and final victory.

all is now made manifest by the appearing of our Saviour Jesus Christ, who hath abolished death, and hath brought life and immortality to light through the Gospel. The full accomplishment and victory comes when He who abolished death by His death on the Cross, and triumphant resurrection, comes again. Paul was the herald of this Gospel to all men, to Jews and Gentiles. It was for this he suffered, and he was not ashamed. He knew all he passed through, all reproach, all afflictions, would not leave him ashamed. He knew the Lord and His power. "For I know whom I believed, and am persuaded that He is able to keep that which I have committed unto Him against that day."

"The Apostle does not say 'in *what* I have believed,' but '*whom*,' an important difference, which pleases us (as to our confidence) in connection with the Person of Christ Himself. The Apostle had spoken of the truth, but truth is allied to the Person of Christ. He is the truth; and in Him truth has life, has power, is linked with the love which applies it, which maintains it in the heart and the heart by it. 'I know,' says the Apostle, '*whom* I have believed.' He had committed his happiness to Christ. In Him was that life in which the Apostle participated; in Him, the power that sustained it, and that preserved in heaven the inheritance of glory which was his portion where this life was developed."*

Verses 13–14. Next he exhorts Timothy to hold fast the form of sound words. "Hold fast the form of sound words which thou hast heard of me, in faith and love which is in Christ Jesus. That good thing which was committed unto thee keep by the Holy Ghost which dwelleth in us." This is one of the most important exhortations of this Epistle, and of special meaning for all believers who, in these days of departure from the truth, contend earnestly for the faith delivered once for all unto the saints. The expression "the form of sound words" is a strong argument for verbal inspiration. The truth of God is conveyed in

*J. N. Darby.

the very words of God, and therefore the form in which the truth of God is made known is to be maintained. It is all to be held fast in faith and love, which are in Christ Jesus. It does not mean a certain creed constructed by man, but the whole truth of God as revealed by Him. And whatever good thing is committed unto the believer, in the form of a gift as a member of the body of Christ, must be kept by the energy and power of the Holy Spirit, who dwells in the believer. What we have received, the knowledge of the form of sound words and the gift imparted, must be used. "In proportion as we do not care to communicate to others the 'sound words' which we have received, we shall find their power over our own souls diminish and their sweetness for us also."

Apostasy starts with the giving up of the form of sound words. Critics and other deniers of inspiration speak of the spiritual meaning of the words of the Bible, and, that the Bible contains the Word of God, instead of *is* the Word of God. And that is the starting point of the ever increasing departure from the truth of God in our days, which will soon culminate in the predicted complete apostasy.

Verses 15–18. All in Asia (the province) had heard the Gospel in years gone by from the lips of the Apostle. And now the great man of God had to write mournfully: "This thou knowest, that all they which are in Asia be turned away from me; of whom are Phygellus and Hermogenes." It would be wrong to conclude from this that they had turned their backs completely upon Christianity and abandoned the profession of it. Such was not the case. Their faith had become weak and they had withdrawn from the Apostle of the Lord Jesus Christ, because he had become a despised prisoner, and with this act they showed likewise that they were departing from the great and blessed doctrines the Apostle had preached unto them. Perhaps some of those in Asia had visited Rome and had repudiated Paul the prisoner. It was an evidence of the spiritual decline which was setting in.

But there was a notable exception. Onesiphorus had also

visited Rome and had diligently sought him and found him finally. There were many thousands of prisoners in Roman dungeons, and we may well imagine how day after day Onesiphorus sought for his beloved brother, going from dungeon to dungeon till he had located Paul. What a meeting that must have been! He had ministered to Paul in Ephesus, which was well known to Timothy, and now he was not ashamed to minister unto the prisoner of the Lord. He prays therefore for his house* and that he may find mercy of the Lord in that day. The reward for his faithfulness to Paul will be mercy, as everything else is mercy in the believer's life.

---

*Strange it it is that the prayer of the Apostle for the house of Onesiphorus is used as an authority to pray for the dead. The assumption that Onesiphorus had died is incorrect.

II. FAITH'S CONFLICT AND THE BELIEVER'S PATH.

CHAPTER II.

1. The Apostle's charge (verses 1–2).
2. As soldier and husbandman (verses 3–7).
3. Identification with Christ (verses 8–13).
4. Exhortation and Warning (verses 14–18).
5. The great House (verses 19–22).
6. The believer's path (verses 23–26).

Verses 1–2. First we find a charge of the Apostle to his spiritual son Timothy. The blessed servant of the Lord knew that he was soon to depart, and therefore he charges Timothy to commit the great truths concerning the Gospel, which he had heard from the lips of the Apostle in the presence of many witnesses, to faithful men, who are able to teach others. To the Apostle it had been given to complete the Word of God (Col. i:25). No new revelation is promised through Timothy, but he is charged to communicate the revealed truth to others, who would be chosen by the Lord, as His gifts to the church, to propagate His truth. This is the only true apostolic succession, not through the church as an organization, nor through certain men who claim ecclesiastical authority, but through those who hold the form of sound words and who minister it to others in the energy of the Spirit of God. Timothy needed for this the strength of the grace that is in Christ Jesus. And so does every servant of Christ.

Verses 3–7. Here the qualities that Timothy ought to possess in order to carry on the work are given by the Apostle. As a good soldier of Jesus Christ, warring a spiritual warfare, he must suffer hardships and many privations. He must beware not to be entangled with the affairs of this life. The soldier's calling is to please him who has called him, and all else, comforts and self-indulgence must be sacrificed. The soldier does this to obtain a corruptible crown, how much more then should the soldier of Jesus Christ do this to gain an incorruptible crown!

The Christian is also a laborer, a husbandman. He must labor first in order to enjoy fully the fruit of his labor. And that requires patience. He urges Timothy to consider what he tells him, with the assurance that the Lord would give him understanding in all things. These are the practical conditions for all who are engaging in service—enduring hardship, self-denial, unentangled, separated from the world and its ways, fighting lawfully and laboring first to be partaker of the fruits.

Verses 8–13. In connection with this he was to remember "that Jesus Christ of the seed of David was raised from among the dead" according to the Gospel, which he calls "my gospel"—"wherein I suffer as an evildoer, even unto bonds; but the Word of God is not bound." Christ suffered, and though He is of the seed of David and has the promises of David's throne, yet it is not yet His; He waits patiently for it upon the Father's throne. In the meantime He, raised from among the dead (the seal upon His blessed work), has given His Gospel of grace and glory to be preached. And suffering is connected with this (Phil. iii:10; Col. i:24).

"The afflictions found in the path of service in the gospel assume here a high and peculiar character in the mind of the suffering and blessed Apostle. It is participation in the sufferings of Christ, and, in the case of Paul, to a very remarkable degree. The expressions he uses are such as might be employed in speaking of Christ Himself as regards His love. As to the propitiation, naturally no other could take part in that: but in devotedness, and in suffering for love and for righteousness, we have the privilege of suffering with Him. And here what part had the Apostle with these sufferings? 'I endure,' He says, 'all things for the elect's sake.' This is truly what the Lord did. The Apostle trod closely on His footsteps, and with the same purpose of love—'that they might obtain the salvation which is in Christ Jesus, with eternal glory.' Here of course the Apostle has to add, 'which is in Christ Jesus;' still, the language is marvellous in the lips of any other person than the Lord Himself. For it is what Christ did."

The servant is identified with his Lord and called upon to go in the same path. "It is a faithful saying, for if we died with Him, we shall also live with Him." While this is true positionally of all believers, all have died in Christ and live in Him, the meaning here is the practical manifestation of it in self-denial and suffering with Him. If we suffer and endure we shall also reign with Him. And if any deny Him He will also deny them before His judgment seat (Matt. x:33). These are solemn words little heeded in our days of laxity and declension. "If we are unfaithful, yet He abideth faithful; He cannot deny Himself," that is, His own nature. "The One we serve must of necessity be served according to the reality of what He is. The Righteous One must be served in righteousness; the Holy One, in holiness; the One who is not of the world, by those who seek no place in the world. We cannot make Christ other than He is, and we cannot make the world other than it is."*

Verses 14–18. These things he was to remember. And if they are remembered they will bring deliverance from the strife about words, vain and unessential disputations in which there is no profit, which only subvert the hearers, It is through disputes about words, and speculations, that Satan brings in his most subtle deceptions. The true way is to strive diligently to show oneself approved of God, a workman that needeth not to be ashamed, "rightly dividing the Word of Truth." What a havoc has been wrought by a wrong dividing of the Word of Truth! Law and grace have been jumbled together, Israel robbed of her promises, and the church impoverished on account of it. The Word of God and the Truth of God have suffered most from the hands of such unskilled workmen, who, not dividing the Word of Truth rightly, have produced confusion worse confounded. The sad division of Christen-

*Numerical Bible.

dom, a carnally minded, professing church, is the fruit of it, and much else. The whole Truth of God has been obscured, and unbelief fostered by it. To insist upon "rightly dividing the Word of Truth" and to practice it both in teaching and living is a most essential requirement of the true workman.

Profane and vain babblings are to be avoided, for they only produce ungodliness. Hymenaeus and Philetus, who held that the resurrection had taken place already and thereby overthrew the faith of some, were examples of it. How true it is that error is like a gangrene, spreading vileness and corruption everywhere.

Verses 19–22. But in the midst of the declension and perversion of the Truth of God, as it began in apostolic days, and is now more fully developed in our own times, there is the foundation of God, which stands firm and unmovable. Christ is the foundation of faith, and of His church. There is a double seal. "The Lord knoweth them that are His"—this is the divine side. This statement is given for the comfort of His own, and it is a most precious comfort, "the Lord knoweth them that are His." But this comforting assurance must lead us into communion with Himself. If He knoweth us as His own, we also know Him and delight ourselves in His fellowship. And so we also know in the days of decline and departure from the truth, that the Lord knows and keeps those who belong to Him. But there is also another side, "Let every one that nameth the name of the Lord depart from iniquity." This is the solemn responsibility of every one who nameth that blessed Name, which is above every name. This is the true evidence that we walk in real fellowship with Him, that He knows us and we know Him.

The great house of which Paul speaks is Christendom. It contains vessels of gold and silver, and vessels of wood and earth, some to honor and some to dishonor. Here we have the two classes found in the professing church, those who are really the Lord's, known of Him, who know Him, who walk in His fellowship and witness to it by departing from iniquity; and the other class, which merely profess His name, who have the outward form of godliness, but deny the power thereof; more fully described in chapter iii:1–5. If the true believer is to be a vessel fit for the Master's use he must purge himself individually from such. This is demanded again by the Apostle when in the above passage, describing the moral character of these vessels to dishonor, vessels of wood and earth, he writes, "from such turn away." This is the solemn responsibility of every true believer; he is not to be in fellowship with such, and when obedient to this call the believer becomes a sanctified vessel, a vessel set apart, separated, and then as such a fit vessel for the Master's use and prepared unto every good work.

The whole of that which calls itself "Christian" is looked at here as a great house. The Christian is of it outwardly, in spite of himself; for he calls himself a Christian, and the great house is all that calls itself Christian. But he cleanses himself personally from every vessel which is not to the Lord's honor. This is the rule of Christian faithfulness; and thus personally cleansed from fellowship with evil, he shall be a vessel unto honor fit for the Master's use. Whatsoever is contrary to the honor of Christ, in those who bear His Name, is that from which he is to separate himself.

By purging himself from all those who are unto dishonor, the servant of God shall be unto honor, sanctified and prepared for every good work. For this separation from evil is not merely negative; it is the effect of the realization of the word of God in the heart. I then understand what the holiness of God is, His rights over my heart, the incompatibility of His nature with evil. I feel that I dwell in Him and He in me; that Christ must be honored at all costs; that that which is like Him alone honors Him; that His nature and His rights over me are the only rule of my life. That which thus separates me unto Him, and according to what He is, separates me thereby from evil. One cannot walk with those who dishonor Him, and, at the same time, honor Him in one's own walk.*

Verses 22–26. Exhortations follow pointing out the way the servant of Christ is to walk and serve as a vessel unto honor, and fit for the Master's use. He is to flee youthful lusts and follow righteousness, faith, love and peace, in true fellowship with all who call on the Lord out of a pure heart. His service, under the direction of the Lord, must be among those who are destitute of the truth and who are ensnared by the devil, though they profess to be religious. The servant of the Lord has a solemn responsibility towards such. How he is to act in this service is given in verses 24–26. And blessed are those servants who, walking in true separation, reach out for the unsaved masses of professing Christendom and labor in love in the great house.

---

*Synopsis of the Bible.

III. THE LAST DAYS AND THEIR PERILS.

CHAPTER III.

1. The Characteristics of the last days (verses 1–7).
2. What the last days mean for the true believer (verses 8–17).
3. The need of the Word of God (verses 14–17).

Verses 1–7. Little comment is needed on these words. They are a prophecy. The Apostle by the Spirit of God reveals what shall come in the last days. It is a description of the moral qualities of the vast number of professing Christians of the last days, "who have the form of godliness," that is, go "to church," profess a creed of some sect, and are outwardly religious, "but deny the power thereof." Three times they are shown to be lovers. "Lovers of themselves"—they live for themselves and know nothing of self-denial, they live and walk in the flesh. "Lovers of money"—this is what the word covetous means. Greed controls their activities so that they can enjoy themselves and live luxuriantly and in pleasure. And therefore "they are lovers of pleasure more than lovers of God." The same class is mentioned in Phil. iii, they are the enemies of the cross of Christ, minding earthly things. Their end is destruction. Compare verses 1–4 with the last verses of the first chapter in Romans. There the characteristics, morally, of heathendom are given, and here the characteristics of the professing masses of nominal Christendom. There is no difference between the two, only the condemnation of the profession, the unsaved, religious element in Christendom is greater. There is no need to point out how this prophecy given by the aged Apostle has come true. We live in the midst of these conditions, and are surrounded by them on all sides. Evil teachers began in apostolic days to creep into houses, winding about silently like a serpent, and captured silly women laden with sins, led away with divers lusts. How much more true this is to-day.

Verses 8–13. What true believers may expect in the closing days of this age, if they walk in separation and are faithful in their testimony, is the theme of these verses. Jannes and Jambres were the Egyptian sorcerers who withstood Moses. Jewish tradition gives the information that the magicians of Ex. vii:11–22 bore these names. The Spirit of God assures us here that this is correct. Another Jewish tradition claims that they were the sons of Balaam. They worked by imitations. They produced by Satanic powers certain miracles which were imitations of God's power. Such is the case in our own days. Christian Science, Spiritism and other systems are the sphere where Satan's power of imitation is manifested. Satan also imitates in a still more subtle way the work of the Holy Spirit. All this will work on till finally (after the church has been called away) the times are reached prophetically described in 2 Thess. ii:3–12. And like the folly and wickedness of Jannes and Jambres were manifest, so will these deceivers and perverters of the Truth be uncovered. This will be when the Lord comes.

How happy in the Lord Paul must have been that he could point to himself as an example. The grace of God had enabled him to be all he writes to his beloved son Timothy. "But thou hast fully known my doctrine, manner of life, purpose, faith, long suffering, charity, patience, persecutions, afflictions, which came unto me at Antioch, at Iconium, at Lystra; what persecutions I endured: but out of them all the Lord delivered me." Paul endured persecutions because he was a faithful minister of the Lord Jesus Christ and did not shun to declare the whole counsel of God. "Yea, and all that will live godly in Christ Jesus shall suffer persecution." If the believer is true to the Lord, if he lives in separation, the world, and especially that which is called "the religious world," with its unscriptural aims and endeavors, will not applaud him, but he will have to bear the reproach of Christ and suffer persecution. Why do so few Christians suffer persecutions? Because they have not purged themselves from the vessels unto dishonor, and are consequently yoked with unbelievers.

"But evil men and seducers (juggling impostors) shall

wax worse and worse, deceiving, and being deceived." Things morally and religiously are therefore not getting better in this age. There is no hope apart from the coming of our Lord.

Verses 14–17. The inspired Scriptures of God are the need, the supreme need of the believer in the last days. Timothy had known the sacred Scriptures* from a child, and of these Scriptures Paul writes "they are able to make thee wise unto salvation, through faith that is in Christ Jesus." He exhorts him therefore, "Abide thou in the things which thou hast learned, and of which thou hast been assured, knowing of whom thou hast learned them." Then the assuring statement of the Holy Spirit, the Author of the Scriptures, that all Scripture is inspired of God. It is well known that the revised version has dropped the "is," so that it reads "every Scripture given by inspiration of God." We do not accept this, for it opens the way to deny that parts of the Scriptures are given by inspiration of God.

"We are told we have to read as, 'Every Scripture inspired of God,' as if it distinguished such from other Scriptures side by side with them, and therefore we had to distinguish in like manner. At once the human mind is set in supremacy over the Scripture, and we become judges of it instead of its judging us. But the apostle has been already pointing out the sacred Scriptures of which he is speaking when he says 'All Scripture.' Nothing is Scripture in the sense he uses the word except that which is in the sacred Scriptures, and nothing that is in them is without that inspiration of God which makes it 'profitable for doctrine, for conviction, for instruction in righteousness'."†

How important it is to hold fast the great truth that the Bible is the Word of God, and therefore "God-breathed." All apostasy starts with the denial of this fact. The Scriptures are the permanent expression of the mind and will

---

*The Old Testament.

†Numerical Bible.

of God. It is not merely that the truth is given in them by inspiration, but they are inspired. They are the expression of His own thoughts. They are our only authority. Upon the constant use of them depends everything. Without adhering to the Scriptures and being obedient to them, we also would be swept along by the current of apostasy. They are the one thing profitable. Note the order: Profitable for doctrine, which we get alone from the Word of God, and which is the foundation of everything. Then follows "reproof" or conviction, and that is followed by correction and instruction for righteousness. It starts with the doctrine and leads, after conviction and correction, to righteousness. And then the man of God, obedient to the Scriptures in all things, is perfect, thoroughly furnished unto every good work.

IV. THE LAST WORDS OF THE APOSTLE.

CHAPTER IV.

1. The last Charge (verses 1–5).
2. His last Testimony (verses 6–8).
3. The last personal messages (verses 9–22).

Verses 1–5. This last chapter is a most impressive one. It is the farewell of this great man of God. Joy and sorrow, confidence and love breathe in his final charge and message. "The sorrow that he might have in his soul was only for those he was leaving, and even that is almost swallowed up in the joyful consciousness of the thought with Whom he was leaving them." And so he delivers one more charge, and that solemnly before God and the Lord Jesus Christ, who is about to judge the living and the dead, and by His appearing and His kingdom. He is as a servant to keep the coming of the Lord, His appearing and His kingdom before his heart.

"The Apostle urges this upon Timothy as what would, amid all the difficulties of the way, be his strength and assurance. It is always according to Scripture, 'yet, but a little while, and He that will come shall come, and shall not tarry.' We look back and see how long it has been, and we take this to make the distance behind us put distance into that which is before us. The Apostle's way for us would be rather that we should say, 'The night is far spent, and the day is at hand.' We may, after all, go to the Lord before He comes to us, but we shall not have missed the good of having been in the meanwhile 'like unto men that wait for their Lord.' The whole character of our Christianity will be affected by our 'holding fast,' or practically losing sight of His coming, as our constant expectation."*

With the thought of the coming of the Lord before his soul, Timothy is charged to preach the Word at all times. The

---

*F. W. Grant in "Numerical Bible."

blessed hope gives energy to continue in the ministry of the Word. Preach the Word! The Word, all the Word of God, the Gospel and dispensational truth, is needed in the days when sound doctrine is no longer endured. And how all has come to pass! As the Apostle testified even so it is today. Sound doctrine no longer endured, "after their own lusts they heap to themselves teachers, having an itching ear." They care nothing for the message of God, but have man's person in admiration (Jude). They admire the teacher, his great swelling words (Jude). And the teachers and preachers are men-pleasers. And as a result of this their ears are turned away from the Truth and are turned to fables, such as evolution, higher criticism, Christian Science and other delusions. In the midst of all this departure from the Truth of God, the Lord still maintains His testimony through those who keep His Word and who do not deny His Name (Rev. iii:8).

Verses 6–8. The martyr's death now looms up, and he pens the never-to-be-forgotten words of his faithfulness and assurance of the crown of righteousness. "For I am already being offered, and the time of my departure is come. I have fought the good fight, I have finished the course, I have kept the faith. Henceforth there is laid up for me the crown of righteousness which the Lord, the righteous judge, shall give me at that day; and not only to me, but also to all that love His appearing." Upon the incorrect translation of the authorized version "I am now ready to be offered" has been founded that strange theory that the Apostle was now ready to die, and had at last the assurance that he was worthy of being a participant in the first resurrection.* The Apostle from the moment he had trusted in Christ had the fullest assurance that he belonged to Christ and was His co-heir; and so every believer knows that he is fitted for glory, not by what he does, or what he has suffered, but through grace alone. To teach that the Apostle Paul received his assurance that he would

*See annotations on Phil. iii.

share the glory of Christ in resurrection, after, and as the result of, his prolonged suffering, is pernicious, inasmuch as it denies all the great revelations in his Epistles concerning the standing of the believer in Christ. But he did not say he was ready; his words are, "For I am already being offered, and the time of my departure is come." Knowing the time of his departure, in which he would have fellowship with His sufferings and be made conformable unto His death (Phil. iii:10), his heart contemplated in joyful expectation the moment when he would depart to be with Christ. In this sense he was being already offered, having his heart set upon the early departure to be with His Lord. He had fought the good fight, finished the course and kept the faith. He had been faithful in all things and resisted the attacks of the enemy.

And now he looks forward to the reward. He knew that there is laid up for him the crown of righteousness. He does not say that this crown would be bestowed upon him immediately after he left the earthly tabernacle. He will receive it from the righteous Judge in that day, and that day has not yet come. At the same time "all that love His appearing" will receive the rewards. The Lord will come for His Saints, as it is promised in the Word of God, and take them to Himself, and the Kingdom which follows the rewards for faithful service will be enjoyed. To be in that glory with the Lord, in the Father's house is the blessed destiny of all who have accepted the Lord Jesus Christ, and who are accepted in the Beloved. No service can secure that destiny. The grace of God puts it on our side. Faithful service will be rewarded in the Kingdom. How great the reward that awaits the Apostle Paul in that day! May it be an incentive to all His people to labor on, to spend and be spent.

Verses 9–22. And now the last messages of the Apostle. How he would have loved to have his beloved Timothy at his side and look into his face once more! "Do thy diligence to come shortly unto me." And once more at the close of the letter he writes, "Do thy diligence to come before winter." It was the cry of deepest affection of one who was deserted by others and yet not a lonely man, for the Lord was with him. Demas, a fellow worker and with Paul in his first imprisonment (Philemon, verse 24; Col. iv:14), perhaps a Thessalonian, had forsaken the prisoner of the Lord. It is a mournful record, "having loved the present age, and is departed unto Thessalonica." It is wrong to conclude from this that Demas ceased to be a Christian and had renounced the Name of the Lord. He, with love for the present age in his soul, would avoid the cross and its shame, and therefore abandoned Paul. What became of Demas? What was his after history? The Lord alone knows this.

And Crescens had also gone away to Galatia. We know nothing else of him. Titus went to Dalmatia. It is supposed that Titus joined Paul at Nicopolis (Tit. iii:12) and accompanied him to Rome, and then went to Dalmatia to preach the Gospel there. Only Luke, the beloved physician, remained with him, and no doubt he ministered in every way to the comfort of Paul. Then Mark is mentioned. It is the same John Mark mentioned in Acts xiii:5 and xv:36–41. For a time after his failure in service Mark was unprofitable. His restoration had taken place, accomplished by the grace of God, and therefore the Apostle desires to have him again at his side, "for he is profitable to me for the ministry." And this John Mark became the chosen instrument to write the Gospel record which bears his name, in which the Spirit of God describes so blessedly the Servant of all, who never failed.

Tychicus he had sent to Ephesus. Winter approaching he feels the need of the cloak which he had left with Carpus in Troas. We see that he paid attention even to so small a matter, and that as to his earthly possessions he was poor. He also wants the books, but especially the parchments. He had opportunity as a prisoner to read and study. We do not know what these books and parchments were.

And then the sad record of Alexander the coppersmith. He warns Timothy against him, for he had done him much evil. It must be the same Alexander mentioned in 1 Tim. i:20. It may be possible that this man became incited against Paul on account of having mentioned his name in the first Epistle, and that he persecuted him for it. "The Lord will reward him according to his works." This is according to God's righteousness. At the time of the Apostle's first defence no one took his part, by standing by him; all forsook him. They left him alone and had not the courage to defend him. Beautiful is his prayer, "that it may not be laid to their charge."

But while all men had forsaken him, one had not forsaken His faithful servant. True to His promise, "I will not leave nor forsake thee," He had stood with Paul and strengthened him. And when he stood before the Roman authorities the Lord had given him another opportunity to proclaim the Gospel he loved so well, "that through me the preaching might be fully known, and all the Gentiles might hear: and I was delivered out of the mouth of the lion."

And then in simple confidence he counted on the help of the Lord to the end. "And the Lord shall deliver me from every evil work, and will preserve me unto His heavenly kingdom: to whom be glory forever and ever. Amen."

He sends his last greetings to his dearest friends and old companions, Prisca and Aquila and to the house of Onesiphorous. Erastus had remained in Corinth, where he was treasurer (Rom. xvi:23). The Ephesian brother Trophimus (Acts xx:4; xxi:29) he had left sick in Miletus. Then the final greetings and the last works of his inspired pen, "The Lord Jesus Christ be with thy spirit. Grace be with you."

"It is evident that this Epistle was written when the Apostle thought his departure near at hand, and when the faith of Christians had grievously declined, which was proved by their having forsaken the Apostle. His faith was sustained by grace. He did not hide from himself that all was going wrong: his heart felt it—was broken by it; he saw that it would grow worse and worse. But his own testimony stood firm; he was strong for the Lord through grace. The strength of the Lord was with him to confess Christ, and to exhort Timothy to so much the more diligent and devoted an exercise of his ministry, because the days were evil.

"This is very important. If we love the Lord, if we feel what He is to the assembly, we feel that in the latter all is in ruin. Personal courage is not weakened, for the Lord remains ever the same, faithful, and using His power for us: if not in the assembly which rejects it, it is in those who stand fast that He will exercise His power according to the individual need created by this state of things."*

---

*Synopsis.

TITUS

CONTENTS

Page

Introduction 205

Division of the Book of Titus 205

Analysis and Annotations 206

The Epistle to Titus.

Introduction.

Titus, to whom this Epistle is addressed, was a Greek convert of the Apostle (Titus i:4; Gal. iii:3). We have little knowledge of him. From the Epistle to the Galatians we know that he accompanied Paul and Barnabas in their journey to Jerusalem to attend the council in which the question of the relation of believing Gentiles to the law was decided (Acts xv). From the Second Epistle to the Corinthians we learn that Paul sent him to Corinth to gather the collection (2 Cor. viii:1–6) and that he discharged the duty in a zealous way. "But thanks be to God, who put the same earnest care into the heart of Titus for you. For indeed he accepted the exhortation; but being more forward, of his own accord he went unto you" (2 Cor. viii:16–17). Paul also stated in the Second Corinthian Epistle that he had no rest when he did not find Titus (2 Cor. ii:13), but when he came Paul was greatly comforted. "Nevertheless God, who comforteth those who are cast down, comforted us by the coming of Titus" (2 Cor. vii:6). The Epistle shows that he was in the island of Crete. Paul visited this island in company with Titus, leaving him there. Titus probably did not stay long in Crete, for Paul asked that he should meet him at Nicopolis (iii:12). This is all that can be said on the person of Titus.

The contents of this Epistle are of the same nature as the Epistles to Timothy, though the departure from the faith so prominent in the Epistles to Timothy is less prominent in this Epistle. That the truth must be after, or according to, godliness is especially emphasized; the truth must be manifested in a godly walk.

The Divisions of the Epistle to Titus.

The Epistle contains practical instructions. We make three divisions.

I. INSTRUCTIONS AND WARNINGS. Chapter i.

II. THINGS WHICH BECOME SOUND DOCTRINE. Chapter ii.

III. IN RELATION TO THE WORLD AND FALSE TEACHERS. Chapter iii.

Analysis and Annotations.

I. INSTRUCTIONS AND WARNINGS.

CHAPTER I.

1. The Salutation. 1–4.
2. Instructions Concerning Elders. 5–9.
3. Warnings against False Teachers. 10–16.

Verses 1–4. Paul calls himself in writing to Titus "a servant of God and an apostle of Jesus Christ," for he speaks in these introductory words of God's elect, and their faith in Him; and the promise of eternal life, God, who cannot lie, gave before the dispensations began; and that His Word is now manifested through preaching which was committed unto him by our Saviour-God. God's elect are those who have trusted in Christ. They have personal faith in God and know His love and are in relationship with Him. But such a faith and relationship demands godliness; therefore the statement, "The acknowledgment of the truth which is after godliness." These two, truth and godliness, belong together. If the truth is given up or not held, then godliness also is given up; the truth must be manifested in godliness. As to statement on the promise of life before the ages began, see annotations on 2 Tim. i:9.

Verses 5–9. Paul had left Titus in Crete. From Acts ii:11 we learn that the inhabitants of Crete were present on the Day of Pentecost and heard Peter preach. These Cretan Jews may have brought the Gospel to the island. Titus is commissioned by Paul to set the things in order which were wanting, and to appoint elders* in every city. We do not find the same intimacy between him and Titus as that intimacy and confidence which existed between Paul and Timothy. He does not open his heart to him as he did to Timothy. He invests Titus with authority to appoint

---

*That bishops are elders, etc., see annotations on 1 Timothy iii.

elders and states the qualifications the elder must possess. These qualifications are also mentioned in the First Epistle to Timothy (1 Tim. iii:1-7). Here is added that their children must be faithful and not accused of riot or of being unruly. The bishop must also be blameless as God's steward, not self-willed (headstrong), not soon angry, not given to wine, no striker, no seeker of filthy lucre. What he is to be is given in verses 8 and 9. "But a lover of hospitality, a lover of good, sober-minded, just, holy, temperate; holding fast the faithful word according to the doctrine taught, that he may be able to exhort with sound doctrine and to convict the gainsayers." Thus we have again that godliness and sound doctrine belong together.

Verses 10-16. He states that there were many unruly and vain talkers and deceivers, especially they of the circumcision. The Judaizing teachers were at work among the Cretans. Titus must have been especially distasteful to them, for he was an uncircumcised Greek. These Cretan Jews who claimed to have accepted Christianity worked evil in the assembly. The Apostle demands that their mouths must be stopped, for they subverted whole houses, teaching things which they ought not, for the sake of base gain. The national traits of the Cretans are then described. One of their own prophets had said, "The Cretans are always liars, evil beasts, idle gluttons." This is a quotation from Epimenides, who lived six hundred years before Christ. The Cretans were classed with the Cappadocians and Cilicians (all beginning in the Greek with a "K") as the most evil and corrupt in the Greek world. And Paul testifies to the truth of it, "This witness is true." They must be rebuked sharply, so that they may be sound in the faith, "not giving heed to Jewish fables, and commandments of men, that turn from the truth." These Judaizing teachers were ascetics, forbidding certain things, making rules for the outward conduct. Certain things were forbidden by their ordinances and commandments; yet though they were fasting and continent, they were, because unregenerated, inwardly defiled and unbelieving. Paul brands these Judaizers in this

Epistle as "defiled and unbelieving," with a confession that they know God, but in works they denied Him. He speaks of them as abominable, disobedient, and to every good work reprobate.

II. THINGS WHICH BECOME SOUND DOCTRINE.

CHAPTER II.

1. Adorning the Doctrine of our Saviour-God. 1–10.
2. The Grace of God and its Work. 10–15.

Verses 1–10. "But speak thou the things which become sound doctrine." The sound doctrine or healthful teaching must be accompanied and witnessed to by the right condition of soul, a godly character. The doctrine of God our Saviour must be adorned in all things. Aged men are exhorted to be temperate, grave, sober-minded, sound in faith, in love and in patience. Sound doctrine must of necessity produce such a character. Aged women are to be reverent in demeanor, not slanderers (1 Tim. iii:11) nor to be enslaved by too much wine. In the First Epistle to Timothy deacons are exhorted "not to be given to much wine." Here the exhortation is in the original in a stronger form, for the Cretans were known, and especially the women, for being slaves of strong drink. They are to be teachers of what is good. This is not contradicting 1 Cor. xiv:34 and 1 Tim. ii:12. The teaching of the aged woman is here defined. She is to teach young women to be sober, to love their husbands and their children, to be discreet, chaste, busy at home, good, obedient to their own husbands; that the Word of God may not be blasphemed. These are important instructions. They show that the Christian woman's sphere is first of all at home. The disregard of this has more than once wrecked Christian families. This is the great danger in these last days to put woman into a place which does not belong to her.

Young men are also to be discreet. Titus who is charged to deliver these exhortations was himself to be a pattern of good works. His example was to confirm his word. In teaching he was to show uncorruptness. Likewise gravity, setting forth the doctrines with dignity and in all seriousness,* and sincerity. "Sound speech that cannot be condemned"—so that those who oppose may be silenced, unable to speak anything evil of the servant of God. When the preacher or teacher does not practise what he preaches it becomes a great detriment to sound doctrine. How great a stumbling block this is!

Servants (slaves) are next exhorted to be obedient to their masters. They were not to forget their place. Though they had been saved and become children of God and heirs of God, their earthly relationship was that of slaves, and as such they were to strive to please their masters in all things, not answering them in contradiction, not purloining but showing all good fidelity, "that they may adorn the doctrine of God our Saviour in all things." Chrysostom said: "The heathen do not judge of the Christian's doctrine from the doctrine, but from his actions and life." The world does the same to-day. And so even slaves in their low estate could bear a witness to the Saviour God by adorning His doctrine.

Verses 10–15. "For the grace of God, bringing salvation for all men, hath appeared, teaching us that, denying ungodliness and worldly lusts, we should live soberly, righteously and godly in the present age, awaiting the blessed hope and appearing of the glory of our great God and Saviour Jesus Christ, who gave Himself for us that He might redeem us from all lawlessness, and purify unto Himself a peculiar people, zealous of good works."

This is a blessed and comprehensive statement of the Gospel and Christianity. It may be looked upon as embodying all the great Apostle taught in his God-revealed Gospel, in a practical way. The grace of God hath appeared, and it appeared in the person of His Son, our Lord Jesus Christ. In Him His grace is made known. His finished work

---

*What a contrast with certain evangelists and preachers of our day, who act like clowns and make sport of sacred things; instead of teaching the young reverence, drag down holy things!

is the source of it. It flows from the cross. And this grace comes to man with salvation. It brings salvation, not to a certain class of men, but it brings salvation for all men. Because all men are lost, and therefore in need of salvation, unable to save themselves; the grace of God bringing an unconditional, a perfect and eternal salvation hath appeared, offering that salvation to all. And when this salvation is accepted by faith in the Son of God and the believing sinner is saved by grace, the same graces teaches how to live and walk here below in newness of life. Grace instructs to renounce all ungodliness and all lusts that find their gratification in this age. But grace does more than that; it supplies the power to do this. It bestows upon the believer a new nature and the Holy Spirit, and walking in the power of all this, the lusts of the flesh are not fulfilled. And renouncing ungodliness and worldly lusts, the believer, saved by grace, is to walk with grace as his guide, instructor and power. That walk as concerning ourselves is to be soberly; as to our fellowmen it is to be righteously; as to God, godly. It teaches something additional. We are to await the blessed hope, "the appearing of the glory of our great God and Saviour Jesus Christ." He who gave Himself for us, to redeem us from all lawlessness,* who has purified us unto Himself a peculiar people, He is coming again. He will appear in glory, and grace has given us the blessed promise that we shall be with Him in glory, beholding His glory and sharing it also.

---

*With respect to the conduct of Christians towards the world, grace has banished violence, and the spirit of rebellion and resistance which agitates the heart of those who believe not, and which has its source in the self-will that strives to maintain its own rights relatively to others. The Christian has his portion, his inheritance, elsewhere; he is tranquil and submissive here, ready to do good. Even when others are violent and unjust towards him, he bears it in remembrance that once it was no otherwise with himself: a difficult lesson, for violence and injustice stir up the heart; but the thought that it is sin, and that we also were formerly its slaves, produces patience and piety. Grace alone has made the difference, and according to that grace are we to act towards others.—Synopsis.

And this blessed hope is the most powerful motive for a sober, a righteous and godly walk in this present age.

These things Titus was to speak, to exhort; and also to rebuke with all authority. This is still the calling of every true servant of the Lord Jesus Christ.

III. IN RELATION TO THE WORLD AND FALSE TEACHERS.

CHAPTER III.

1. Instructions. 1–8.
2. Warnings. 9–11.
3. Directions. 12–15.

Verses 1–8. He asks Titus to remind all believers to be subject to rulers, principalities and powers* (Rom. xiii:1), to yield obedience and to be ready for every good work. An ancient historian (Diodones Siculus) speaks of the riotous insubordination of the Cretans. They were to speak evil of no man, nor were they to be contentious, but show all gentleness and all meekness towards all men. Our own rights must be yielded, but never the rights of God. If authorities demand what is against sound doctrine then God must be obeyed more than man. This is indicated by the exhortation "to be ready for every good work." Meekness towards all men is to characterize those who are no longer of the world, but who are still in it. Such meekness towards all, not only towards fellow-believers, but towards all men, adorns the doctrine of our Saviour-God, and is a commendation of the grace of God which offers salvation to all men.

Then follows an additional reason why Christians should be gentle and meek towards all men. "For we ourselves were once foolish, disobedient, deceived, enslaved by divers lusts and pleasures, living in malice and envy, hateful and hating one another." It is a look backward, what they were in their unregenerate condition. These are the true characteristics of man in the flesh. Here is an answer to the question, What is sin? Sin is foolishness, disobedience, deception, slavery to lusts and unsatisfying pleasures, a life of malice, envy and hatred. It is lawlessness. And such is the natural man in all ages. What was true of these Cretans nineteen hundred years ago is true to-day of every

*Greek: Magistracies and authorities.

unregenerated person. And then follows a "but"—(See Ephes. ii:14). "But when the kindness and love to man* of our Saviour-God appeared, not by works of righteousness which we have done, but according to His mercy He saved us through the washing of regeneration and renewing of the Holy Spirit, which He has shed upon us richly through Jesus Christ our Saviour; that having been justified by His grace, we might be heirs according to the hope of eternal life." For such as the Cretans were, and we all are, the kindness and love of our Saviour-God appeared; and this Saviour-God is Christ Himself, He by whom and for whom all things were created. All who have believed and trusted in the kindness and love of God as manifested in Christ can testify in fullest assurance, "according to His mercy He saved us," and own it likewise that it is "not by works of righteousness which we have done." And this is accomplished by the washing of regeneration and the renewing of the Holy Spirit. The washing (or bath) or regeneration is the new birth. Of this our Lord spoke to Nicodemus (John iii) and also to His disciples when He washed their feet. "He that is washed (bathed) needeth not save to wash his feet, but is clean every whit; and ye are clean, but not all" (John iii:10). He spoke in these words of the fact that His disciples, except Judas, were born again, and therefore they were clean every whit. The washing has nothing whatever to do with water-baptism; water-baptism cannot save nor help in the salvation of a sinner, nor produce regeneration. What is the renewing of the Holy Spirit? It is distinct from regeneration. The Holy Spirit is the active agent in the new birth; imparts the new nature and then indwells the believer, and as such He does His blessed work by renewing the inward man day by day (2 Cor. iv:16). He is shed upon us richly through Jesus Christ our Saviour, and gives power to all who walk in the Spirit. On the fact that

---

*"Love to man" in the Greek is "Philanthropy." Our Lord Jesus Christ is the great Lover of men—Philanthropist, as no human being could ever be.

the word "regeneration" is found only once more in the New Testament (Matt. xix:28) the late F. W. Grant made the following interesting comment in connection with this passage.

"The Lord promises to the twelve that 'in the regeneration, when the Son of man shall sit upon the throne of His kingdom,' they also shall 'sit upon twelve thrones, judging the twelve tribes of Israel.' 'The regeneration' is in this passage the millennial state; but thus we may see already the difference between it and the idea of new birth, whatever the connection may be between these. The millennial regeneration is not a new life infused into the world, but it is a new state of things brought about by the new government over it. Thus, the Lord speaks of the throne of the Son of man and of thrones for His disciples. The throne of the world in the hands of the perfect Ruler is, in fact, what brings about the regeneration. Righteousness now *reigns.* In the new earth it will *dwell;* but in the millennium there is yet neither the full reality, nor, therefore, the full permanence of deliverance from evil. Righteousness reigns, and evil is not suffered any more, but the full blessing waits to be manifested in that which is eternal and not millennial. The subjugation of evil, Christ's foes put under His feet, goes on through the millennium, in different stages, towards completeness. It is the preparation for eternity, but not the eternal state itself.

"It is plain, therefore, that there is a parallel between the stages of God's preparation of the earth for blessing and that of the individual man. The present stage of the earth is that out of which the Christian has been delivered, the state of bondage to corruption, the dominion of sin. The present state of the Christian is that which the earth itself waits for, the time when the power of sin will be broken and righteousness will reign. For us righteousness reigns now, but the conflict with sin is not over. This, in the millennium, will be fully seen at the end, when there is once more the outbreak of evil, Satan being let loose. What follows this is the dissolution of the present heavens and earth and the coming of the new earth, in which dwelleth righteousness, just as the dissolution or the change of the body makes way for the perfect eternal state with us. Thus there is a complete parallel, which we cannot be wrong in accepting as that which will help us with the expression here. 'The washing of regeneration' is the deliverance from the power of sin, which is no more tolerated, but which is not, by any means, wholly removed. 'The renewing of the Holy Spirit' is that which is constantly needed to supplement this, although the word used does not speak of a mere reviving or refreshing constantly, but rather of a change into that which is new—thus, of ways, habits—as the light more and more penetrates, and the word of God manifests more and more its perfection and its power for the soul."

Being then saved according to His mercy by the washing of regeneration and receiving the Holy Spirit and having been justified by His grace, we become also heirs according to the hope of eternal life.

The practical side, godliness in life and walk, is once more connected with these preceding statements of sound doctrine. "This is a faithful saying, and these things I will that thou affirm constantly, that they which have believed in God might be careful to maintain good works. These things are good and profitable unto men."

Verses 9–11. Foolish questions and genealogies, contentions and striving about the law must be avoided, for they are unprofitable and vain. How many of these things are about us! Some are more occupied with the ten lost tribes and their supposed recovery, according to the Anglo-Israel hallucination, than with the grace and glory of God; and others are given to questions of law, like Seventh-day Adventism—that evil system. All these things are indeed unprofitable and vain. The heretic is one who sets up his own opinions and then causes division in the body of Christ. If such a one after a second admonition continues in his ways, he is to be rejected, for he proves that he is self-willed and not subject to the Word of God—"Knowing that he that is such is subverted, and sinneth, being condemned of himself."

Verses 12–15. In the closing directions and greetings Artemas is mentioned first; his name does not occur elsewhere. Tychicus is mentioned in 2 Tim. iv:12. He was sent by Paul to Ephesus; he probably was sent later to Crete to take the place of Titus. Zenas the lawyer and Apollos (Acts xviii:24) were travelling companions, and the Apostle expresses his loving care and interest in them.

"Observe also that we have the two kinds of laborers: those who were in personal connection with the apostle as fellow-laborers, who accompanied him, and whom he sent elsewhere to continue the work he had begun, when he could no longer carry it on himself; and those who labored freely and independently of him. But there was no jealousy of this double activity. He did not neglect the flock that were dear to him. He was glad that any who were sound in the faith should water the plants which he himself had planted. He encourages Titus to shew them all affection, and to provide whatever they needed in their journey. This thought suggests to him the counsel that follows: namely, that it would be well for Christians to learn how to do useful work in order to supply the wants of others as well as their own."*

Then the final exhortations, once more "to maintain good works" and his final greeting. "All that are with me salute thee. Greet them that love us in the faith. Grace be with you all."

*Synopsis.

PHILEMON

CONTENTS

Page

Introduction.................................... 221

Analysis and Annotations....................... 223

The Epistle to Philemon.

Introduction.

This beautiful little letter addressed by Paul to Philemon does not occupy the right place in the New Testament. It should be put after the Epistle to the Colossians, for it was written at the same time as that Epistle. Tychicus carried from Rome the two epistles to the Ephesians and Colossians. Onesimus, his travelling companion, received from the prisoner of the Lord this personal letter to Philemon. It was therefore written at the same time as Colossians, during the first imprisonment of the Apostle Paul, about the year 61 or 62. Its genuineness cannot be doubted, though some critics have done so. Dean Alford says: "The internal evidence of the Epistle itself is so decisive for its Pauline origin—the occasion and object of it so simple, and unassignable to any fraudulent intent, that one would imagine the impugner of so many of the Epistles would have at least spared this one, and that in modern times, as in ancient, according to Tertullian and Jerome, '*Sua illam brevitas defendisset.*' "* The objections raised against this Epistle we do not need to state nor investigate, for they are pure inventions and do not require an answer.

The occasion and object are both plainly indicated in the Epistle itself. Onesimus, a slave, probably a Phrygian, who were considered the lowest of all, had run away from his master, Philemon, who was a Christian. It is more than probable that he had stolen money from Philemon (verse 18). He was attracted to Rome, the great world-city, thinking perhaps he would be undetected there. What happened to him in Rome and how he came in touch with Paul is not made known in the Epistle. He may have been in dire want and destitution. Perhaps he had heard Paul's name mentioned in his master's house and learning of his presence in Rome as a prisoner, he got in touch with him. This we know, that he heard the Gospel preached by the Apostle, and believing, he was saved. He then told the Apostle his story and Paul sent him back to his master with this precious letter. And Onesimus who returns to Philemon is no longer "unprofitable"; "not now as a servant, but above a servant, a brother beloved" (verse 16).

The Epistle itself shows the sweet and tender character of the great man of God who penned it under the guidance of the Holy Spirit. It has been remarked, "Dignity, generosity, prudence, friendship,

---

*"Its own brevity would be its defence."

affection, politeness, skillful address, purity are apparent. Hence it has been termed with great propriety, 'the polite Epistle.' "

Suggestive are Luther's words on this letter to Philemon: "The Epistle showeth a right noble, lovely example of Christian love. Here we see how St. Paul layeth himself out for the poor Onesimus, and with all his means pleadeth his cause with his master; and so setteth himself, as if he were Onesimus, and had himself done wrong to Philemon. Yet all this doeth he not with power or force, as if he had right thereto; but he strippeth himself of his right, and thus enforceth Philemon to forego his right also. Even as Christ did for us with God the Father, this also doth St. Paul for Onesimus with Philemon; for Christ also stripped Himself of His right, and by love and humility enforced the Father to lay aside His wrath, and to take us to His grace for the sake of Christ, who lovingly pleadeth our cause, and with all His heart layeth Himself out for us. For we are all His Onesimi, to my thinking."

Analysis and Annotations

1. The Greeting. 1–3.
2. Recognition of Philemon's Faith and Love. 4–7.
3. Concerning the Reception of Onesimus. 8–21.
4. The Conclusion. 22–25.

Verses 1–3. He speaks of himself as a prisoner of Christ Jesus; the Lord had made him a prisoner. He addresses Philemon (meaning: friendly, loving), the beloved, and his fellow-laborer. Apphia was probably the wife of Philemon; Archippus is called "fellow soldier;" he ministered in the Colossian assembly (Col. iv:17). Greeting is also extended "to the church" which was gathered in the house of Philemon. While the Epistle is addressed to Philemon personally and Paul appeals to him in behalf of Onesimus the gathered assembly was equally to be interested in this runaway slave, who was now returning as a brother beloved and therefore to be received by them in Christian fellowship. The Lord had received Onesimus and he had become through grace, a member of the body of Christ; he belonged to the Colossian assembly. Therefore in addressing the Colossians Paul had written of Onesimus as "a faithful and beloved brother, who is one of you" (Col. iv:9).

Verses 4–7. He thanked God for Philemon, making mention of him always in his prayers. He did not know Philemon personally, but had heard of his love and faith toward the Lord Jesus, and toward all saints. And he prayed for him "that the fellowship of the faith may become effectual by the acknowledgment of every good thing that is in us toward Christ Jesus." His faith was to manifest itself still more by exhibiting every good thing which Christians possess to the glory of Christ. With these words of commendation, recognition and encouragement, he opens the way to plead for Onesimus.

Verses 8–21. For this reason, because of love which was in Paul's heart for Philemon, he did not use his authority to enjoin upon him what was meet as to the reception of a good-for-nothing slave, who had been saved by grace and accepted in the Beloved. He beseeches instead, and that "for love's sake"—his love for Philemon and Philemon's love for Onesimus, for he was entitled to this love, being a Saint in Christ. And he beseeches, "being such an one as Paul the aged, and now also a prisoner of the Lord." Courteously he repeats "I beseech thee," and then he mentions him who was so dear to his own heart—"I beseech thee for my child, whom I have begotten in my bonds, who in times past was to thee unprofitable, but now profitable to thee and to me." Onesimus (meaning helpful) shows the power of the Gospel of Jesus Christ. A miserable, unprofitable slave, a runaway thief, had become a child of God, born again, and the loving servant of the Lord presses him to his bosom, calls him "my child" and speaks of him as being now profitable to him and to Philemon. Oh! the wonders of divine grace.

"Whom I have sent again; thou therefore receive him, that is, mine own bowels. Whom I would have retained with me, that in thy stead he might have ministered unto me in the bonds of the gospel; but without thy mind would I do nothing; that thy benefit should not be as it were of necessity, but willingly." What loving words these are! He gives Philemon to understand that Onesimus had endeared himself in such a way that he was as dear to him as his own heart. He would have liked to retain him and keep him at his side in Rome, for he would have performed all the service for Paul which Philemon would have rendered to him if he were in Rome. But without Philemon's consent he would do nothing, so that his action might not be of necessity, forced by what Paul had done, and not voluntarily.

"For perhaps he therefore departed for a season, that thou shouldest receive him forever; not now as a servant, but above a servant, a brother beloved, specially to me, but how much more unto thee, both in the flesh and in the Lord?" How delicately he expresses it all! He does not speak of Onesimus as having run away, as trying to escape forever from serfdom, but that "he departed for a season." God's providence is beautifully touched upon, when Paul thus states that he perhaps departed for a season (Greek, an hour) so that Philemon might receive him forever, not now as a slave, but above a slave, a brother beloved. And so that Philemon might not take offense at Paul asking him to receive his runaway slave as a brother beloved, he tells Philemon that he is a beloved brother especially to himself—and then how much more to Philemon who had a claim on him.

Human slavery, so universal in apostolic days, so full of misery, is indirectly dealt with in this letter to Philemon. It may be rightly called the first anti-slavery document and petition ever written and presented.

"Paul lays here broad and deep the foundation of a new relation between master and servant, a relation in which, while there is subordination of the one to the other, there is also a common brotherhood to be acknowledged and an equality before God to be maintained. Christianity would melt the fetters from the enslaved by the fervour of its love. Men's method commonly is, to strike them off by armed revolution."*

And he continues, "If thou count me therefore a partner, receive him as myself. If he hath wronged thee, or oweth thee aught, put that on mine account." Verse 17 connects well with verse 12. If Philemon counted Paul as in Christian fellowship, he is to receive Onesimus as if he were Paul, "receive him as myself." Onesimus had probably confessed his theft to Paul, and again he uses the choicest words to approach this delicate matter. He does not call it "theft" outright, but writes "if he hath wronged thee" and that again he softens to "or oweth thee aught," then he declares himself ready to make good the loss and assume the debt in place of the slave Onesimus—"put that on mine account." These five words "put that on mine

*Prof. Moorehead.

account" are translated in Rom. v:13, by the word "impute." How blessedly this illustrates the Gospel. Indeed this Epistle to Philemon is a perfect and practical illustration of the Gospel of Grace, the Gospel Paul preached, and which is unfolded in the larger Epistles. What the Gospel does for the poor slave of sin, how he becomes a son and a brother, profitable instead of unprofitable, a member of the body of Christ, may be traced in these verses.

He wrote this Epistle, not as he usually did, by an amanuensis, but with his own hand! That shows again what a fine character he was. He had full confidence in Philemon not alone that he would grant him his request, but that he would even do more than he had asked.

We do not know from Scripture what became of Onesimus. According to the "Apostolical Canons" he was emancipated by his master. Another tradition says that he became a servant of the Lord ministering in Macedonia, and that he was martyred in Rome. We shall meet him with all the other saints in glory.

Verses 22–25. Paul during his first imprisonment always anticipated his release; he and others prayed for it (Phil. ii). And so he expects to come to Colosse, and asked Philemon to prepare him a lodging. The salutations from Epaphras, Marcus, Aristarchus, Demas and Lucas, with the word of blessing, conclude the Epistle.

HEBREWS

CONTENTS

	Page
Introduction	229
Division of the Book of Hebrews	234
Analysis and Annotations	236

The Epistle to the Hebrews.

Introduction.

This Epistle presents many problems. Some refuse to call it an Epistle and look upon it as a treatise, but the leading question is about the author of this document. It is anonymous; the writer has carefully concealed his identity. It is the only portion of the New Testament of which this can be said. What was a possible motive for doing this? We may answer that He who inspired this great message guided the pen of the instrument to put himself out of sight. Dr. Biesenthal in a very learned work on Hebrews, advances an interesting theory why the writer did not mention himself. He shows that the teaching of Christianity that animal sacrifices, once foreshadowing the great sacrifice and now completely ended and no longer necessary, was being felt in Heathendom. In consequence the many sacrifices used in heathen worship at births, marriages and different other occasions were being more and more neglected. The priestly class which lived by these sacrifices and the very large industry of cattle raising was being threatened with utter ruin, on account of which a bitter antagonism was being stirred up against Christianity and its advocates. On account of this, Dr. Biesenthal, concludes, the writer of Hebrews kept his name a secret. Furthermore, this scholarly Hebrew Christian, advancing the strongest arguments for the Pauline authorship are here seen,* shows additional reason why the Apostle Paul had very valid reasons to keep himself in the background. His heart was filled with such burning love for his Hebrew brethren that he was constrained to send to them a special message of love and entreaty. At the same time he was deeply concerned about those who had believed. Under heathen persecution, as well as through ignorance concerning the full meaning of Christianity, a tendency towards Apostacy threatened these Hebrew Christians, especially those who lived in Jerusalem before the destruction of the temple and the Jewish worship. And Paul knowing how he was disliked by the Jews, and how he had been discredited by the Judaizing teachers, whose evil work he had exposed and so severely condemned in the Epistles to the Galatians and Corinthians, feared that if his name was made prominent, the message would at once be discarded. He therefore omitted his name.

The Question of Authorship.

The question of the authorship of Hebrews is of much interest. Many volumes have been written on it. Origen wrote, "The thoughts are Paul's, but the phraseology and composition are by someone else. Not without

*This work, "Das Trostschreiben an die Hebraer—The Message of Comfort to the Hebrews," has, as far as we know, never been translated into English.

reason have the ancient men handed down the Epistle as Paul's, but who wrote the Epistle is known only to God." The question is then, did Paul write Hebrews and if he did not, who wrote this Epistle? Some are very positive that Paul did not write Hebrews, as will be seen by the following statement:

"The only fact clear as to the author is that he was not the Apostle Paul. The early Fathers did not attribute the book to Paul, nor was it until the seventh century that the tendency to do this, derived from Jerome, swelled into an ecclesiastical practice. From the book itself we see that the author must have been a Jew and a Hellenist, familiar with Philo as well as with the Old Testament, a friend of Timothy and well-known to many of those whom he addressed, and not an Apostle but decidedly acquainted with Apostolic thoughts; and that he not only wrote before the destruction of Jerusalem but apparently himself was never in Palestine. The name of Barnabas, and also that of Priscilla, has been suggested, but in reality all these distinctive marks appear to be found only in Apollos. So that with Luther, and not a few modern scholars, we must either attribute it to him or give up the quest."*

This is very sweeping, and quite incorrect and superficial. It is not the final word. To follow the controversy in our brief introduction is quite impossible. All that has ever been written on it may be condensed as follows:—1. There is no substantial evidence, external or internal, in favor of any claimant to the authorship of this Epistle, except Paul. 2. There is nothing incompatible with the supposition that Paul was the author of Hebrews. 3. The preponderance of the internal, and all the direct external evidence, go to show that the Epistle was written by Paul. The Pauline authorship can hardly be questioned after the most painstaking research.

Origen's words, that only God knows who wrote this Epistle, has been taken as final by many. But to whom did Origen refer when he said, "not without reason have the ancient men handed down the Epistle as Paul's?" He undoubtedly referred to the Greek Fathers, who, without one exception ascribed this Epistle to Paul. It appears that in no part of the Eastern church the Pauline origin of this Epistle was ever doubted or suspected. The earliest of these testimonies, that Paul wrote Hebrews, is that of Pantaenus, the chief of the catechetical school in Alexandria about the middle of the second century. This witness is found in Eusebius, the church-historian, who quotes Clement of Alexandria that Hebrews was written by Paul originally in the Hebrew language and that Luke translated it into the Greek. Clement of Alexandria was the pupil of Pantaenus and had received this information from him. Pantaenus was a Hebrew Christian and in all probability living only a hundred years after Paul, received, what he taught Clement, by tradition. Apart from other similar testimonies that of Pantaenus and Clement is quite sufficient to show that the early church believed Paul to have written Hebrews.

*Weymouth.

And the internal evidences are overwhelmingly for the Pauline authorship. As to doctrine the parallels with his other Epistles are numerous and some of the peculiarities are also in full harmony with the teaching of the Apostle Paul. The personal allusions are altogether Pauline. These likewise show that Paul is the writer. The writer was a prisoner for he writes, "ye took compassion of me in my bonds" (x: 34); and he hopes to be liberated "but I beseech you the rather to do this, that I may be restored to you the sooner" (xiii: 19). Here is the same thought as expressed in Philippians (Phil. I: 25); in Philemon (verse 22). And this prisoner is in Italy for he writes "they of Italy salute you." It was probably written from Rome. The writer also was well acquainted with Timothy whom he mentions in the Epistle (xiii: 23). All these personal words have a decided Pauline stamp.

But some have said that Christ is not mentioned in Hebrews as the head of the body, not a word is said of that union with a risen and glorified Christ, one Spirit with the Lord, that cardinal doctrine so prominent in the great Apostle's testimony. From this omission it has been argued that another than Paul must be the author. But this inference is without foundation. For though Paul alone develops the mystery concerning Christ and the Church, it is only in the Epistles to the Ephesians and Colossians, with the First to the Corinthians practically, and in that to the Romans allusively. In the rest of his Epistles we find "the body" no more than in that to the Hebrews, and this is as distinctly in the ordering of the Holy Spirit, as in those which contain it fully. Each Epistle or other book of Scripture is prepared for the purpose God had in view when He inspired each writer. As the main object is that to the Hebrews in Christ's priesthood with its necessary basis, due adjuncts, and suited results, and as this is for the Saints individually, the one body of Christ could not fall fittingly within its scope, if it were a divinely inspired composition, whether by Paul or by any other. Its central doctrine is, not as one *with Him* as members of His body, but the appearing before the face of God *for us.**

Peter's Significant Statement.

At the close of his second Epistle the Apostle Peter wrote "and account that the long suffering of our Lord is salvation, even as our beloved brother Paul also, according to the wisdom given unto him, hath written unto you" (2 Pet. iii: 15). Now Peter wrote to those of the circumcision, to believing Hebrews in the dispersion. He does what our Lord commanded him "to strengthen his brethren." And in the above words he speaks of the fact that Paul also wrote unto them. We do not hesitate to give this as an argument of the Pauline authorship of Hebrews. No other Epistle of Paul answers to this statement of Peter. There is but one Epistle addressed to the Hebrews and Peter no doubt meant this Epistle, and he

---

*Wm. Kelly.

also knew that Paul was the writer. So that this in itself is quite conclusive. As another has said "Where do we find beside the Apostle a man who could have written this Epistle? Who beside him would have ventured to write it with such decided apostolic authority? And who had greater reason to write anonymously to Israel than the Apostle who loved his people so fervently, and who was so hated by them that they refused to listen to his voice and to read his writings?"*

His Last Visit to Jerusalem and this Epistle.

It seems to the writer that Paul's last visit to Jerusalem also explains this Epistle. As we learn from the Book of Acts, Paul went up to Jerusalem against the repeated warnings given by the Spirit of God. His arrest was the result of having gone into the temple to purify himself with the four men who had a vow on them. This he was asked to do and to show that he walked orderly and kept the law.† He did wrong in this. It is true he acted through zeal and love for his brethren; yet he also knew that a believer, be he Jew or Gentile, is dead to the law and that all the ordinances of the law were fulfilled and ended. Yet the Jewish believers in Jerusalem still clung to the law, were zealous for the law, went to the Temple and made use of the ordinances. When in Rome as prisoner the Spirit of God moved him to write this letter in which the greater glory and the better things of the new covenant are unfolded with solemn warnings not to be drawn back into Judaism. And at the close of the Epistle the final and important exhortation is given "Let us go forth therefore unto Him without the camp (Judaism), bearing His reproach" (xiii: 13). May not this Epistle have been written in view of Paul's failure in Jerusalem, showing these Jewish-Christians the necessity of separating from the shadow things of the Old covenant?

To Jewish Christians.

That this Epistle was addressed to Jews who professed the name of the Lord Jesus is shown by its contents. This fact and their peculiar state must not be lost sight of in the study of this Epistle. We may assume that the Epistle was especially addressed to the Church in Jerusalem. As already stated these Jewish believers were all zealous of the law. They observed the ordinances of the law with great zeal; they went daily into the Temple and were obedient to all the ceremonial law demanded of a good Jew. Then there arose a persecution against them. Some of them were stoned and they suffered great affliction and humiliation. The Epistle speaks of this. They were made a gazing stock both by reproach and afflictions; they endured joyfully the spoiling of their goods. (x: 33-34)

---

*Mallet.

†See Acts of the Apostles, an Exposition by A. C. G. Chapter XXI.

They were being treated in a shameful way by their brethren and looked upon as apostates. They were excluded from the temple worship and the ordinances, unless they abandoned faith in the Lord Jesus Christ and forsook the assembling of themselves.

"We can scarcely realize the piercing sword which thus wounded their inmost heart. That by clinging to the Messiah they were to be severed from Messiah's people was indeed a great and perplexing trial; that for the hope of Israel's glory they were banished from the place which God had chosen, and where the divine Presence was revealed, and the symbols and ordinances of His grace had been the joy and strength of their fathers; that they were to be no longer children of the covenant and of the house, but worse than Gentiles, excluded from the outer court, cut off from the commonwealth of Israel,—this was indeed a sore and mysterious trial. Cleaving to the promises made unto their fathers, cherishing the hope in constant prayer that their nation would yet accept the Messiah, it was the severest test to which their faith could be put, when their loyalty to Jesus involved separation from all the sacred rights and privileges of Jerusalem."*

They were under great pressure. They loved the nation, their divinely given institutions, their traditions and their promised glory. They did not possess the full knowledge of the better things of the new covenant; that they had as believers in Christ, the substance of what the old covenant only foreshadowed. There was grave danger for them to turn back to Judaism and therefore the repeated warnings and exhortations to steadfastness. They needed instructions, teachings, to lead them on to perfection, and they needed comfort in their trying position. Both are abundantly supplied in this Epistle.

The Vision of Christ.

Hebrews gives a wonderful vision of the Lord Jesus Christ. He is revealed as the Son of God, and Son of Man; as the heir of all things; higher than the angels. We can trace His path of humiliation to death and what has been accomplished by the death on the Cross. All the blessings put on the side of the believer are made known in Hebrews. But above all the great message is the Priesthood of Christ. This is the great center of this sublime Epistle. It is an Epistle of contrasts. There is the contrast between the Lord Jesus Christ and the angels; between Him and Moses, between Him and Aaron, between the Priesthood of Melchisedec and that of Aaron; between the offerings of the old covenant and the one great offering of Christ. This was the supreme need of these Jewish-Christians, to know Christ in all His fullness and glory. This knowledge would make them perfect, steadfast and fill them with comfort. And this is still our need. May the Lord bless us in meditating on this wonderful document.

---

*A. Saphir

Divisions of the Epistle to the Hebrews.

"Commencing in the style of a doctrinal treatise, but constantly interrupted by fervent and affectionate admonitions, warnings, and encouragements, this grand and massive book concludes in the epistolary form, and in the last chapter the inspired author thus characterizes his work: "I beseech you, brethren, suffer the word of exhortation; for I have written a letter unto you in few words."

"We are attracted and riveted by the majestic and sabbatic style of this epistle. Nowhere in the New Testament writings do we meet language of such euphony and rhythm. A peculiar solemnity and anticipation of eternity breathe in these pages. The glow and flow of language, the stateliness and fulness of diction, are but an external manifestation of the marvellous depth and glory of spiritual truth, into which the apostolic author is eager to lead his brethren."

With these well chosen words Adolf Saphir, the Hebrew Christian scholar, begins his exposition of this epistle.

The division of Hebrews is difficult to make because the different sections of this document often overlap and form a solid unity. It has been well said that "one feels as if he were endeavoring to dissect a living organism when he seeks to sever part from part in this marvellous Scripture."

The Lord Jesus Christ, the promised Messiah, in the fullness of the glory of His Person as the living and eternal realization of Jewish promise and type, is the most blessed theme of this epistle or treatise. This necessitated the various contrasts in which this document abounds and which we shall point out in the annotations. The glory of Christ, all He is, as well as His sympathy, grace and power as the true high priest who has entered heaven itself, is so fully made known to help, first of all, the weak faith of the Jewish Christians who received this message, that by it they might be established in their heavenly calling and become completely separated from Judaism, which was about to pass away. The two opening chapters introduce the great theme of the epistle and are the foundation of the doctrine developed. The first chapter reveals the glory of the Person of the Messiah, that He is the Son of God. The second chapter unfolds His glory as the Son of Man. He, who is above the angels, was made a little lower than the angels to suffer and to die. He partook of all sufferings and temptations and is now as the glorified Man in God's presence, crowned with glory and honor, awaiting the time when all things are put under His feet. The fact that He suffered, and was tempted opens the way for the development of the central truth of the epistle, His priesthood. He is called the Apostle and High Priest and shown to be greater than Moses and Joshua. Then follows the main section of the epistle, which reveals Him as the true priest who has opened the way into the Holiest, where He is exercising now His priesthood. The contrast is made in this portion (chapter iv:14–.x) between Him and the priests and sacrifices of the Jewish dispensation. With the eleventh chapter begin the practical instructions and exhortations to walk in faith, to be steadfast and to leave the camp of Judaism. We divide, therefore, this epistle in four sections.

I. CHRIST, THE SON OF GOD AND HIS GLORY.
Chapter i–ii:4.

II. CHRIST, THE SON OF MAN, HIS GLORY AND HIS SALVATION.
Chapter ii:5–iv:13.

III. CHRIST AS PRIEST IN THE HEAVENLY SANCTUARY.
Chapter iv:14–x.

IV. PRACTICAL INSTRUCTIONS AND EXHORTATIONS.
Chapter xi–xiii.

The analysis which follows shows the different subdivisions, paranthetical sections and contrasts, found in these main sections.

Analysis and Annotations.

I. CHRIST, THE SON OF GOD AND HIS GLORY.

CHAPTER i-ii:4.

1. The Son in Whom God hath spoken. 1–4.
2. So much better than the angels. 5–14.
3. Admonition and Warning. Chapter II: 1–4.

Verses 1-6.—Sublime is the beginning of this precious document. God who in many measures and in many ways spake of old to the fathers in the prophets, at the end of these days hath spoken to us in a Son, whom He constituted heir of all things, by whom also He made the worlds; who being the effulgence of His glory and the expression of His substance, and upholding all things by the word of His power, having made (by Himself) purification of sins, sat down on the right hand of the Majesty on high, having become so much better than the angels, as He hath by inheritance a name more excellent than they."

It is an abrupt beginning with no words of introduction, no salutations or words of thanksgiving and prayer. Only one other epistle begins in a similar way; the first epistle of John. The foundation upon which all rests, the Word of God, is the first great statement we meet. It tells us that God has spoken of old to the fathers in the prophets. The prophets were not, as so often stated by the deniers of Divine inspiration "Jewish patriots and visionaries," but they were the mouthpiece of Jehovah "holy men of God who spake as they were moved by the Holy Spirit." (2 Pet. i:21). The words they uttered are the words of God. And this is true of Moses, the author of the Pentateuch and of all the other instruments used in the production of the Old Testament scriptures. And He spoke in many measures (or parts) and in many ways, in histories, ordinances, divinely appointed institutions, visions, dreams and direct prophetic utterances, which have a fragmentary character; they are not in themselves complete and final. And therefore we find in this epistle the Law, the Prophets and the Psalms more frequently quoted than in any other portion of the New Testament. It is a striking characteristic of Hebrews that the names of the prophets, like Moses, David, Isaiah, etc., are omitted. God is the speaker. He spoke in the prophets concerning Him, who is now fully revealed in His glory, that is His Son, the promised Messiah. Our Lord declared of the Old Testament scriptures "they are they which testify of Me." (John v:39). Before He ever came into the world He also bore witness of this fact "in the volume of the Book it is written of Me." (Heb. x:7). God's speaking in the Old Testament culminated in the manifestation of this Person. "At the end of these days hath spoken to us in a (or the) Son." The end of these days is the present dispensation as distinguished from the preceding Jewish dispensation. The words "to us" mean primarily in this epistle the children of the fathers to whom God spake by the prophets.* "Jesus Christ was a minister of the circumcision for the truth of God to confirm the promises made unto the fathers." (Rom. xv:8). It was to the Jew first. He came to the lost sheep of the house of Israel and manifested in their midst the power of the kingdom promised to that nation. The promised One came and God spoke in Him, who is God the Son. The original has no article in connection with the word "Son." It is simply "in Son." The reason for this omission is because the character of the One in whom God hath now spoken, and not so much the person, is to be emphasized. The prophets were servants, angels were servants, but He in whom God speaks now is Son; such is His relationship, One with God.

The declaration of the glory of His Sonship follows. He is eternally Son of God, the Only—Begotten, very God in eternity. He is Son of God in incarnation, taking on the form of man, making purification of sins and He is in resur-

---

*In a general way it applies, of course, to all believers during this dispensation. The opinion of some that Hebrews, the Epistle of James, the Epistles of Peter have no meaning and no message to the Church is pernicious.

rection the first begotten, declared Son of God by resurrection from among the dead. It is a marvellous revelation of Himself, corresponding to the similar statements in the beginning of the Gospel of John and the first chapter of Colossians. He is constituted the heir of all things as He created all things and is the creator. All things in heaven and on earth are His. He possesses all things which exist. This is God's eternal purpose concerning Him. All things are by Him and for Him. By Him the worlds were made.* The vast universe is the work of His hands and He himself as very God is "the effulgence of His glory and the expression of His substance." He makes the invisible God visible. He is the perfect impress of God; God is fully revealed in His person who came from glory and dwelt among men. Furthermore, He is upholding all things by the Word of His power.

And He who was all this, and is all this, became man, appeared on earth, assuming manhood, to accomplish the work which He alone could do. By Himself He made purification of sins. The Son of God alone did this and none was with Him. What a blessed, sure, eternally secure foundation of our salvation! The passage shows the personal and perfect competency of the Son of God to effect this mighty work. It was done in the cross, in the death in which He glorified God and which has glorified Him forever. And therefore He arose from the dead and "sat down on the right hand of the Majesty on high." It is significant that nothing is said in the text of His resurrection, in the sense as it is spoken of in other scriptures, that God raised Him from the dead and gave Him glory (1 Pet i:21). Nor is it said that He was told to sit down, but He sat down and took Himself the exalted place at the right hand of God. It is presented in this way because His character as Son is here in view. The place He has taken at the right hand

---

* Literally "the ages"; Hellenists understood by it the universe. Its meaning then is equivelent to creation. It is used thus in the Greek translation of the O. T. known as the Septuagint.

of the Majesty on high is only proper and possible for a divine person. The fact that He took this place and sat down attests the perfection, the completeness and acceptation of the work He undertook and finished on the cross. He is now on the throne of God. David's throne and His own throne He will receive when as the First-begotten He returns from the glory. Such is the Messiah. the Christ, promised to Israel; He is God, the creator and upholder of all things, the heir of all things, come down from heaven, in whom God spoke on earth and is still speaking from heaven, who made purification of sins and has gone back to heaven.

Constituted now heir of all things, destined according to God's eternal decrees to be head of all things, He, as the glorified Man, has "become so much better than the angels, as He hath by inheritance a name more excellent than they." The contrast between Him and angels is now made. The epistle being addressed to Hebrews explains this comparison and contrast of Christ with angels. In the estimation of a Hebrew, next to Jehovah Himself, angels were looked upon as the highest and holiest beings. Then furthermore the law was given through angels. (Acts vii:53; Gal. iii:19) and other angelic ministrations had been prominent in Israel's history, so that these beings occupied a high place in the Jewish mind. But Christ, the man Christ Jesus, has become so much better than the angels; He is above the angels. His name is above every other name. He is on the right hand of the Majesty on high in the form and likeness of Man. As the Only Begotten He is the creator of angels. In incarnation He was made a little lower than the angels, and now having finished the work for which He became man, He has received by inheritance that highest position and a more excellent name than angels. Into this wonderful place He takes His own people for whom He suffered and died. In Him all believers are above the angels. Angels are but servants, never said to occupy a throne, for they cannot reign. But Christ has a throne and His redeemed shall reign with Him.

Verse 5-14. Upon this the Spirit of God quotes seven passages from the Scriptures in which He speaks of Christ and His exaltation and glory in contrast with angels. All seven are taken from the Book of Psalms. Psalms ii; lxxxix; xcvii; civ; xlv; cii and cx. The destructive criticism declares that there are no Messianic predictions in the Book of Psalms. That blessed portion of the Old Testament has suffered much from the hands of these destroyers of the faith. They say that the second, the forty-fifth, the one hundred and tenth Psalms have nothing to say about Christ, that the King mentioned in these psalms was some other unknown King, but not the King Messiah. How significant that the Holy Spirit quotes now from these very psalms telling us that the Messiah, Christ, is predicted in them. The Hebrews had no difficulty in accepting this for they know these psalms speak of the promised Messiah.*

The first quotation is from the second psalm. Never did God address angels in the way He is addressed of whom this psalm bears witness. "Thou art my Son, this day I have I begotten Thee." This psalm reveals the royal glory and world-wide dominion of Christ, the one whom the people (Israel) and the nations reject. He is to be enthroned as King upon the holy hill of Zion. As Son He will receive the nations for His inheritance and the uttermost parts of the earth for His possession. The title here refers to His incarnation, and, secondarily, to His resurrection from the dead. (Acts xiii:33–34). It is therefore not the fact of His eternal sonship which is before us in this statement; it speaks of Him as Son of God in time. The eternal Son of God became incarnate; but this did not lower His eternal Sonship. It is therefore His birth, His entrance into the world of which this psalm bears witness. "But it is of all moment for the truth and His own personal dignity to re-

---

*The Lord Jesus used the CX. Psalm in confounding the Pharisees. He showed that that Psalm speaks of himself and that it is the testimony of the Spirit. Such is "higher criticism" it sets aside the testimony of the Son of God and of the Spirit of God.

member that His Sonship when incarnate as well as in resurrection is based on His eternal relationship as Son, without which the other could not have been."

Psalm lxxxix:26, 2 Sam. vii:14 and 1 Chron. xvii:13 are mentioned next. It brings out the relationship in which the incarnate Son of God, the promised Messiah, is with God. God accepts and owns Him. "I will be to Him a Father and He shall be to me a Son." And this relationship was audibly declared and confirmed at His baptism and when on the mount of transfiguration. Such a relationship could never be the portion of angels. In Psalm lxxxix:27 His future glory is made known as it is in the second psalm. "Also I will make Him, my Firstborn, higher than the Kings of the earth." He is the Firstborn; He will have the pre-eminence.

The next quotation and argument is from Psalm xcvii:7. "And again when He brings in the Firstborn into the habitable earth, He saith, let all the angels of God worship Him." This no longer refers to His incarnation, but to His second coming. He is to be brought into the world and then He will receive the worship of the angels of God. Some have applied this to His first coming. But then He came as the "Only Begotten" and was sent into the world. Here it is said that as the First Begotten (from the dead) He will be brought into the world. He, who was cast out from the world and rejected by man, will re-enter it in power and glory; God will bring Him back into the habitable earth. When this event takes place the angels will bow in worship before Him, for He comes with His holy angels. It is therefore not His first advent, but His second, which is here contemplated. When He was born, angels praised the sender and not the sent One, but when He comes again He will be the object of angelic worship. This shows His glorious superiority to all the angels.

Psalm civ speaks of angels as servants. "He maketh His angels spirits, and His ministers a flame of fire." They are spirit and not flesh. They are made to do His will and can never be anything else but servants. And then the contrast is shown what the Son is by the quotation from the forty-fifth psalm. Angels are servants and cannot reign nor can they ever occupy a throne, "but unto the Son He saith, Thy throne of God is forever and ever, a sceptre of righteousness is the sceptre of thy kingdom." He is addressed as God in this psalm in which He is revealed as the coming King Messiah. He has a throne which is forever and ever, and as Messiah, and the promised King, He will have an earthly throne and rule with a sceptre of righteousness. He loved righteousness and hated iniquity when down here and therefore He is anointed with the oil of gladness above His fellows. Thus we learn from this psalm His Deity. He has a throne forever and ever. His humanity: He was on earth and loved righteousness and hated iniquity. Who are the fellows mentioned? Angels are not His fellows and could not be. His fellows are all they who are made one with Him through grace and who will be ultimately conformed to His image. It includes the believing remnant of Israel and all who put their trust in Him.*

Still more remarkable is the sixth quotation from Psalm cii. Wonderful as His glory is in the forty-fifth psalm the one hundred and second psalm surpasseth it. No human being would have ever known the real meaning of this psalm if it had not pleased the Spirit of God to give it in this chapter. The little word "and" shows that in verses 25-27 the Son of God is addressed by God as the creator of all things. It is Jehovah's answer to the prayer of His Son suffering as man and dying. "He weakened my strength in the way; He shortened my days. I said, O my God, take me not away in the midst of my days, thy years are throughout all generations." These words as well as verses 1–11 in this psalm are the expressions of the Man of sorrows,

*"This is a remarkable passage, because, while on the one hand the divinity of the Lord is fully established as well as His eternal throne, on the other hand the passage comes down to His character as the faithful man on earth, where He made pious men—the little remnant of Israel who waited for redemption, His companions; at the same time it gives Him (and it could not be otherwise) a place above them."—*Synopsis.*

the suffering Messiah. And Jehovah answers Him and owns Him is His humiliation, approaching the death of the cross, as the Creator. He was ever the same; His years cannot fail. He, the Son of God, had laid the foundation of the earth and the heavens are the works of His hands. And He will do, as the sovereign One, what God attributes to Him. "They shall perish, but Thou abidest; they shall grow old as doth a garment; and as a vesture shalt Thou roll them up, and they shall be changed, but Thou art the same, and Thy years shall not fail." Such is He, whose glory the Spirit of God reveals in the Holy Scriptures, who became Man, suffered and died, and risen from the dead, sits at the right hand of God. He is the unchangeable One, creator and sustainer of the universe.

The final quotation is from the one hundred and tenth psalm, which is more frequently quoted in this epistle than elsewhere. The preceding psalm, the one hundred and ninth, predicts His rejection by His own. In the opening verse of this psalm the Messiah is seen again in His Deity and Humanity. He is David's Lord and David's Son. His work is finished on earth. He has taken His place of rest (the symbol of the work done) sitting down at His right hand and waiting for the hour when God makes His enemies the footstool of his feet by bringing in again the Firstbegotten into the world. To no angel did God ever say, "Sit on my right hand."

Once more are angels spoken of as ministers. "Are they not all ministering spirits sent forth to minister to them who shall be heirs of salvation?" They minister now to those who are the heirs of salvation, who bear the title of sons in His Son and who possess His life. How little God's people make use of this comfort An active and simple faith is needed to perceive in what men carelessly regard as accidents of time and place, the positive workings of angels' ministry. They minister to God's people now in a way unknown to us. "It is a truth which brings the shadow of God's majesty with a peculiar nearness over the believer's soul. That we are seen of angels is an assurance to which the Spirit elsewhere practically bids us heed. (1 Cor. xi:10). A happy thought, yet one of sobering effect to be thus seen; to be the objects of near gaze, and very contact, to those holy visitants of watchful love, who, standing as the bright apparitions of heavenly majesty beside the throne on which the Son of God now rests, are sent forth to speed upon their way the pilgrim brethren of the Lord."*

Chapter ii-1-4.—This is the first parenthetical exhortation of this epistle, well suited to the condition of those Hebrews to whom is was first addressed. They are exhorted to give more earnest heed to the things which they had heard, that is the gospel of salvation in this Christ, whose glory is displayed in the opening chapter. This salvation was at first spoken by the Lord when He was on earth. He began its proclamation. It was continued by those who heard Him, that is by His apostles, and finally God the Holy Spirit had put His witness to it with signs and wonders and gifts. If then the word spoken through angels (the law dispensation) was steadfast and every transgresssion and disobedience received a just retribution "how shall we escape if we neglect so great a salvation?" It is a warning to Jews who were halting between two opinions and to those who had in a measure accepted outwardly the truth of Christianity without having laid hold in earnest and in faith of that salvation. If this great salvation, which God offers now not through angels, but in His Son, is rejected or neglected there can be no escape.

*A. Pridham

II. CHRIST, SON OF MAN, HIS GLORY AND HIS SALVATION.

CHAPTER 11:5-18

1. The Man crowned with Glory and Honor. 5–9.
2. His Humiliation, Suffering and the Results. 10–18.

Verses 5–9.—Angels are once more mentioned and the fact is stated first of all that angels are not called of God to reign "unto the angels hath he not put in subjection, the world to come whereof we speak." "The world to come" is not heaven or the eternal state. The literal translation is "the habitable world to come;" it is the existing earth, inhabited by human beings in the dispensation which will follow the present age. The world in the dispensation to come, called in Ephesians "the dispensation of the fullness of time" is not put in subjection to angels. A quotation from the eighth psalm follows from which we learn that man is to have dominion and to rule over this world to come. Dominion over the earth was given to Adam (Genesis i:28) but sin coming in, and death also, this dominion and rule was lost; the glory and honor which rested upon Adam was changed into shame and dishonor. Through man's fall Satan became the usurper, the prince of this world. Adam was the figure of Him that was to come, the second Man in whom and through whom the lost dominion is restored. The eighth psalm* reveals this second Man, the Lord from Heaven, the creator in creature's form. He was made a little lower than the angels. The Son of God took the position of man to make peace in the blood of His cross "to reconcile all things unto Himself, whether they be things

*It is interesting to study the order of the psalms with which the book of psalms begins, divinely arranged by an unknown instrument. The righteous Man in Psalm I is the Lord Jesus; the second Psalm shows Him as the Messiah—King. Then Psalms III–VII show the suffering, sorrows and soul-exercise of the godly during the time when He does not yet reign, especially the suffering of the Jewish remnant during the tribulation and then comes Psalm VIII, Christ, The Second Man set over all things. The Annotated Bible on the Psalms follows this more fully.

in earth or things in heaven." (Col. i:20). All things are therefore put in subjection under His feet and nothing is left that is not put in subjection under Him. He will have dominion over all and His name will be excellent in all the earth. Satan knows that the dominion of the earth will not be left forever in his horrible grasp. He offered the kingdoms of the world and their glory to the Son of Man, attempting to keep Him from going to the cross, in which, through the death of Christ, the devil, who has the power of death, is brought to nought.

The work is done. Christ is the second Man; He will have dominion over the earth in the world to come, the dispensation to come. He will reign and rule and His fellows, the partakers of His salvation, will reign with Him. "But now we see not yet all things put under Him." The time is not in this present age in which Satan is god and ruler. Only when the Firstbegotten is brought back from the glory, in His second coming, will all things be put under Him. Faith knows this from the unfailing promises of God. But faith also has another vision; while Satan is not yet dethroned and Christ enthroned "we see Jesus crowned with glory and honor, who was made a little lower than the angels on account of the suffering of death; so that by the Grace of God He should taste death for all things." Glorious vision! He suffered death. He perfectly glorified God on the earth where God had been dishonored. He came down and took the lowest place and now He is exalted to the highest. The Man who suffered and died fills the throne and is crowned with glory and honor. And as surely as He is there now, so will He in God's own time occupy His own throne with all things put under his feet. He tasted death for that—for all things—for a ruined creation which He has redeemed and will restore.

Verses 10–18.—This salvation work is now more fully mentioned in the second part of this chapter. He is spoken of as the captain (author) of the salvation of the many sons He is bringing to glory. And as the originator and leader of their salvation He had to suffer and die. Not

His person was to be perfected, for He is perfect; but He had to be perfected through suffering as a Saviour. "For it became Him for whom are all things and by whom are all things in bringing many sons unto glory to make the captain of their salvation perfect through suffering." Here God's eternal purpose is wonderfully revealed. He purposed before the foundation, knowing the coming ruin of man, to bring many sons unto glory. This is divine love. But God's holiness had to be vindicated, and therefore the Son of God became man to suffer as the captain of their (the many sons) salvation. As disobedience had led man from life to death, so, by obedience unto death the sinless Lamb of God had to win in righteousness the path of endless life for those who trust in Him as the originator and captain of their salvation. And those who accept Him are the many sons, whom God is bringing through Him, to glory everlasting. And both He who sanctifieth and they who are sanctified are all of one. It is a wicked perversion of the truth when it is taught, that He, and all the human race are of one. This is the common error taught so much in the so-called theory of "the Fatherhood of God and Brotherhood of man." The statement shows the wonderful relationship which divine grace has established between the captain of salvation and those who are saved by Him. He, Christ, is the sanctifier, setting those apart unto God, who accept Him as Saviour. Such are born of God and become children of God, destined to be brought by Him as sons to glory. In this sense He who sanctifieth and they who are sanctified by Him arc of One, that is, of God. Higher still is the truth revealed in the epistles to the Ephesians and Colossians, that believers are not only "of one" but are one with Him.

Again quotations from the Scriptures follow. The first is from the twenty-second psalm. "For this cause He is not ashamed to call them brethren, saying I will declare Thy name unto my brethren in the midst of the church will I sing praise unto Thee." (Ps. xxii:22). This psalm shows first Christ on the cross as sin-bearer. In verses 20 and 21 is the prayer of the suffering One. And He was heard. God's answer was His resurrection from the dead. That resurrection and His exaltation is revealed in the second portion of this psalm (verses 22–31). The beginning of this section is quoted here. And when He was risen from the dead He gave this blessed new message at once. "But go unto my brethren and say unto them, I ascend unto my Father and your Father, and my God and your God" (John xx:17). Here we learn the blessed identification of Him that sanctifieth and with them that are sanctified, and that on the ground of resurrection.* And therefore He is not ashamed to call us brethren, which, however, does not authorize believers to call Him "brother" as it is done so often. And by His Spirit He is in the midst of those who are gathered unto His name, the church, and sings praise unto God, as they praise God in His blessed and worthy name. The twenty-second psalm also speaks of "the great congregation," Israel, gathered unto Him and of the ends of the earth and the nations who shall remember and shall worship before Him. It is His coming glory when all things are put under Him in the age to come.

The next quotation is from Psalm xvi.† "I will put my trust in Him." It is the prophetic expression of His personal faith on earth. As man He trusted in the Lord and waited for Him (Isaiah viii:17). "The Seed of David, and the object of the promises, is thus represented as awaiting, in perfect confidence, the righteous award which in due time should be made to Him who alone is worthy, by the God whom He had glorified in perfect obedience; although for an appointed season His gracious labor might seem to have been spent for nought and in vain, while man and Satan appeared only to prevail." (Is. xlix).*

---

*Never before His death and resurrection did He address His disciples as "brethren." Only once did He hint before his death at this relationship to come, in Matthew xii:48-50.

†It may also be brought in connection with Is. viii:17. The Septuagint has it "I will trust in Him." 2 Sam. xxii:3.

The last quotation is from Isaiah viii:18. The children, which the Lord had given to Isaiah, were for signs and wonders in Israel from the Lord. The two sons of Isaiah had received their names of significant meaning from Heaven. Believers are children, belong to Him and are signs and witnesses both to unbelieving Israel and the world. In a special sense this passage, no doubt, applies to the believing remnant of Israel, which owned Him, while the nation rejected Him. And some day, the day of His glory, He will declare triumphantly "Behold I and the children which God gave unto me." Then He will be glorified and admired in all that believed (2 Thess. i:10) and the redeemed will be for signs and wonders in a still more blessed way.

Then follows a restatement of the fact of His incarnation and its special bearing on the calling of the children, God has given Him, the many sons He brings to glory. "Forasmuch then as the children are partakers of flesh and blood, He also in like manner took part of the same (His incarnation) that through death He might bring to nought him who hath the power of death, that is the devil, and deliver as many as through fear of death were all their lifetime subject to bondage." It was for the children's sake, all who accept Him and whom God brings through Him to glory, that He took on flesh and blood† and by doing so He arrayed Himself for death. Satan's work is perfected in death. "That the Lord Jesus might enjoy the children as the gift of God, He must first take away the yoke of the oppressor. But because the right of Satan to destroy was founded on the victory of sin, which made man the lawful prey of death, He, who loved the children though as yet they knew Him not, took also flesh; that in their stead He might undergo that death which should forever spoil the devil of his claim."* The limit of this work of the Lord Jesus to the children as its object, should be carefully observed.

---

*A. Pridham.

†He took on flesh and blood apart from sin.

Jewish saints in the Old Testament, believing the promise and expecting the Messiah, were in bondage and in fear of death. "The sting of death is sin, and the strength of sin is the law," but the death of Christ once for all to sin has received the sting and brought to nought him who has the power of death. A believer is delivered from the fear of death, for he no longer dies the sinners death, but falls asleep in Jesus and that with the promise to awake in due time in His likeness. "For verily it is not angels upon whom He taketh hold, but he taketh hold of the seed of Abraham." And who were they whom He took hold on? Not angels, but the seed of Abraham. Those are the children for which He came, took on flesh and blood and wrought His work on the cross. The expression "seed of Abraham" is as a generic term, descriptive of the whole family of faith. Believers of Jews and Gentiles are comprehended in this term. They that are of faith the same are the children of Abraham, and they that are of faith are blessed with faithful Abraham.

His priesthood is next introduced for the first time in this epistle. He was made like unto His brethren in all things "that He might be a merciful and faithful highpriest in things pertaining to God to make propitiation for the sins of the people. For in that He Himself hath suffered being tempted, He is able to succor them that are tempted," and thus in suffering and temptation (apart from sin) in His humanity, He was fitted to be the priest to sympathise with His own in all their trials and conflicts.*

*He suffered—never yielded. We do not suffer when we yield to temptation: the flesh takes pleasure in the things by which it is tempted. Jesus suffered, being tempted, and He is able to succour them that are tempted. It is important to observe that the flesh, when acted upon by its desires, does not suffer. Being tempted, it, alas! enjoys. But when, according to the light of the Holy Spirit and the fidelity of obedience, the Spirit resists the attacks of the enemy, whether subtle or persecuting, then one suffers. This the Lord did, and this we have to do. That which needs succour is the new man, the faithful heart, and not the flesh. I need succour against the flesh, and in order to mortify all the members of the old man.—*Synopsis.*

CHAPTER III

1. As Son over the house of God, greater than Moses. 1–6.
2. The Danger of Unbelief. 7–13.
3. The Need of Faith. 14–19.

Verses 1–6. He now addresses believing Hebrews as "holy brethren and partakers of the heavenly calling," and exhorts them to consider the Apostle and Highpriest of our confession, Christ Jesus." Hebrews address each other as "brethren" (Acts ii:29, vii:2 xxii:i). Believing Hebrews are here addressed by the Spirit of God as "holy brethren" Trusting in Christ they were sanctified and belonged to those whom He is not ashamed to call brethren. They are called "partakers of the heavenly calling" in contrast with their former "earthly calling" of Israel. The two titles of the Lord Jesus, Apostle and Highpriest, correspond to the preceding opening chapters of the Epistle. As Apostle (a Sent One) the Son of God, came from God to man. And then as Man who suffered and died, He has gone from man to God as Highpriest, typified by Aaron. As the Lord Jesus Christ is in this Epistle called the Apostle, the Spirit of God may have, for this reason, kept the pen of the Apostle, who wrote this document, from calling himself an Apostle.

Then follows the contrast with Moses. Moses was faithful in all his house (the tabernacle) but only as a servant. Christ is over God's house, which He has built, for He is God. And in this house He is not a servant, but a Son. Both the universe and the church, as the House of God, are here blended together. The house in the wilderness, the tabernacle, was a type of the universe. "And every house is built by some one, but He that built all things is God." Christ is the builder of the universe, the house, and the upholder of it and so He is counted worthy of greater honor than Moses, inasmuch as He who hath built it hath more honor than the house. The Apostle of our confession, the sent One of God, the Son of God, is also the Highpriest. After His finished work on the cross, having made propitiation for the sins of the people, He passed through the heavens into the Holiest not made with hands.* Ultimately in virtue of redemption, all having been cleansed by the blood, God will dwell in the house. "Behold the tabernacle of God is with men, and He will dwell with them and they shall be His people, and God Himself shall be with them, and be their God." (Rev. xxi:3).

"And Moses verily was faithful in all his house as a servant, for a testimony of those things which were to be spoken after." And those things have come and are given through Christ, who is Son over His house, whose house are we. This is His spiritual house, the house of God composed of living stones, the sanctified, the holy priesthood. The Son of God, the builder of all things, has now as Highpriest, His own house, which are we "if we hold fast the confidence (boldness) and the rejoicing of the hope firm unto the end." It is a warning to those Hebrews who had confessed Christ, who were facing trials and many difficulties, not to give up the confidence and the rejoicing in the hope. They are urged to hold it fast and are solemnly warned against unbelief. They were in danger of forsaking Christianity, and turning back to Judaism. And these words of warning are also given to us, for they are needful for the exercise of the conscience.† A true believer will continue in confidence firm to the end. Such a continuance is the proof of the reality of our confession.

Verses 7–13. The danger and calamity of unbelief is next called to their remembrance. Ps. xcv is quoted. The Holy Spirit saith "Today if ye will hear His voice harden not your hearts." Such was the word of warning addressed

---

*The three parts of the Tabernacle, the outer court, the holy part and the Holiest typify the first, the second and the third heaven.

†"It is clearly not our standing which is in question; for this being wholly of God and in Christ is settled and sure and unchanging. There is no "if" either as to Christ's work or as to the gospel of God's grace. All there is unconditional grace to faith. The wilderness journey is before us (as the next verses show). Here it is that "if" has its necessary place, because it is our walk through the desert, where there are so many occasions of failure, and we need constant dependence in God."

to Israel in the past, but it also has its application in the present. The word "today" expresses God's wonderful patience and long suffering towards Israel as well as towards all during this age of grace. The "today" is now; the great morrow comes, when the "today" ends and the kingdom of power and glory with its attending judgments upon those who did not obey the gospel of Jesus Christ comes, and the once rejected King Messiah appears. The fathers of the Hebrews had tempted God in the wilderness. He was wroth with that generation and swore in His wrath "they shall not enter into my rest." It was God's solemn sentence of exclusion from His rest. They hardened their hearts, did not obey His voice and their unbelief shut them out from God's rest. Even so these Hebrews, professing Christianity were in the same danger. "Take heed brethren, lest there be in any of you an evil heart of unbelief in falling away from the living God." But while it was "today," God still waited to be gracious and so they were to exhort each other daily, lest any of them be hardened through the deceitfulness of sin. Danger surrounded them on every side. "The heart of unbelief which barred the land of Canaan from their natural fathers was yet within their flesh. Not only were the lusts of nature in their ordinary shape forever combating against the will of God, they were exposed also to a more specious, and therefore a more dangerous form of evil in the still existing rivalry which they who made their boast in their traditions were opposing to the cross of Christ. Of all the evils with which Satan can afflict the heart, atheism, religion, without faith in God, is by very much the worst. For it lulls the conscience, while it weaves its web of unblessed, unsanctifying exercises about the heart's affections so as effectually to exclude the light of God. It was to this peace-corroding yet seductive evil that these Hebrew Christians stood practically exposed."

"Now the remedy and safeguard of all evil is the truth of God. It is only by listening to the word of Him who speaks to us as children with a knowledge of our need, that believers can be kept in their true place. The possession of truth in the way of doctrine is not enough. God daily speaks and must be daily heard if we would really know him."*

All this is true of God's people at all times, for faith and obedience are the essential conditions of blessing and the tests of profession. God is faithful and will certainly not permit that any of His own perish. Faith reckons with this, but also heeds the warning, knowing and owning the the tendency of the flesh to depart from God, and hence the need of His constant and never-failing grace is recognized and a walk in godly fear is the blessed result. There are teachers who claim that these solemn exhortations have no meaning for Christians today and even have made the statement that this epistle was not for the church at all. Such claims show a deplorable ignorance of the truth of God. All believers must heed the warning "that none of you be hardened through the deceitfulness of sin."†

Verses 14–19. The need of faith, the holding fast of the beginning of our confidence unto the end, is now more fully presented. All Israelites came out of Egypt. But with whom was he wroth for forty years? It was with them that sinned, whose carcases fell in the wilderness. Their sin was unbelief. And those who believed not were kept out of His rest. "So we see that they could not enter in because of unbelief." What the rest of God is we shall follow in the annotations of the next paragraphs.

---

*A. Pridham on Hebrews.

†"Sin separates us from God in our thoughts; we have no longer the same sense either of His love, His power, or His interest in us. Confidence is lost. Hope, and the value of unseen things, diminish; while the value of things that are seen proportionately increases. The conscience is bad; one is not at ease with God. The path is hard and difficult; the will strengthens itself against Him. We no longer live by faith; visible things come in between us and God, and take possession of the heart. Where there is life, God warns by His Spirit (as in this epistle), He chastises and restores. Where it was only an outward influence, a faith devoid of life, and the conscience not reached, it is abandoned."—*J. N. D.*

CHAPTER IV

1. What the Rest of God is. 1–11.
2. The Power of the Word of God. 12–13.

Verses 1–10.—Let us therefore fear, lest, a promise being left of entering into His rest, any one of you might seem to come short of it. For unto us was the gospel preached as well as unto them, but the word preached did not profit them, not being mixed with faith in them that heard it." These words of exhortation belong properly to the preceding chapter.

What is the rest of which these verses speak? It is generally explained as the rest which the true believer finds and has in the Lord Jesus Christ in believing; that his conscience has rest. It is frequently identified with Matth. xi:28-29. While it is blessedly true that all who come to the Lord Jesus Christ as Saviour find rest in Him from the curse of the law and the burden of sin, while it is equally true that those who follow Him in obedience and learn of Him find rest day by day for their souls, yet it is not this present rest which is before us in these verses. The rest which is meant is called by God "My rest"; it is the rest of God and is future, the rest in coming glory, an eternal rest. It is God's rest, because He made it Himself and He will enjoy it in glory with those who have believed in Christ, in whose perfect work God has His rest, because it satisfies His holiness and His love. Into this rest the believer enters at His coming. Then work will be over and all burdens cease. Righteousness reigns and groaning creation is delivered and all the promised glory will be accomplished. God rests then in His love and rejoices. (Zeph. iii: 17). Till that day God works, for sin and the curse is unremoved, but all will be changed when His Son appears in glory and all things are put in subjection under Him. The perfect, complete rest of God is in the new heaven and earth, when God dwells among men and sin and death are forever gone. He then is all in all. This is the rest which remains for the people of God.

"God must rest in that which satisfies His heart. This was the case even in creation—all was very good. And now it must be in a perfect blessing that perfect love can be satisfied with, with regard to us, who will possess a heavenly portion in the blessing which we shall have in His own presence, in perfect holiness and perfect light. Accordingly all the toilsome work of faith, the exercise of faith in the wilderness, the warfare (although there are many joys), the good works practised there, labour of every kind will cease. It is not only that we shall be delivered from the power of indwelling sin; all the efforts and all the troubles of the new man will cease. We are already set free from the law of sin; then our spiritual exercise for God will cease. We shall rest from our works—not evil ones. We have already rested from our works with regard to justification, and therefore in that sense we have now rest in our consciences, but that is not the subject here—it is the Christian's rest from all his works. God rested from His works—assuredly good ones—and so shall we also then with Him.

"We are now in the wilderness; we also wrestle with wicked spirits in heavenly places. A blessed rest remains for us in which our hearts will repose in the presence of God, where nothing will trouble the perfection of our rest, where God will rest in the perfection of the blessing He has bestowed on His people.

"The great thought of the passage is, that there *remains* a rest (that is to say, that the believer is not to expect it here) without saying where it is. And it does not speak in detail of the character of the rest, because it leaves the door open to an earthly rest for the earthly people on the ground of the promises, although to christian partakers of the heavenly calling God's rest is evidently a heavenly one."*

The argument and exhortation of verses 3-11 is therefore easily understood. God had rested in creation on the seventh day from all His work. But that rest was broken and is also the type of another rest of God to come. Those who believe not cannot enter into that coming rest and it is shown that Joshua† and the rest in Canaan is not the

*Synopsis.

†Verse 8. Not Jesus, but Joshua.

true rest of God, for if it had been why should David, long after Joshua, have spoken of it again? Nor has this rest come now for the people of God; it is still in the future. A Sabbath-keeping remaineth for the people of God. We are on the road toward it, beset by dangers and difficulties as Israel was when passing through the wilderness. And therefore the exhortation to be diligent to enter into that rest and not to be unbelieving and disobedient. Entrance into the rest is by faith. We who have believed do enter into rest. While the believer is assured of this future entrance into the rest of God, he also uses diligence and earnestness while on the way, watching and praying. True faith is evidenced by such a walk.

Verses 12–13.—The Word of God and its divine living power is here introduced by the Holy Spirit. It is the method of God, to use His Word, to bring to light and judge the unbelief and workings of the heart. It judges everything in the heart which is not of Him. Its use, its constant use, is the supreme necessity of those who believe and are on the way to the rest of God, for it is His divine Word which brings us into God's presence. It is a searching Word and under its power the conscience becomes aroused and the blessed and needed work of self-judgment begins. Life, power and omniscience, three great attributes of God, are here given to His Word.* The Word also gives power and spiritual energy.

---

*"Soul and spirit" as thus named together can only be the two parts of the immaterial nature of man; which Scripture, spite of what many think, everywhere clearly distinguishes from one another. The soul is the lower, sensitive, instinctive, emotional part, which, where not, as in man, penetrated with the light of the spirit, is simply animal; and which also, where man is not in the power of the Spirit of God, will still gravitate towards this. The spirit is intelligent and moral, that which knows human things (1 Cor. ii. 11). In the "natural man," which is really the *psychic* man, the man soulled (1 Cor. ii. 14), conscience, with its recognition of God, is in abeyance, and the mind itself becomes earthly. Important enough it is, therefore, to divide between "soul and spirit." "Joints and marrow" convey to us the difference between the external and the internal, the outward form and the essence hidden in it."—*Numerical Bible.*

III. CHRIST AS PRIEST IN THE HEAVENLY SANCTUARY

CHAPTER IV:14-X.

1. The Great High-Priest. 14-16.

With this statement the main section of the epistle begins, and the great theme, the Priesthood of Christ, is introduced. This section covers six chapters, ending with the tenth. Here we learn that Christ, the true priest, has passed through the heavens and is now in a heavenly sanctuary, the way into which His own work has blessedly opened. The different contrasts with the priests and sacrifices of Judaism, the old covenant and the new, are made in these chapters. The concluding verses of the fourth chapter, one might say, contain all the truth of His Priesthood which the succeeding chapters develop and expand.

He is the great high priest who is passed through the heavens. He has entered heaven itself, the third heaven, the Holiest. The earthly tabernacle in which Aaron and his successors ministered had three parts. Through these Aaron passed as he entered into the Holiest and these parts are typical of the heavenly things. Christ also passed through, but not through the places made by hands —He passed through the heavens and into the Holiest. "Christ is not entered into the holy places made with hands, which are the figure of the true, but into heaven itself, now to appear in the presence of God for us." (ix:24.) And He who passed through the heavens is Jesus, the Son of God; He who was made a little lower than the angels and after His sacrificial death arose, is now clothed with a glorified human body in the presence of God. His priestly ministry there is in behalf of His people. He is, as high priest, touched with the feeling of our infirmities; He was in all points tempted as we are, apart from sin.* He lived on earth

*"Yet without sin" is an incorrect translation and is responsible for the very erroneous teaching that our Lord, while He did not sin, might have sinned. It was absolutely impossible for Him to sin, for He is the Son of God and God cannot sin.

and passed through life; He suffered and was tempted; He experienced all the trials His people have to pass through in their lives and infinitely more than His saints can ever suffer, and therefore He sympathises with all our infirmities. In all the difficulties, perplexities, trials and sorrows, the Saint of God finds perfect sympathy in Him as priest. His heart filled with that love which passeth knowledge, is touched, beyond our finite comprehension, with the feeling of our infirmities.

As to sin, temptation from within, the lust of an evil heart, He knew absolutely nothing. He knew no sin. He was tempted in all things, apart from sin. Sin, therefore, is excluded.* Nor does a child of God desire sympathy with indwelling sin. It must be judged, put into the place of death, and not sympathised with. And this fact that He is the great High Priest touched with the feeling of our infirmities, our weaknesses and our trials; the knowledge that He, who is exalted in glory, concerns Himself about us and our trials down here, gives encouragement to hold fast our confession. He will not leave, nor forsake, nor fail His Saints.

And while we are not told to go to this great High Priest (He is constantly occupying Himself about us) we are told to come boldly to the throne of grace. We look to the Lord Jesus Christ, trust His love and sympathy, and knowing that He is there we can go with boldness to the throne of grace. And there we find all we need.

---

*We have evil temptations from within; Christ had none. Temptation from sin was absolutely incompatible with His holy person. By a miracle he was even as to humanity exempt from the taint of evil. It is of holy temptations this Epistle treats, not of our unholy ones. The Epistle of James distinguishes them very definitely in Chapter I. Compare verses 2, 12, on the one hand, and verses 13–15 on the other. We know the latter too well. Jesus knew. But he knew the former as no other before or since. He was in all things tempted according to likeness, *i.e.* with us, with this infinite difference 'apart from sin.' He knew no sin. He is therefore the more—not the less—able to sympathize with us. For sin within, even if not yielded to, blinds the eye, and dulls the heart, and hinders from unreserved occupation with the trials of others."—J. H. D.

CHAPTER V

1. What the High Priest is and represents. 1–4.
2. The Fulfillment in Christ Made High Priest. 5–10
3. The Spiritual Condition of the Hebrew-Christians. 11–14.

Verse 1–4.—In developing the priesthood of Christ and showing how it excels the earthly priesthood and is more glorious than the priesthood of Judaism, the principles of priesthood of the levitical system are first stated. Upon this follows the comparison of the priesthood of Christ with that of Aaron. The transcendent priesthood of Christ is thus established by this contrast. These opening verses have nothing to do with our Lord. They show how the high priest was taken from among men and being merely a man who was to exercise forbearance toward the ignorant, himself clothed with infirmity, he was obliged not alone to offer sacrifices for the sins of the people, but also for himself. This can, of course, never apply to the Lord Jesus Christ, inasmuch as He is sinless. He therefore cannot be meant in these introductory words of this chapter. And the earthly priests did not take this honor to themselves. God's call was necessary.

Verses 5–10.—How the priesthood foreshadowed in Aaron was first of all fulfilled in Christ is the theme of this section. Here we have His call to be priest. "So Christ also hath not glorified Himself to be made an high priest; but He that said unto Him, Thou art My Son, today I have begotten Thee (Ps. ii.). As He saith also in another place, "Thou art a priest forever after the order of Melchisedec." (Ps. cx.) His call from God is to be King-Priest. The second psalm reveals Him as Son of God, King to be enthroned and to rule over the nations, and He is priest after the order of Melchisedec. This name is here mentioned for the first time. His Melchisedec priesthood the Spirit of God unfolds fully in the seventh chapter. The call of Him is according to the eternal purposes of God. He came to offer Himself as the sacrificial Lamb on the Cross. This was indicated when He went into Jordan, baptized by John. It was then that the Father's voice was heard declaring His Sonship.

He had to pass through death and rise again to be the priest after the order of Melchisedec.

His suffering and death are therefore next mentioned in these verses: "Who in the days of His flesh having offered up prayers and supplications with strong crying and tears to Him who was able to save Him out of death and having been heard for His godly fear, though He were a Son, yet learned He obedience by the things which He suffered." These words refer chiefly to the portal of the Cross, Gethsemane. There He prayed with strong crying and tears, alone with His Father in deepest agony, fallen on His face, and His sweat became as great drops of blood falling down on the ground. He went into all the anguish of death, deprecating the cup He had to drink, yet in meek and perfect submission. What a terrible weight was there upon His holy soul! And He was heard for His godly fear. He was saved, not from dying, for that would have left man in his sins and unredeemed; He was saved out of death. His prayer was answered by His resurrection. It was in that agony that He learned obedience. Though Son of God, He learned obedience from the things which He suffered. Having come to obey and to suffer (which as Son of God was unknown to Him), He obeyed in everything and submitted to everything. He did not save Himself, but drank the cup and died the sinner's death.

What He is in resurrection, the results of His sacrificial death, are next stated. "And being made perfect, He became, unto all that obey Him, author of eternal salvation; being saluted (or welcomed by God) of God as high priest after the order of Melchisedec." In the second chapter we saw that the captain of our salvation had to be made perfect through sufferings. (ii:10.) Here we meet the same statement, that He has been made perfect. It means the completeness of His work through sufferings, in resurrection and heavenly glory. And through this finished work in which He is perfected as Saviour, He also became unto all that obey Him (all who believe on Him and own Him thus as their Saviour) the author of eternal salvation. Returning to glory, God saluted, or welcomed Him as priest after the order of Melchisedec.

Verses 11–14.—Here another parenthesis begins which closes with the end of the sixth chapter. The seventh chapter resumes the instructions concerning Melchisedec and the priesthood of Christ. Their spiritual state was that of babes as still under the ordinances and requirements of the law. They clung to Judaism and could not fully break loose from the shadow things of their system. They were dull of hearing and while they ought to have been teachers (having believed in Christ) there was need of teaching them again what are the elements of the beginning of the oracles of God. They needed milk and were not fit for the "solid food." They had not gone on in the gospel, into that maturity which the Holy Spirit has revealed as to the believer's standing and perfection in Christ. As long as they were occupied with ordinances they were but infants and in danger of apostasy.

Ritualistic Christendom today corresponds to the state of many of these Hebrew-Christians of the first century, only ritualism is worthy of greater condemnation.* The fearful evil of ritualism (Romish and so-called Protestant) is that it takes and imitates Jewish forms and ordinances and through these things sets aside and corrupts true Christianity. It is the bondage of the flesh.

---

*We may observe that there is no greater hindrance to progress in spiritual life and intelligence than attachment to an ancient form of religion, which, being traditional and not simply personal faith in the truth, consists always in ordinances, and is consequently carnal and earthly. Without this people may be unbelievers; but under the influence of such a system piety itself—expressed in forms—makes a barrier between the soul and the light of God: and these forms which surround, pre-occupy, and hold the affections captive, prevent them from enlarging and becoming enlightened by means of divine revelation. Morally (as the Apostle here expresses it) the senses are not exercised to discern both good and evil.—*Synopsis*

CHAPTER VI

1. Return to Judaism the Crucifixion of the Son of God afresh. 1–8.
2. Persuaded of Better Things. Comfort and Hope. 9–20.

Verses 1–8.—A solemn warning follows, addressed to these Hebrews who were halting and in danger of turning back to Judaism, and doing so would crucify the Son of God afresh. "Therefore leaving the word of the beginning of Christ, let us go on to full growth; not laying again a foundation of repentance from dead works and faith in God, of a teaching of baptisms, and of laying on of hands and of resurrection of the dead, and of eternal judgment." It is of much importance to see that these things are not "the principles of the doctrine of Christ" (as the authorized version erroneously states). These things mentioned are the elementary things which the Jews had before Christ came and as they were still occupied with them, He exhorts to leave the word of the beginning of Christ, the Messiah, and to go on to full growth. The full growth is Christianity as revealed in the finished work of Christ, the glory of His Person, His Priesthood and the fact that the believer is in Christ and complete in Him. While these Hebrews had believed in Christ, that He had come, they had not gone on to this maturity and lacked the spiritual knowledge of what Christ had done and the blessed results of His work and priesthood. They were therefore to leave the elementary things which they had and believed in as Jews, and abandoning them, reach the true Christian maturity. And these elementary things consisted in repentance from dead works and of faith in God. This was known and taught in Judaism. But it is faith in God, but nothing is said of faith in the Lord Jesus Christ. When baptism is mentioned and laying on of hands it has nothing whatever to do with Christian baptism, and much less does the laying on of hands mean "confirmation."* The word "baptism" is in the plural—

---

*Confirmation as practiced in the Roman Catholic, Lutheran, Episcopal and several other Protestant denominations is a merely ecclesiastical invention without the slightest scriptural foundation.

"baptisms"—the different washings the Jews practice in connection with the ceremonial law, and so also the Jewish imposition of hands. These Jewish washings and purifications were only shadows of what was to come. It had come; and yet these Jews, though believing that Christ had come, still lingered in these things. Resurrection of the dead and eternal judgment, the things concerning the future were likewise the teachings they had in Judaism. But Christianity gives a higher truth, namely, "the resurrection from among the dead" and that the believer is passed from death unto life and shall not come into judgment.—"And this will he do if God permit"—that is in the coming unfolding of true Christianity, the full growth, as given in chapters vii-x.

Before the author of the epistle does this he shows what it would mean if these Hebrews turn back to Judaism altogether, and instead of going on to full growth would abandon the Christian ground they occupied as professing believers in Christ. Such a course would make it impossible to renew them again to repentance, for they crucified, by falling away, afresh for themselves the Son of God, putting Him to open shame. They committed the crime, which was done by them through ignorance (Luke xxiii:34; Acts iii:17), now knowingly of their own will and choice. For such a wilful falling away there was no remedy. The things mentioned in verses 4 and 5 show the possibility that a person may be enlightened, and have tasted, and even participated, by listening to the testimony of the Spirit concerning Christ, and seen miracles, the powers of the age to come—without having fully accepted the offered salvation.

"The warning here has been a sore perplexity to many who are far as possible from the condition which is here contemplated. The description of these apostates, solemn as it is, does not speak of them as children of God, as justified by faith, or in any way which would imply such things as those; and the apostle, after describing them, immediately adds, as to those whom he is addressing; 'But, beloved, we are persuaded better things of you, even things that accompany *salvation*, though we thus speak.' This is the most distinct assurance that he had no thought of one who had known salvation incurring the doom of an apostate."*

All the blessings offered upon Christian ground are to such outward professors like rain, which instead of bringing forth from the ground useful herbs, brings thorns and briers, worthless, nigh unto cursing, and then the end, to be burned. Of a true child of God this can never be said.†

Verses 9–20.—Words of comfort and hope conclude this chapter. He addresses them now as "beloved", of whom he is persuaded of better things, the things which accompany salvation. Their true faith had been manifested by works. And God is not unrighteous "to forget your work and labour of love, which ye have showed towards His name in that ye have ministered unto the Saints and do minister." These are things which accompany salvation. He encourages them to be followers of them who through patience and faith inherit the promises. He calls their attention to Abraham, the father of the faithful. He endured patiently and obtained the promise. And He gave not only the promise of His Word, but also His oath. "For when God made promise to Abraham, because He could swear by no greater, He swore by Himself." What assurance therefore—God's Word and God's oath. And this makes manifest to the heirs of promise (believers) the mmutability of His counsel, so that we might have strong consolation. Therefore those who trust and hope for future glory have a strong and satisfying consolation. But there is more than that. There is a personal guarantee, for the Lord Jesus as a forerunner has entered into heaven,

*Numerical Bible.

†"When once we have understood that this passage is a comparison of the power of the spiritual system with Judaism, and that it speaks of giving up the former, after having known it, its difficulty disappears. The possession of life is not supposed, nor is that question touched. The passage speaks, not of life, but of the Holy Ghost as a power present in Christianity. To "taste the good word" is to have understood how precious that word is; and not the having been quickened by its means. Hence in speaking to the Jewish Christians he hopes better things and things which accompany salvation, so that all these things could be there and yet no salvation. Fruit there could not be. That supports life."—*Synopsis.*

where He now is as high priest after the order of Melchisedec. He, who is our Hope, is there as a forerunner and this is the anchor of the soul; it anchors in Him who hath entered within the vail. He who is seated in glory is the promised One, the object, bearer and dispenser of all the promises of God. In Him and His work all is made secure. His presence there speaks of the ultimate realization of all the promises of glory for His people.

CHAPTER VII

1. The Priesthood of Melchisedec in Contrast with the Levitical Priesthood. 1–19.
2. The Holy and Heavenly Priesthood of Christ. 20–28.

Verses 1–19.—The interrupted argument concerning the priesthood of Christ is now resumed. It connects with chapter v:10. There we find Melchisedec mentioned for the first time, and here the historical Melchisedec is first of all described. The record is given in Genesis xiv:18-20. He met Abraham, who returned from the smiting of the Kings, and blessed him. Abraham gave him the tenth of all. His name means "King of Righteousness"; but he was also King of Salem, that is, "King of Peace." First righteousness and peace afterward. This is God's order—not peace and righteousness, but righteousness and peace. It is so spiritually for the believer; it will be so in millennial times when "righteousness and peace will kiss each other." Who was Melchisedec? Some have said he was Shem and not a few maintain that he was the Lord Himself, one of the theophanies, a pre-incarnation manifestation of the Son of God. The latter view is certainly wrong, for Scripture states that Melchisedec is "made like unto the Son of God", that is, he is a pattern, a similitude of Him; Melchisedec was therefore not the Lord Himself. It is vain to speculate on the identity of this King-Priest, for the Holy Spirit on purpose does not mention who he was. When we read, "Without father, without mother, without descent, having neither beginning of days nor end of life," it does not mean that Melchisedec had no father and no mother, etc. But it means that Scripture gives no record of these facts; Moses being divinely guided in omitting it all in the book of Genesis, and thus making Melchisedec appear as a man without father and mother, without descent, having no beginning and end of days, who has a priesthood invested in himself. And this for the purpose of furnishing a type of our Lord as the royal priest.

Melchisedec foreshadows fully the millennial glory of the Lord Jesus Christ. See Zech. vi:9-13. He will receive His own throne and be a priest upon that throne. Significantly he appeared suddenly when Abraham was returning from smiting the allied kings.* And then he blessed Abraham and made known to him God as the Most-High (the millennial name of God), the possessor of heaven and earth. Even so the true Melchisedec will some day appear, and after the smiting of the kings (the battle of Armageddon, Rev. xvi:14-16; xix: 19) will begin His glorious rule. Nor must it be overlooked that Melchisedec brought to Abraham bread and wine, the blessed emblems of the great sacrificial work of the true Melchisedec, which points us, who are by faith the children of Abraham, to the blessed memorial feast, in which His love and grace, as well as glory, are remembered. Christ is therefore now for His own the Priest after the order of Melchisedec; the full display of His Melchisedec Priesthood arrives in the day of His coming glory.

The chief object of bringing forward the Person of Melchisedec and his connection with Abraham is, to show first, the superiority of Melchisedec to Levi and his Priesthood as better and higher than the Levitical priesthood. Abraham gave him the tenth part of all the spoil. The whole Levitical priesthood was then not in existence, inasmuch as Levi, unborn, was in the loins of Abraham; in Abraham, Levi, therefore, gave tithes to Melchisedec. Melchisedec, as priest, blessed the father of the nation, and therefore he was greater than Abraham, for "without controversy, the less is blessed of the greater." The priesthood of Melchisedec

*Genesis XIV gives the record of the first war of the Bible.

was therefore superior to that of the sons of Levi, the Aaronic priesthood.

After this argument another one is introduced. The question is concerning the Levitical priesthood, if it could give perfection. The one hundred and tenth psalm announced the coming of a priest after the order of Melchisedec and therefore superior to Aaron. If then perfection were by the Levitical priesthood, what need was there that this other priest of a higher order than Aaron should arise? Because perfection was not by that earthly priesthood, nor by the law,* therefore this better priest had to come to bring the needed perfection and that necessitated a change of the law also. The law in all its ordinances was a witness of imperfection, though it foreshadowed the good things to come. The law was therefore not to abide. With the cessation of the Levitical priesthood the entire law-covenant would terminate. And He of whom these things are spoken (the Lord Jesus Christ) "pertaineth to another tribe, of which no one hath given attendance at the altar (as priest). For it is certain that our Lord sprang out of Juda; of which tribe Moses spake nothing concerning priesthood." His coming, therefore, has taken from the tribe of Levi the honor and set aside their priesthood. And He who sprang out of Judah, the priest after the similitude of Melchisedec (combining priesthood and royalty) hath been made, not after a law of fleshly commandment, but after the power of an indissoluble life. His priesthood is not a thing of time and change, a fleshly priesthood like Aaron's, but it is a priesthood in the power of an indissoluble life. He has passed

*"The law, doubtless, was good; but separation still existed between man and God. The law made nothing perfect. God was ever perfect, and human perfection was required; all must be according to what divine perfection required of man. But sin was there, and the law was consequently without power (save to condemn); its ceremonies and ordinances were but figures, and a heavy yoke. Even that which temporarily relieved the conscience brought sin to mind and never made the conscience perfect towards God. They were still at a distance from Him. Grace brings the soul to God, who is known in love and in a righteousness which is for us."—*J. N. D.*

through death, and now in heaven, not on earth, He is the Melchisedec priest, who has no end of days, who lives eternally.

Then follows a conclusion, a summing up of the whole argument. In the stated fact that the Lord Jesus Christ is a priest forever after the order of Melchisedec, "There is a setting aside of the commandment going before (the law and its ordinances) on account of weakness and unprofitableness (for the law made nothing perfect) and the bringing in of a better hope through which we draw near to God." The law is then set aside on account of its weakness and unprofitableness, for it could not perfect anything. All the priestly ordinances and ministrations could not make atonement, nor could bring nigh unto God. It was all imperfection. Yet perfection and bringing His children nigh unto Himself is God's gracious and eternal purpose. And God has accomplished this now in the person of His ever blessed Son, the priest after the order of Melchisedec. This is the bringing in of a better hope; by Him we draw near unto God. This truth is more fully developed later.

Verses 20–28.—An additional argument is given. The priesthood of Christ was established by an oath, while that of Aaron was not. Swearing an oath God said as to Him, who sat down at His own right hand, "The Lord hath sworn, and will not repent, Thou art a priest forever, after the order of Melchisedec." How superior, then, this priesthood! By so much, also, hath Jesus become surety of a better covenant." And furthermore, they were many priests, for they were mortal men and died. But Christ continueth forever and hath the unchangeable priesthood. And this ever-living priest is able to save to the uttermost those that come unto God by Him, seeing that He always liveth to make intercession for them." He saves completely and keeps His own by His priestly, all-powerful intercession, for eternal glory. And what a high priest He is! Such a high priest Well may His own in holy joy and praise cry out—"Such a high priest!" He is holy, harmless, undefiled, and separate from sinners. "In His official dignity and glory

He is made higher than the heavens." And He has no need, day by day, as the earthly high priests, first to offer up sacrifices for His own sins, then for those of the people. This He did once for all when He offered up Himself. What a contrast with the Jewish priests. They were sinners—He, separate from sinners and absolutely holy; they with the many sacrifices, which could accomplish nothing for man—He with the one great sacrifice which has accomplished all. And so He maketh intercession for them who have believed in Him, the many sons He brings to glory. He is holy and heavenly—even so are all His own, saved by grace, holy and partakers of the heavenly calling. (iii: 1.)

CHAPTER VIII

1. Christ, the High Priest. 1–6.
2. The Old Covenant and the New. 7–13.

Verses 1–6.—The new priesthood which the better priest exerciseth in heaven furthermore implies also a change in the sacrifices and in the covenant. This is now more fully developed in the last three chapters of this section. There is first of all a summary. The priest we have is not ministering on earth but "we have such an high priest, who is set on the right hand of the throne of the Majesty in the heavens; a minister of the Sanctuary, and of the true tabernacle, which the Lord has pitched, and not man." Every high priest had to offer gifts and sacrifices, so it was of necessity that He also should have something to offer. What He has offered is brought out in the ninth and tenth chapters. As high priest He offered up Himself on the cross and then, as the high priest who had brought this perfect offering, He passed through the heavens and into heaven itself. If He were upon the earth and His priesthood went no further than the earth, he would not be a priest. He has no place among the Levitical priests, the priests who offered according to the law, whose office and ministrations were but shadows of heavenly things; but He hath obtained a more excellent ministry, because He is the mediator of a better covenant, which has for a foundation better promises. As Christ came not from

Aaron's family He could not be a priest after that pattern; His priesthood is wholly different, for it is heavenly and exercised in glory. With this more excellent priesthood, foreshadowed in the earthly Levitical priesthood, the latter has been completely set aside. This is the truth these Hebrew believers needed more fully to lay hold on, because the earthly tabernacle was still standing and the earthly priests were still exercising their empty and meaningless functions. And that which is put away, which is gone, because the one great offering was brought, and the true high priest has entered into the Holiest and is in the presence of God for His people, Satan has successfully introduced and established upon Christian ground as one of the most soul-destroying inventions. Ritualistic Christendom with a priesthood patterned after the extinct Jewish priesthood, with a worship more or less after the model of Israel's worship, is the shade of the departed shadow. It is apostady from the truth of the Gospel of grace; it is a wicked denial of the Gospel of our salvation. This priestly assumption of men is the worst possible corruption of the doctrine of Christ.

Verses 7–13. The preceding verse showed that Christ is the mediator of a better covenant. This leads next to a contrast between the first (the old) and the new covenant. A covenant contains the necessary principles established by God under which man may live with God, in which He deals with man. There are only two covenants. The old covenant which was established at Sinai, the law-covenant, and the new covenant which in its fullest meaning has not yet been ratified, for it also relates to the people of Israel as we shall soon learn from this chapter. Strictly speaking the gospel, the proclamation of the salvation of God, is not a covenant. Still those who accept the gospel possess all the spiritual blessings of this new covenant, and much more than Israel can ever possess, when at last as a converted nation this new covenant will be established with them.

The argument is simple. The fact that a new covenant is promised shows that the old covenant was insufficient.

"For if that first one had been faultless, then would no place have been sought for the second." It could not accomplish what was in God's heart to bring His people into the closest and nearest relationship with Himself. The first covenant, the law, could not do this, and therefore "finding fault, He saith unto them, Behold the days come, saith the Lord, when I will make a new covenant with the house of Israel and the house of Judah. Not according to the covenant that I made with their fathers in the day when I took them by the hand to lead them out of the land of Egypt, because they did not continue in my covenant, and I did not regard them, saith the Lord." This first covenant was conditional, and the people did not keep this covenant and the Lord, because they were disobedient, did not regard them. That first covenant was unto their condemnation. And therefore the Lord had announced through the prophet Jeremiah that a new covenant was to be consummated for Israel and Judah, the same people with whom the first covenant was made. "For this is the covenant that I will make with the house of Israel after those days, saith the Lord, I will put my laws in their mind, and with them in their hearts; and I will be God unto them, and they shall be my people. And they shall not teach every man his neighbor, and every man his brother, saying, know the Lord: for all shall know me of the least to the greatest. For I will be merceiful to their unrighteousness, and their sins, and their iniquities I will remember no more." (Jeremiah xxxxi: 31–34). This new covenant is unlike the old one in that it has no condition attached to it. In it the Lord speaks alone in words of sovereign grace—"I will." It is the same what Jehovah promised to the nation through the prophet Ezekiel (Chapter xxxvi). And this grace covenant awaits its fulfillment for that nation in coming days. The ground of this new covenant is the sacrificial death of Christ, His blood, as we learn from His own words when He instituted His supper. Because He died for that nation (John xi:51–52) all Israel—the house of Israel and the house of Judah—will be brought into the promised blessings through this grace covenant.

In the meantime, while Israel has not yet entered into this new covenant, Gentiles, who are by nature aliens from the commonwealth of Israel, and strangers from the covenants of promise (no new covenant being promised to Gentiles), believing in Christ, are made nigh by the blood of Christ (Eph. ii:12–13), enjoy every spiritual blessing in heavenly places in Christ, become members of the body of Christ and joint heirs with the Lord Jesus Christ. When the fullness of the Gentiles has come in (Rom. xi:25) then God will turn in mercy to His people Israel, whom He hath not cast away, and this new covenant will be fully established and all the promises as to restoration, temporal blessings, as well, spiritual blessings, so richly promised throughout the Old Testament prophetic word, will through grace come upon them. Then their sins and iniquities will be remembered no more. It all comes to pass when He comes again, who alone can turn away ungodliness from Jacob. What light and joy these facts of the old covenant set aside* and the promises of the new covenant must have brought to the hearts of these Hebrew believers who read first this great message.

---

*"Modern Judaism (both rabbinical and rationalistic) is not able "to account for the cessation of sacrifices and the Levitical dispensation. The former acknowledges that in the destruction of the temple and the present condition of Israel without high priest and offerings, divine judgment on the nation's sin is expressed: the idea of atonement through a vicarious sacrifice is not quite extinct, as appears in the rite of the cock performed on the eve of the day of atonement, though devoid of all Scriptural authority. Rationalistic Judaism has departed still further from the truth. Rejecting the idea of substitution and expiation in connection with sacrifices, it regards the present condition of Israel as a more spiritual development, misinterpreting the protests of David and the prophets against a mere external view of the ceremonial law. (Ps. xl. 7; Hos. vi. 6; Jer. vii. 21–23.) The old has indeed vanished; but according to the will of God, because the true light now shineth, because the substance has come in Christ."—A. Saphir.

CHAPTER IX

1. The First Tabernacle and its Worship. 1–10.
2. The Blood; and the Perfect Work Accomplished. 11–23.
3. The Priest in Heaven. 24–28.

Verses 1–10. The Spirit of God now brings forth the greatest and most blessed facts concerning Christ, the offering He brought, and what has been accomplished by that offering. First the worldly sanctuary, the tabernacle, which was connected with the old covenant is briefly mentioned. It was erected by divine command, exhibiting divine wisdom and foreshadowed, like the levitical priesthood, the better things to come. Yet it was a "worldly sanctuary," that is, it was tangible according to this present world and built of materials of the earth. The antithesis to worldly is heavenly, uncreated, eternal. Everything in this tabernacle had a spiritual meaning. But it is not the purpose here to explain these things, the shadows of spiritual realities, for the apostle writes "of which we cannot now speak particularly." He does not give a complete description of the tabernacle at all. Nothing is said of the outer court, nor of the brazen altar, the golden altar of incense and other details. His object is not to explain the tabernacle but to demonstrate one great fact. He speaks of the two principal parts of the tabernacle, divided by the interior veil. Into the second the highpriest entered in only once every year, not without blood—"the Holy Spirit signifying this, that the way into the Holiest was not yet made manifest, while the first tabernacle had yet its standing." This is the truth he demonstrates. The way into the Holiest, into God's presence was barred; the veil was in the way and concealed Him. All the gifts and sacrifices brought in that tabernacle could not give perfection as to the conscience—they could not lead the people into the Holiest and give peace to the conscience.

Verses 11–23. With verse eleven begins the setting forth of the perfection which now has come. From here to the close of the tenth chapter we have the heart of this great epistle. The most blessed truth of the great work of Christ accomplished for His people is now gloriously displayed. The greatest contrast between the old things and the new is reached. Two little words of deep significance stand at the beginning of this section—"But Christ—." The gifts and offerings, the meats and drinks, the divine washings, the carnal ordinances, all and everything could not do anything for sinful man—but Christ. It is well for the understanding of what follows to give a summary of what is here taught. "But Christ having come, a highpriest of the good things that are come, by the better and more perfect tabernacle, not made with hands, that is to say, not of this building (creation)—neither by the blood of goats and bulls, but by His own blood, He hath entered in once for all into the holy places, having found an eternal redemption." Christ having come, perfection has come through His own precious blood. The blood of Jesus has opened the way into the Holiest and the believer is admitted into the presence of God by that new and living way which He has consecrated for us through the veil, that is to say, His flesh. The next chapter brings this out more fully, that believers on earth have a free, a full, a perfect access to God. The believer can now go in perfect liberty, not into an earthly tabernacle, but into heaven where His holiness dwells and be perfectly at home there in virtue of the work of Christ and His own presence there. Such is the believers position in the presence of God through the entrance of our highpriest into the heavenly sanctuary.

And the believer can go in without doubt and fear, for he has no more conscience of sin, his conscience is made perfect before God through Christ who through the eternal Spirit offered Himself without spot to God. The question of sin is settled forever. "A perfect conscience is not an innocent conscience which, happy in its unconsciousness, does not know evil, and does not know God revealed in holiness. A perfect conscience knows God; it is cleansed, and, having the knowledge of good and evil according to light of God Himself, it knows that it is purified from all evil according to His purity. Now the blood of bulls and goats, and the washing is repeated under the law, could never make the conscience perfect. They could sanctify carnally, so as to enable the worshipper to approach God outwardly, yet only afar off, with the veil still unrent. But a real purification from sin and sins, so that the soul can be in the presence of God Himself in the light without spot, with the consciousness of being so, the offerings under the law could never produce. They were but figures. But, thanks be to God, Christ has accomplished the work; and is present for us now in the heavenly and eternal sanctuary, He is the witness there that our sins are put away; so that all conscience of sin before God is destroyed, because we know that He who bore our sins is in the presence of God, after having accomplished the work of expiation. Thus we have the consciousness of being in the light without spot. We have the purification not only of sins but of the conscience, so that we can use this access to God in full liberty and joy, presenting ourselves before Him who has so loved us.*

And thus these Hebrews (as well as we) know that the true highpriest is in the sanctuary above, not with the blood of sacrifices, but He has put away sin by the sacrifice of Himself. As man on earth, in the perfection and value of His person, He offered Himself, by the eternal Spirit, without spot, to God. And therefore every sinner who comes to God through Him is purged from dead works to serve the living God. Being therefore perfectly cleansed, perfectly brought into God's presence, in possession of an eternal (in contrast with earthly) redemption and an eternal inheritance, the believer can serve the living God. All this was unknown in the legal covenant. It is then that through the death of Christ and the subsequent bestowal of the Holy Spirit believers are constituted true worshippers in the heavenly sanctuary, a holy Priesthood. Christ is the perfect mediator. And therefore no earthly priesthood is needed. The attempt to introduce priestly meditation of sinful men between Christ and His people, whom He is not

*Synopsis.

ashamed to call brethren is anti-Christian, the offspring of Satan. Adolph Saphir,* the author of an able exposition of Hebrews has exposed the Romish blasphemy in aping the defunct Judaism in words, which are worthy to be quoted.

"What a marvellous confusion of Jewish, Pagan, and Christian elements do we see here! Jewish things which have waxed old, and vanished away; preparatory and imperfect elements which the apostle does not scruple to call beggarly now that the fulness has come—revived without divine authority, and changed and perverted to suit circumstances for which they were never intended. Pagan things, appealing to the deep-seated and time-confirmed love of idolatry, and of sensuous and mere outward performances; the Babylonian worship of the Queen of Heaven; the intercession of saints and angels, the mechanical repetition of formulas, the superstitious regard of places, seasons, and relics. Buried among these elements are some relics of Christian truth, without which this ingenious fabric could not have existed so long, and influenced so many minds—a truth which in the merciful condescension of God is blessed to sustain the life of His chosen ones in the mystical Babylon. This so-called Church, vast and imposing, opens its door wide, except to those who honor the Scriptures, and who magnify the Lord Jesus. It can forgive sins, and grant pardons and indulgences, extending the astounding assumption of jurisdiction even beyond the grave; yet it cannot bring peace to the wounded conscience, and renewal to the aching heart, because it never fully and simply declares the efficacy of the blood of Jesus, by which we obtain perfect remission, and the power of the Holy Ghost, who joins us to Christ. This community speaks of sacrifice, of altars, of priesthood, and stands between the people and the sanctuary above, the only High Priest, who by His sacrifice has entered for us into the holy of holies. And in our day this great

*A Hebrew Christian, whose insight in the Scriptures is most extraordinary. Read "The Epistle of Hebrew" in 2 volumes.

apostasy has reached a point which we would fain regard as its culminating point, when it places the Virgin Mary by the side of the Lord Jesus as sinless and pure, and when it arrogates for man infallible authority over the heritage of God.*

Verses 15–23.—These verses introduce once more the question of covenant. The covenant of which the Lord Jesus Christ is the Mediator is now identified with a testament of which He is the testator. When there is a testament there must also of necessity be the death of the testator, before the rights and possessions acquired in the testament can be possessed and enjoyed. The first covenant was inaugurated by blood. "For when Moses had spoken every commandment to all the people according to the law, he took the blood of bulls and goats, with water and scarlet wool and hyssop (Leo. xiv: 4. Num. xix: 6) and sprinkled both the book and the people, saying, this is the blood of the covenant which God hath enjoined unto you." So also the tabernacle and the vessels were sprinkled with blood. Yea, almost all things are according to the law purified with blood "and without shedding of blood is no remission." The blood was used in a threefold manner. The covenant itself is founded on the blood. Defilement is washed away by the blood and the guilt is taken away through the blood that hath been shed. And all this is only fully realized through the blood shed by the Lord Jesus Christ, He died and all the blessings of the new and better covenant are righteously willed to the believer.

Verse 24–28.—"For Christ is not entered into the holy places made with hands, the figures of the true; but into heaven itself, now to appear in the presence of God for us." After His great sacrifice He entered heaven itself, where He now is, appearing in the presence of God

---

*Dr. M. Luther describes the Romish harlot in these excellent words: "The Church of Rome is not built upon the rock of the divine word, but on the sand of human reasoning." It is a rationalistic church. And Lutheranism, Episcopalianism and other sects are turning back to it and support the Satanic counterfeit of a man made priesthood.

for His people. "Nor yet that He should offer Himself often, as the high priest enters into the holy place every year with blood of others; for then must He often have suffered since the foundation of the world, but now once in the consummation of the ages hath He appeared to put away sin by the sacrifice of Himself." The sacrifice He brought needs not to be repeated, it is all-sufficient for all eternity. If He were to offer again it would be necessary also to suffer again. Both are impossible.* At the completion of the ages of probation,† when man's utter ruin and hopeless condition had been fully demonstrated, He appeared in the fullness of time (the completion of the ages) and put away sin by the sacrifice of Himself. And here let us remember that the full and complete results of this work are not yet manifested. Sin will ultimately be blotted out of God's creation. The blessed words which came from His gracious lips, when He gave Himself on the cross—"It is finished"—will find their fullest meaning when all things are made new, when the first heaven and earth are passed away and a new heaven and new earth are come, when all things are made new. Then His voice will declare once more "It is done." (Rev. xxi: 1–6).

But now for those who believe sin is put away. It is appointed unto men—natural men—once to die and after this the judgment. From the latter the believer is exempt. His own words "He that heareth my words, and believeth in Him that sent Me, hath everlasting life and shall not come into judgment, but is passed from death unto life" (John v: 24) assure us of this. And when the believer dies, it is no longer as penalty. A day will come at last when it will be fulfilled "Behold I show you a mystery, we shall not all sleep, but shall be changed in a moment, in the twinkling of an eye." And He who was once offered to bear the sins

---

*The Romish assumption of the Lord's Supper being a sacrifice and that the blasphemous mass is an unbloody sacrifice are completely refuted by Verse 26, by this entire chapter and by the teaching of the New Testament.

†The Age before the Law and the Age under the Law.

of many (those who believe in Him) shall appear the second time." Unto them that look for Him shall He appear the second time, apart from sin, for salvation." It is His second coming. When He comes again He has nothing to do with sin, as far as His people are concerned. This was settled forever in His first coming. But He comes for their salvation their complete deliverance from all the results of sin, and His own will be changed into His image.*

CHAPTER X

1. The All-Sufficiency of the One Offering. 1–18.
2. Exhortations. 19–25.
3. Warning. 26–31.
4. Encouragements. 32–39.

Verse 1–18.—The precious truth the Apostle has unfolded in the preceding chapters concerning Christ, His one offering He made, His own blood by which He entered once for all into the holy place, the one all sufficient sacrifice, which has an eternal value and can never be repeated, is now still more practically applied. This one offering sanctifieth and it hath perfected forever them that are sanctified, so that the believer thus sanctified and perfected can enter into the Holiest as worshipper. The sacrifices brought in the first covenant did not make the worshippers perfect. If such had been the case there would have been no need to repeat

*"Without sin" is in contrast with "to bear the sins of many." But it will be remarked, that the taking up of the church is not mentioned here. It is well to notice the language. The character of His second coming is the subject. He has been *manifested* once. Now He is *seen* by those who look for him. The expression may apply to the deliverance of the Jews who wait for Him in the last days. He will appear for their deliverance. But we expect the Lord for this deliverance, and we shall see Him when He accomplishes it even for us. The apostle does not touch the question of the difference between this and our being caught up, and does not use the word which serves to announce His public manifestation. He will appear to those who expect Him. He is not seen by all the world, nor is it consequently the judgment, although that may follow. The Holy Ghost speaks only of them that look for the Lord. To them He will appear. By them He will be seen, and it will be the time of their deliverance; so that it is true for us, and also applicable to the Jewish remnant in the last days."—*Synopsis.*

them year by year continually. The repetition of these sacrifices in the law dispensation was a memorial of sin. "In those sacrifices there is a remembrance again of sins every year." The day of atonement was repeated every year and each time the highpriest entered in the Holiest with the blood of others. But the worshippers were not purged by it; the conscience as to sins remained, and those worshippers could not enter in themselves. For it was not possible that the blood of bulls and goats should take away sins. Yet the sins of Jewish believers before the cross were forgiven, not because the blood of an animal was sprinkled on the mercy-seat, but in anticipation of the one great offering, known to God in all its value and meaning.*

All is now changed. The one offering has been brought; by His own blood He entered the heavenly sanctuary, and all who believe are purged, the conscience is cleansed, we draw nigh and enter the Holiest, not by the blood of bulls and goats, but by the blood of Jesus.

Verses 5–9 are of deep interest. It reveals what passed between God the Father and God the Son. When about to enter the world these words were spoken by Him to the Father: "Sacrifice and offering Thou wouldest not, but a body hast Thou prepared Me; in burnt-offerings and sacrifices for sin Thou hast had no pleasure. Then I said Lo, I come (in the volume of the book it is written of Me†) to do Thy will, O God. It is a startling revelation, the Spirit of God acquainting us with what transpired between the Father and the Son. He comes into the world to do God's eternal will.

"He is the Son of God from all eternity, and in that mysterious eternity before the creation of the world, in His pre-mundane glory, this mind was in the Son, that He would humble himself, and take upon Himself the form of a servant,

*See Romans III:25. The remission of sin's that are past are the sins of Old Testament believers. The work of Christ on the Cross declares God's righteousness in having passed over the sins of those who believed the promise.

†The Old Testament Scriptures. What a testimony the Son of God bears as to the character of these Scriptures! As He said on earth "they testify of Me."

and obey the whole counsel of God concerning the redemption of fallen man. His whole life on earth, embracing His obedience and His death, His substitution for sinners, was His own voluntary resolve and act.

True, the Father sent Him; but such is the unity and harmony of the blessed Trinity, that it is equally true to say, the Son came. The love of the Lord Jesus, the sacrifice of Himself in our stead, the unspeakable humiliation of the Son of God, have their origin not in time but in eternity, in the infinite, self-subsistent, co-equal Son of the Father. He took on Him our nature. By His own will He was made flesh. From all eternity He offered Himself to accomplish the divine will concerning our salvation, He must needs be God, to have the power of freely offering Himself; He must needs take upon Him our nature to fulfil that sacrifice. Only the Son of God could undertake the work of our redemption; only as man could He accomplish it."*

He speaks of "a body hast Thou prepared Me." This means His virgin—birth. The body the Son of God took on was a prepared body, called into existence by a creative act of the Holy Spirit. (Luke I: 35).

The sentence "a body hast Thou prepared Me" is the Septuagint translation, or paraphrase, of the Hebrew, "ears hast Thou digged for Me" (Ps. xl:6.) This reading, or interpretation, is here fully sanctioned by the Holy Spirit. The ear is for learning, and the opened ear stands for obedience. (Is. l.:5.) In taking on the human body He took the form of a servant. See also Exodus xxi* And thus He offered Himself, as One who had the power to do so, out of love for the glory of God, to do His will. He undertook of His own free will the accomplishment of all the will of God and He took on the prepared body in incarnation in order to accomplish the eternal will of God. In this prepared body He lived that blessed life of obedience, suffering from man for God, and then He gave that body, according

†A. Saphir on Hebrew.

*Annotations on Ex. XXI. Vol. I.

to the will of God, in His death, when He suffered from God for man, in being made sin for us. "God's rights as the Lawgiver have been fully satisfied by the unsullied and complete obedience of the Lord Jesus. He magnified the law which man had taken and dishonored. Having fulfilled it in His life, He gave Himself to death, that He might silence forever its demand on the believing sinner's life. By man and for man the will of God has been fulfilled. In the life and death of the Lord Jesus the active measure of both grace and truth has been attained. God's will was the redemption of His people. But that His grace might triumph, His holiness must first be satisfied. The Cross of Christ has effected this. God's will, when finished, is thus found to be atonement. Blood has been shed, in obedience to His commandment, which is of virtue to remove all sin. It pleased Him to bruise His Son for sinners. He has laid upon Him the iniquity of all His people. By making Him an offering for sin, He has finished His intention of salvation. He has established grace in perfect righteousness."* And thus "He taketh away the first (the ordinances of the law, the burnt-offerings and sacrifices) and established the second (the will of God perfectly done). "By the which will we have been sanctified through the offering of the body of Jesus Christ once for all." This is a great and most blessed truth. His people, those who believe in Christ, are according to the will of God, to be sanctified, that is set apart to God. And this sanctification of all who believe is accomplished by the offering of the body of Jesus Christ once for all. The will of man has no part in this; the work by which believers are sanctified is absolutely and wholly of God. It was done once for all when Christ died on the Cross; before we were in existence it was all done. In this faith rests, knowing that He hath sanctified us, that His work, not ours, nor our experience, has accomplished our sanctification. Believers belong to God for ever according to the efficacy of the offering of the

---

*A. Pridham.

body of Jesus Christ once for all. And this setting aside abides; it is as settled and permanent as the peace which was made, the peace with God, the abiding possession, of all who are justified by faith. There is also for those who are sanctified in Christ, a practical sanctification which is wrought by the Spirit of God in the believer. (Chap. xii:14.)

Once more a contrast is made between Him and the levitical priests. The priests stood ministering, always bringing the same sacrifices over and over again. And they could never take away sins. But He having offered one sacrifice for sins, sat down forever* at the right hand of God. The work is accepted and believers are accepted in Him. Those who are sanctified are perfected in perpetuity by what He has done. He is forever seated, we are forever perfected by virtue of His work. And there at the right hand of God He is also waiting in patience till it pleases God to make His enemies the footstool of His feet. That will be when He comes the second time. And the Holy Spirit bears witness to it. That witness is in the Word of God; there the Spirit of God speaks. "If we could have heard the counsel of eternity, the word of the Father to the Son, ere time began, we could have no greater certainty than now. when we listen to Scripture, the echo in time of the counsel in eternity." We see here in this chapter up to verse 15 the three persons of the Godhead in connection with redemption. The will of God is the source of the work of redemption; the Son of God accomplished it; the Holy Spirit bears witness of it. Here again is an allusion to the new covenant in verses 16–17. (Sec. viii:10-12). Blessed assurance which all believers have "their sins and their iniquities will I remember no more." This is the witness of the Holy Spirit.

Verses 19–25. And now the great truth is reached which the Holy Spirit wanted these Hebrew Christians to lay hold of and for which He so wonderfully prepared the way. He has shown that by the sacrifice of Christ the believers

*It is not "eternal," but continuously, without interruption; He is at rest, His work is finished.

sins are put away; a perfect and everlasting cleansing has been made, remission assured and an eternal redemption obtained. By the will of God believers are sanctified by the offering of the body of Jesus Christ once for all; they are perfected and therefore in the eyes of a holy God, believers are without sin. This gives liberty to come into God's presence. The veil is rent and we can enter in. There is no more barrier; we have a free and unfettered access. "Having therefore, brethren, boldness to enter into the holy places by the blood of Jesus, a new and living way which He hath consecrated for us through the veil, that is to say, His flesh." And we do not go in alone but we find Him in the Holiest who has done the work. He is there as a great highpriest to welcome us and to minister in tenderness to our needs. Upon this follow three exhortations. 1. "Let us draw near with a true heart in full assurance of faith, having our hearts sprinkled from an evil conscience, and our body washed with pure water (corresponding to the washing of the priests, Ex. xxix: 4, and typical of regeneration)." We are then a holy priesthood fit and fitted in Christ to offer up spiritual sacrifices. 2. 'Let us hold fast the confession of the hope without wavering for He is faithful who hath promised." And we shall hold fast if we draw near and constantly realized our nearness, our blessings and privileges in Christ. 3. "Let us consider one another to provoke unto love and good works; not forsaking the assembling of ourselves together, as the custom is with some, but encouraging one another, and so much the more as ye see the day approaching. It is the public confession of God's people that they are one and belong together. And they saw the day approaching which is here not the day when His people will be gathered together unto Him, caught up in clouds to meet Him in the air, but the day of His appearing.

Verses 26—31. A solemn warning is now once more added. It warns against deliberate apostasy of those who have known the truth (though not regenerated). They are enemies, adversaries and for such wilful going astray there remaineth no longer any sacrifice for sins "but a certain fearful looking for judgment and fiery indignation, which shall devour the adversaries." This was the great danger for these Hebrews who had professed faith in Christ, yet lingered around the levitical institutions as the temple with its worship was still standing. If they renounced the truth of Christianity by turning back to Judaism they trampled under foot the Son of God and counted the blood of the covenant, wherewith they were sanctified* an unholy thing; for such horrible, deliberate contempt there was no repentance and no remedy. They cannot escape judgment. It is a fearful thing to fall into the hands of the living God—He who hath said "Vengeance is mine, I will recompense."

Verses 32–39. Words of encouragement and comfort conclude this main section of the epistle. They had suffered for Christ's sake and he calls to their remembrance their former days. They had endured even with joy the spoiling of their goods, because they knew that they had in heaven a better and enduring substance. He exhorts them to be patient and not to cast away their confidence. The promise was sure. "For yet a little while, and He that shall come will come and wi l not tarry." Hab. ii: 3–4 is quoted. He was sure that they are not of them who draw back unto perdition, but of them that believe (literally: of faith) to the saving of the soul. The chapter which follows describes the action of this faith through the example of their forefathers who walked and lived according to the same principle.

---

*"Observe here the way in which sanctification is attributed to the blood; and, also, that professors are treated as belonging to the people. The blood received by faith, consecrates the soul to God; but it is here viewed also as an outward means for setting apart the people as a people. Every individual who had owned Jesus to be the Messiah, and the blood to be the seal and foundation of an everlasting covenant available for eternal cleansing and redemption on the part of God, acknowledging himself to be set apart for God, by this means, as one of the people—every such individual would, if he renounced it, renounce it as such; and there was no other way of sanctifying him. The former system had evidently lost its power for him, and the true one he had abandoned. This is the reason why it is said, 'having received the knowledge of the truth.' "—*Synopsis.*

IV. PRACTICAL INSTRUCTIONS AND EXHORTATIONS.

CHAPTER XI-XIII

1. Faith in Regard to Creation and Salvation. 1–7.
2. The Patience of Faith. 8–22.
3. The Energy of Faith. 23–40.

Verses 1–7. The disastrous effect of unbelief has been pointed out in the earlier part of this epistle (iii:12; 19. iv:2) as well as the necessity of faith. After the great theme of the epistle, the sacrificial work and priesthood of Christ had been fully demonstrated, faith, in the closing verses of the previous chapter is mentioned once more "the just shall live by faith." To live and walk by faith is inseparably connected with the possession and enjoyment of the good things which have come, the perfection the believer has in Christ. And now the Spirit of God gives a remarkable record of the saints of old and shows how prominent faith was in their lives and experiences. It is one of the great and marvellous chapters, not only of this epistle, but of the whole Word of God. There is a divine order here in the way the names are mentioned as well as many and deep spiritual lessons into which we cannot fully enter.* First three antedeluvians are mentioned—Abel, Enoch and Noah. The main part of the chapter is devoted to Abraham and his life of faith, trust and patience, Isaac, Jacob and Joseph are also mentioned. That those who lived before the inauguration of the law covenant and the levitical institutions. are prominently used in this faith-chapter is not without meaning. These illustrious heads of the Hebrew nation had the promise; the grace-covenant had been established with them, the covenant which was to remain. They had no law and carnal ordinances, no tabernacle, no priest and yet they pleased God by their faith. And now in possession

*The purpose of our work makes this impossible. Saphir on Hebrews, A. Pridham and others will be helpful in a more analytical study of this chapter.

of the promise, fulfilled in Christ, these Hebrew Christians were to live in faith and manifest the patience of faith, even as Abraham (whom they called "our father Abraham") did.

The first statement speaks of faith, not so much as a definition, but as a declaration of the action and power of faith. The revised version is better in its rendering than the King James translation. "Now faith is the assurance (or substantiation) of things hoped for, the conviction of things not seen." Faith makes real to the soul that which we hope for and is a demonstration of that which we do not see. It is therefore assurance and a settled conviction respecting things hoped for, though unseen. "It is the soul's hand that grasps the promised blessings and makes them its very own. Faith lays hold on what is future, but sure, and brings it into the life of the believer, so that in the presence and power of it he lives and walks. It is far-sightedness. It sees and forsees. It pierces into the unseen, it seizes the promised riches of God and makes them a present reality, and and therefore the life of the believer may become opulent with noble deeds, because ruled and stimulated by a great motive." It is by faith we know that the worlds were framed by the Word of God, so that things which are seen were not made of things which do appear. God called all things into existence. Matter is not eternal; the universe is not a producing cause. God has created all things by Him and for Him, who is the eternal Word. (Heb. i:2; John i:1). Man is unable by searching to solve the mystery of creation. How ridiculous have been the cosmogonies of ancient nations. The evolution theories are equally absurd.* "In the beginning God created the

*It would be a good thing if the men of science to-day would give heed to such a text as this Take Darwin's "Origin of Species," where he never gets, indeed, to the origin, and owns that he cannot prove that any species ever did originate after the fashion he decrees. And think of originating in his manner Eve out of Adam! Given even the rib, she could not have sprung out of that simply. There must have been what did not appear—the power of God. If it is not perfectly scientific to believe that in her

heavens and the earth." This we believe that the worlds were framed by the Word of God. Abel is next mentioned. The truth of salvation is seen in his case. Sin and death had come in. By faith, trusting in the promise, acknowledging his true condition, he brought a more excellent sacrifice than Cain. He approached God with that more excellent sacrifice. He obtained witness that he was righteous. He was justified by faith. And Abel himself who died by the hand of his brother is a type of the Lord Jesus Christ and His sacrifice.

Enoch was translated by faith that he should not see death. In Abel the truth of righteousness by faith is illustrated. Enoch, walking with God, believing God and prophesying (Jude. verses 14–15) went to heaven without passing through death. The power of death was destroyed in his case; the power of that life he possessed was manifested in his translation. How blessedly Abel and Enoch show forth that by faith Righteousness and life are bestowed upon those who believe. The great sacrifice, typified by Abel's more excellent sacrifice and also by his death, has conquered death. Through death Christ has destroyed him who had the power of death. (Heb. ii: 14).

Enoch is a type of the church. He prophesied of coming judgment (the deluge) but did not pass through that judgment. Even so the true church, when the Lord comes, will be taken from earth to glory without dying, before tribulation, wrath and judgment come upon this age, which ends

---

case, we may as well give up Scripture at once, for you cannot expunge the miraculous out of it. If it be only a question of less or more, how unreasonable to measure out the power of God, and how enormous the pretence of being able to say just how much this power, or how or when it shall be fitting for it to be displayed!

After all, Scripture is at once the most scientific and rational of books, while it is, besides, a miracle of the most stupendous kind, always ready to hand, and with its own power of conviction for any who will examine it. And this one may say in the face of all the higher critics in the world, who are simply the Darwinians of theology, and who, like them, theorize after the most stupendous fashion and then talk about the credulity of faith. —*Num. Bible.*

like the days of Noah. Enoch also received testimony before he was translated that he pleased God, for he walked in faith in His presence and in His fellowship. This is the walk into which all God's people are called and which faith and the power of the indwelling spirit make possible. Without faith (a faith which clings close to Him, trusts in His word and is obedient) it is impossible to please Him.

Verse 7 speaks of Noah and his faith. In this verse we find mentioned the ground of faith (warned of God); the realm of faith (things not seen); the exercise of faith (he feared); the work of faith (he prepared an ark); the result of faith (he saved his house); the testimony of faith (he condemned the world) and the reward of faith (heir to righteousness). It is the most remarkable verse in the whole chapter. Enoch was caught up to heaven before the deluge came. Noah was warned of the unseen judgment to come (which Enoch had warned would come) and was roused with godly fear. He is a type of the godly remnant of Jews at the end of this present age, who will pass through tribulation and judgment, after the true church has left the earth, and having passed through the judgment, as Noah did, will inherit the earth. Noah represents the faith and exercise of this Jewish remnant, which will be saved out of the judgments at the close of this age.

Verses 8–22. The obedience and patience of faith is the theme of verses 8–22. Obediently Abraham went out, not knowing whether he was going. He obeyed the voice, believed the promise of God. Faith made of him a stranger in the land of promise as in a foreign country. He had no permanent place, but as a pilgrim he dwelt in tents with Isaac and Jacob—"for he waited for the city which hath foundations, whose architect and maker God is." God revealed to him the heavenly city and in patience he waited for that city, and while he waited he dwelt there content in perfect reliance on God. It was by faith that Sarah received strength to conceive seed "because she counted Him faithful that promised." And then they died in faith "not having received the promises, but having seen them (by the eyes of faith) afar off and embraced them, and confessed that they were strangers and pilgrims on earth." This faith in its power and action is examplified. By faith Abraham offered up Isaac. He manifested in this act that absolute confidence in God, which, at His command, can renounce even God's own promises as possessed after the flesh, confident that God would restore them through the exercise of His power, overcoming death.* By faith Isaac and Jacob acted. And Joseph, a stranger in a strange land, yet believing the promises as to the land, reckoned in faith on their fulfillment and thus gave commandment concerning his bones. (Gen. l: 25).

Verses 23–40. Faith in this section illustrates the energy connected with it which surmounts any obstacle and difficulty, and, trusting, brings forth the manifestations of God's power in deliverance. Such was the faith of the parents of Moses. They hid the child and were not afraid. "Faith does not reason; it acts from its own point of vision and leaves the result to God." And how this energy of faith is illustrated in Moses himself. His faith renounced the wealth, power, glory and splendor of Egypt. He gave up a princely position, the possibility of an earthly throne and identified himself with the people who had become slaves, because he believed them to be the people of God. Faith taught him not to fear the wrath of the king; faith fears nothing, but God and faith has nothing to fear. The secret was "he endured as seeing Him who is invisible." By faith he celebrated the passover and the sprinkling of blood, that the destroyer of the firstborn might not touch them. And

---

*Observe here that, when trusting in God and giving up all for Him, we always gain, and we learn something more of the ways of His power: for in renouncing according to His will anything already received, we ought to expect from the power of God that He will bestow something else. Abraham renounces the promise after the flesh. He sees the city which has foundations; he can desire a heavenly country. He gives up Isaac, in whom were the promises: he learns resurrection, for God is infallibly faithful. The promises were in Isaac: therefore God must restore him to Abraham, and by resurrection, if he offered him in sacrifice.—*Synopsis.*

what more? The Red Sea, the walls of Jericho, the harlot Rahab.* God's power opened the way to faith through the Red Sea for the salvation of His people while the unbelieving Egyptian perished. Jericho's walls fall and Rahab's house, standing upon the wall, is preserved because she believed. And then Gideon, Barak, Samson, Japhtha, David, Samuel and the prophets and the heroes of faith which follow. Their names are not given, but God knows them all as well as the countless thousands of martyrs who are constantly added to this list. "The strongest thing in the world is faith—is has an eagle's eye and lion's heart. It has a lion's heart to confront dangers and hardships, and an eagle's eye to descry the unseen glories and the sure victory. The heroism of faith is a wonderful thing. It may suffer indescribable tortures and agonies, as often it has, but it is unconquerable, invincible. Some were tortured (tympanized, i. e., stretched in a wheel as the drumhead), 'that they might obtain a better resurrection,' as were the mother and her seven sons who were put to death one after the other, and in sight of each other, by the Syrian monster, Antiochus Epiphanes (2 Macc. vii). Some were stoned, as Zechariah (2 Chron : xxiv) and Jeremiah, according to tradition. Some were sawn asunder, as was Isaiah under Manasseh. Some were slain with the sword, as Urijah, (Jer. xxvi: 23), and James the brother of John (Acts xii). They might have rustled in silks and velvets and luxuriated in the palaces of princes had they denied God and believed the world's lie. Instead, they wandered about in sheepskins and goatskins, themselves accounted no better than goats or sheep, nay, they like these reckoned fit only for the slaughter. The world thought them unworthy to live here, while God thought them worthy to live with Him in glory."†

*Rahab the harlot! Those who seek for proofs of the divine authorship of Scripture may find one here. Was there ever an Israelite who would have thought of preferring that woman's name to the names of David and Samuel and the prophets, and of coupling it with the names of the great leader and prophet of the Jewish faith "whom the Lord knew face to face." And what Jew would have dared to give expression to such a thought! —*Sir R. Anderson, K.C.B*

†Prof. Moorhead.

"God having provided some better thing for us, that not apart from us should they be made perfect." The Old Testament saints who died in faith have not yet been raised from among the dead; their spirits are in His presence. New Testament saints constituting the church, the body of Christ, have provided for themselves "some better thing." But the Spirit of God does not here enlarge upon this and only gives the information that the perfection of the Old Testament saints in resurrection from among the dead will not be apart from us, the New Testament saints. And that will be when the Lord comes for His saints with the shout. (1 Thess. iv:13-18).

CHAPTER XII

1. Looking Away Unto Jesus. 1-2.
2. The Contradiction of Sinners. 3-4.
3. Chastened as Sons. 5-11.
4. Exhortations. 12-17.
5. The End of Faith. 18-24.
6. The Final Warning. 25-29.

Verses 1-2. Therefore seeing we also are compassed about with so great a cloud of witnesses, let us lay aside every weight, and the sin which doth so easily beset us, and let us run with steadfastness the race lying before us."

Some teach that the Old Testament saints are spectators of us and that they look upon us now from heaven. Dean Alford also states that they are lookers on and adds "Whosoever denies such reference, misses, it seems to me, the very point of the sense." Others have gone so far as to say that they not only look on but help the believer in his conflict on earth. But this view is unscriptural. We know that angels are spectators (1 Cor. iv:9; xi:10); angels are ministering spirits to minster unto the heirs of salvation, but the disembodied spirits of the righteous are neither spectators not do they minister to the saints on earth. The preceding chapter contains "the cloud of witnesses;" they witness to us by their lives and the victory of their faith and this is the encouragement for us. The Christian's life is a race; the glory at His coming is the goal. The runner of the race does not burden himself with weights, unnecessary things. Everything that impedes spiritual progress must be laid aside, as well as the sin that so easily besets us, which is the sin of unbelief. Against this sin they had been emphatically warned. "It is a sin that easily besets us, because it is but the mind of nature acting, according to its instincts, against the will of God." And the runners eyes are to be on the goal. (Phil. iii). The believer runs the race with steadfastness and divests himself of every weight and the sin that easily besets, if he looks away from everything and looks away "unto Jesus, the author and finisher of faith (Leader and Perfecter), who, for the joy that was set before Him, endured the cross, having despised the shame and is set down at the right hand of the throne of God." He is the great examplar of faith. He is to be constantly before us, and His people are to follow Him in the path of faith and trust. What light these words shed on His blessed life and especially His death on the cross! He endured the cross and despised the shame, connected with it, for the joy that was set before Him. See Isaiah liii:10–12. The joy set before us is to be with Him forever. Oh, for the daily vision of that goal.*

Verses 3—4. The believers life is also a conflict, trials which come from sin in the world, a world which is always, and always will be, antagonistic to Christ. Those Hebrews had their share of it; they were persecuted and hated for His Name's sake (x: 32–34). Peter also wrote about these persecutions they endured. And now they are called to

---

*"The flesh, the human heart, is occupied with cares and difficulties; and the more we think of them, the more we are burdened by them. It is enticed by the object of its desires, it does not free itself from them. The conflict is with a heart that loves the thing against which we strive; we do not separate ourselves from it in thought. When looking at Jesus, the new man is active; there is a new object, which unburdens and detaches us from every other by means of a new affection which has its place in a new nature: and in Jesus Himself, to whom we look, there is a positive power which sets us free."—*J. N. D.*

consider Him who endured such contradiction of sinners against Himself, lest they would be wearied, disheartened and fainting in their minds. These persecutions were the fellowship of His sufferings; and they had not yet resisted unto blood, striving against sin. Looking away unto Him gives strength to resist and to conquer.

Verse 5–11. In these verses the trials of the believer are viewed as chastenings from the Lord. As a loving father, who loves his children, He chastised them. They were not to forget this, that He speaks to them, not as to sinners, but as unto sons, "My son, despise not thou the chastening of the Lord, nor faint when reproved by Him, for whom the Lord loveth He chastiseth and scourgeth every son whom Hereceiveth." The chastening they were to endure. God,as Father, permits trials and tribulations to come to believers for their own good. Such experiences are not an evidence of divine displeasure, but evidences of sonship. "God dealeth with you as with sons; for who is the son whom the father chastiseth not. But if you are without chastening, of which all are made partakers, then are ye bastards and not sons." And therefore chastisements must not be despised, nor viewed as a discouraging experience; for the chastisement is for our eternal good and He does it in love. Paul's thorn in the flesh was such an experience which was needful for Him. Grace sustains in all chastisements. Then we have a contrast between the chastising of earthly fathers and that of the heavenly Father. The one is father of our flesh; God is the Father of spirits, the Creator and source of life, spiritual and ever-lasting, as well as physical and temporal. The one for a brief period; God during our whole lifetime. The one with imperfect knowledge, in much infirmity "after their own pleasure;" God with unerring wisdom, and in pure love. The aim of the one, our earthly future; the aim of God, to make us partakers of His holiness. Yet imperfect as is the earthly father's discipline, we gave it reverence, "as was right" and according to God's will, and for our safety. How much more ought we to be in subjection unto the Father of spirits, of whom is our true life.

And when we are disciplined it is not a joyous experience; it brings heart-searching, humiliation, confession, repentance and self-loathing, but afterward it yieldeth the peaceable fruit of righteousness unto them which have been exercised in this way.

Verse 12–17.—Words of exhortation and encouragement follow. The first three exhortations refer to ourselves (Verse 12–13); to others and to God. (Verse 14). To follow peace (pursue peace) with all men is to characterize those who have peace with God and who know the way of peace. Holiness must also be pursued, for without that none shall see the Lord. In Christ, believers are sanctified once for all, as this Epistle has so clearly demonstrated. The Holiness which qualifies a man to see the Lord, is Christ, and His blessed finished work. Abiding in Him the believer pursues the way of holiness, practical holiness, separation from evil in all things. It does not mean a certain "holiness experience" by which a believer is fitted, by erradication of the old nature, or by something else, to see the Lord. In Christ the believer is sanctified; as Martin Luther used to say "My Holiness is in Heaven." The exhortation here means to pursue that Holiness into which grace has called us, which grace has given and for which grace gives daily, power. Closely connected with this is the warning which follows in verse 15–17. The man who falls short of the grace of God, who lacketh that grace which is in Christ Jesus, his heart not resting in Him, is a mere professing believer and possesseth not the holiness, which grace alone can give. He is a root of bitterness and a profane, and earthly-minded person, as Esau was who sold his birthright.

---

*The time came when he regretted that for a paltry gratification he forfeited his right. Afterwards, when he would have inherited the blessing, he was rejected. For though he sought carefully with tears to change his father's mind he found (in Isaac) no place for change of mind. This seems to be the meaning of this difficult passage. Esau is never represented as an apostate, as one who professed and appeared to be a believer, and then

Verses 18–24. These verses contain a great contrast· The grace of God has brought and is bringing believers to better things than those which characterize Judaism. What the end of faith will be, the goal of glory is here unfolded. Believers have nothing now to do with Sinai, the the law and its terror. Then follows a marvellous enumeration of the earthly and heavenly glories to which we have come through faith and which faith beholds. First Mount Zion is mentioned. It is the place the Lord has chosen for His rest (Ps. cxxxii: 13–14). When that promised new covenant is fully established with the house of Israel and Judah, when sovereign grace has manifested its powers in the salvation and restoration of His people Israel, then Zion will be the earthly center, and God's appointed King will establish His rule there. (Ps. ii.) From the glory of the coming millennium we are taken to the glory above "the city of the living God, the Heavenly Jerusalem." It is the city for which Abraham looked in faith, the eternal home of the Saints of God.

"And to an innumerable company of angels, the universal gathering;" we shall know and behold all the tenants of the unseen world. "The church of the firstborn ones which are written in heaven"—this is the church in particular; there will be an unbroken and eternal fellowship with all the saints who constitute the body of Christ. "And to God the Judge of all," whose grace in Christ has put His own beyond all condemnation and who will, in His Son, judge the world in righteousness. "The spirits of just men made perfect" are the Old Testament saints, distinguished in this way from "the church of the firstborn ones;" they receive their perfection when the church is gathered home (xi:40). "And to Jesus the mediator of the new covenant, and to the blood of sprinkling that speaketh better than Abel." Through

fell away. So (apart from other reasons) the meaning of the apostle cannot be that Esau, as an apostate, was not able to find repentance. But we know that, notwithstanding his vehement and urgent entreaties, Isaac could not change his mind, or repent him of what he had done in conferring the blessing on Jacob, which God approved of.—*Saphir.*

Him and His precious blood these earthly and heavenly glories will be accomplished. And faith looks to these. It is the blessed goal for the heirs of God, the many sons He brings to glory.

Verse 25–29. A final warning follows, not to refuse Him that speaketh. (Compare with chapter ii:3). He that spoke on earth (giving the law) is the same that speaketh from heaven—the Son of God. To refuse Him means no escape from perdition. His voice then shook the earth. The prophetic word predicts another shaking of earth and heaven. (Hag. ii: 6). That will be when He comes again. Then follows the judgment of all who obeyed not the Gospel of our Lord Jesus Christ. The things that can be shaken will be removed and things that cannot be shaken remain. "Therefore let us, receiving a kingdom which cannot be shaken, have grace whereby we may serve God acceptably with reverence and fear; for our God is a consuming fire."

CHAPTER XIII

1. The Practical Walk. 1–6.
2. The Call to Separation. 7–16.
3. Conclusions. 17–25.

Verses 1–6. No comment is needed on the simple exhortations with which this concluding chapter of this epistle begins. Brotherly love stands in the foreground. Hospitality and loving kindness to prisoners and those who suffer adversity is especially enjoined. The great high priest in glory sympathises with such a condition of His saints and we too are to be sympathisers as well as intercessors with Him. The life is to be clean and undefiled. Walking in faith there should be not coveteousness but happy contentment in view of His never failing promise.

Verses 7 15. The first exhortation in these verses is that they should remember their leaders who had spoken the Word of God to them, to follow their faith and to consider the issue of their walk. These leaders had passed away from the earthly service into the presence of the Lord. One abides the same. He must be exalted above everything and He alone can satisfy the hearts of His people. "Jesus Christ is the same yesterday, and today, and forever." He is the unchanging Jehovah who had spoken of old "I am the Lord who changeth not." What a One to follow and to trust. From Him and His gracious riches the enemy tries to lead away God's people and ensnare them. Christ is the person whom Satan hates and all wicked and strange doctrines are invented by him to dishonor that worthy name and to spoil God's children.

Then follows the call to separation, the great exhortation at which the Holy Spirit aimed from the beginning of this document and which He now presses upon the conscience. "We have an altar whereof they have no right to eat who are serving the tabernacle." That altar is Christ for those who have left the shadow things behind and who have found in Him their all in all.

Those who still cling to the Jewish things have no right of access; they have no right to eat if they serve the tabernacle, for everything has passed away since the substance in Christ has come. They had put Christ outside. All had been done as foreshadowed by the legal sacrifices. "Wherefore Jesus also, that He might sanctify the people with His own blood, suffered without the gate." And now all is done and the whole Jewish system has no more meaning. To remain in it and practice the old things, which are gone, is a denial of Christ and His work as the sin-bearer. The camp is the people who continued in the things of the law, who denied thereby that the new sacrifice had been brought; who still used an earthly priesthood and denied thereby that the new and living way into the holy place had been made by the blood of Jesus, the rent veil. Ritualistic Christendom with its man-made priesthood, its so-called "saving ordinances," its legal principle, so prominent, not only in the worst form of apostate Christendom (the Romish church), but in other systems and sects, is but another camp in which the truth of Christ and His all sufficient work is denied. Outside of the camp is found the Cross of Christ with all its grace and glory. And therefore the exhortation, which seems to us was the all-important message for these Hebrews (and for us as well) "let us go forth therefore unto Him without the camp, bearing His reproach. For here we have no continuing city, but we seek one to come." In other words, leave all behind, be separate from all, which denies the cross and the work accomplished there. And "outside the camp" must mean "inside the veil," to enjoy the perfection in Christ, to be in God's holy presence as a true worshipper. "For we are the circumcision who worship God in the spirit, and rejoice in Christ Jesus, and have no confidence in the flesh." (Phil. iii-3).

This priesthood of which Peter speaks (1 Pet. ii:5) is mentioned here also. By Him therefore (not by an earthly priest or in an earthly tabernacle) let us offer up a sacrifice of praise to God continually that is the fruit of our lips, giving thanks to His name." And besides this, which is done inside the veil, there is another aspect to the sacrifice we bring in His name—"to do good and to communicate forget not, for with such sacrifices God is well pleased."

Verses 17-25. They were to obey the leaders and submit themselves. These leaders watched over their souls as those that shall give account in the coming day of Christ. And by obedience and submission they honored Him who has made them the overseers of the flock of God. Well it would be if all workers would never loose sight of the fact that they are accountable to the Lord. The writer of the epistle, no doubt the apostle Paul, requests their prayers, "pray for us."* In true humility, so characteristic of Paul he writes "for we persuade ourselves that we have a good conscience, in all things desiring to live honestly." Most

*"The fact is that none need the prayers of God's people more than those who are active and prominent in the Lord's work. Practically occupied with preaching and teaching others, how great the danger is of going on with a conscience not good about themselves! And what can more decidedly defile or harden?"

ask prayer because their conscience is bad. "He beseeches them that they may do this, so that by their prayer of intercession he might be restored to them the sooner. (See Philemon, verse 22). He valued the prayers of the saints.

Then follows that blessed prayer so well suited to this epistle and its great truths. "Now the God of peace that brought up from the dead our Lord Jesus Christ, the great Shepherd of the sheep, through the blood of the everlasting covenant, perfect you in every good work to do His will, working in you what is pleasing in His sight through Jesus Christ, to whom be glory forever and ever (unto the ages of the ages). Amen."

In the final words the apostle beseeches them to bear with the word of exhortation as contained in the letter. The mention of Timothy is another evidence that Paul wrote Hebrews. Brief salutations and the benediction closes this wonderful portion of the Word of God. "Grace be with you all. Amen."

THE EPISTLE OF JAMES

The Epistle of James

Introduction

The Epistles of James, First and Second Peter, the three Epistles of John and the Epistle of Jude constitute the so-called Catholic, or General Epistles. They were thus named in earliest days, and in the ancient manuscripts these seven Epistles are grouped together as we have them in our English version; however, they always follow the Book of Acts. It is claimed that they were named General Epistles because Christians in general are addressed in them, which does not hold good with the second and third Epistles of John, for these were addressed to individuals. The first Epistle in this group, following the Book of Acts in the manuscripts, is the Epistle of James.

Its Peculiar Character

That there is a great difference between the great Pauline Epistles and the Epistle of James is seen at a glance. If one reads even the Epistle to the Hebrews, addressed to the same class of people, believing Hebrews, to whom the Epistle of James is also addressed, and reads James immediately after, a great and notable change is seen at once. The character of the Epistle of James is essentially *Jewish*. In the second chapter the word synagogue is used as the place of their assembly, "If there come unto your *synagogue* a man, etc." They were then still in the synagogue. Nothing about the church, the body of Christ is mentioned in this Epistle, nor do we find here the great doctrines of Christianity and the corresponding Christian relationship. The law is also prominent; and there are other Jewish features which will be pointed out in the annotations. The character of the entire Epistle corresponds with those to whom the Epistle was originally addressed "the twelve tribes which are scattered abroad." It is evidently a document written at an early date during the transition period and before the great doctrinal Epistles of the Apostle to the Gentiles had been produced, in which the fulness of redemption, the body of Christ, the church, and its unity and other cardinal doctrines of our faith are revealed.

What do we mean by "*transition period*"? That the beginning of Christianity had a decidedly Jewish cast is known to all Bible students. For years all the believers were Jews. There was a great Jewish-Christian assembly in Jerusalem and many more throughout Judea. As we learn from the Book of Acts there were many thousands of Jews who believed, but who were also zealous for the law; they still made use of the temple worship, went there at the accustomed hours of prayer. There were also many priests who at one time were obedient to the faith, believed that the Crucified One was the Messiah; they also continued undoubtedly in their priestly ministrations in the temple. They still had their great national hope of a restoration of the kingdom. That hope indeed was preached by Peter in Acts iii:19-20.

That the Epistle of James is put in all the ancient manuscripts next to the Book of Acts is therefore of significance. We breathe in this Epistle the same Jewish-Christian atmosphere which we find in the beginning of the Book of Acts.

James, the Author of the Epistle

What we have stated above identifies the author of this Epistle. Who is James (Greek: *Jacobos*—Jacob)? Certainly not James, the Apostle, the son of Zebedee. He was martyred in the year 44, as recorded in Acts xii:2. Nor can the author be James, the son of Alphaeus, another Apostle. His name is mentioned for the last time in the New Testament in Acts i:13. We hear nothing more about him, and it is inconceivable that he should have held a position of authority which belongs to the author of this Epistle. There is another James, who is designated as "the brother of the Lord." He has been generally accepted, even by critics, as the author of the Epistle.

The Apostle Paul speaks of him in Gal. i:19. Three years after his conversion he returned to Jerusalem to interview Peter, and Paul adds, "but of the other Apostles saw I none, save James, the Lord's brother."

James, the brother of the Lord, belongs to those mentioned in John vii:5: "For neither did His brethren believe in Him." James and his brethren did not believe on Jesus, the Virgin-born Son of God, as the Messiah. But in the first chapter of Acts we find mentioned among those who waited in Jerusalem for the promise of the Father "Mary, the mother of Jesus, and His brethren." They had been converted and were now believers. How were they convinced that Jesus was the Christ? There can be no question that the James mentioned, distinct from the Apostles, in 1 Cor. xv:7, to whom the risen Christ appeared, is the brother of the Lord. He saw the Lord risen from the dead; He had appeared to him and that became the great turning point in his life and he and his brethren believed.

He early held in Jerusalem the position as leader. When Peter had been miraculously led forth from prison and appeared in the midst of a company of believers, he said, "Go show these things unto James and to the brethren" (Acts xii:17). He was the acknowledged head of the Jewish-Christians in Jerusalem. He is the spokesman in the first council held in Jerusalem, in the language of our day "the presiding officer" (Acts xv:13). Through him the Holy Spirit gave a very important revelation. Years later when Paul undertook the fateful journey to Jerusalem and had reached the city, he called on James, and after salutation reported to him "what things God had wrought among the Gentiles by his ministry." And James spoke the fatal words which enticed the Apostle Paul to conform to the keeping of the law, when James told him, "Thou seest, brother, how many thousands of Jews there are which believe, and they are all zealous for the law" (Acts xxi:19-26).

According to ancient sources, like Eusebius, James was a godly man and a strong observer of the ceremonial law, and, though he was ready to see the hand of God in the ministry of Paul and Barnabas among the Gentiles (confirmed by the second chapter of Galatians), he adhered closely to the law and the Judaistic form of Christianity to the end of his life. Dr. Schaff* remarks, "Had not a Peter and above all Paul arisen, Christianity would perhaps never have completely emancipated from the veil of Judaism and asserted its own independence. Still, there was a necessity for the ministry of James. If any could win over the ancient covenant people it was he. It pleased God to set so high an example of Old Testament piety in its purest form among the Jews, to make conversions to the Gospel, even at the eleventh hour (preceding the destruction of Jerusalem), as easy as possible for them. But when they would not listen to the voice of this last messenger of peace, then was the measure of divine patience exhausted, and the fearful and long-threatened judgment broke forth. And thus the mission of James, the brother of the Lord was fulfilled. According to Hegesippus James died a year before the destruction of Jerusalem." The Jewish historian Josephus records this in the following paragraph: "Festus was now dead, and Albinus was but on the road, so he assembled the Sanhedrim or judges, and brought before them the brother of Jesus, who was called Christ, whose name was James, and some others. And when he had formed an accusation against them as breakers of the law, he delivered them to be stoned."†

For various reasons this Epistle was, even among the church fathers, treated with suspicion. It seems that the uncertainty as to the writer, and that it was addressed entirely to Jewish believers, raised these doubts. These doubts were revived during the Reformation and Luther especially called it "an Epistle of straw," meaning by it that it did not contain the wheat.

"On the whole, on any intelligent principles of canonical reception of early writings, we cannot refuse the Epistle a

---

*Dr. P. Schaff-Kirchengeschichte.

†Josephus Book XX.

place in the canon. That that place was given it from the first in some parts of the church; that, in spite of many adverse circumstances, it gradually won that place in other parts; that when thoroughly considered, it is so consistent with and worthy of his character and standing whose name it bears; that it is marked off by so strong a line of distinction from the writings and Epistles which have not attained a place in the canon; all these are considerations which, though they do not in this, any more than in other cases, amount to demonstration, yet furnish when combined a proof hardly to be resisted, that the place where we do now find it in the New Testament canon is that which it ought to have, and which God in His providence has guided His church to assign to it."*

When Was It Written

James lived and labored in Jerusalem. There is no likelihood that he ever left the city of his fathers, hence we cannot doubt that the Epistle was written by him in Jerusalem and sent forth from there. As to the exact date scholars have been divided on that. That it was written before the destruction of Jerusalem, and not after, is obvious, for James died before the city was taken by the Romans. But does not the Epistle of James refer to Paul's teachings in Romans as to righteousness by faith, and therefore, it is argued, James must have written the Epistle after Romans, and perhaps also Hebrews, had been written. But the argument is weak. James did not answer Paul's teaching at all; he was guided by the Spirit of God to emphasize a holy life, as a justification of real faith before man. That he cites Abraham, as Paul did in Romans, is no evidence that he had the Epistle to the Romans in his possession. "It is much more probable, that all which James saith respecting works and faith has respect to a former and different state and period of the controversy, when the Jewish Pharisaic

*Dean Alford Prolegomena.

notions (as to the boast in the law) were being carried into the adopted belief in Christianity, and the danger was not, as afterwards, of a Jewish law-righteousness being set up, antagonistic to the righteousness which is by faith of Jesus Christ, but of a Jewish reliance on exclusive purity of faith superseding the necessity of a holy life, which is inseparably bound up with any worthy holding of the Christian faith." Some of the most painstaking scholars, like Drs. Neander and Schaff have assigned to the Epistle a very early date. The absence of any mention of the decision at the church council (Acts xv) in the Epistle strengthens the early date. The date must be put around the year 45 A. D. and this makes the Epistle perhaps the earliest of the New Testament writings. Why should it not be so, considering that the Judaistic church in Jerusalem was the beginning of Christianity and the message of the Epistle harmonizes so fully with the character of that church?

The Twelve Tribes Scattered Abroad.

As already stated James addressed the Epistle "to the twelve tribes scattered abroad." We hear much in our days about "the ten lost tribes." But were they lost when James wrote his Epistle? If they were lost how could he have addressed this Epistle to them? But furthermore he addresses also those among the twelve tribes who were believers, so that it is but logical to assume that the twelve tribes, perhaps remnants of them, were known in the days of James, and that a number of each of the tribes had accepted Christ, the Messiah. Of course, like so much else, the term "twelve tribes" has been spiritualized as if it meant "the real Israel of God," that is, all believers, Jews and Gentiles. But this cannot be done. The fact that the literal tribes of Israel are addressed has been recognized by most expositors. James as the head of the Jerusalem church came in touch with many Israelites, who, according to their age-long custom, came up to Jerusalem to the feasts. Perhaps many of these visitors becoming acquainted with James and their believing brethren were also convinced that Jesus was the promised Messiah and believed on Him. They went back to their different communities in Central Asia and beyond, in the dispersion, and formed their synagogues. Later James learned from them the spiritual conditions in these different centers in the dispersion and addressed this Epistle to them as well as to those who were not believers.

We must also remember that a similar Jewish-Christian remnant will be in existence once more in Palestine during the coming great tribulation; it is the godly remnant, which we have pointed out many times in the prophetic Books and in the Psalms. Then the Gospel of the Kingdom will again be preached, and as it was in the Jewish beginning of the age, signs and miracles will follow, in healing (James v:14) and otherwise. The Epistle of James will then have a special meaning for this remnant.

Is the Epistle of James for us?

The Jewish character of this Epistle has lead some to say "It is for the Jews and not for us." We have known believers who refuse to read this Epistle. But that is a serious and deplorable mistake. Here are written great and needed truths which are as needful for us as they were for those to whom the Epistle was originally addressed. The Christian who passes by the Epistle of James rejects a most important part of the Word of God and as a result he will suffer loss. We quote from another: "I am persuaded that no man, I will not say despises, but even attempts to dispense with the Epistle of James except to his own exceeding loss. Luther would have been none the worse, but all the stronger, for a real understanding of this writing of James. He needed it in many ways; and so do we. It is, therefore, a miserable cheat that any should allow their own subjective thoughts to govern them in giving up this or any portion of the Word of God; for all have an important place, each for its own object. Is it too much to ask that a document be judged by its express and manifest design? Surely we are not to take Paul's object in order to interpret James. What can be conceived more contrary, I will not say to reverence for what claims to be inspired, but even to all sense and discrimination, than such a thought? And it is thus that men have stumbled and fallen over this—it is little to say—precious and profitable, and above all, practically profitable position of the Word of God.

"At the same time we must read it as it is, or rather as God wrote it; and God has addressed it, beyond controversy, not merely to Christian Jews, nor even to Jews, but to the twelve tribes that were scattered abroad. Thus it embraces such of them as were Christians; and it gives a very true and just place to those who had the faith of the Lord Jesus Christ. Only it is a mistake to suppose that it contemplates nobody else. People may come to it with the thought that all the Epistles were addressed to Christians, but this is simply wrong. If you bring this or any other preconception to the Word of God, no wonder His Word leaves you outside its divine and holy scope. For He is ever above us, and infinitely wise. Our business is to gather what He has to teach us. No wonder, therefore, when persons approach the Scripture with preconceived thoughts, hoping to find confirmation there instead of gathering God's mind from what He has revealed—no wonder that they find disappointment. The mischief is in themselves and not in the divine Word. Let us prayerfully seek to avoid the snare."*

The exhortations in this Epistle are, therefore, of great value; and there are many precious gems to be found scattered throughout the Epistle of James, the brother of the Lord.

---

*William Kelly.

The Divisions of the Epistle of James

We have already pointed out that this Epistle is not a doctrinal document. Addressed as it is to the twelve tribes in the dispersion it has nothing to say about Gentile believers, nor about their place in the church, the body of Christ. They were believers, yet distinctly Jewish believers. This is seen in the opening verse in which James calls himself "the servant of God," an Old Testament expression; but he adds "of the Lord Jesus Christ." He and those to whom he wrote were serving God, still zealous for the law, adhering to it in every way, yet they believed on the Lord Jesus Christ and served Him. Their national hope as the people of God was theirs still. The Epistle is taken up entirely with the difficulties these Jewish believers had; it refers to the trials (like Peter's first Epistle) they were undergoing, exhorts them to faith. It points out their serious errors in their lives as believers; while they believed their lives did not correspond with such a belief. The correction of the faults, while common to all believers, has a striking Jewish aspect. They had respect of persons, looked to outward circumstances, and they are reminded of the royal law of the Scriptures, and insistence is made that their faith in the Messiah must be evidenced by works. They are exhorted to be more than mere hearers of the Word, by which they had been begotten anew, but to be doers of it. Many of them evidently wanted to be teachers, had great ambitions, but their Jewish character, looseness of their tongues in speaking evil, had become prominent and that is corrected. There is a repeated reference in the Epistle to the godly of their nation, to Abraham and Isaac, to Rahab, Job and Elijah. There is also quite a little which links with the Sermon on the Mount. Finally there are exhortations to godliness, prayer, the life of trust and a reminder of the Coming of the Lord. The prominent word seems to be the word "**patience.**" We find it five times. The trying of faith is to work patience (i:3); patience is to have her perfect work (i:4); they are to be patient unto the coming of the Lord (v:7); and be like the husbandman who waits in patience, and finally they are reminded of the patience of Job. The exhortations may be grouped around this word patience. I. Exhortations to Patience in Suffering God's Will (i:1-18). II. Exhortation to Patience in Doing God's Will (i:19; iv:17). III. Exhortation to Patience in Awaiting God's Will (v:1-20). We shall follow in our analysis and annotations the chapter division as we have them in our Bibles.

I. **TRIALS AND THE EXERCISE OF FAITH.** Chapter I.

II. **THE ROYAL LAW: FAITH AND WORKS.** Chapter II.

III. **THE EVILS OF THE TONGUE CORRECTED.** Chapter III.

IV. **FURTHER EXHORTATIONS TO RIGHT LIVING.** Chapter IV.

V. **THE COMING OF THE LORD AND THE LIFE OF FAITH.** Chapter V.

Analysis and Annotations

I. TRIALS AND THE EXERCISE OF FAITH

CHAPTER I.

1. Trials and the Power of Faith. 1-4.
2. The Resources of Faith. 5-8.
3. The Realization of Faith. 9-11.
4. The Conquest of Faith. 12-15.
5. The Result of Faith. 16-27.

I. Trials and the Power of Faith: Verses 1-4. The first verse is the introduction. The writer is James, but he does not add, as he might have done, "the brother of the Lord." It would have identified his person at once, and being the Lord's brother, he had a perfect right to call himself thus. But he did not. His humility shines forth in this omission; others called him by that title, but he avoided it. He is "servant of God," and he served God as "servant of the Lord Jesus Christ," a godly believing Jew. He writes to the twelve tribes in the dispersion of like faith. But the beautiful words of greeting in other Epistles "Grace and peace be unto you," are not used by him. Greetings only are sent, and in this respect it is like the Apostolic document which was issued by the council in Jerusalem in Acts xv (see Acts xv:23).

The practical character of his letter is at once apparent. "Count it all joy when you fall in divers temptations." They were all undergoing trials and tests as believing Jews, who had accepted the Lord Jesus Christ as the Messiah. The First Epistle of Peter, which is also addressed to believing Hebrews tells the same story. They were in heaviness through manifold temptations. Their faith was severely tried as with fire (1 Peter i:6-7). James exhorts these sufferers not to be grieved or disturbed over these trials, but rather to count it a joy. These trials were the evidences of their sonship and that their faith was real. Faith must be tried; the trial itself worketh patience, that is, endurance. This belongs to the practical experience of a believer. "For even hereunto were ye called; because Christ also suffered for us, leaving us an example, that ye should follow His steps" (1 Peter ii:21). If endurance has its perfect work, if the believer continues steadfast and in patience he will be perfect and complete, lacking nothing. The word "perfect" has been misinterpreted by some as if it meant an assumed Christian perfection or sinlessness. It does not mean that, but it means the perfect work of patience, enduring to the end, when self-will is subdued and the will of God is fully accepted. The result is that there is no deficiency in the practical life of the believer. The Lord Jesus is an example of it. He never did His own will, but patiently waited for the will of God and yielded a perfect obedience. Faith is power to suffer and to endure trials and testings.

2. The Resources of Faith: Verses 5-8. Such endurance is impossible without prayer. In the midst of trials and hardships, the various perplexities which come upon the believer, they, as well as we, lack wisdom; we often do not know what to do. Wisdom is needed, not human wisdom, but that wisdom which is from above. This wisdom enables us to discern His will and to follow the right guidance. It is obtained by an utter dependence on God, and the expression of that dependence is prayer. He giveth to all liberally, nor does He upbraid. We can come to Him at all times, and habitually wait on Him for guidance and direction; and as we wait on Him thus and count on Him there will be no disappointment. Often believers think they have divine guidance, but it is but following some kind of an impression, certain impulses, which may come from ourselves, or from the enemy. But constant waiting on the Lord and trusting in Him, this is wisdom. All this necessitates childlike faith, which means counting on His faithfulness and on an answer from Him. If we doubt His faithfulness or question His answer we cannot receive anything from Him. Hesitance about God, a doublemindedness, depending upon something else besides God is in reality unbelief: "For he that wavereth (is not positive in his utter confidence and dependence) is like a wave of the sea driven with the wind and tossed. For let not that man think that he shall receive anything of the Lord. A double-minded man is unstable in all his ways." If the believer is double-minded, looking to the Lord and at the same time looking elsewhere, he dishonors Him, and He cannot honor the believer and answer his prayer. How blessedly it was expressed by David, which perhaps was remembered by these believing Jews, when the inspired king wrote: "My soul, wait thou only upon God; for my expectation is from Him" (Psalm lxii:5).

3. The Realization of Faith: Verses 9-11. Faith makes things real. It lifts above the circumstances of life. The brother of low degree in the midst of his trials can glory in realizing faith that he is exalted, while the rich believer can rejoice in faith in his trials, that he is made low, that he can suffer loss, and learn from it his own poverty and lowness, realizing that all his riches are but for a moment, transitory "because as the flower of the grass he will pass away." This is the realization of faith in the believer; the believer of low degree in the midst of trials realizes that he is exalted, he glories in that, while the rich learns his low estate, that riches will fade away, but that he possesses an inheritance that fadeth not away.

4. The Conquest of Faith: Verses 12-15. Here is a beatitude: "Blessed is the man that endureth temptation; for when he is proved, he shall receive the crown of life, which the Lord hath promised to them that love Him." Overcoming faith will be rewarded. As the poor believer, or the rich believer, endures temptation, is proved and overcomes through faith, the Lord will give to him the promised crown of life.

The sources of temptations are mentioned in connection with this beatitude. There are two sources of temptations. There are temptations, the trial of faith which comes from God for our own good; there is a temptation of the flesh, of inward evil, which is not of God, but of the devil. Trial of faith God permits, but when it comes to temptations of evil, to do evil, to be tempted in this fashion, God never is the author of that. God cannot be tempted with evil, nor tempteth He any man.

This passage settles the question with which so many believers are troubled: "Could the Lord Jesus Christ sin?" They generally quote in connection with this Hebrews iv:15, that He was tempted in all points as we are. They claim that "all points" includes temptation to sin coming from within. Even excellent Christians are at sea about this question. Our Lord Jesus Christ is very God. Being manifested in the flesh does not mean that He laid aside His Deity. James says, "God cannot be tempted with evil," for God is absolutely holy. Therefore our Lord could not be tempted with evil. He had nothing of fallen man in Him; the prince of this world (Satan) came and found nothing in Him. Furthermore, the correct translation of Hebrews iv:15 is as follows: But was in all points tempted like as we *are, apart from sin.* In all other points our blessed Lord was tempted, but never by indwelling sin, for He was absolutely holy in His human nature, given to Him by the Holy Spirit.

It is otherwise with man fallen, he is drawn away of his own lust and enticed. The working, as revealed in verses 14-15, is illustrated in the case of David when lust brought forth sin and death (2 Sam. xi).

5. The Result of Faith: Verses 16-27. Evil has been traced to its source, and now we come to the other side. From God cometh every good and perfect gift and He is a God who does not change; with Him there is no variation, neither shadow that is cast by turning. The greatest good and the greatest gift from such a God is the gift of His Only Begotten Son. Those who believe Him that sent the Son of God into the world (John v:24) are born again by the Word of Truth (see John iii:5; 1 Peter i:23; Ephes. i:13) to be a kind of first fruits of His creatures. His own holy nature is thus communicated to those who believe; it is the result of faith. Of that new nature, the divine nature, it is written in 1 John iii:9: "He that is born of God doth not commit sin; for his seed remaineth in him; and he can not sin, because he is born of God." It means that there is no evil in the new nature; it is a holy nature, it will never tempt to sin. But the believer has an old nature, and that is evil, nor can it ever be anything else, "for that which is born of the flesh is flesh." Thus, begotten again by His own good and gracious will, we are the first fruits of that new creation which in God's own time will be revealed.

This new nature must produce the fruits of righteousness, hence the practical exhortation, "Wherefore, my beloved brethren, let every man be swift to hear, slow to speak, slow to wrath. For the wrath of man worketh not the righteousness of God." Hearing is the attitude of true faith, ever listening to that which God speaks in His Word; then slow to speak, because speech gives expression to what we are; and it needs caution not to let the old nature express itself; and slow to wrath, which is the flesh. Wrath does not work that practical righteousness which is pleasing to God. Then there is to be, as a result of true faith, a laying aside of all filthiness, all superfluity of naughtiness; this is the same putting off of which we read in the Pauline Epistles (Col. iii, etc.). This putting off is not the working of the law, but it is the result of the implanted Word, which received in meekness, saves; it is both the means of true salvation and the working out of that salvation into results of righteousness. But it needs more than hearers of the Word; we must be doers of it.

"But whoso looketh into the perfect law of liberty, and continueth, he being not a forgetful hearer, but a doer that worketh, this man shall be blessed indeed." What is the law of liberty? It is not the law of Moses as some have imagined. The perfect law of liberty is explained in the context. It is the Word of God by which the believer is begotten again, it is the implanted Word, which teaches, instructs, guides and directs; it is the life which flows from the new nature, subject to the Word of God. It has often been very aptly described as a loving parent who tells his child that he must go here or there; that is, the very places which he knows perfectly the child would be gratified to visit. Such is the law of liberty; as if one said to the child: 'Now, my child, you must go and do such and such a thing,' all the while knowing you cannot confer a greater favor on the child. It has not at all the character of resisting the will of the child, but rather of directing his affection in the will of the object dearest to him. The child is regarded and led according to the love of the parent, who knows what the desire of the child is—a desire that has been, in virtue of a new nature, implanted by God Himself in the child. He has given him a life that loves His ways and His Word, that hates and revolts from evil, and is pained most of all by falling through unwatchfulness into sin, if it seemed ever so little. The law of liberty therefore consists not so much in a restraint of gratifying the old man, as in guiding and guarding the new; for the heart's delight is in what is good and holy and true; the Word of God on the one hand exercises us in cleaving to that which is the joy of the Christian's heart, and strengthens us in our detestation of all that we know to be offensive to the Lord."*

This is the law of perfect liberty and in doing this there is blessedness. Then follows a definition of pure and undefiled religion before God and the Father. Religion does not mean here the inner life, but the outward manifestation of it. The fatherless and the widows are God's special objects of love and care; to visit such in their affliction is Christlike. How often this is quoted by those who do not believe in the Gospel of Grace and in the Cross of Christ, as if works of kindness were the true religion, by which man is saved and pleasing to God. The whole chapter shows how erroneous such an application is. And the other definition "to keep himself unspotted from the world," a true life of self surrender and separation, is generally overlooked.

---

*Kelly on James.

II. THE ROYAL LAW. FAITH AND WORKS.

CHAPTER II.

1. The Faith of Christ With Respect to Persons. 1-5.
2. The Royal Law. 6-13.
3. Faith Must be Manifested by Works. 14-26.

1. The Faith of Christ with Respect to Persons. Verses 1-5. Here we have the synagogue mentioned, sufficient evidence that these Jewish believers were still gathering together in the Jewish fashion, and were not an ecclesia, an assembly, gathered out. The Epistle to the Hebrews, written many years after the Epistle of James, exhorted them to leave the camp behind and go outside of it (Hebrews xiii:13). Now in the synagogue among unbelieving Jews the rich man with his gold ring and fine clothing was accorded all honor, received the foremost place, while the poor man was told to stand up.* Such a practice is not according to the faith of our Lord Jesus Christ, the Lord of Glory, who Himself became poor so that by His poverty we might be rich. Faith, so prominent in the opening chapter of this Epistle, is here again insisted upon. Their action, even, in so small a matter as preference of the rich and influential, was not according to that faith, which worketh by love. "Hearken, my beloved brethren, Hath not God chosen the poor of this world, rich in faith, heirs of the kingdom which He hath promised to them that love Him?"

2. The Royal Law. Verses 6-13. They had despised the poor, who were believers and walked in faith, while the rich oppressed them and dragged them before the judgment-seats. These of course were not believers, but mere professors, which again shows the mixed conditions of their gatherings. Furthermore, these rich people with their shameful behavior had blasphemed "that worthy Name" by which they were called, the name of the Lord of Glory. This respect of persons was a sin against the royal law:

*The same spirit prevails in many "churches" too, with their pew rents, sometimes auctioned off to the highest bidder, while the poor are not welcomed in such aristocratic surroundings.

"Thou shalt love thy neighbor as thyself." "If ye have respect to persons ye commit sin, and are convicted by the law as trangressors." If it is the matter of keeping the law, it must be kept in every detail and the entire law "for whosoever shall keep the whole law, and yet offend in one point, he is guilty of all." They were in their consciences still under the law, not having fully seen "the law of liberty" which is the perfect law, flowing as we have learned from the first chapter, from the new nature guided by the Holy Spirit, producing the walk in the Spirit, thus fulfilling the righteousness of the law. James, therefore, appeals to the ten commandments as a witness to arouse their consciences. Then he mentions once more the law of liberty. "So speak ye, and so do, as they that be judged by the law of liberty. For judgment shall be without mercy to him that hath shown no mercy. Mercy rejoiceth over judgment." The perfect law of liberty produces mercy in the believer, but where no mercy is shown, no mercy can be expected, but judgment. "With what measure ye mete, it shall be measured to you again." (Matthew vii:2).

3. Faith Must be Manifested by Works. Verses 14-26. This section of the Epistle has produced much perplexity in the minds of some and led to a great deal of controversy. As it is well known, Dr. Martin Luther, thinking that James tried to answer and contradict Paul's statement in Romans, called James "an Epistle of straw." Others also hold that James corrects the Epistles to the Romans and Galatians, the one being the inspired statement unfolding the Gospel of grace, the other the defense of that Gospel. But how could James answer either Epistle when they were not at all in existence, but written years later? When Paul wrote Romans and Galatians he knew James' Epistle. But did Paul try to correct James' argument? Not by any means. Both James and Paul wrote under the guidance of the Holy Spirit. Any thought of correcting a mistake impeaches the inerrancy of the Word of God.

There is no difficulty at all connected with this passage. The Holy Spirit through James shows that true faith which justifies before God must be evidenced by works. "What should it profit, my brethren, though a man may say that he hath faith, and have not works? Can faith save?" What kind of faith does he mean? It is a faith which assents to certain dogmas, consisting in a mental, intellectual assent, but it is not the living faith. A living faith manifests itself in works. That is what James insists upon. In their synagogue were those who professed to believe, but they did not show by their actions that they had the faith given by God; they only said that they had faith, works, as the proof of true faith were absent. "If a brother or a sister be naked (the fatherless and widows of the closing verse of the previous chapter), and destitute of daily food, and one of you say unto them, Depart in peace, be ye warmed and filled; notwithstanding ye give them not those things which are needful to the body; what doth it profit?" The answer to this question is, it certainly profits nothing. Such a behavior shows that the professed faith is dead. "So also faith, if it have not works, is dead in itself." The quality of faith is defined in the nineteenth verse. "Thou believest there is one God"—that which the Jew boasts of, that he believes in one God, and not like the heathen in many gods—"thou doest well; the demons also believe and tremble." Demons who also believe are still demons; so a man may believe and still be the natural man, live and act as such. The seal of true faith is works.

This the Holy Spirit now illustrates through the case of Abraham and Rahab, so different from each other, the one the Father of the faithful, the other the harlot of Jericho. The works of both bear witness to the character of true faith which produced them. In the case of Abraham he offered up his only son. Of Abraham it was said "he believed God." That he acted as he did, in unquestioning and unhesitating obedience, was the proof that he believed God. What he did was the seal put on his faith, by which he was justified before God. Rahab also believed, and her faith was demonstrated when she received the spies, hid them and associated herself with the people of God, while she separated herself from her own people. Thus faith was seen as a perfect faith, as the true faith, by works. This is what the Holy Spirit teaches through James. In Romans justification before God is taught, which is by faith only. James does not say that our works justify us before God; such are not needed before an omniscient God, for He sees the faith of the heart, which man does not see. It is in exercise with regard to Him, by trust in His Word, in Himself, by receiving His testimony in spite of everything within and without—this true faith God sees and knows. But when our fellow-men ask, show me, then that faith shows itself by works. It is our justification before man. The argument is concluded by the terse comparison: "For as the body without the spirit is dead, so faith without works is dead also."

III. THE EVILS OF THE TONGUE CORRECTED

CHAPTER III.

1. The Tongue and its Work. 1-12.
2. The Wisdom which is earthly and the Wisdom that is from above. 13-18.

1. The Tongue and its Work: Verses 1-12. The practical character of this Epistle is still more evidenced by the contents of this chapter. The tongue is the member of the human body which is made prominent. The human tongue is a great and wonderful gift of the Creator; with which no other earthly creature is endowed. It is written: "Out of the abundance of the heart the mouth speaketh." It therefore reveals the real condition of the heart and by what it is governed.

The opening verse exhorts to caution as to teaching: "My brethren, be not many teachers, knowing that we shall receive a greater judgment." Here another Jewish characteristic is mentioned. They are naturally forward and love to be heard, taking leadership. It seems as if many wanted to be teachers and exercise public ministry. Perhaps this may refer to the "speaking in tongues" also, and the abuse of it as mentioned in 1 Corinthians xiv:20-33. In the first chapter the exhortation was given "slow to speak"; here it is applied to teaching. The exhortation is interesting in its bearing. First, is the warning not to assume leadership in teaching for self-display; even teaching as given to the members of the body of Christ must be carefully exercised, for it carries with it great responsibility, for one may preach to others and be himself disapproved (1 Cor. ix:27). If one is a teacher he must also practice what he teaches, otherwise he shall receive a greater judgment, not as to salvation, but as to disapproval before the award seat of Christ. In the second place, the exhortation shows that ministry among these Jewish Christians was in perfect liberty; they did not possess among themselves a special class in whom public teaching was vested. The next verse broadens and refers to speaking in general. The perfect man is he who does not offend in a word and therefore is able to govern the whole body. This introduces the tongue and its twofold possibility. "Behold we put bits in the horses mouths, that they may obey us; and we turn about their whole body. Behold also the ships, which though they be so great, and are driven of fierce winds, yet are they turned about with a very small helm, whithersoever the governor listeth. Even so the tongue is a little member, and boasteth great things. Behold how great a matter a little fire kindleth! And the tongue is a fire, a world of iniquity; so is the tongue among our members, that it defileth the whole body, and setteth on fire the course of nature when it is set on fire by Gehenna." Horses, with their powerful bodies, are governed, led about and directed by the bit in their mouths; great ships which are driven about by gales and hurricanes, are steered by a small rudder, and so the human tongue is a little member which controls the whole man. It is like a tiny spark, yet that spark can set everything on fire and produce a disastrous conflagration. "Behold how much wood is kindled by how small a fire"—this is the correct rendering of the text. The tongue of the natural man, unrestrained by anything, is a fire. It defiles the whole body. Our Lord speaks of this. "That which cometh out of the man, that defileth the man. For from within, out of the heart of men, proceed evil thoughts, adulteries, fornications, murders, thefts covetousness, deceit, lasciviousness, an evil eye, blasphemy, pride, foolishness; all these evil things come from within, and defile the man" (Mark vii:20-23).

The tongue is the medium to reveal all these evils of the heart, and by its use for evil becomes the seducer of others. It can set everything on fire, if it is set on fire by Gehenna, (translated, hell); when it is under the control of the author of sin.

"For every kind of beasts and birds, of creeping things and things in the sea, is tamed and hath been tamed of mankind; but the tongue can no man tame; it is a restless evil, full of deadly poison. Therewith bless we the Lord and Father, and therewith curse we men, made after the likeness of God. Out of the same mouth cometh forth blessing and cursing. My brethren, these things ought not so to be. Doth the fountain send forth out of the same opening sweet and bitter? Can a fig-tree, my brethren, yield olives, or a vine figs? Neither can salt water yield sweet."

James vehemently attacks this evil, yet in the spirit of love, as seen by the repeated address, "My brethren." Sins of the tongue are especially prominent among Jews; evil speaking, back-biting and lying, so frequently mentioned in their own Scriptures. He speaks of the power man has to tame every kind of beasts and birds, even the creeping things, as serpents and things in the sea; but man, the conqueror of the brute creation, is helpless when it comes to the taming of the tongue; the tongue can no man tame. David knew of this, for he wrote: "I said, I will take heed of my ways, that I sin not with my tongue; I will keep my mouth with a bridle, while the wicked is before me" (Psa. xxxix:1). All resolutions man makes to keep his tongue in subjection are unsuccessful. But if man has a new nature with the Holy Spirit dwelling there, the tongue can be governed and its evils overcome. Yet what sin is more frequently found among God's people than the sins of the tongue. It needs a constant watching and words must be weighed. Idle words, words which are not according to truth, or which reflect upon the character of another child of God, insinuating evil, magnifying faults, or words which belittle, words of envy and strife—are the sins of the tongue prevalent among God's people. How well then to consider constantly the exhortation of the first chapter of this Epistle: "Let every man be swift to hear, slow to speak, slow to wrath" (i-19). The tongue is a restless evil; it is unceasingly at it and carries in its sinful use deadly poison.

Blessing and curse may be expressed by the tongue. While on the one hand, the tongue is an instrument of evil and for evil, the tongue of the believer, on the other hand, should be an instrument of righteousness and for the glory of God. What greater occupation on earth is possible than true worship in Spirit and truth! Through the tongue we can praise and exalt the Lord, bear testimony to that worthy Name, tell others of Him and become channels for eternal blessing. But how quickly, if uncontrolled, it may be used in the service of sin. Peter uttered with his tongue his great, God-given confession, "Thou art the Christ, the Son of the living God." But a short time after, that same tongue became the mouthpiece of Satan, when he rebuked the Lord for saying that He would go to Jerusalem to suffer and to die. What an inconsistency the tongue of man reveals! No such thing is found in nature anywhere. A tree does not produce two kinds of fruit; a fig tree bears no olives; a vine does not produce figs; nor does the same fountain gush forth salt water and sweet water.

2. The Wisdom that is Earthly and the Wisdom that is From Above: Verses 13-18. "Who is wise and understanding among you? Let him shew out of a good behavior his works in meekness of wisdom. But if you have bitter envying and strife in your heart, boast not and lie not against the truth. This is not the wisdom which cometh down from above, but it is earthly, sensual, demoniacal. For where envying and strife is, there is disorder and every evil thing." This exhortation, also, is suited to the Jewish believers to whom it was originally addressed. They are noted still for their jealousies, their strife and self-exaltation, these fruits of the fallen nature of man, the works of the flesh; they are, of course, also found among Gentile believers. Envyings, the sectarian spirit, the party spirit, producing bitterness and contentions, these things are not the manifestations of the wisdom which is from above, the fruit of the new nature and of the Spirit, but it is the earthly wisdom, springing from the natural man, behind which stands the author of sin.

"But the wisdom which is from above is first pure, then peaceable, gentle and easy to be entreated, full of mercy and good fruits, without contention, without hypocrisy; and the fruit of righteousness is sown in peace for those who make peace." This is the other side, the manifestation of the wisdom from above, the true fruits of the new nature and of the Spirit of God. It is first pure and then peaceable. It is pure, because it comes from God and leads to God. That which is from God cannot tolerate evil; it repudiates it. It aims at the glory of God and maintains His holy character. As a result it is peaceable, it seeks the fruits of peace among men, through the exercise of that love which the Holy Spirit describes in 1 Corinthians xiii. It is gentle: "Let your gentleness be known to all men" (Phil. iv:5); it is easy to be entreated, ready to yield. It knows nothing of stubbornness, prejudice and opinionativeness, the sources of so much strife and contention among believers. When a man is conscious that his wisdom is of a superior kind, one can understand his unwillingness to have his mind or will disputed; but the truth is, that there is nothing which so marks the superiority of grace and truth and wisdom, that God gives, as patience, and the absence of anxiety to push what one knows is right and true. It is an inherent and sure sign of weakness somewhere, when a man is ever urgent in pressing the value of his own words and opinions, or caviling habitually at others. The fruit of righteousness is sown in peace, and produces peace.

IV. FURTHER EXHORTATIONS TO RIGHT LIVING.

CHAPTER IV.

1. Fightings and Worldliness Rebuked. 1-6.
2. The Godly Walk. 7-17.

1. Fightings and Worldliness Rebuked: Verses 1-6. A strong rebuke follows the statements concerning the wisdom from beneath and the wisdom from above. It must be borne in mind that these exhortations are addressed to the twelve tribes scattered abroad; to say that these words mean believers only would be a serious mistake; while Christians are contemplated, those of the tribes of Israel who are not believers are equally in view. It applies therefore to those who were born of God, real believers, and to those who were not, an entirely different matter from the Pauline Epistles, which are exclusively addressed to the saints.

There was much strife and contention amongst them. Whence come wars and fightings? Certainly not from the wisdom which is above, which is first pure and then peaceable. But wars and fightings are the fruits of the old nature, the flesh. They come from the pleasures which war in the members. The gratification of the lusts of the natural man produces fightings and not the new nature, that which is from above; this includes all forms of lusts, not only those of the flesh, but the lust for power, the lust for pre-eminence and leadership; the lusts of the mind. "Ye lust and have not;" there is nothing that can satisfy the heart of man; any kind of lust will end in disappointment and remorse. "Ye kill and covet and cannot obtain." This is the way of the world in sin and away from God; it shows that James speaks to the unbelieving of the twelve tribes, and pictures their condition. "Ye fight and war. Ye have not because ye ask not. Ye ask and receive not because ye ask amiss, that ye may consume it in your pleasures." The natural man is also religious and as such prays. But their prayers sprang from the old nature, the desires of the flesh; they received not because they asked amiss. They prayed for selfish things, incited by selfish motives, so that they might gratify their sinful natures. Even true believers often ask and receive not, because they ask amiss, out of selfish reasons, to minister to their own pleasures and gratification. If the Lord would answer such prayers He would minister to that which is evil.

The world and its unsatisfying pleasures controlled those described in the foregoing words, some of whom may have been professing believers. The wisdom which is earthly, sensual and demoniac, they followed. And now the writer breaks out in a passionate exclamation: "Ye adulteresses, know ye not that the friendship of the world is enmity with God? whosoever therefore would be the friend of the world maketh himself an enemy of God." Here others than unbelievers are contemplated. The sphere of the natural man is the world; his walk is according to the course of this world; he is governed by the lust of the flesh, the lust of eyes and the pride of life. As such he is an enemy of God by wicked works and by nature a child of wrath. (Ephesians ii:1-3). The true believer, saved by grace, is not of the world, even as our Lord was not of the world (John xvii:16). Grace has severed the believer from the world; the Cross of Christ has made him dead to the world and the world dead unto him. Hence the exhortation in John's Epistle "Love not the world, neither the things of the world. If any man love the world, the love of the Father is not in him. For all that is in the world, the lust of the flesh, and the lust of the eyes, and the pride of life, is not of the Father, but is of the world" (1 John ii:15-16). And believers may turn back to the world, like Demas, and love it for a time. James calls such adulteresses; they leave Him to whom they are espoused, even Christ, and turn to another. The term must have reminded the Israelites of the Old Testament passages in which unfaithful, apostate Israel is pictured as an adulteress and playing the harlot (Jeremiah iii:9; Ezekiel xvi:23; Hosea ii). It is a solemn exhortation which every true believer should consider carefully; friendship with the world means enmity against God. Verse 5 should be rendered as follows: "Or think ye that the Scripture speaketh in vain? Doth the Spirit, who dwelleth in us, long unto envying?" All the Scriptures testify that worldliness and godliness cannot exist together; think ye then that these Scriptures speak in vain? And the Holy Spirit, who dwells in the believer, does not lust unto envy, for He opposes the flesh and those who walk in the Spirit do not fulfill the lusts of the flesh. But he giveth more grace, yea grace sufficient to overcome by faith the world, for faith is the victory that overcomes the world. He quotes Proverbs iii:34. God resisteth the proud, but giveth grace unto the humble.

2. The Godly Walk: Verses 6-17. Exhortations to a godly, holy walk follow. Submit yourselves, therefore to God; be subject unto Him, have no friendship with the world, but be His friend. There is one who would drag the believer back into the world, as Pharaoh tried to get Israel back to Egypt. Guard against it by resisting the devil and he will flee from you. This is a blessed promise which all His faithful people have tested at all times. We are not to flee from the devil, but to resist him and as we do so in the name of our Lord, the enemy will be helpless and flee from us. Another blessed exhortation follows. "Draw nigh to God and He will draw nigh to you." Next James addresses again those who had not yet fully turned to the Lord. It is a call to repentance. "Cleanse your hands, ye sinners; and purify your hearts, ye doubleminded. Be afflicted, and mourn, and weep; let your laughter be turned to mourning, and your joy to heaviness. Humble yourselves in the sight of the Lord, and He shall exalt you."

The attitude towards other brethren is made clear in verses 11 and 12: "Speak not one against another, brethren." Speaking evil, the sin of the tongue is once more mentioned by James. There are seven verses in which exhortations to guard the tongue and speech are given: i:19, 26, ii:12, iii:9, 16, iv:11 and v:9. It seems that this must have been the besetting sin of these believing Jews. Evil, of course, must always be judged, whether it is unsound doctrine or an evil conduct; this belongs to the responsibility of a believer. But God alone, the righteous Judge, knows the heart and its motives. Speaking against a brother and judging him, that is, pronouncing a sentence of condemnation upon him, is the same as speaking against the law and judging the law. But if one judges the law, the same is not a doer of the law, but a judge; doing this we take the place of Him who is both, the lawgiver and the judge, that is the Lord. The final paragraph urges dependence on the Lord and warns against making plans for the future without looking to the Lord and His will concerning His people. "Go to now, ye that say, Today or tomorrow we will go into this city, and spend a year there, and buy and sell, and get gain; whereas ye know not what shall be on the morrow." Such a language shows self-will, forgetfulness of God, and self-confidence. It is planning with God left out. No one knows what the morrow may bring forth; but God knows. "For what is your life? It is even a vapor, that appeareth for a little time, and then vanisheth away. For that ye ought to say, If the Lord will and we live, we will also do this or that." The child of God who walks in godly fear, trusting the Lord, planning as under Him, will constantly remember that all depends on the Lord and on His will. It is a wholesome habit to add always, when we speak of the future, "if the Lord will and we live"; this is pleasing in His sight and a testimony of our submission to Him and dependence on Him. Otherwise it is the boasting, vain-gloriousness of the self-secure world, which boasts and plans, without thinking of God and His will. The last verse must not be detached from what goes before. "To him, therefore, that knoweth to do good and doeth it not, to him it is sin." Sin does not consist only in doing evil, but if we do not the good we know, it is also sin. If we do not act according to the fact that we are entirely dependent on God as to the future, we sin.

"This verse should forever settle the question of sinless perfection for a Christian: 'To him who knoweth to do good, and doeth it not, to him it is sin.' This is much more, of course, than the prohibition of positive evil. There is a negative evil which we have carefully to keep before us. The responsibility of knowing what it is good to do is one that, while we may in a general way allow it, yet deserves far deeper consideration than we often would even desire to give it. How solemn it is to think of all the good that we *might* do, and yet have *not* done! How slow we are to recognize that this, too, is sin! We are so apt to claim for ourselves a kind of freedom here which is not Scriptural freedom; and there is no doubt, also, that we may abuse a text like this to legality, if there be legality in our hearts. We are to be drawn, not driven. Yet the neglect of that which is in our hand to do—which we, perhaps, do not realize our capacity for, and that only through a spirit of self-indulgence or a timidity which is not far removed from this—such neglect, how hard it is to free ourselves of it, and how much do we miss in this way of that which would be fruitful in blessing for ourselves as well as for others! for, indeed, we can never sow fruit of this kind without reaping what we have sown; and the good that we can do to others, even if it requires the most thorough self-sacrifice, yet will be found in the end to have yielded more than it cost, and to have wrought in the interests of him who has not considered even or sought this."*

V. THE COMING OF THE LORD AND THE LIFE OF FAITH

CHAPTER V.

1. The Oppression by the Rich and their coming Doom. 1-6.
2. Be Patient unto the Coming of the Lord. 7-12.
3. The Prayer of Faith and the Life of Faith. 13-20.

The Oppression by the Rich and their Coming Doom: Verses 1-6. The two classes whom James addresses stand out very prominently in this final chapter of his Epistle.

---

*Numerical Bible.

The rich oppressors certainly are not believers but the unbelieving rich; they are not addressed as "brethren"; but others are in verse 7 and exhorted to patience. Both classes, the unbelieving rich and the believing remnant are confronted by the coming of the Lord. "Go to now, ye rich, weep and howl for your miseries that are coming upon you. Your riches are corrupted and your garments are motheaten. Your gold and your silver are rusted; and their rust shall be for a testimony against you, and shall eat your flesh as fire. Ye have heaped together treasures in the last days."

The present age, which began with the death and resurrection of our Lord, and the coming of the Holy Spirit, is spoken of as "the last days" and "the last time" (see Heb. i:2 and 1 John ii:18); this age will be followed by the dispensation of the fullness of times, the times of restoration as promised by God's holy prophets (Eph. i:10; Acts iii:19-20), the age of the Kingdom when Christ reigns and His saints with Him. And this present age will end with the coming of the Lord to execute judgment, to right all wrong and judge all unrighteousness. These rich Israelites heaped treasures together, and, as we shall see later, acted outrageously, thereby showing that they did not believe in the day of the Lord, when He will be manifested in judgment glory. Yet their own Scriptures announced exactly that which James here states. See Isaiah ii:10-20 and especially Zephaniah i:14-18. In anticipation of that coming day he calls on them to weep and howl, and announces the fate of their treasures.

Let us remember that the Epistle was written years before the destruction of Jerusalem. When Jerusalem fell, and even before its fall, many of the rich Jews became paupers; they were ruined, tortured and murdered, as Josephus tells us. The fall of Jerusalem with its awful horrors, in the year 70 A. D., was a judgment of the Lord, but not the day of the Lord and the Coming of the Lord. What happened then to the stubborn unbelieving masses will happen again, only on a larger scale during the coming great tribulation and when the Lord returns in power and in great glory. We believe therefore, that this exhortation to the rich has a special bearing for the future, during the very end of the age.

But they were oppressing the poor as well. "Behold, the hire of the laborers who mowed your fields, which is of you kept back by fraud, crieth out; and the cries of them that reaped have entered into the ears of the Lord of Sabaoth. Ye have lived delicately on the earth, and taken your pleasure; ye have nourished your hearts in a day of slaughter. Ye have condemned, ye have killed the Just One; he doth not resist you." Oppression of the poor, yea, the poor of their own people, is another characteristic of the Jewish people. The Prophet Amos rebuked it in his day, when the poor were downtrodden and robbed by the rich. It is so today and will be so in the future. And the money which was taken from the poor was used by the rich to live in luxury and wanton pleasures. The spirit they manifested in heaping treasures together, oppressing the poor and needy, robbing them, and living in pleasure, is the same which condemned and killed the Just One, the Lord Jesus Christ, who did not resist. To apply these words primarily and altogether to our Lord can hardly be done. What was done to the Lord of Glory these unbelievers did to His true followers. It will be so again during the great tribulation, under Antichrist, when the godly remnant will be persecuted by those who side with the false Messiah. See Psalm lxxix:1-3; Daniel xii:1; Matthew xxiv:9-25; Revelation xi, xii and xiii.

2. Be Patient unto the Coming of the Lord: Verses 7-12. "Be patient therefore, brethren, until the coming of the Lord. Behold the husbandman waiteth for the precious fruit of the earth, being patient over it, until it receive the early and latter rain. Be ye also patient; stablish your hearts; for the coming of the Lord is at hand." He addresses in these words the believers, the suffering remnant amongst the unbelieving masses which attended the synagogue. They are to be patient and suffer in patience, without resisting. The coming of the Lord, which is mentioned twice in these verses, is His visible and glorious manifestation, the same which our Lord speaks of in Matthew xxiv:30-31. The first Epistle to the Thessalonians, which contains that unique revelation of the Coming of the Lord for His Saints, the resurrection of the holy dead and the sudden transformation of the living saints, to be caught up together in clouds to meet Him in the air (1 Thess. iv:13-18) had not yet been given. The mystery "we shall not all sleep but be changed in a moment, in the twinkling of an eye" (1 Corinth. xv), was then unknown. And let us note here, that this is one of the mysteries nowhere made known in the Old Testament. The coming of the Lord, we repeat, is that coming which is so many times announced in the Prophetic Word of the Scriptures. "The first generation of Christians expected to witness in the near future the personal reappearance of Christ on earth to close the old dispensation by punishing unbelievers, and delivering the Christians. These expectations were partly realized when the fall of Jersusalem closed the old Jewish dispensation by the destruction of the Temple and the final cessation of the Levitical worship of Jehovah. At the same time misery and ruin befell the Jewish nation which had rejected and crucified our Lord. As regards any more exact fulfilment, the statements of the New Testament must be interpreted according to the principle laid down in 2 Peter iii:8 and 1 John ii:18."* That the destruction of Jerusalem and the judgment of the nation was predicted by our Lord is known to all, that the event when it came in the year 70 is the coming of the Lord, is not true.

James exhorts his suffering brethren to be like the husbandman who has to wait between the sowing time and the harvest. But here is another wrong interpretation. The latter rain of which James speaks has been foolishly interpreted as meaning a spiritual latter rain, another Pentecost. This is one of the star arguments of present day Pentecostalism with its supposed revival of apostolic gifts. The

*From New Century Bible. One is grateful to find this paragraph in a work which is more or less on the side of the Destructive Criticism.

former and latter rain of which James speaks has no such meaning; it is purely the rainfall in nature. In Palestine there are two distinct rainy seasons, one in the Spring, the other in the Fall. (See Deut. xi:14.)

Then follow other words of encouragement. "Murmur not, brethern, one against the other, that ye be not judged; behold the judge standeth before the door." Among themselves they were to guard against any friction and fretfulness, always remembering Him who is the Judge, and who standeth before the door. They were also to remember the examples in suffering and patience of the prophets, who spoke in the name of the Lord, the patience of Job, and how blessedly his suffering ended through the pity and mercy of the Lord. There is a warning also against oath making, such a common thing amongst the Jews. (See our Lord's warning in the Sermon on the Mount, Matthew v:33-37.)

3. The Prayer of Faith and the Life of Faith: Verses 13-20. The Epistle closes with practical exhortations to prayer and the exercise of faith. "Is any among you suffering? Let him pray." A short but weighty instruction. Instead of murmuring, as their forefathers did, instead of complaining in suffering, prayer must be exercised. The godly in Israel always made prayer their refuge and especially are the Psalms rich in this direction. "Is any cheerful? Let him sing psalms." The Psalms were used extensively in the synagogue. To teach upon this statement, as has been done, that the church should sing nothing but the Psalms, and reject the great hymns of the saints of God of all ages, born often in adversity and in deep soul exercise, is far fetched. Much in the Psalms does not express true Christianity at all. "Is any among you sick? Let him call for the elders of the assembly; and let them pray over him, anointing him with oil in the name of the Lord; and the prayer of faith shall save him that is sick, and the Lord shall raise him up; and if he have committed sins, they shall be forgiven him." This exhortation demands a closer scrutiny and examination. Of late this instruction by James has been greatly misapplied by faith-healers. There are many extremists who teach that here is a commandment to the church how sickness among the Saints should be dealt with; that means, to alleviate bodily ills, must be fully discarded and if they are used, it is unbelief in the power of God and a hindrance to faith. There are men and women all over Christendom, who go about with a message of healing of diseases, who anoint the sick by the hundreds and thousands, claiming that this is the only way that illness is to be treated. Then these same healers claim miraculous cures which are, after careful investigation, mostly found to be falsehoods. Some of these advocates of this method of healing, denouncing means and the use of physicians, were taken sick and had to use means to overcome their bodily ills. The entire subject of "Faith-Healing" we cannot examine here; nor can we enlarge upon the claims of "Christian Science" and other metaphysical cults and systems. Supernatural healing of diseases is claimed by Romish Catholicism, by the shrines and holy places of the Greek Orthodox church, by Spiritism, Mormonism and in many pagan systems. We confine our remarks to the passage before us.

It has been explained by some that the words of James mean that which should be done in case sickness unto death has seized upon a believer. It is then interpreted to mean "Prayer shall save the dying man from the punishment of his sins; and after his death, the Lord will raise him up in resurrection." This view we reject. No prayer of faith is needed for the coming physical resurrection of a believer. Romanism has made out of it "the sacrament of extreme unction" which is another invention.

Inasmuch as "the anointing with oil" seems to be the point most stressed by divine healers, we shall examine this first. What does it mean? Here we must remember the Jewish character of the Epistle. We have shown before that the believers whom James addresses were still closely identified with Judaism, hence they practised many things peculiar to Judaism. Anointing with oil was extensively used in the ceremonies of the Jews. Kings and priests were anointed, oil being liberally poured upon the head, denoting outwardly the fact of consecration to office, and symbolically the Spirit of God, which they needed for the exercise of their functions. Furthermore, oil was also very widely used for health and comfort. It was and is still a great remedial agent in the Orient. The Good Samaritan poured into the wounds of the man who had fallen among the thieves oil and wine. Oil was used in cases of fever and most generally in skin diseases. Anointing the sick with oil was a general practice, as can be shown from talmudical literature. In Mark vi:13, we read "And they cast out many demons, and anointed with oil many that were sick, and healed them." Would they not have been healed if they had not been anointed with oil? The anointing with oil was an old custom which the disciples made use of, but the Lord in commissioning them in connection with the Kingdom message did not tell them that they should anoint the sick with oil; they did it, for such was the universal practice. If James commands these Jewish believers who were sick to be anointed with oil he re-affirmed therefore this old Jewish custom. Oil is something beneficial to the body, a remedy, just as wine is recommended by the Spirit of God as a remedy for the ills of the body (I Timothy v:23). It is therefore an open question whether oil may not stand here also for legitimate means to be used in case of illness. Divine healers carry with them a small bottle of oil and daub the forehead with a drop of oil, but this is not the anointing commanded here. Where is the authority to say that a drop of oil must be put on the forehead?

But it is very striking that apart from this passage, in this transition epistle, nowhere else in the New Testament (except in Mark vi:13), do we read anything about this anointing with oil in case of sickness. Why did not Paul write to Timothy, who often had infirmities, "Call the elders, let them anoint you with oil," but, instead of it, the divinely given remedy. "a little wine," is urged upon him. And Paul was sick himself, suffered with his eyes, which probably was the thorn in the flesh. Trophimus was sick in Miletus. But nowhere this Jewish ceremony, anointing with oil, is mentioned. The Epistles which are the high-water mark of divine revelation, are the Epistles to the Ephesians and Colossians; we find nothing in these Epistles about healing of diseases by anointing and prayer. Nor is it mentioned in any of the other Pauline Epistles. In Corinthians the gift of healing is found among the gifts of the Spirit, but he who possessed that gift had no need of using oil besides. Our conclusion, then, is that the anointing with oil in this passage is something customary with the Jews, which is not meant to be perpetuated in the church, for if such were the fact the Holy Spirit would have stated it elsewhere. We pass over the question as to true elders, which are to be called. Many of those who go about as divine healers are women. Who has ever heard of "women elders"? In fact, in the public healing services which have become such a common thing in our days, the question of elders is entirely ignored. Big advertisements appear in the papers that services for the healing of the sick are to be held. As a result hundreds come and are ready to do anything, to believe anything, if only some hope is held out that they might be cured. They readily submit to the ceremony of having a little oil put on their foreheads, but the command, that the sick person, is to call for the elders of the church, those of authority, is ignored. The question is, "Do we still have the elders in the Apostolic sense?" These are matters which are completely set aside by modern faith healers.

But the emphasis in the passage is on "the prayer of faith." The prayer of faith, not the anointing with oil, shall save the sick. No believer denies the efficacy of believing prayer, yet always guarded by the condition "if it be His will." In case of sickness the child of God will not send for a physician in the first place, but the believer turns to the Lord and puts himself in His gracious and merciful hands. The passage here seems to be the matter of sickness as a chastening from the Lord on account of specific sins committed. In such a case when self-judgment has brought the matter into His light, the promise can be claimed "the prayer of faith shall save the sick."

"Was it intended to be a direction universally applicable to all cases, and to be carried out at all times, in all places, and under all conditions? Surely—most surely not. For note that there is no question at all as to the result: 'the prayer of faith *shall save* (it is certain) the sick and the Lord will raise him up.'

"Now, we know perfectly well that this is not and *cannot* be the invariable outcome of all sickness. The vast majority of mankind—yes, of Christians—has died as the result of some sickness: has this been because 'elders' have not been called? Have they come to the end of that life here because they were not anointed with oil, and the prayer that always goes up from loving hearts was not the prayer of faith, and since not of faith, was sin? Who would not reject such conclusions with abhorrence? Yet are they inevitable, if this Scripture be pressed as being the one divinely given direction in the case of all sickness.

"In it every act, every movement, must be in faith: that is recognizing the Lord's hand in the sickness, and the Lord's mind in removing it. But where is the great and precious promise on which faith can always rest, that shall make healing sure? In one case only, and that is if the sickness does not come from constitutional weakness, as with Timothy, or the hardship of a Christian devotion as with Epaphroditus, or any other natural cause—but as *a chastening of the Lord* for some specific sins committed, and this confessed and put away, the chastening ceases.

"And this is naturally enough the point of view of such a writer as James. Freedom from sickness consequent on obedience was interwoven in the first covenant: "And the Lord will take away from thee all sickness, and will put none of the diseases of Egypt, which thou knowest upon thee; but will lay them upon all that hate thee"—is that what the Christian desires today: his diseases put on anyone else who may hate him? yet is that involved in that covenant.

"What, then, more natural than that this writer, who, although Christian, is still on the ground of a regenerate and sincerely pious Jew, should regard sickness in a light that is common to both Christian and Jew—as a chastening for sin."*

With this we leave this portion of the Epistle, which has led to so much misunderstanding. To help the reader in getting the true conception we add in a brief appendix, at the close of these annotations, the comment as it is given in the "Numerical Bible."

"Confess, therefore, your sins one to another, that ye may be healed." This brings out fully the fact that the sickness in view is on account of specific sins. When the sins are confessed and judged, grace intervenes, and God in mercy heals. Rome builds upon this passage the miserable invention of the confessional. But it does not mean confession to a man-made "priest," but a simple confiding of believers among themselves.

The great value of prayer is next pointed out by James. "The supplication of a righteous man availeth much in its working"; this is a rendering adopted by many. He cites the case of Elijah. He was a man "of like passions with us" as we learn from the historical record of the Scriptures, which tells us of his great infirmities, as well as of his remarkable faith. He prayed fervently and rain was withheld, he prayed again and God answered his faith. The God of Elijah is our God still, who delights to answer the fervent prayer of the righteous man; the power of prayer can never be separated from the character of him who prays.

"My brethren, if any among you do err from the truth, and one convert him; let him know, that he which converteth a sinner from the error of his way shall save a soul from death, and shall cover a multitude of sins." With this the Epistle ends abruptly. Faith must be manifested by love towards those who err. The exhortation finds an application in a general way, but primarily to those who know the truth

*F. C. Jennings in "Our Hope."

and have backslidden. This is learned from the words "if any among you"; the application in a general way is also fully warranted. The ending without greeting has led some critics to assume, that the Epistle is made up of passages from sermons, compiled quite late, by a man by the name of James. The internal as well as the historical evidences refute this assumption.

APPENDIX
James v:14-16

By F. W. Grant

The anointing with oil in the name of the Lord seems to be the claim of an authority which those of whom we are speaking would be the last to assert. No doubt the emphasis is laid here upon the "prayer of faith," to save the sick; and the prayer of faith certainly should not be lacking with us. We need not doubt how much we should gain if there were a more simple and constant reference to the Lord in these matters, and we cannot but remember the example of old of one who sought not to the Lord, but to the physicians, and died. The use of means that are in our hand may easily be perverted to the slighting of this way of faith; and it would certainly be far better to leave out the means in any case rather than to leave out the Lord. The distinct and united acknowledgment of our dependence upon Him in all these cases is due from us, and we suffer loss if God is not acknowledged; but then for this, no elders or anointing can be needed, and the prescription of these things makes it evident that something more is contemplated here than simply the prayer of faith. Even so, there is no *prohibition* of means, if there be no *prescription* of them; and in God's ordinary way of working He certainly works by them. He could sustain us at any time without food, but we do not ordinarily expect Him to do this, although the food may profit nothing except the Lord please to use it. We cannot but remember in this way the prescription of a little wine to Timothy, while at the same time he was in the very midst of an assembly which had its regularly appointed elders. In Judaism let us remember how, at the beginning of it, God was pleased to act miraculously in a marked way; and in the beginning of Christianity in Jerusalem, we find the same signs and miracles accompanying the Word. This was a most suited testimony to the new doctrine being published, a testimony which was also recognized in our Lord's case by the Jews as that which was to establish a new doctrine (Mark i:27). The waning of all miraculous powers when once the testimony was established is marked, and cannot be denied. People may impute it, as they do impute it, to a lack of faith on the part of Christians; but with regard to such things one might certainly expect faith to be manifested as much as in other things. In fact, they would be things most earnestly clung to, for the manifest benefit and the display of power in them. On the other hand, the prevalence of corrruption which, whatever may be our own individual views of truth, cannot be but acknowledged, would naturally make it less suited that the Church so failing should still preserve her ornaments; but the reason for the decline of miracles is evidently other than this. In the history of the Acts we find an apparent absence of such things, where, for instance, as in Berea, men were employed with the Word itself to test the doctrine by it. Although in general, as the Lord promised, miraculous signs did follow at the beginning those who believed, yet even then this was never universally true. It could not be pleaded as the necessary mark of Christian faith. "Are all workers of miracles?" says the apostle; and the question in itself supposes a negative answer. Thus, if a whole assembly lacked, there was no *necessary* failure, and need be no disappointment in this case; while in Corinth their "coming behind in no gift" was no necessary evidence of a right state of soul. It seems even, one would say, a matter of course that God never meant our daily lives to be full of manifest miracles. He never meant to demonstrate the truth after that fashion. He would leave it, rather, to its own inherent and spiritual power. Men easily crave miracles;

but the whole generation in the wilderness, the constant witness of these, nevertheless perished for their unbelief. The miracles work no faith, although they might, and would, awaken attention to that which God presented as an object for faith; yet to those who believed in Christ, when they saw the miracles, He did not commit Himself (John ii:23-25). Every way it should be plain to-day that what goes for such amongst men commonly is no longer the mark upon true faith or the truth itself which calls for faith. The same things exactly can be wrought by those who deny Christian fundamentals as by those who profess them; and where is the evidence then? No set of men in the present day can be found who can adjust broken bones without surgery. If God wanted to show what He was doing, do we think that a broken bone would be a greater difficulty to Him than anything else?

Moreover, the signs and wonders of the time of the end are spoken of as rather giving evidence to falsity than to truth, to Antichrist than to Christ; and there will be signs and wonders wrought yet, which, as the Lord has said, would deceive, if it were possible, even the very elect. Thus, then we can easily understand (and especially in such an epistle as the present—an epistle to that nation to whom God had testified by signs and wonders of old, and would repeat to them now, in evidence that Christ was in nothing behind Moses) how we should find a reference of this kind to powers which might connect themselves with the elders of the Christian assembly, and yet understand why James should leave us, as it were, at a loss how to apply these things to ourselves. We can never be wrong in believing that the prayer of faith is still really the power that will save the sick, let means be used or not used; but the use of means seems in general rather according to the Lord's mind than against it. His common way is to work through that which He has Himself ordained, and there are plainly herbs for the healing of men. The very presence of such powers is proof that the Lord has given them; and if He has given them, it is for us. Faith can acknowledge Him in these, as well as be perfectly happy in trusting Him apart from all consideration of these. The prohibition of them, if God designed it, would surely be furnished to us.

Moreover, God at no time intended that things should be left, as it were, absolutely in man's hands, even though it were the hand of faith, as the doctrines taught suppose. The prayer of faith may be that which saves the sick, and yet, after all, that be far from meaning that we can find in every case a faith which should do so. God has His own will and His own way; and while we can always reckon upon Him to answer the soul that looks to Him, yet the way of His answer we do not always know. The apostle prays that the thorn in the flesh might depart from him, but it did not depart. God turned it to greater blessing. That was an answer to the prayer, but it was not such an answer as men usually count as that. Could any one suppose that among Christians, if everything were absolutely right, the sick would always be raised up, that death would hardly obtain at all, except in the extremest old age? We may imagine any such fancies, but fancies they are, and nothing else. Yet it is plain there is an appeal to God advocated here which we are always right in making, and from which we may always expect an answer in the goodness of Him whom we address. More than this, the Lord may give distinct light as to His mind that will enable one, as to anything, to ask with assurance, without the possibility of denial. If we are near enough to God for this we have cause indeed to be thankful; but we had better be humble about it, and be very sure that we have it before we claim it.

THE FIRST EPISTLE OF PETER

The First Epistle of Peter

Introduction

The genuineness of this epistle is confirmed by the most ancient sources. Polycarp, who was personally acquainted with the Apostle John, cites the Epistle of Peter. Papias of Hierapolis made use of the Epistle likewise. This was about the middle of the second century. Two quotations of Peter's Epistle are found in a very ancient source, "The Teaching of the Twelve Apostles," a kind of manual going back to 100 A. D. All the other documents of the first and second centuries show that the Epistle was unanimously known and accepted as Peter's.

The critics have not left it unattacked. We do not need to quote the different theories advanced by Cludius, Eichhorn (the man who coined the phrase "higher criticism"), De Wette, Bauer, Davidson, Pfleiderer, Harnack and others. The main objection seems to be that the expressions used in this Epistle are too much like the thoughts and expressions of the Apostle Paul as used in his Epistles, so, as it is assumed, Peter could not have written it. This theory was expanded into the hypothesis that some one must have written it who had spent considerable time with Paul, so that he adopted Pauline ideas and phrases; John Mark has been suggested by some to be that person. Critics have pointed out many parallels with different Pauline Epistles. "In considering these parallels, allowance must be made for ideas and phraseology, hymns, prayers, confessions of faith, and other matter, which was the common property of the primitive church; and would introduce a degree of similarity into the writings of different authors. But much of the thought and language of First Peter belongs to what was characteristic of the teaching of Paul and his followers as distinct from that of the Palestinian or Jewish churches. The parallels in any case, show a dependence upon Pauline teaching. But we may go further. There is a great variety of opinion as to the precise character and extent of the dependence of First Peter on the writings of Paul. It has been suggested that it is just possible that Paul himself was the author of First Peter, the passages in which Peter's name occurs being later insertions; and again that this Epistle and Ephesians were the work of one author. But that dependence, especially on Romans, is very widely recognized."* All these objections, speculations, and theories denying the Petrine authorship are answered by the fact of inspiration. Peter no doubt knew and read the Epistles of Paul; in fact he speaks of them in his second letter (2 Peter iii:15-16). But that does not mean that he copied and reproduced the statements found in some of Paul's Epistles; nor does it mean that he depended on Paul when he wrote his Epistle. The Holy Spirit who guided Paul's pen guided also the hand of Peter; all is the direct work of the Holy Spirit. If Peter uses some of the great truths found in the Epistles of Paul it was because the Spirit of God desired to have them restated. If we examine these parallels closely we discover that they cover the most essential truths of Christianity and are used for practical exhortations. Those whom Peter addressed needed these truths and the practical application. On the other hand there are many internal evidences which prove that none but Peter wrote this Epistle. It has been pointed out that there is a similarity between Peter's statements in the Book of Acts and in this first Epistle. Compare Acts iv:11; ii:32; iii:15 with I Peter ii:7; i:3, 4, 8 and v:i. He also uses a peculiar word for the cross. It is the word "*Tree*" (the Greek word *Xulon*). See Acts v:30; x:39; I Peter ii:24. Furthermore, the writer speaks of having been an eyewitness of the Lord's sufferings (v:1). He describes these sufferings, how He was reviled and reviled not, how He suffered and threatened not. And Peter was an eyewitness of all this. Nor is it without significance that in this Epistle alone the Lord Jesus Christ is called "the chief Shepherd." On the shores of Lake Tiberias the risen Lord

*New Century Bible.

restored Simon Peter to service and told him "shepherd My sheep," hence Peter speaks of the Lord as the chief Shepherd, and also exhorts the elders to be faithful in feeding the flock of God. As it is with all other critical objections to the traditional belief as to the inspired authorship of the different Bible books, the objections against the Petrine authorship of this Epistle are wholly worthless. Peter wrote this Epistle. The date cannot be definitely settled, but must be placed between 62 and 65 A. D.

SIMON PETER

A brief review of the life and service of the Apostle Peter will be helpful in understanding his writings. He was born at Bethsaida in Galilee, from which Philip came also (John i:44, 45). His name was Simon (or Simeon, Acts xv:14) and his father's name was Jonas. He had a brother by name of Andrew, and the three, the father, Simon and Andrew were fishermen at Capernaum. There Simon Peter had his home, as he was a married man (Matthew viii:14; 1 Cor. ix:5). His brother Andrew was a disciple of John the Baptist and when he pointed out the Lord Jesus as the Lamb of God, Andrew followed Him. Andrew brought Peter to the Lord (John i:35-43). When the Lord beheld Him he revealed His omniscience, for He said: "Thou art Simon the son of Jona, thou shalt be called Cephas," which is the Aramaic word for stone. When later Peter, in answer to the question "Whom say ye that I am?" said: "Thou art the Christ the Son of the living God," the Lord Jesus said to him, "Thou art Peter, and upon this rock I will build my church; and the gates of Hades shall not prevail against it" (Matthew xvi:17-18). The Greek word *Petros* means a small rock, or piece of a rock; the Greek for rock is *Petra*, the word our Lord used when He designated the foundation of the church. It is not Peter, but Christ Himself, who is the rock. In his Epistle Peter contradicts by the Spirit of God the miserable invention that he is the rock upon which the church is built, as claimed by Rome and even by Protestant expositors. (See I Peter ii:4-8.) The Gospel records, as well as the Epistle to the Galatians, give us a good description of his peculiar character. He was impulsive, forward and self-confident, yet he was true, loving and faithful. Before he denied the Lord, the Lord Jesus announced Peter's great failure and assured His disciple of His prayer, when Satan would sift him as wheat. In connection with this our Lord gave him a commission. "When thou art converted, strengthen thy brethren." His denial, his bitter repentance, his restoration at the lake of Tiberias, the still greater commission to shepherd the sheep and the lambs of the flock of God, are so well known, that we need not to enlarge on them. The Lord also committed to him the "keys of the kingdom of the heavens," not to heaven, nor to the church, but to the kingdom of the heavens, that is to that which is now on earth. The Book of Acts gives us the history of the use of the keys. He used the keys in connection with the Jews on the day of Pentecost, when he preached to them and, in preaching, opened the door to those who heard him; then he used the keys once more in the household of Cornelius (Acts x) and then by preaching he opened the door to the Gentiles. This is what our Lord meant. Here is another significant fact, in writing his Epistles he never mentioned this commission of the keys. According to Rome and other ritualistic churches he should have stated in the beginning of his Epistle that he is the supreme holder of the keys of the kingdom of heaven. But not Peter was to be the great Apostle to the Gentiles; the Lord called Paul to this position. Peter is the prominent actor in the beginning of the Book of Acts, when the Gospel was preached "to the Jew first." After Jerusalem rejected that Gospel and the Apostle to the Gentiles had been called, Paul becomes the prominent figure in Acts. Peter is mentioned only once more in connection with the council held in Jerusalem (Acts xv). In Galatians chapter ii his Jewish character in withdrawing from the Gentile believers after he had fellowshipped them is rebuked by Paul. In that chapter we also read that Peter with James and John were to minister to those of the circumcision, that is the Jews; while Paul and Barnabas were to go to the Gentiles.

After this incident we hear nothing more about Peter. The Spirit of God might have given us a complete account of what he did, where he went, but all is passed over in silence. The omniscient Spirit saw what would come in Christendom. He knew that ritualism would give to Peter a place of supremacy in the body of Christ which does not belong to him at all. Therefore Peter's life and service are passed over by the Holy Spirit and we hear nothing more about him in the inspired records. But we hear from him in the two Epistles which bear his name and which he wrote.

But while Scripture is silent, tradition is not. It is claimed by the historian Eusebius that he was Bishop of Antioch, the church which he founded. But the latter statement is contradicted by Acts xi:19-21 and the former is equally incorrect. Other ancient sources declare that he was very active in Asia Minor. That he must have ministered widely may be gained from 1 Corinthians ix:5: "Have we not power to lead about a sister, a wife, as well as other apostles, and as the brethren of the Lord, and Cephas?" But the entire ministry he rendered is not revealed.

Another tradition claims that he settled in Rome to oppose the Samaritan sorcerer Simon Magus (Acts viii). Justin Martyr in his writings states that Simon Magus was worshipped in Rome as a god on account of his magical powers. On account of it they erected a statute on an island in the River Tiber inscribed "*Simoni Deo Sancto.*" Actually there was found in the year 1574 in the Tiber a stone with the inscription "*Semoni Sanco Deo Fidio Sacrumi.*" i.e. "to the god Semo Sancus," the Sabine Hercules, which is definite proof that Justin Martyr was mistaken. Upon this rests the legend that Peter went to Rome to oppose Simon Magus. It is claimed that Peter was Bishop in Rome for 25 years and founded what is called "the Holy See," which later developed into the abominable papacy with its lies. Peter never saw Rome. As we shall show later in this introduction, there is sufficient Scriptural authority to contradict this legend. Another legend states that he was martyred in Rome, where the Lord appeared to him, when Peter had left the city to escape death. That he should die the martyr's death had been announced by our Lord, as well as the manner of his death by crucifixion. Nobody knows where that death took place. When he wrote his second Epistle it was a brief time before his death (2 Peter i:14); but that Epistle was not written from Rome.

Did Peter Write from Babylon or from Rome?

At the close of the Epistle we read the following salutation: "The church that is in Babylon, elect together with you, saluteth you, and so does Marcus my son." "*The church that is*" does not appear in the original text; it has, therefore, been explained that Peter meant his wife, though it appears more probable that he meant the other elect ones who were with him in Bablyon. The fact is established that when he wrote this Epistle Peter was in Babylon. But does this mean the literal Babylon on the banks of the Euphrates or the mystical Babylon, which is Rome? Roman Catholic writers claim that it means the city of Rome, and a large number of Protestant commentators side with this view. They claim that he was in Rome with Mark. They say that Babylon has the same meaning as the word has in the Book of Revelation, that is, not the literal Babylon, but Rome. There is no definite proof that Rome was universally called "Babylon" before John received it in his Patmos vision; it is claimed that the persecution under Nero led Christians to call Rome by the name of Babylon; but it is more likely that the name Babylon was widely used for Rome after John had written the Apocalypse. The Apocalypse was written some 25 or 30 years after Peter had written his Epistle, how, then, could he have used this mystical name for Rome? Furthermore, a mystical name is out of keeping in an Epistle. It would be the only instance in the entire epistolar testimony where a place is camouflaged in this way. The use of a mystical name in an Epistle appears strained. It therefore must be the literal Babylon in Mesopotamia. And why should this not be? We read in the second chapter of Acts that among those who were in Jerusalem when the Holy Spirit came to earth were "Parthians, Medes, Elamites and dwellers in Mesopotamia." They heard Peter's testimony and some of them must have been converted. Many Jews dwelt there, and while in 41 A. D. Caligula instituted a persecution against the Jews in Babylon and many left, there was still a large company of them in the fast decaying city.

But the most conclusive evidence against Babylon, meaning Rome, is the complete silence of the Apostle Paul about Peter being in Rome. Paul sent his Epistle to the Roman Church in the year 58 A. D. In that Epistle he greets many believers who were in Rome. If Peter had been there, why did he not mention him also? He went to Rome as a prisoner in the year 61, but there is not a word about meeting Peter in Rome. Finally, when Paul penned his very last Epistle from Rome he makes the significant statement: "Only Luke is with me" (2 Tim. iv:11). This silence about Peter in the Pauline Epistles can only be explained by the fact that Peter was not in Rome at all.

Addressed to Believers in the Dispersion

The Epistle is addressed to the sojourners in the dispersion, that is, to Jewish believers who were scattered throughout Pontus, Galatia, Cappadocia, Asia and Bithynia, provinces in the northeastern part of Asia Minor. Many assemblies had been founded there and there were many believing Jews. They probably had their own gatherings, keeping aloof from the assemblies formed by believing Gentiles. They were the remnant and yet in having believed they were members of the body of Christ.

THE PURPOSE AND MESSAGE OF THE EPISTLE

When Peter wrote this Epistle he fulfilled the request of

the Lord, when he told him "when thou art converted strengthen thy brethren." They needed strengthening and comfort for they were passing through all kinds of persecutions; their faith was being severely tested. As believers they were pilgrims and strangers on earth, their portion and calling was different from the unbelieving Jews about them, among whom they suffered. The Lord Jesus Christ who suffered in their behalf is repeatedly presented as a pattern for them in their persecutions, and blessed exhortations are linked with the Person and holy character of our Lord. The Epistle is not doctrinal, though the great doctrines of Christianity are in view throughout the Epistle. It is, like the Epistle of James, a practical Epistle, abounding in exhortations and references to Old Testament history suited to believing Jews in their trials. The keynote is "*Suffering and Glory.*" The words suffering and suffer occur fifteen times and the word glory ten times.

The same error has been taught by some extremists in Biblical interpretation which we have pointed out already in the introduction to the Epistle of James, namely, that it has a Jewish character and does not belong to the Epistles in which the church and the heavenly calling are revealed, and therefore the church should not consider it. This is a most vital mistake. The first Epistle of Peter has an important message also for all believers at all times; to pass it over and not to heed its blessed message, its comfort and exhortations, would mean a very serious loss. A one-sided Bible reading produces a one-sided Christian character and a one-sided Christian service. And there are only too many of such in the church today.

The Divisions of First Peter

As stated in the introduction the keynote of the Epistle is "Suffering and Glory." The end of their pilgrimage, when all suffering ends, will be salvation and the possession of an inheritance incorruptible, undefiled and that fadeth not away. This salvation was the object of inquiry and searching by their own prophets. The Spirit of Christ who was in them testified beforehand the sufferings of Christ and the Glory that should follow. So they as being His and identified with Him would also have suffering which in due time will be followed by Glory. The Glory comes with His revelation, His appearing, when He comes again.

We divide the Epistle into five sections, but somewhat different from the five chapters into which the Epistle is divided in our Bibles.

I. THE SUFFERING OF BELIEVERS AND EXHORTATION TO HOLY LIVING. i:1-21.

II. THE BLESSINGS AND PRIVILEGES OF ALL BELIEVERS. i:22-ii:10.

III. CHRIST THE PATTERN FOR HIS SAINTS. ii:11-iii:9.

IV. THE COMFORT IN THE MIDST OF TRIALS AND SUFFERING. iii:10-iv.

V. EXHORTATION CONCERNING SERVICE AND CONFLICT. v.

Analysis and Annotations

I. THE SUFFERING OF BELIEVERS AND EXHORTATIONS TO HOLY LIVING.

CHAPTER I:1-21.

1. The Introduction and Doxology. 1-5.
2. Suffering and the coming Glory. 6-9.
3. As revealed in the Prophets. 10-12.
4. Exhortations to Holy Living. 13-21.

1. The Introduction and Doxology: Verses 1-5. As stated in the introduction, Peter writes to believing Jews in the dispersion throughout the provinces mentioned in the first verse. There is at once pointed out a contrast between them as true believers and their former condition. The nation to which they belonged was an elect nation, but they were "elect according to the foreknowledge of God the Father." It is something infinitely higher than a national election. Here is an individual election; they were foreknown of God the Father. In the Old Testament the Lord called Israel nationally "my first-born son," but no individual Israelite knew God as his Father, nor did an Israelite know himself individually as a son of God and a member of the family of God. They had received something better. The nation had been set aside while those who believed were brought individually into the family of God, knowing God as their Father, while they became His children. Israel as a nation was set apart externally and by ordinances; but their setting apart, or sanctification, was through the Spirit. Their sanctification was unto the obedience and sprinkling of the blood of Jesus Christ. Their setting apart was vastly different from that separation which God had accorded to the nation as such. The Holy Spirit had set them apart unto the obedience of Christ, called them to obey as He obeyed, not to an obedience of the law. Connected with this obedience is the sprinkling of the blood of Jesus Christ, that precious blood typified by their former sacrifices which were unable to cleanse from sin, but the blood of Christ assures perfect forgiveness and justification, and that gives confidence and boldness before God, and liberty and power to practice the obedience of Christ, for which the believer is set apart.

"Blessed be the God and Father of our Lord Jesus Christ, who, according to His great mercy, hath begotten us again unto a living hope by the resurrection of Jesus Christ from among the dead." This is the doxology. It declares the new relationship into which they had been brought; for these Jewish believers it is no longer the God of Abraham, Isaac and Jacob, but "the God and Father of our Lord Jesus Christ." They were begotten again unto a living hope by the resurrection of Jesus Christ from among the dead. It is a joyful song of the better hope. We may think of what it meant to Peter, as well as to the other disciples. They had believed on Jesus as their promised, national Messiah. Their hope was in Him. As the two said on the way to Emmaus, "we trusted that it had been He which should have redeemed Israel." They hoped He would be King and take the throne of His father David. Then He who was their hope died on the shameful cross, and hope died. But the third day came and Christ arose from among the dead. Hope revived, yea, they were begotten again unto a living hope. His ressurrection was a begetting again to a living hope, no longer the hope of the earthly kingdom but a living hope "unto an inheritance incorruptible and undefiled that fadeth not away." And this living hope by the resurrection of Jesus Christ from among the dead, the hope which centers in Him as the living, risen and glorified One, is the hope of all His people. Israel as a nation possessed an earthly inheritance, the promised land and with it corresponding earthly blessings. But now as the elect, according to the foreknowledge of the Father, they have a better inheritance. Earthly things are corruptible; the heavenly inheritance is incorruptible. Earthly things are defiled, pollution clings to the fairest and choicest; the coming inheritance is undefiled, nor can it ever be polluted by sin and its curse, it is eternally pure. Here on earth everything is fading, every beautiful flower has its roots in a grave, all is passing and fading away; but that inheritance which we shall receive is never-fading, it is always fresh and beautiful. And this inheritance is "preserved in heaven for you;" it is more than *reserved*, as we have it in our Bibles. It is with Him in the Glory and He preserves it for His Saints, so that the cruel hand of Satan cannot touch it nor take it away from man. And while that inheritance is preserved by the never-failing Lord in Glory, Saints are kept for the inheritance by the power of God through faith. Here is the real perseverance of the Saints; the power to persevere and to keep is not in us but in God. That inheritance is ready to be revealed in the last times, that is when the Lord comes for His Saints.

2. Suffering and the Coming Glory: Verses 6-9. The way to the promised land for the literal Israel led through the desert sands with trials and testings. The way of the elect in Christ also leads through the desert with its wilderness experiences; faith too must be honored and glorified by testings. Faith is not only a precious thing for us, it is precious to God as well. It is His gold, that in which He rejoices. To bring out its value various trials are permitted by Him: "that the trial of your faith, being much more precious than of gold that perisheth, though it be tried with fire, might be found unto praise and honor and glory at the appearing of Jesus Christ." The goal of the hope, when the inheritance will be bestowed, is the appearing of Jesus Christ. This is His visible appearing. Peter writes as the Apostle of circumcision and he does not write about the church as the body of Christ, the heavenly calling and destiny of the church, and therefore he does not say anything about the rapture preceding the revelation. Peter always speaks of His appearing or revelation; salvation as used in this chapter means the manifestation in glory, when He appears in visible glory and when we shall be manifested with Him in glory. Having mentioned His appearing, the Spirit of God directs the attention at once to the Person of Christ. He must ever be the object of faith and occupation for the true believer. This brings into view the true character of Christianity.

"Whom having not seen ye love." It is a strange sound and fact at first, but in the end it is precious. Who ever loved a person that he never saw? We know that in human relations it is not so. In Divine things it is precisely what shows the power and special character of a Christian's faith. "Whom having not seen, ye love, in whom, though now ye see Him not, yet believing, ye rejoice with joy unspeakable and full of glory: receiving the end of your faith, the salvation of your souls." This at once gives us a true and vivid picture of what Christianity is, of signal importance for the Jews to weigh, because they always looked forward for a visible Messiah as an object, the Son of David. But here it is altogether another order of ideas. It is a rejected Messiah who is the proper object of the Christian's love, though he never beheld Him; and who while unseen becomes so much the more simply and unmixedly the object of his faith, and the spring of "joy unspeakable and full of glory."*

3. As Revealed in the Prophets: Verses 10-12. He directs their attention to the Prophets. The Spirit of Christ was in them and they testified before of the sufferings of Christ and the glories that should follow. This is the great message of these holy men of God who spoke as they were moved by the Holy Spirit. When our Lord said to the Jews "Search the Scriptures . . . they are they which testify of Me" He called attention to the same fact. They prophesied of the grace which was to come and then they did not understand their own prophecies, they sought diligently, they studied what they had written, searching and always searching, to find out what time, near or far, these things should come to pass. But they knew one thing, "To whom it was revealed, that not to themselves, but to us did they minister the things which are reported to you by those who have preached the Gospel unto you by the

---

*W. Kelly on Peter.

Holy Spirit sent from heaven, into which things the angels desire to look." They knew that it was not for themselves, nor for their own times, that which the Spirit had announced, but for another time. The passage is illustrated by comparing Isaiah lxiv:4 with 1 Corinthians ii:9-10. The Spirit having come down from heaven after Christ had died and was raised from among the dead, has made known the fullness of redemption. And the angels desire to look into these things; they seek to explore and to fathom the wonders of that redemption and the coming glories which are connected with it.

4. Exhortations to Holy Living: Verses 13-21. The first exhortation is to gird up the loins of the mind. The man who girds the loins of the body is getting ready for service; the girding of the loins of the mind means to set the mind on these things, the things spiritual and unseen. To be sober means to be watchful and temperate, thus walking soberly, and "set your hope perfectly on the grace that is to be brought unto you at the revelation of Jesus Christ" (the correct translation). As they were now "obedient children" in the family of God, their responsibility and calling is to live and act as such. A holy God demands a holy people; this was God's call to His people Israel in the Old Testament, it is His call to the elect in the New Testament (Leviticus xi:44). This necessitates a walk in the Spirit as it is so fully revealed in the Epistles to the Romans and Galatians.

Next we find two great reasons for walking in holiness; the first reason is the relationship which believers have as children, God being their Father; the second, the redemption price which was paid.

"And if ye call on Him as Father, who without respect of persons judgeth according to each man's work, pass the time of your sojourn in fear, knowing that ye were redeemed not with corruptible things, with silver or gold, from your vain manner of life handed down from your fathers; but by precious blood, as of a lamb without blemish and without spot, the blood of Christ, foreknown indeed before the foundation of the world, but was manifested at the end of the times for your sake, who through Him believe in God, who raised Him from among the dead and gave Him glory, so that your faith and hope might be in God."

He has called us by His Grace and we call Him Father. As Father, the head of His family, to which we belong, He must govern His house. As Father He exercises judgment in government regarding His children; He must chasten His children if they do not walk as it becometh those who are in possession of the divine nature. And though that government is one of love and grace, the Father's dealing with a beloved child, we must pass the time of our sojourn with fear. But this is not a slavish fear, nor a fear which has in it the elements of uncertainty as to salvation, a fear which trembles before a holy God, fearing His wrath. It is a godly, a holy fear, a fear that we might not please Him. This holy fear should be a passion to measure up to our calling as children and not to displease Him who is our Father, so that He does not need to exercise a Father's judgment upon us. While the first reason to walk in holiness has to do with our conscience, the second concerns the affections. That blessed redemption by the blood of Christ, the Lamb without spot and blemish, foreknown before the foundation of the world, is the other great incentive to please God. It is not by silver or gold that He has redeemed us from all the vain things, whether vain religious traditions, or vain manner of life and all that goes with it, but by that which is the dearest, the most blessed and the most precious thing in the eyes of God and to the heart of God—the Blood of Christ. No finite mind can understand the price God paid for our redemption. By Him we believe in God, who raised Him from among the dead and gave Him glory. And that acquired Glory He received He has given to His own (John xvii:22).

II. THE BLESSINGS AND PRIVILEGES OF ALL BELIEVERS

CHAPTER I:22: II:10.

1. The New Birth. Verses 22-25.
2. Spiritual Growth. ii:1-3.
3. The Privileges of Believers as the holy and royal Priesthood. 4-10.

I. The New Birth: Chapter i:22-25. The relationship of those who are thus redeemed, whose faith and hope is in God, who raised Him from the dead and gave Him glory, whose souls are purified by obedience to the truth, unto unfeigned love of the brethren, is stated first: "Love one another with a pure heart fervently." All the elect through the foreknowledge of God the Father are covered by the same love, are redeemed by the same Lamb, washed in the same precious blood, have the same Father. They are one; they are brethren and as such love must characterize them. But this love, loving one another out of a pure heart fervently, is the fruit of the new nature which all possess who have believed and are redeemed by the precious blood of the Lamb. "Being born again, not of corruptible seed, but of incorruptible, by the Word of God, which liveth and abideth for ever." The Word of God, living and abiding, under the operation of the Spirit (the Word is "the water" of which our Lord spoke to Nicodemus) is the agent of the new birth. It is not corruptible seed, but incorruptible, hence the nature is an incorruptible, a holy nature. There are three incorruptible things mentioned in this chapter. An incorruptible inheritance, an incorruptible redemption price, and an incorruptible seed giving an incorruptible nature. And that new nature must love that which is of God, therefore the exhortation of loving one another, which is more fully developed in the great "family Epistle," the first Epistle of John.

But the new birth carries with it another blessing. "For all flesh is as grass and all the glory of it as the flower of the grass. The grass hath withered and the flower fallen, but the Word of the Lord endureth forever, and this is the Word which by the Gospel is preached unto you."

The old creation is left behind, the world with all its glory and boastings, is judged. All is as grass and the glory of man as the flower of the grass. Those born again do no longer belong to this world, as He prayed: "They are not of the world, as I am not of the world." The words concerning the grass and the flower of the grass are a quotation from Isaiah (Isa. xl:6, 8). But the quotation is changed a little. In Isaiah we read: "The grass withereth, the flower fadeth," and here it is, "The grass hath withered and the flower fallen," that is how faith must look upon the world and all its glory, as withered and fallen, with no more attraction for the heart which knows God. But those who are born again are linked with that which abideth for ever, the Word of the Lord, preached in that ever blessed Gospel.

2. Spiritual Growth: ii:1-3. "Wherefore, laying aside all malice and all guile and hypocrisies and envyings and all evil-speakings as new born babes desire earnestly the pure milk of the Word that ye may grow by it unto salvation, if ye have tasted that the Lord is good."

Those who are born again of incorruptible seed, in possession of a new nature, are still in the world, though they are no longer of it. Evil is on all sides and there is still the old nature, the flesh, in every child of God though believers are reckoned as being no longer in the flesh (Rom. viii:9). The old things of the flesh must be put off, completely laid aside. This is the necessary thing for spiritual growth; if there is no putting off of these there can be no progress. Peter speaks of believers as "new-born babes." The sense in which this expression is used here differs from the use of it in 1 Corinthians iii:1: "And I, brethren, could not speak unto you as unto spiritual, but as unto carnal, even as unto babes in Christ." The spiritual growth of the Corinthians had been arrested and dwarfed; they never developed, but remained babes, a spiritual monstrosity. But the meaning here is entirely different. Believers should be at all times like new-born babes hungering for that which the Lord has provided for spiritual growth, the milk in all its purity as found in His Word. The mother by which we are begotten again, that is the living and abiding Word of God, has also the nourishment for the life we have received. In this sense the child of God must always be like a healthy babe, always craving, hungering and thirsting for the pure milk as provided in His Word. All that we need, yea, every need is provided there, and as we go to that fountain which never runs dry, which never fails nor disappoints, we shall grow thereby. One of the most subtle delusions is found among some pentecostal sects, who imagine that they are so filled with the Spirit that they can dispense with the reading of and feeding on the Word. In the authorized version two words are missing which belong in the text; they are the words "*unto salvation*" . . . "that ye may grow thereby unto salvation." They were omitted in some manuscripts, but belong here. Salvation here has the same meaning as in the first chapter, it looks forward to the end in glory.

And if we have felt that the Lord is gracious, have tasted of His loving kindness, we shall desire more and more of it, crave for still more. Peter surely had tasted that the Lord is gracious. We think of his denial, and when the Lord turned and looked upon him, Peter went out and wept bitterly. He had tasted that the Lord is gracious, and more so, when the Lord dealt so graciously with him at the meal His blessed hands had prepared for His disciples on the lake-shore (John xxi), and His loving voice asked: "Simon, son of Jonas, lovest thou Me more than these?" The sentence, "If so be ye have tasted that the Lord is gracious," is a quotation from the Psalms (Psalm xxxiv:8). David, like Peter, had shamefully failed and like Peter he had tasted that the Lord is gracious. All His saints have had the same experience of the graciousness of the Lord.

3. The Privileges of Believers: Verses 4-10. The testimony of Peter which follows is of great importance. The fisherman of Galilee knew nothing of what would happen centuries later. He did not know that ritualism would exalt him to a position of supremacy, claiming that he was and is the rock upon which the church is built, that he was a Bishop who communicated in Rome his apostolic authority to another, as it is claimed to one by name of Linus, and Linus handed over the same authority to Cletus and Cletus to Clemens, Clemens to Anacletus, Anacletus to Sixtus and so on from one generation to the other, each adding a little more till the harlot system of the mystical Babylon, the papacy became what it is today. But while Peter did not know the future, the Holy Spirit knew and He inspired his pen to write that which is the complete refutation of popery and a man-made priesthood.

Not Peter is the living Stone upon which everything rests, but the Lord Jesus Christ is the rock foundation, the Stone upon whom all is built. Not Peter was rejected by men, then chosen of God and precious, but it is the Lord Jesus Christ. The Scriptures had announced this fact beforehand. Isaiah xxviii:16 is quoted in Verse 6. This is followed by a quotation from Psalm cxviii:22 and Isaiah viii:14. The Lord Jesus while on earth had made use of these prophecies given by His Spirit (Matthew xxiv:42). The Holy Spirit after Pentecost reminded the rulers, elders and scribes of the people once more of this great prophecy concerning the rejection of the Messiah by the nation (Acts iv:9-12). And when the Lord Jesus quoted this prophecy from Psalm cxviii He added, what is cited here in Verse 8, "whosoever shall fall on this stone shall be broken," that is what happened to the nation Israel. The second half of this statement of our Lord in Matthew xxi:44 is still unaccomplished—"but on whomsoever it shall fall, it will grind him to powder." This will happen at the close of the Times of the Gentiles, when the stone strikes the feet of the prophetic image (Dan. ii). Israel had rejected the Stone and therefore was unfit as a nation to build the spiritual house, as the Lord had likewise announced: "the kingdom of God shall be taken from you, and given to a nation bringing forth the fruit thereof." They had as a nation a house called "The House of the Lord," where He delighted to dwell, but it was not a spiritual house, but a house made with hands, a shadow of the better things to come. When Israel rejected the Messiah and the kingdom He had offered, when they had delivered Him up and He died, after His resurrection from among the dead and His exaltation to the right hand of God, the third person of the trinity, the Holy Spirit, came to earth for the purpose of building amongst men the habitation of God, a spiritual house, and that house is the church. Thus Peter bears witness to Christ as the living Stone, the rock upon which the church "the spiritual house" is being built. He with all other believers, including ourselves, are the living stones. As mentioned in the introduction, Christ is the *Petra, the rock,* Peter and every other child of God is a *Petros,* a little rock, a living stone with Himself (Matt. xvi:17-18). And His Son whom man dishonored and rejected is precious to God; He is His delight; He is precious to those who have believed; He is our delight. While God says that His delight is in Him, we too confess that all our delight is in the Lord Jesus Christ.

Furthermore, all believers constitute a holy Priesthood. Peter does not claim an exclusive Priesthood vested in him, but His inspired testimony is that all members of the body of Christ, the living stones, are a priesthood. In the Old Testament the Priesthood of Christ was foreshadowed in Aaron and the Priesthood of believers by the sons of Aaron. (See Annotations in Leviticus.) No longer are needed sacrifices of animals, for He has brought the one sacrifice, by which He has made the new and living way by His blood into the Holiest, so that every believer can draw nigh with a true heart and full assurance of faith, with hearts sprinkled from an evil conscience and bodies washed with pure water (Hebrews x:19-22). This completely disposes of the ritualistic priesthood, vested in "ordained" men, that system which has been and still is and always will be, the corruption of Christianity. It also answers the blasphemous mass, which is an act of idolatry.

The function of the holy priesthood of believers consists in bringing spiritual sacrifices acceptable to God by Jesus

Christ. "By Him therefore let us offer the sacrifice of praise to God continually, the fruit of our lips, giving thanks to His Name" (Hebrews xiii:15). It is worship in the Spirit and Truth; it is praise and adoration as well as the ministry of intercession.

Once more Peter mentions the fact of the Christian Priesthood. "But ye are a chosen generation, a royal Priesthood, a holy nation, a peculiar people; that ye should shew forth the excellencies of Him who hath called you out of darkness into His marvellous light; which in time past were not a people, but are now the people of God; which had not obtained mercy, but now have obtained mercy" (Hosea ii:23). Israel was chosen, Israel was called to be a kingdom of priests and a holy nation, they were called "to shew forth His praises." They never attained it, because they were not a holy nation, though constituted a separated nation by God's calling. But these believing Jews through grace in Christ had become a chosen generation, a royal Priesthood, a holy nation, a peculiar people. As a remnant of the nation they possessed now what the nation never possessed. Of course that remnant was embodied in the church, and is a part of the body of Christ. Yet the application to them as a remnant must not be lost sight of. Nor must we forget that there will be a future remnant of the nation, the nation which is now dispersed, which will become a holy nation, a royal priesthood in connection with the other nations. The promises, the gifts and callings of God, will all be accomplished, and those who had not obtained mercy will yet obtain mercy; that will be when He whom they pierced comes again and when they shall look upon Him in that day. Apart from this application to them as believing Jews, to whom the Epistle was addressed, all believers, whether Jews or Gentiles, have a royal Priesthood. Christ is a holy Priest and a royal Priest; both aspects of His Priesthood believers share in Him. We are holy priests to go in to God to represent man before God; we are royal priests to represent God before man, to shew forth His excellencies. The royal Priesthood of Christ, is the Priesthood after the order of Melchisedec. He was the King-Priest who came to Abraham and made known God and His Glory to Abraham. Thus in Christ we behold the Glory of God and as identified with Christ, indwelt by Him, our royal Priesthood is to make Him and His excellencies known among men.

III. CHRIST THE PATTERN FOR HIS SAINTS

CHAPTER II:11-III:9.

1. Abstinence and Submission. ii:11-17.
2. Christ the Pattern for those who suffer. 18-25.
3. Glorifying Christ in the Marriage relation. iii:1-7.
4. True Christian Character. 8-9.

1. Abstinence and Submission: Chapter ii:11-17. The first exhortation is addressed to them as strangers and pilgrims. Such all true believers are. Because we belong to a heavenly home we cannot be at home in a world which lieth in the wicked one, which has cast out the Lord of Glory, and which continues to reject Him. And it is only as a stranger here that we can do what we are exhorted to do, "to abstain from fleshly lusts which war against the soul." If our heart is where He is, if our affections are set upon the things on high, if we lose sight of the "vain things" which charm the natural man, and we realize in faith the heavenly calling and the heavenly home, then we shall not fight the lusts of the flesh, but willingly and joyfully abstain from them, fleeing them, as Paul exhorted Timothy.

A general exhortation follows. Their conversation is to be honest among the Gentiles who often spoke of them as evil-doers, accusing Christians of their own shameful conduct, as unsaved Gentiles, so that it might bring reproach upon "that worthy Name." By their godly lives the Gentiles should see their good works and when the day of visitation came, they would then glorify God. Does this mean a visitation in judgment, or the visitation in Grace? It means the latter, though a visitation by the chastening hand of God is not excluded. When sorrows come, when earthly hopes are blasted, when sickness makes the enjoyment of the material things impossible, then the unbelievers often turn to the people of God for help and comfort, the grace of God will then be manifested in the day of visitation; this glorifies God.

Exhortation to submission is linked with this. "Submit yourselves therefore to every ordinance of man for the Lord's sake, whether unto the king as supreme; or to governors as sent by Him for the punishment of evil-doers, and for the praise of them that do well." We must remember that the kings and rulers mentioned here, under whom these believing Jews lived, were heathen and idolators. Yet they were to obey and to manifest patient submission. The exhortation has a special meaning for them as Jews, for naturally they were a rebellious people. The exhortation given to them before their captivity in Babylon, "to seek the peace of the city" where they would dwell has generally been disobeyed. These believing Jews probably were tempted to resist the powers which ruled.* Therefore the exhortation to submit for the Lord's sake, though there are limitations to such submission. Such submission is "the will of God, that with well-doing ye may put to silence the ignorance of foolish men." Brief, but weighty, exhortations follow.

2. Christ the Pattern for Those Who Suffer: Verses 18-25. The exhortation after that is addressed to the servants, that is, to those Jewish believers who were slaves. To such the choicest words are addressed, God knowing that His own beloved Son had been on earth as a servant, that He was here not to be ministered to, but to minister and to give His life as a ransom for many. They were in the blessed position to "follow His steps." But the exhortation does not mean servants or slaves exclusively, it is written for all

*It is a significant fact that many of the radicals, anarchists, or as they used to be called in Russia, nihilists, are apostate Jews. Many of the persecutions of the Jews, in which the innocent have to suffer with the guilty, are produced by Jews meddling with the politics of the nations among whom they are strangers and trying to overthrow these governments.

believers. "For this is acceptable, if a man for conscience toward God endure grief, suffering wrongfully. For what glory is it if, when ye sin, and are buffeted for it, ye take it patiently? but if, when ye do well and suffer, ye take it patiently, this is acceptable with God." To suffer wrongfully and take it patiently, without murmuring and without strife, is whereunto believers are called. It is then that they can show forth His excellencies and follow after Him. "Because Christ also suffered for you, leaving you an example that ye should follow His steps." And what an example has He left for us? He was the holy, spotless Son of God. Suffering for His own sins was an impossibility, for He was spotless. He knew no sin, neither could He sin. Yet He suffered. "Who did no sin, nor was guile found in His mouth; who when reviled, He reviled not again; when He suffered, threatened not; but committed Himself to Him who judgeth righteously." Such is the pattern. But there is more than that. He knew no sin, did not sin and all His suffering, the shame and the suffering connected with the cross, was on account of our sins. "Who His own self bare our sins in His own body on the tree, that we, being dead to sins, should live unto righteousness; by whose stripes ye were healed. For ye were as sheep going astray; but are now returned unto the Shepherd and Bishop of your souls." The rendering, or, rather, paraphrase, some have adopted that Christ bore our sins "up to the tree" is erroneous and misleading. Our Lord did not bear our sins in His holy life before the cross, but He bore them on the cross, in His own body. And He bore them that "we, being dead to sins," not as revealed in Romans to *sin*, but to sins, that is, the practical giving up of our own wills, should live unto righteousness. The Fifty-third chapter of Isaiah is used by Peter in this paragraph. There it is written: "By His stripes we are healed," and the confession, "all we like sheep have gone astray." Of late the so called "divine healers," men and women who claim gifts of healings, if not gifts to work miracles, speak of the sentence, "By His stripes we are healed," as meaning the healing of diseases. They claim that

Christ died also for our bodily ills and that the stripes laid upon Him were specifically for the healing of our bodies, which Scripture so clearly states are "dead on account of sin." This is a most dangerous perversion of the truth. Christ died for our sins according to the Scriptures, but nowhere is it written that He died for our bodily diseases.

These believing Jews were in possession of the truth as revealed in Isaiah liii. They foreshadow that other Jewish remnant of the future which will some day use the Fifty-third chapter of Isaiah as their great confession of Him whom they despised and rejected, and by whose stripes they also will be healed. Then Peter speaks of our Lord as Shepherd, the Shepherd who died for the sheep, the great Shepherd brought again from among the dead. He loves His sheep and shepherds them. Bishop means overseer. He is the only Bishop, who watches over all and guards all His blood-bought sheep.

3. Glorifying Christ in the Marriage Relation: iii:1-7. The practical exhortations are now extended to the marriage relation, how wives and husbands should be royal priests, showing forth His excellencies in their divinely sanctioned union, as man and wife. The wife is mentioned first, for her place is the highest, the place of submission, which in God's eyes is the place of honor. The case of a wife is stated who has an unbelieving husband. Is she to submit to him, who is an unbeliever? Must she be obedient to such a one? How often wives placed in this position have listened to the evil councils of others, and, instead of submitting to the demands of an unbelieving husband, have resisted him, and as a result misery came upon them. Let it be noticed that the Holy Spirit insists on obedience; the fact of the disobedient husband is given as a reason for submission. Then there is a promise. The unbelieving husband is to be won without the Word, that is, without preaching in a public service, by the godly life of meekness and submission of the believing wife. This is the advice of the Holy Spirit, and many times the promise given to the believing wife has been made good.

Furthermore, there is a word concerning dress. The adorning is not to be outwardly in braiding of hair, wearing of gold, or putting on of apparel, but inwardly, "the hidden man of the heart, in that which is not corruptible, even the ornament of a meek and quiet spirit, which in the sight of God is of great price." The positive side is emphasized more than the negative. The greatest ornament a woman can wear is "a meek and quiet spirit," for it shows that in manifesting meekness and quietness, they learned and received from Him, who on earth was "meek and lowly of heart." This applies to every believer likewise. Wherever a meek and quiet spirit is manifested God is well pleased with it. What a contrast with the conditions in the world today. Women claim equality with men; in every walk of life they clamor to be heard; the female sex is breaking down the barriers set by the Creator and the Redeemer, demanding leadership in every sphere. The result will be disaster. But it must not be overlooked that here is also exhortation for the Christian woman to dress outwardly as becomes a follower of the Lord Jesus Christ. There should be a difference between the daughters of the world and those who are Christ's. On the other hand, shabbiness of dress, an unclean appearance, is no more an honor to the Gospel, than a dress which is after the latest fashion of the world

And the husband is exhorted next. He is not told to claim submission, or to insist upon it as his peculiar right. He is exhorted to give the wife honor as the weaker vessel, hence he must show to her, as the weaker one, kindness, tenderness, consideration and loving sympathy, as we read in Ephesians: "Husbands, love your wives as Christ loved the church." The believing husband and the wife are "heirs together of the grace of life." Where this is practised there will be sweet companionship and fellowship in the Lord, nothing hindering them from bowing the knees together in His presence, expressing together their praise, their mutual needs and those of others.

4. True Christian Character: Verses 8-9. General exhortations follow. What is found in these two verses constitutes a true Christian character.

IV. THE COMFORT IN THE MIDST OF TRIALS AND SUFFERING

CHAPTER III:10-IV.

1. The Comfort in Suffering. Verse 10-17.
2. Few saved as illustrated by Noah's Preaching. 18-22.
3. The new life in its transforming Power. iv:1-11.
4. Suffering and Glory. 12-19.

1. The Comfort in Suffering: Verses 10-17. The words which stand in the beginning of this section are quoted from Psalm xxxiv:12-16. It is interesting to note that the Spirit of God quotes from the three main divisions of the Hebrew Bible in the first three chapters of this Epistle. The Hebrew Bible is composed according to Jewish division of the Law, the Prophets and the Writings. In the first chapter the Law is quoted; in the second the Prophets; and in the third we have a quotation from the Psalms. If we practice righteousness, the result of the new nature, produced by the new life, the promises of the Lord will not fail. To Israel in the Old Testament the Lord promised earthly blessings, and while to His heavenly people heavenly, spiritual blessings are vouchsafed, the earthly blessings are not excluded. It was true in olden times that "the eyes of the Lord are over the righteous, and His ears are open unto their prayers." It is so today, for He changes not. He looks for practical righteousness. Equally true is it that in His righteous government the face of the Lord is against them that do evil. And there is the comfort if we do right that none can harm us, for the Lord is on our side.

Suffering for righteousness' sake must be, but there is a "blessedness" connected with it. The Lord pronounced this in one of the beatitudes of the sermon on the mount (Matt. v:10). How fitting it is that in this Epistle, in addressing these Jewish believers as a remnant of the nation, this should be mentioned. It is the comfort in persecution, "be not afraid of their terror, neither be troubled." The quotation in verse 15 is from Isaiah viii:12, 13. There it is a prophecy concerning the future remnant of Israel during their coming great tribulation, foreshadowed in Isaiah by the Assyrian invasion.

2. Few Saved, as Illustrated by Noah's Preaching: Verses 18-22. "For Christ also hath once suffered for sins, the just for the unjust, that He might bring us to God, being put to death in flesh but quickened by the Spirit: in which also He went and preached to the spirits in prison, who before time were disobedient when the long suffering of God waited in the days of Noah, while the ark was preparing; in which few, that is, eight souls, were saved through water; which figure does also now save you, even baptism (not the putting away of the filth of the flesh, but the request as before God of a good conscience), by the resurrection of Jesus Christ, who has gone into heaven and is at the right hand of God; angels and authorities and powers being subjected unto Him."

This difficult and much misunderstood passage demands a closer attention. It is the passage upon which Rome has built her obnoxious and unscriptural doctrine of a purgatory. Protestant expositors have also misinterpreted this passage; in some quarters of "Protestantism" a kind of a "Protestant purgatory" is now being taught. Many errors, like a second probation, another chance for the lost, the restitution of the wicked, are linked with the wrong exposition of the above words. Even sound believers have adopted that which Peter does not mean at all, and which is unknown in the rest of the Word of God. Their teaching founded upon these statements by Peter is as follows: The Lord descended into Hades, the place of the departed spirits and preached there. The visit took place after His death and before His physical resurrection, that is, He made the visit in His unclothed state, while His body still rested in the tomb. As to the preaching, the opinions of these exegetes are divided. Some believe that He went to Hades to announce the certain doom of the lost. Others state, and they are not a few, that He preached, offering to the lost salvation, while still others claim that the spirits in prison are the righteous dead to whom Christ announced that their redemption had been wrought out for them, and that He announced His victory. As to the result of the preaching, the teaching is that it was successful; this is by inference, as they say, otherwise it could not be mentioned among the blessed results of Christ's suffering. They also claim that inasmuch as early Christian literature has much to say about that fictitious "Descent into Hades" (or, as generally stated, hell), it must be the true meaning of the passage. In giving these views on the meaning of the passage before us we give a very few; there are many others, like the late Bullinger's view, that the spirits were the fallen angels, and that He went to herald His triumph to them. Pages could be filled with the fanciful and unscriptural interpretations of this passage.

The chief question is: Did our Lord go to Hades in a disembodied state? In fact, all depends on the question of what is the true meaning of the sentence, "quickened by the Spirit." Now, according to the interpretations of the men who teach that the Lord visited Hades, the spirits in prison, during the interval between His death and the morning of the third day, He descended into these regions while His dead body was still in the grave. Therefore, these teachers claim that His human spirit was quickened, which necessitates that the spirit which the dying Christ commended into the Father's hands had also died. This is not only incorrect doctrine, but it is an unsound and evil doctrine. Was the holy humanity of our Lord, body, soul and spirit dead? A thousand times *No!* Only His body died; that is the only part of Him which could die. The text makes this clear: "He was put to death in flesh," that is, His body. There could be no quickening of His spirit, for His spirit was alive. Furthermore, the word quickening, as we learn from Ephesians i:20 and ii:5-6, by comparing the two passages, applies to His physical resurrection, it is the quickening of His body. To teach that the Lord Jesus was made alive before His resurrection is unscriptural. The "quickened by the Spirit" means the raising up of His body. His human spirit needed no quickening; it was His body and *only* His body. And the Spirit who did the quickening is not His own spirit, that is, His human spirit, but the Holy Spirit. Romans viii:12 speaks of the Spirit as raising Jesus from among the dead. We have shown that it was an impossibility that Christ was in any way quickened while His body was not yet raised, hence a visit to Hades is positively excluded between His death and resurrection. There is only another alternative. If it is true that He descended into these regions, then it must have been after His resurrection. But that is equally untenable. The so-called "Apostle's creed" puts the descent between His death and resurrection and all the other theorists follow this view. We have shown what the passage *does not* mean. It cannot mean a visit of the disembodied Christ to Hades, for it speaks of the quickening by the Spirit, and that means His physical resurrection.

What, then, does the passage mean? It is very simple after all. He preached by the Spirit, or in the Spirit, that is, the same Spirit who raised Him from among the dead, the Holy Spirit of Life and Power, to the spirits who are *now* in prison. But when the preaching occurred they were not in prison. And who were they? All the wicked dead for 4,000 years? The text makes it clear that they are a special class of people. They were living in the days of Noah. It is incomprehensible how some of these teachers, misinterpreting this passage, can teach that it includes all the lost, or angels which fell, or the righteous dead. The Spirit of God preached to them, that is, the Spirit who quickened the Body of Christ, the same Spirit preached to the generation of unbelievers in the days of Noah. The time of the preaching, then, did not occur between the death and resurrection of Christ, but it took place in Noah's day. Christ was not personally, or corporeally present, just as He is not present in person in this age when the Gospel is preached; His Spirit is here. So was He present by His Spirit in the days of Noah. It is written: "My Spirit shall not always strive with man, for that he also is flesh; yet his days shall be one hundred and twenty years" (Gen. vi:3). His Spirit was then on the earth. In long-suffering God was waiting for one hundred and twenty years while the ark was preparing. His Spirit preached then. But He needed an instrument. The instrument was Noah; in him was the Spirit of Christ and as the preacher of righteousness (2 Peter ii:5) he delivered the warning message of an impending judgment to those about him, who did not heed the message, passed on in disobedience, were swept away by the deluge and are now the spirits in prison. As the Spirit of Christ was in the prophets (chapter i:11) testifying beforehand of the suffering of Christ and the glory that should follow, so the Spirit of Christ preached through Noah. This is the meaning of this passage, and any other is faulty and unscriptural.

This interpretation is in full keeping with Peter's testimony. It is to "strengthen his brethren," to encourage and comfort those who were suffering persecution and passed through many fiery trials. They thought it strange that they had to suffer, that they were few in number who were saved, while they lived in the midst of the vast multitudes which rejected the Gospel and live on in sin and disobedience. For this reason the Spirit of God reminds them that such was also the case in the days of Noah, as it will be again at the close of the age, as the Lord Himself had announced. The multitudes in the days of Noah despised the warning; only eight souls were saved out of the judgment.

It must also be remembered that Peter's Epistle is not a doctrinal Epistle. He does not teach, but exhort. It is true many of the exhortations have for a foundation doctrines stated elsewhere in the Pauline Epistles. If it were Christian doctrine that Christ went to the prison of the wicked dead, such a doctrine should then be more fully stated somewhere else in the New Testament. But such is not the case. The passage in Ephesians iv, concerning Christ leading captivity captive has nothing to do with Peter's statement. (See annotations on Ephesians iv.)

The concluding words, linked with this statement, are

a typical comparison of the deluge and the ark with baptism. It has also been misunderstood, and some teach on account of it that baptism is a saving ordinance, which is another error. We quote a paragraph from the "Synopsis of the Bible" which clears this up in a way which cannot be improved upon.

"To this the apostle adds, the comparison of baptism to the ark of Noah in the deluge. Noah was saved through the water; we also; for the water of baptism typifies death, as the deluge, so to speak, was the death of the world. Now Christ has passed through death and is risen. We enter into death in baptism; but it is like the ark, because Christ suffered in death for us, and has come out of it in resurrection, as Noah came out of the deluge, to begin, as it were, a new life in a resurrection world. Now Christ, having passed through death, has atoned for sins; and we, by passing through it in spirit, leave all our sins in it, as Christ did in reality for us; for He was raised up without the sins which He expiated on the cross. And they were our sins; and thus, through the resurrection, we have a good conscience. We pass through death in spirit and in figure by baptism. The peace-giving force of the thing is the resurrection of Christ, after He had accomplished expiation; by which resurrection therefore we have a good conscience."

In other words our good conscience is not in having obeyed an ordinance, but it is by what Christ has done, who has gone into heaven and who is exalted at the right hand of God.

3. The New Life in its Transforming Power: iv:1-11. The opening sentence of the fourth chapter connects with chapter iii:18. The sufferings of Christ are thus brought to their attention once more. The reason is obvious. They were Jews and had been taught that earthly, temporal blessings, were the marks exclusively of divine favor; trials, sufferings and persecutions, on the other hand, according to Jewish conceptions, were evidences of disfavor. They were therefore disheartened and greatly perplexed when persecutions arose and they had to suffer. But these sufferings were the evidence that they followed Him who also suffered in the flesh. He suffered for us, that is for our sins, and therefore believers must arm themselves with the same mind. They must expect suffering, not for sins, but from the side of an evil world. "For he that hath suffered in the flesh hath ceased from sin." The death of Christ for sin (not sins) demands from the believer that he also cease from sin, from living after the old nature. If the Christian gratifies the old nature and yields to it, it will not entail any suffering, but if the believer lives as "dead unto sin," walks in separation from this evil age, the result will be that he has to suffer in some way. The life he lives is no longer "in the flesh to the lusts of men, but to the will of God." Such a walk brings with it the contradiction of sinners, the hatred of the world, such sufferings through which Christ also passed. Once they did as the heathen, the Gentiles, about them, walking in lasciviousness, lusts, excess of wine, revelings, banqueting, and abominable idolatries. But now their lives had been transformed; no longer did they run with them and do what the Gentiles did. Their former associates in sin and in the lusts of the flesh thought it strange that such should be the case, and they spoke evil of them. What evil they spoke about them is not stated. But for this they will have to give account to Him who is ready to judge the quick and the dead, even Christ.

The next verse has perplexed many, and has been misused by teachers of error and unsound doctrines, like the passage about the spirits in prison. "For to this end was the Gospel preached also to the dead, that they might be judged as regards men after the flesh, but live according to God in the Spirit." It is strange that expositors should detach a verse like this from the context and then, without considering its connection, build upon one verse a new and vital doctrine. So it is claimed that the dead mentioned are those who died before the Gospel was preached, or who never had a chance to hear the Gospel, but who hear it now in the abode of death, to obtain eternal life. But this is only one of a number of other interpretations.

The Apostle had spoken in the preceding verse of the

judgment of the living and of the dead. He now mentions the dead to whom the Gospel had been preached. It is a thing of the past and means that those who are dead now while they lived had heard the preaching of the Gospel. He means only the righteous dead and the other dead are not in view at all. Those who are now dead passed through the same experience, as the living pass through it, judged according to men in the flesh, but living according to God in the Spirit. Thus the preaching to the dead as dead is not taught at all in this verse. If there were such a thing as preaching to the physical dead we should find it in the Epistle to the Romans, in that great document of the Gospel, or somewhere else in the Pauline Epistle; but there is nothing mentioned about this anywhere.

The new life which is dead to sin and suffers with Christ must be manifested. Of this we read in the exhortations which follow (verses 7-11). The end of all things is at hand, the fact that this age will end must always be kept before the heart and mind. And if it was true then that the promised end is at hand how much more true is it now. As a result of waiting for His Coming, expecting Him at any time, we are to be sober and watchful unto prayer, and manifest fervent love among and towards fellow-believers. There is to be hospitality without murmuring, ministering one to another, according as each has received. Public ministry in preaching or teaching is to be as the Oracles of God, in dependence upon Him, as of the ability which God supplieth, that is,as enabled by His Spirit.

4. Suffering and Glory: Verses 12-19. "Beloved, think it not strange concerning the fiery trial which cometh upon you, as though some strange thing happened unto you; but rejoice, inasmuch as ye are partakers of Christ's sufferings; that, when His glory shall be revealed, ye may be glad also with exceeding joy." With what love and tenderness, dear Peter, by the Spirit of God, touches again on their sufferings and trials! How perplexed they must have been when they read their own Scriptures and remembered the promises made to Israel as to earthly blessings; and here they were suffering want and privation, were persecuted and slandered by those about them. He writes to them not to think it strange, as if a strange thing happened unto them, when passing through fiery trials. It is the path the Shepherd went and the sheep must follow Him. He suffered, it is the believer's privilege to suffer with Him. When sufferings and trials come, then is the time for rejoicing and not for being disheartened. Sufferings become sweet and precious when we remember they constitute us partakers of Christ's sufferings. And there is coming a revelation of His glory. In anticipation of that we can rejoice, for that revelation will bring the end of all suffering, and glory as well.

"If ye are reproached for the name of Christ, blessed are ye, for the Spirit of Glory and of God resteth upon you; on their part He is evil spoken of, but on your part He is glorified." Instead of trying to escape sufferings with Christ, a little reproach, a little contempt for Christ's sake, we should welcome all most gladly. There is a blessing in it, even when people call us narrow or by any other name of contempt, because we exalt Christ and are true to Him. The Spirit of Glory and of God rests upon us whenever we are reproached for the name of Christ. And if we were but more faithful, more separated, more loyal and devoted, we also would have more reproach, and as a result know more of the blessed experience that we are the resting and dwelling place of the Spirit of glory.

But there are sufferings which are inconsistent with Christ's sufferings and with the character of a Christian. "But if any suffer as a Christian, let him not be ashamed; but let him glorify God on this behalf." It means to count reproach and suffering for Christ an honor and a glory. Peter had made this experience when with his fellow-apostles he had been beaten, "they departed from the presence of the council, rejoicing that they were counted worthy to suffer shame for His name" (Acts v:41).

"For the time is come that judgment must begin at the house of God, and if it first begin at us, what shall the end be of them that obey not the Gospel of God? And if the righteous scarcely be saved, where shall the ungodly and sinner appear?" The sufferings of believers are permitted by the Lord for their own good likewise; they are His loving chastenings. Thus He deals as a loving Father with His house, whose house are we (Hebrews iii:6), permitting and using afflictions, sorrows, losses, that we may be partakers of His holiness. But if such is the case with His house, with those who belong to Him and whom He loves, what shall be the end of those that disobey the Gospel of God? If the righteous, the sinner saved by grace, in his walk through the wilderness can scarcely be saved, if it needs the very power of God to keep him, what shall be the fate of the ungodly and the sinner? Therefore, when the believer suffers he commits his soul to Him who is able to sustain and carry him through.

1. EXHORTATIONS CONCERNING SERVICE AND CONFLICT

CHAPTER V.

1. As to Christian Service. 1-7.
2. Conflict and Victory. 8-14.
3. The Conclusion. 12-14.

1. As to Christian Service: Verses 1-7. Peter now speaks in great tenderness exhorting to service. The exhortation is addressed to the elders and he speaks of himself as a "fellow-elder." Does he mean by this an official title or does he mean simply his age and experience? He is not writing in any official capacity, but the word elder has the meaning of old in years. He assumes no ecclesiastical authority to dictate, but speaks out of a ripe experience and a heart of love. How different from what ritualism has made him to be. He takes his place among the other elders and calls himself a fellow-elder, not claiming any authority or superiority whatever. He was a witness of the sufferings of Christ; he knew he would be a partaker of the glory which shall be revealed. The Lord had given him this assurance. (Matt. xix:28, 29).

He gives some important exhortations. We give it in a better rendering. "Tend the flock of God which is among you, exercising the oversight, not of constraint, but willingly; not for filthy lucre, but readily; neither as lording it over the charge allotted to you, but being ensamples to the flock." Believers here are called "the flock of God." In John x:16 the Lord had given the announcement that there should be one flock (not one fold, as the authorized version). The flock of God is the church, the body of Christ. The language so frequently heard in Christendom when preachers and pastors speak of those to whom they preach as "my flock" or "my people," is unscriptural and should be avoided. God's children do not belong to anybody but the Lord. As the Lord had commissioned Peter: "Feed my sheep" and "Feed my lambs," so Peter writes to the elders to tend the flock of God. It is the same Greek word used here which we find in John xxi:16 and is really "shepherd"—shepherd the flock of God. It is not to be done for filthy lucre's sake, on account of gain, for money considerations. All is prophetic, for exactly that which was not to be done is being done in Christendom today, hence many of those who claim to be shepherds of the flock are in reality nothing but hirelings; and often it happens that the hireling for the sake of better financial conditions will exchange "his flock" for another. Furthermore, there is to be no lording over the allotted charge (or over your allotments). The elder who has the oversight of the flock, called to shepherd the flock, minister to the flock as a servant, is not to take a place of superiority or spiritual dignity, claiming authority. This also is done in Christendom with its "Lord Bishops" and other titles of ecclesiastical authority. The word translated in the authorized version with "heritage" is in the Greek "*Kleros*", and means an allotment. From this word comes our English "Clergy." There is no such thing in the body of Christ as a "Clergy" and a "Laity."

Instead of lording over their allotted charge, the elders are to be ensamples to the flock, in a godly life. Then comes the promise, "when the chief shepherd is manifested, ye shall receive a crown of glory that fadeth not away." The sheep of Christ for which He laid down His life are very precious to Him, and those who serve His sheep, who minister to their need, will be honored by Him and rewarded with the crown of glory in the day of His manifestation. There is to be submission by the younger to the elder, that is, the younger in years are to be subject to those older in years. The same rule of loving submission extends to all the flock of God, "be subject one to another." Humility is to be the right clothing for the saints of God. "They are to gird themselves with humility in this way, humility being that which will keep everything rightly adjusted, as the girdle the robe, and which would thus enable for such activity as all are called to; for humility is a grand help against discouragement by the difficulties of the way, and necessarily against all that would search out any remnant of pride in us."* Self-exaltation is the very essence of sin. God cannot tolerate it in His people. The example of Christ, who made of Himself no reputation, forbids it. God resisteth therefore always and in every way the proud, while He giveth grace to the humble. "Humble yourselves therefore under the mighty hand of God, that He may exalt you in due time." How little these great exhortations are considered in our times! Even among those who have the truth and believe in the revelation of God, while there is much increase in knowledge, there is little evidence of true humility. Humility will never leave us ashamed. We do not need to exalt ourselves; the Lord will do it for us.

Then there is the sweet comfort: "Casting all your care upon Him, for He careth for you." All means all—all cares, whatever they are; all burdens, all anxieties we can roll upon Him, with the perfect assurance that He does care. Alas! our anxieties, our heavy feelings, our worry and our hurry, all speak the same language of unbelief "Lord, doest Thou not care?" Well, it is if we look upon all burdens He permits to be laid upon us, as tokens of His love, by which

*F. W. Grant.

we may learn His faithfulness afresh. Instead of murmuring then, we should sing and rejoice, being anxious for nothing, knowing He carries us and our burdens and cares as we can never do.

2. Conflict and Victory: Verses 8-11. Once more we hear His exhortation: "Be sober, be watchful!" Why? Because there is an adversary and a conflict. In those days of persecution he was the roaring lion; in our days he sneaks about as an angel of light. No longer is it the persecution of the church; it is the corruption of the Truth which is the work of the adversary today. But in Peter's day the enemy was engaged in active persecution, seeking to devour God's people. Once more he will assume this character during the coming great tribulation, the time of Jacob's trouble. Then the faithful Jewish remnant, like this remnant to whom Peter wrote, will have to face the roaring lion, as we read so frequently in the Book of Revelation.

Then follows Peter's benediction, quite a different thing from the fraudulent benedictions, which come from the counterfeit successors of Peter: "But the God of all grace, who hath called you unto His eternal glory in Christ Jesus, when ye have suffered a little while, Himself shall perfect, stablish, strengthen and settle you. To Him be glory and dominion for ever and ever."

3. The Conclusion: Verses 12-14. The Epistle was sent to them by Silvanus. It is the same Silvanus whose back had been lacerated in the prison of Philippi, whose feet had been in stocks, and who sang the praises of the Lord with beloved Paul in that night of pain and suffering. He knew what suffering with Christ meant and could equally sympathize with his brethren.

There is greeting from the other elect ones in Babylon, as we have shown in our introduction, in literal Babylon on the banks of the Euphrates. Salutation from Marcus is also given. This is John Mark, the cousin of Barnabas, whose failure in the Book of Acts is recorded, and on account of whom the Apostle Paul had a falling out with Barnabas;

it is the same Mark who wrote the Gospel which bears his name. The kiss of love is mentioned (Rom. xvi:16; 1 Cor. xvi:20; 2 Cor. xiii:12; 1 Thess. v:26). It was universally observed for centuries. "Peace be with you all in Christ Jesus. Amen."

THE SECOND EPISTLE OF PETER

The Second Epistle of Peter

Introduction

The authenticity of this second Epistle of Peter has occasioned a great deal of controversy and many are questioning it, as it has been done in the past. It is true the most ancient sources of post-apostolic writings do not mention this Epistle. What we have pointed out in the introductions of most of the other New Testament books, that their authenticity is confirmed by references in the fragments of the writings of the church fathers, such as Polycarp, Papias, Clement of Rome and others, cannot be done with this Epistle. Some scholars in their research claim that traces of this Epistle are discernable in the testimonies of Polycarp, Ignatius, in the letter of Barnabas and in the testimony of Clement of Rome, but they are so very faint and fanciful, that they are not reliable. But not finding a direct allusion in these sources does not mean anything at all. The greater portion of the writings of the men who were in touch with the Apostles and the direct disciples of the men who knew Peter and Paul, have been lost. If we had all they have written we would probably find in them references to this Epistle.

The Epistle is not found in the Peshito version. According to Bishop Westcott in his Canon of the New Testament there are in existence two classes of manuscripts of this version. Both omit the second and third Epistles of John, the second Epistle of Peter, the Epistle of Jude and the Book of Revelation, but include all the other books. This Canon seems to have been generally maintained in the Syrian churches. It is reproduced in the Arabic version of Erpenius, which was taken from the Peshito. Cosmas, an Egyptian traveller of the sixth century, states that only three of the so-called "Catholic" Epistles were received by the Syrians. Later sources charge the Syrian churches with mutilating the New Testament by not having these books in their Bibles.

The Epistle is also omitted in the Latin Version, that is, in the oldest editions. That the Vulgate is unreliable is well known. Westcott makes the following argument about the missing second Epistle of Peter in the Latin version: "If we suppose that it was once received into the canon like the first Epistle, it would in all probability have been translated by the same person, as seems to have been the case with the Gospel of Luke and the Acts (both written by Luke), though their connection is less obvious; and while every allowance is made for the difference in style in the original Epistles, we must look for the same rendering of the same phrases. But when on the contrary, it appears that the Latin test of the Epistle not only exhibits constant and remarkable difference from the text of other parts of the Vulgate, but also differs from the first Epistle in the rendering of words common to both, when it further appears that it differs not less clearly from the Epistle of Jude in those parts which are almost identical in the Greek; then the supposition that it was admitted into the Canon at the same time with them becomes at once unnatural. It is indeed possible that the two Epistles may have been received at the same time and yet have found different translators." But this argument does not mean at all that this Epistle is spurious and should be excluded from the New Testament.

But while the Epistle is not mentioned in the Muratorian fragment, in the writings of Polycarp, Papias, Irenaeus and others, and while it is missing in the Peshito and the earlier editions of the Vulgate, Hippolytus (living in the first half of the third century) was evidently acquainted with the Epistle, for in writing on the Antichrist he makes use of 2 Peter i:21. Eusebius, the church historian, gives incontrovertible testimony that the Epistle was positively known at the close of the second century as the second Epistle of Peter. He shows that Clement of Alexandria (about 190 A.D.) knew the Epistle as the work of Peter and used it. The successor of Clement, Origen, according to Eusebius, wrote: "Peter has left one acknowledged Epistle, and possibly also a second, for it is disputed." It was through Jerome's (Eusebius Hieronymus, born 390 A.D.) efforts that the Epistle was added to the Vulgate, He wrote: "Peter wrote two Epistles, which are termed Catholic, the second of which is denied by most to be his, because of the disagreement of its style with that of the former Epistle." On account of these historical facts opinions among scholars have been very much divided. Many reject the Petrine authorship of this Epistle, but other scholars accept it without any question. Among those who defend the Epistle against those who deny it are scholars of the highest reputation like Alford, Olshausen, Keil and others.

The Sufficiency of Internal Evidence

The fact is that external evidences to confirm the authenticity of Second Peter are not needed, for the internal evidences are beyond controversy of such a nature as to establish the Petrine authorship. The Epistle starts with the name of Peter. In the Greek the name Simon is spelled "Symeon" or "Simeon." If we turn to Acts xv:14 we read that James called Peter "Symeon," the Aramaic form for Simon. Then the writer refers to the fact that he would have soon to put off this tabernacle "even as our Lord Jesus Christ hath showed me." He was now an old man, and the Lord had spoken to him at the lakeside "When thou art old thou shalt stretch forth thy hands" (John xxi). Still stronger is the reference of the writer to the transfiguration, where Peter was present, and he speaks of it as being an eyewitness of His Coming and of His Majesty. And, finally, the writer says: "This *second* Epistle, beloved, I now write unto you" (chapter iii:1).

Critical Claims and Evasions

This internal evidence destructive critics try to evade and offset. They claim that the writer was not Simon Peter, but that some unknown author, using Peter's name, wrote this document. It is the same foolish invention advanced by Old Testament critics as to the authorship of the Book of Daniel.

To establish this theory they point to the fact that there was a tendency in the early church to use Peter's name in different pseudo documents, such spurious writings as "The Gospel of Peter; The Revelation of Peter; the Acts of Peter and the travels of Peter." But the fact of these forgeries, some of which cover some of the text of the second Epistle of Peter, is an evidence that a genuine writing exists. According to the opinions of the men who reject the authorship of Peter, the writer of this Epistle to give standing to his production, thought best to impersonate the Apostle Peter and so he started right in the beginning by saying he is Peter. And he is careful to select the Aramaic form of Peter's name, the name Symeon. Would a forger not rather have avoided that uncommon use of Peter's name? But, furthermore, he also tells us that the Lord had told him about his death; and yet this man was not Peter, nor had the Lord ever told him, what he had spoken to Peter about the time and manner of his death. Then the writer of the Epistle claims to have been on the Mount of Transfiguration, that he beheld His glory there and heard the voice of the Father speaking. He is positive that he was present and was an eyewitness, the strongest possible claim. Yet if it was not Peter who wrote this Epistle, then it must have been either John or James, because there were only three eyewitnesses of the transfiguration. But would John or James write thus, hiding his identity under the name of Peter? Then the writer, assuming the name of Peter, declares that he had written the first Epistle, which Peter beyond doubt wrote, yet he had *not* written that Epistle. Here are three (in plain English) *lies*. A man writes an Epistle claiming to be Peter, but he is not Peter at all; hence he is a fraud. The same man claims that he was at the lake of Tiberias, that the Lord told him about his death; yet he was not there, for he was not Peter; therefore this impersonator is a fraud. This is an especially strong point. The fact that the Lord had announced Peter's death was known to but a few at that time, when the Epistle was written, which we take was about the year 65 A. D. The Gospel of John where the Lord's prophecy as to Peter's future is recorded had not yet been written. Furthermore, he says that he saw the transfiguration, which he did not see; hence he lied. The fourth lie is his claim that he wrote the first Epistle, which he did not write. It is astonishing what inventions the enemies of the Bible can bring forth simply to discredit the Word of God and to deny its authenticity. If Peter is not the writer of this Epistle the whole Epistle is a miserable fraud, a dishonest piece of work, a forgery of the worst kind, which every honest man must despise. The foolish babblings of critics: "it is a useful document and should be read by all Christians, though Peter did not write it himself," is ridiculous. Either Peter wrote it and then it must be accepted; or Peter did not write it and in such a case the whole business is a forgery and a fraud. But would a fraud ever have written such a wonderful message as the one with which this second Epistle begins? Would a conscious fraud have warned against apostasy as found in the second chapter? Would he, could he, have exhorted fellow-believers in the way as it is done in this Epistle? It is a moral impossibility.

The Character of the Second Epistle

One of the critics makes the following statement in denying the Petrine authorship: "The fact that the only allusions to the incidents in the Lord's life found in the Epistle are such as would support the character as one writing as Peter does become, in view of the silence of the Epistle as to the passion, the resurrection, the ascension, and of the absence from it of allusions to the Lord's teaching as recorded in the Gospel, are a serious ground for questioning the Petrine authorship of the Epistle" (Chase). Like most critics this one lacks in spiritual discernment. In fact, if critics had some spiritual insight in the majestic scope of God's holy Word, they would not be critics, but worshipers. All second Epistles, except second Corinthians, have a peculiar character. Second Thessalonians, second Timothy, second and third John, and the little Epistle of Jude are in reality prophetic. They all speak of the future, the coming evils in professing Christendom, the apostasy, and all warn against these things. The second Epistle of Peter shares the same character with the other second Epistles and Jude's Epistle. There was no need for Peter to refer again to the passion, the resurrection and ascension of Christ, for besides being outside of the scope of this second letter, he had given his witness and testimony as to these facts so abundantly in his first Epistle. The Two Epistles harmonize in many ways.

Another Supposed Difficulty

Another supposed difficulty is the similarity that exists between the second chapter of this Epistle and the Epistle of Jude. This difficulty will be taken up more fully, in connection with the annotations of the chapter and in the introduction to Jude's Epistle. The learned scholars have spent much time on the question whether Jude copied from Peter or Peter copied from Jude. Some claim that Peter had Jude's Epistle and used it; others claim that Jude imitated Peter. Even so good a scholar as the late Dean Alford says: "It is well known that, besides various scattered resemblances, a long passage occurs, included in the limits Jude 3-19; 2 Peter ii:1-19, describing in both cases the heretical enemies of the Gospel, couched in terms so similar as to preclude all idea of entire independence. If considerations of human probability are here as everywhere else to be introduced into our estimate of sacred writings, then either one saw and used the text of the other, or both drew from a common document or a common source of oral apostolic teaching." This in reality affects the truth of inspiration, and leans towards criticism. If Peter sat down and copied Jude, what Peter wrote was not inspired, but copied. And if Jude sat down and wrote after the pattern of Peter, copied him, and worked over his testimony, then Jude is not inspired. But both, Peter and Jude were inspired, and therefore they wrote independent of each other, the Holy Spirit guiding their respective pens, in giving the same testimony of warning.

The Divisions of Second Peter

This second Epistle of Peter may be looked upon as an appendix or complement of the first Epistle. It introduces a testimony as to the future, connected with the Coming of the Lord, which the first Epistle so frequently mentions. While the first Epistle is silent as to the coming evils preceding the Coming of the Lord, this second Epistle sounds the warning and gives, as already stated in the preceding introduction, a prophetic picture of the conditions of Christendom when the age closes. Here, too, we find the exhortations of Peter, similar to those in the first letter. Peter himself states the purpose when he wrote: "This second Epistle, beloved, I now write unto you, in both of which I stir up your pure minds by way of remembrance." While the language may differ in some respects from the language of the first Epistle, the style and development of the Epistle is just like the first, which is even noticeable in our English version. He writes first of the gracious provisions, which are made for those of like precious faith through the righteousness of God and our Saviour Jesus Christ, which includes present provisions in precious promises, and the gift of all things that pertain unto life and godliness, as well as the gift of the Word of Prophecy.

The second chapter unfolds the coming dangers of the last days of this age. The false teachers and their pernicious doctrines are revealed with the corresponding warnings to beware of them. The concluding chapter is prophetic; it reveals the future, including the coming great transformation when the physical earth will pass through a judgment by fire, to come forth in an eternal resurrection glory as a new earth, surrounded by new heavens. We follow, therefore, in our annotations the division of the Epistle in three chapters as we have it in our Bibles.

I. **THE GRACIOUS PROVISIONS OF GOD.** Chapter I.

II. **THE EVILS TO COME THROUGH FALSE TEACHERS.** Chapter II.

III. **THE FUTURE OF THE EARTH AND THE CONCLUSION.** Chapter III.

Analysis and Annotations

I. THE GRACIOUS PROVISIONS OF GOD.

CHAPTER I.

1. God's gracious provisions in Christ. 1-4.
2. The Development of the Divine Nature. 5-11.
3. The Promises of Prophecy. 12-21

1. God's Gracious Provisions in Christ: Verses 1-4. We are not left in doubt who the writer is, not a pseudo Peter, but Simon Peter, the fisherman of Galilee. With this second Epistle he finishes the task given him by the Lord "to strengthen his brethren." The opening verse of the third chapter shows that the Epistle is addressed to the same persons to whom he wrote the first Epistle. He gives first his old name, Simon (or as in the Greek, Symeon), followed by the new name given him by the Lord, Peter. He calls himself a servant first before he mentions his apostleship. The word servant is the same as the word by which Paul designated himself, that is, a slave. Evidently Peter estimated his servantship higher than his apostleship.

He addresses his brethren no longer as he did in his first Epistle as strangers and elect by the foreknowledge of God. His purpose is a different one. No longer does he mention their trials, sufferings and persecutions; this was done abundantly in the preceding document. He addresses them instead as those "that have obtained like precious faith," that is, the faith in the Lord Jesus Christ, the Son of God, Saviour and Lord. This faith is obtained "through the righteousness of God and our Saviour Jesus Christ." In Romans the righteousness of God is the great theme as the ground of the believer's justification (see annotations on Romans iii). Here it has a somewhat different meaning. It is not the question of justification, but the question of God having been righteous, that is, faithful to His promises by Him who is Jehovah, their own promised Messiah. It was the faithfulness of the God of Israel which had bestowed upon them as a believing remnant this faith, which was now so precious to them, the faith in Jehovah-Jesus as Saviour.

Then follows the greeting: "Grace and peace be multiplied unto you through the knowledge of God, and of our Lord Jesus Christ." This form of greeting using the word "multiplied" is confined to the two Epistles of Peter and the Epistle of Jude. It is not without significance. When believers suffer, as seen in the First Epistle of Peter, they can count on God to multiply grace and peace. But Second Peter and the Epistle of Jude look forward to the last days, the end of the age, with its predicted apostasy, and for those days God promises to multiply to His own grace, peace and mercy. But it must be noticed that this multiplication is "through the knowledge of God, and of our Lord Jesus Christ." It is not independent of a real heart knowledge of God and His Son, our Lord. There may be a head knowledge of God and of Christ, a barren knowledge which brings no fruit unto God. Of this we read in chapter ii:20-22 of our Epistle. The knowledge of God is in Jesus Christ; through Him we know God in all His gracious fullness (see 1 John v:20). The real heart knowledge of Him produces fruit because it carries with it divine power, which has given to the believer "all things that pertain to life and godliness, through the knowledge of Him that hath called us by glory and virtue." Life and glory are the gifts of grace; life is bestowed in the new birth which fits for glory, but godliness and virtue are the practical results of that grace in the life of the believer. The divine power for godliness and virtue which are to be manifested in the believer's life, that power which is able to act in us and give us the victory, must be laid hold on by faith. "How precious it is to know that faith can use this divine power, realized in the life of the soul, directing it toward glory in the end! What a safeguard from the efforts of the enemy, if we are really established in the consciousness of this divine power acting on our behalf in grace! The heart is led to make glory its object;

and virtue, the strength of spiritual life, is developed on the way to it. Divine power has given all that is needed."*

Having called us by glory and virtue, He has in connection with it given us exceeding great and precious promises. These promises relate to both, glory and virtue. Through these promises we are made partakers of the divine nature, by the divine power acting in us, with the glory as the blessed goal. But by the same power promised unto us, we escape and are delivered from the corruption that is in the world through lust. Here is the real victorious life of a believer. It is not in some kind of a fixed "holiness experience" by which the old nature is eradicated, a teaching which is altogether against Scripture. The heart must be occupied with Christ and the glory by which we are called, as a result the divine power, the Holy Spirit in us, acts and victory over sin results.

2. The Development of the Divine Nature: Verses 5-11. While God promises to His people to add, that is, to multiply, daily grace and peace, they themselves in the faith which realizes the divine power and the glory to come, must add to that faith virtue, and that is to be done "by giving all diligence." The divine nature which the believer has received loves the will of God; it is a holy nature, and therefore abhors the corruption which is in the world by lust. But that divine nature is subject to growth and development in the life of the child of God, and that requires all care and diligence. If Christians say that they possess a new nature, are born again, saved by grace, and continue to live according to the old nature, enjoying the world and its sinful pleasures, without manifesting godliness and virtue, they are not only in a very unscriptural attitude, but on dangerous ground. It would prove that they belong to the class of professors described in chapter ii:20-22.

Seven things are to be added to faith. "Add to your faith virtue." This word means something different from its general meaning in English. It means moral courage, a

*Synopsis.

courage which refuses the gratification of the old nature. It is the soldier's courage, who stands manfully against all opposition. It is an energy by which the heart is master of itself, and is able to choose the good, and to cast aside the evil, as a thing conquered and unworthy of one's self. Such courage to stand and withstand, this energy to deny one's self, makes full communion with God possible. If such virtue is added to faith it leads to knowledge, the next thing. The truth of God and the things of God are known and learned by obedience, by walking in them. Knowledge gained, without virtue practised, only puffs up and leads to hypocrisy. A true knowledge of God is heart acquaintance with Him. This knowledge leads to temperance, which means self-restraint. And self-restraint, the government of the will, must be followed by patience, which means endurance. How easy it is to endure reproach, wrongs inflicted by others, sufferings—to endure it all in patience when faith looks to Him Who endured more than we are ever called upon to do. If such is the case, godliness will not be lacking. It is a walk with God, communion with Him, child-like trust and obedience and reverence. Out of such a heart of faith, which has moral courage, practises self-restraint, knowing God, endures and is godly—affections towards fellow-believers flow forth and brotherly love is added. This is what the knowledge of God teaches, "Ye yourselves are taught of God to love one another" (1 Thess. iv:9). But there is something still higher than brotherly kindness and affection, and that is "Love." It means divine Love, which is the very nature of God Himself. "If divine love governs me, I love all my brethren; I love them because they belong to Christ; there is no partiality. I shall have greater *enjoyment* in a spiritual brother; but I shall occupy myself about my weaker brother with a love that rises above his weakness and has a tender consideration for it. I shall concern myself with my brother's sin, from love to God, in order to restore my brother, rebuking him, if needful; nor, if divine love be in exercise, can brotherly love be associated with disobedience. In a word, God will have His place in all my relationships."*

Here, then, is food for self-examination and self-judgment. Does my faith in Christ, in whom all things are freely supplied pertaining to life and godliness, produce moral courage—does it produce heart knowledge of God, self-restraint, endurance in meekness, godliness and brotherly love and is all governed in me according to love, the very essence of God Himself? These things should be not only in us, but abound. It will not leave us barren or unfruitful. "But he that lacketh these things is blind, and cannot see afar off (short-sighted) and hath forgotten that he was cleansed from his former sins." There is not only the blindness of the natural man, but there may be a blindness and short-sightedness of a believer. It means that a believer whose new nature does not develop and manifest itself in these things, is short-sighted in respect to the heavenly things, the seen things which surround him are the objects which absorb his mind. Such a one forgets that he was cleansed from his former sins. The joy and peace in the Holy Spirit are no longer a present possession; his own heart condemns him and he lacks the reality of His salvation; the joy of it is gone, he has forgotten his cleansing from his former sins. When a believer remembers what God has done for Him in redemption, he will also long for a practical manifestation of that salvation in a godly life and walk.

He speaks next of making our calling and election sure. But is this not sure already? As far as God, who has called and elected us, is concerned, it is sure. To have a consciousness of our calling and election, the sureness of it, requires diligence to walk in the path which the Holy Spirit through the pen of Peter has so beautifully described. Those who walk thus will not stumble, and, finally, "an entrance shall be ministered unto you abundantly into the everlasting kingdom of our Lord and Saviour Jesus Christ."

3. The Promises of Prophecy: Verses 13-21. Having

---

*John N. Darby.

mentioned the coming kingdom of Christ, the Holy Spirit now enlarges upon this. We pointed out in the first Epistle that salvation to be revealed, as repeatedly stated, means the visible and glorious appearing of our Lord to establish His kingdom on earth. Peter does not teach the coming of the Lord for His Saints at all. He knew it, of course, for the Lord had revealed it through Paul. Inasmuch as Peter writes to this remnant of believing Jews, and that remnant is also representative of another remnant, which will, during the great tribulation, suffer and wait for the coming of the King, the second half of this chapter is therefore taken up with the kingdom in manifestation, as revealed in prophecy and foreshadowed by the transfiguration.

He speaks first of His coming departure; the Lord had told him about that long ago. But there was no doubt a special intimation from the Lord that this event would now soon be and he would have "to put off this tabernacle." So before his departure he was anxious to give them instructions by the Spirit of God, so that they might have these things always in remembrance. This makes it clear once more that Peter did not look for a chain of successors to become guardians and instructors of the faith.

He and the other Apostles had not followed cunningly devised fables when they made known the power and coming of the Lord Jesus Christ. They had been eye witnesses of His majesty. But where and how? He speaks of the scene on the holy mount, when the Lord Jesus Christ was transfigured before them, when they heard the voice of the Father from the excellent glory. He stood upon that mount clothed with the glory of the Father; with Him Moses and Elijah, the one who had died, the other who went to heaven without dying. It was a foregleam of His coming glory and a fulfillment of the promise given in the last verse of Matthew xvi. As He stood upon that mountain, so He will appear in His glory on earth again, bringing His saints with Him. It is His visible and glorious appearing to which Peter refers, and which was foreshadowed in the transfiguration, and not that coming promised to His own in John xiv:1-3, to take them into the Father's house.

"We have also a more sure word of prophecy" should be rendered, "We have the word of prophecy made more sure." The Word of prophecy is, of course, in the Old Testament. But is not this sure enough? Why should it be made more sure? It must be understood in the sense of attesting, or confirming the word of prophecy. The transfiguration confirmed the prophecies in the Old Testament. The prophets describe such a scene like the transfiguration, when the Son of Man comes from heaven in power and glory; hence the word of prophecy has been confirmed, made more sure, by the scene on the holy mount. Let it be stated again that the Old Testament prophetic Word does not reveal that coming for His saints, which is for the church "that blessed Hope." When Paul speaks of it in 1 Corinthians xv he speaks of it as a mystery; it was hidden in former ages (1 Cor. xv:51). Yet in the verse before us Peter alludes to it when he speaks of the morning star. There is a difficulty connected with this verse, and some have read it as if it meant that the morning star must arise in the heart of the individual, as it has been stated in the following comment: "The day star arising in our hearts will be the inner premonitions which announce the coming, as the day star heralds the dawn; such premonitions might be occasioned by observing the various signs of the coming." But it does not mean this at all, nor does it mean that prophecy is only to be used for encouragement till we possess the proper Christian hope. The suggested rendering in the "Numerical Bible" removes the difficulty. "We have also the prophetic Word confirmed, to which ye do well in taking heed (as to a lamp that shineth in an obscure place, until the day dawn and the morning star ariseth) in your hearts. It does not mean that the morning star is to arise in the heart of the believer; it means that we should take heed to prophecy in our hearts. And how the entire prophetic Word, that blessed lamp, is needed in these darkening days!

The day dawn is preceded by the rising of the morning

star, or day star, and the morning star is the blessed emblem of the coming of the Lord for His saints. He is both the morning star and the sun of righteousness. He appears as the morning star for His saints and afterward in full glory as the sun of righteousness.

The closing statements of this chapter are also of much importance. "Knowing this first, that no prophecy of Scripture is of private interpretation. For no prophecy ever came by the will of man; but men spake from God, being moved by the Holy Spirit." Prophecy never could be produced by the will of man; God only knows the future and He has spoken concerning the future. The fact of prophecy is one of the great evidences of the supernaturalness of the Bible. The men who were used to communicate prophecy spoke from God; they were moved by the Holy Spirit. For this reason the pernicious school of destructive criticism has always aimed at the prophetic Word, for if they concede that there is prophecy, they acknowledge their defeat. What denials and theories they have used in order to get rid of prophecy we cannot follow here. The next chapter shows what results have been brought about through the rejection of the truth stated by Peter, that God hath spoken. Of equal importance is the divine statement, "that no prophecy of Scripture is of private interpretation." Rome has used the word "private" to uphold its awful lie, that Scripture should never be interpreted by a private individual. As a result Rome discourages in every way the reading of the Word of God. In the past that system burned the Bibles, often chaining the Bible to the martyr at the stake, burning the hated Book with the hated witness. Give Rome her old time power and she will do it again. The prophetic Word only is here in view. Prophecy shows a divine unity that is wonderful. Some have said that history must interpret prophecy, but that is not so. History is predicted in advance by prophecy. In interpreting prophecy, prophetic Scripture must be compared with prophetic Scripture. Prophecy must be taken as a whole. We have no business to say, as it is often done, "I think it means this or that." Prophecy starts in Genesis iii:15. The consummation of all prophecy is the Kingdom of Christ, the victory of God in His Son, the complete defeat of Satan. Every prophecy is a part of prophecy, having one and the same object and can, therefore, not be interpreted by itself, independent of the rest of prophecy. All the confusion which is in the professing church today as to the prophetic forecasts of the Word of God is the result of having ignored this important injunction.

II. THE EVIL TO COME THROUGH FALSE TEACHERS

CHAPTER II.

1. The Source of the Evil. 1-3.
2. The Lessons from the Past. 4-10.
3. The Description of the Apostates. 11-22.

1. The Source of Apostasy: Verses 1-3. Tbe Apostle Peter is now being used by the Spirit of God to prophesy. He predicts the coming evil for the professing church, that apostate teachers would do their vicious work. As pointed out in the introduction every other writer of the Epistles bears the same witness and that witness is mostly found in the second Epistles and in the Epistle of Jude (see 1 Tim. iv:1-2; 2 Tim. iii:1-5; iv:1-4; 2 Thess. ii; 1 John ii:18-23; iv:1-6; 2 John, verses 7-11; Jude). He reminds them that among their own nation Israel there were false prophets. The false prophets appeared mostly, if not altogether, when judgment was impending for the nation, as we learn from the prophecies of Jeremiah and Ezekiel. These false prophets opposed the true prophets of God, who preached the God-given message, while the false prophets rejected the Word of the Lord and belittled it. They spoke out of their own hearts and spoke vanities and lies (Ezek. xiii:2, 8). Their message was "peace" when there was no peace. As a result the people of Israel did not believe the Lord and His Word; they rejected Him. The same, it is predicted, would be repeated in this Christian age, only with this difference, that not false prophets should appear, but "false teachers." And as this dispensation draws to its close apostasy would set in (consult annotations on 2 Thess. ii). These false teachers, like the false prophets, reject first of all the Word of God; they, too, speak out of their own hearts, that is, vanities and lies. As a result they bring in "privily destructive heresies." All heresies have but one goal, and that is the denial of Christ and the Gospel. Therefore Peter predicts "denying even the Master, who bought them." This is the way of destructive criticism. One looks in vain among the many preachers and teachers who deny the Virgin birth and with it the Deity of Christ, for one who believes that the Bible is the inerrant Word of God. All those who deny the Master who bought them began with criticism of the Bible, rejecting first the writings of Moses, casting doubt upon other books, and finally abandoning any kind of faith in the Bible as the Word of God. Well is it called "the destructive criticism," for it is in the end destructive of everything. It is this which is poisoning everything in Christendom today and there is no denomination in which this leaven is not at work. Thus Peter's prediction is increasingly fulfilled in our days and will be much more as this age draws rapidly to its close. We must also notice that it does not say that they deny "the Lord who redeemed them"; but "the Master who bought" or purchased "them." The difference between "purchase" and "redemption" is, that purchase is general, while redemption is limited to those who believe on Him and are thus redeemed by His precious blood. These false teachers never believed on Him as Lord, and, therefore, they are not redeemed by Him, though He paid the purchase price in their behalf. By denying Him they disowned the purchase. And for such there is in store swift destruction. This pronounces the sentence of eternal doom upon all false teachers, upon destructive criticism as well as upon the cults which teach damnable heresies and, by doing it, deny the Master who bought them.

Here is also a prediction of the wide-spread success of these false teachers. "Many shall follow their pernicious (dissolute or lascivious) ways, through whom the way of truth shall be blasphemed." They speak of making the world better, they pose as teachers of morality and righteousness, but their ways are branded as pernicious. How can they be righteous when they deny that which alone can give righteousness to man? How often it has been brought to light that those who deny the Truth and yet claim to be teachers of morality, were miserable hypocrites. Unbelief produces worldliness and immorality. Then the way of truth is being blasphemed and "that worthy Name" is being dishonored.

"And through covetousness shall they with feigned words make merchandise of you; whose judgment now from of old lingereth not, and their destruction slumbereth not." The people of God are their prey. They are covetous, seeking their own gratification in money, social standing, fame and everything else that the natural heart loves and desires. All is abundantly verified in the conditions about us. But retribution will surely come upon them.

2. The Lessons from the Past: Verses 4-10. Here we reach the section of second Peter, which is so much like the greater part of Jude's Epistle, that critics have claimed that one must have copied from the other. We have shown in the introduction that Peter and Jude wrote independently of each other as the direct instruments of the Holy Spirit. The correspondence of Peter's testimony with Jude's Epistle is more fully examined in the introduction to Jude.

The Spirit of God calls attention through Peter to that which happened in past history, showing that God deals with apostates who defy Him and are disobedient, while the godly He delivers. In Jude we shall find out, that while there is much similarity, the purpose of the testimony is quite different from that of Peter. First, mention is made of the angels who sinned and who are cast down to hell, the word being Tartarus (the very lowest pit), where they are kept in chains of darkness for the coming judgment. It is evident that this passage does not mean Satan and the angels who joined in his rebellion before ever man was created.

Satan and the fallen angels are not now in the lowest pit awaiting there in a helpless condition the judgment; they are not in chains, but loose, and Satan, as the prince of this world, uses his angels in the pursuit of his work. Who, then, are these angels? They are the beings described in Genesis vi:1-4 as the "sons of God" (a term which in the Old Testament means angels) who came down and mingled with the daughters of men. These angels, as Jude tells us, did not keep their first estate, left their assigned place, and by their disobedience became the means of corrupting the race in such a manner that the judgment of God had to act in the deluge. God has not been pleased to give a complete revelation of this sinister event. That it means this episode is learned that Peter at once speaks of the old world, which was not spared by God, "but saved Noah, the eighth person (with seven others), a preacher of righteousness, having brought in the flood upon the world of the ungodly." This testimony is closely linked with what Peter had written in the first Epistle (1 Peter iii:19-20). And here we are told that Noah was a preacher of righteousness. He and his house had found grace in the sight of the Lord, while the mass of the ungodly world who rejected His Truth and His Spirit, who strove with them, were not spared but dealt with in judgment. It is so now. Another day is coming in which the Lord will judge the ungodly and unbelieving, while His people will be saved.

Sodom and Gomorrah are cited also as examples of God's holy judgment. These cities were turned into ashes, as an example of all those who live ungodly. The awful fruit of sin in the most terrible, unutterable corruption was manifested in these cities; the same corruption is found still in the world, and that mostly in the great centers of Christendom. (Romans i:27 mentions the same corruption so often referred to by classic writers of Rome and Greece.) Lot, who was in Sodom, though not of Sodom, is called, nevertheless, righteous, was vexed from day to day with their lawless deeds. The Lord delivered him. It is another warning to the false teachers with their denials and heresies, for the rejection of God's Word brings in the flood of immorality, licentiousness and lawlessness. The God who turned Sodom and Gomorrah into ashes, by raining upon them fire and brimstone, will also deal with the apostasy at the close of this age, and with the teachers who deny the Master who bought them, in spite of their self-flattery that they are moral. That judgment comes "when the Lord Jesus shall be revealed from heaven with His mighty angels, in flaming fire taking vengeance on them that know not God and that obey not the gospel of our Lord Jesus Christ; who shall be punished with everlasting destruction from the presence of the Lord and from the glory of His power" (2 Thess. i:7-9). These false teachers sneer at these words of Paul and call them quotations taken from the apocalyptic literature of the Jews, or something else; but the day will surely come when the Lord will vindicate His Truth. In the meantime He knows the righteous, watches over them and knows how to deliver them.

3. The Description of the Apostates: Verses 11-22. This is one of the most solemn portions of the Word of God. It is prophetic, for here we have a description of the false teachers of the last days. Here is a startling picture of the baptized infidels of Christendom. It corresponds in a measure with 2 Timothy iii:1-5. They are bold (daring), self-willed, and tremble not to rail at dignities. They are unbridled in their talk and in their conduct. They are daring enough to assail every part of the Truth of God, they call His revelation a myth, the Virgin birth a legend, and despise the atoning work of the Son of God; they do what angels would never do, railing at dignities.*

As we read on let us remember that not Peter, but the

*Jude has more to say about this; it is a well-known fact that some of the liberal theology leaders have joined hands with socialism in its worst form, that is, the anarchistic side of it. They speak of helping the masses and they rail against existing law and order, and advocate their overthrow. The ringleader of an attempt in Western Canada against the government was an apostate preacher of an honored denomination. The so-called "parlor-bolshevists" belong to this class.

Holy Spirit speaks. They are compared to beasts, just born to be caught and to be destroyed; they speak evil of the things of which they know nothing whatever. The meaning is that they were never born again, and therefore follow the flesh, though it may be under the guise of culture and learning. They shall perish in their own corruption. They count it pleasure to revel in the day-time, they delight in luxurious and sinful pleasures. More than that, they claim a Christian profession and fellowship, by attending the love-feasts of believers, which they dishonor by their presence as spots and blemishes, while at the same time they glory in their deceivings, their false teachings and denials of the Master. The right (or straight) way which they professed to have taken, when they took the name of Christ upon themselves, they have now left, having gone astray. Therefore they have eyes full of adultery and cannot cease from sin; they entice unstable souls, leading them astray as they have gone astray themselves.

They are also following in the way of Balaam, who was rebuked for his iniquity by the speaking of the dumb ass. The love of money controls them, as it controlled the heathen prophet. Verses 17 and 18 give additional descriptions of the character of these false teachers. They are springs without water, men look to them for the refreshing water of life, because they profess to be teachers; "the hungry sheep look up and are not fed." They know nothing of the water of life. They are nothing but obscuring mists driven by the tempest of their natural hearts. The great swelling words is the divine estimate of empty, human rhetoric by which thousands are swayed, but they are words of vanity, instead of bringing souls to Christ and the knowledge of redemption, they allure them through the lusts of the flesh, while they promise liberty to others, they are themselves slaves of corruption. Such is the character of the false teachers, who deny the Master that bought them.

"For if, after having escaped the pollutions of the world through the knowledge of the Lord and Saviour Jesus Christ they are again entangled therein and overcome, the latter end is worse with them than the first. For it had been better for them not to have known the way of righteousness, than, having known it, to turn back from the holy commandment delivered unto them." Does this mean that these persons were at one time really begotten again, having received life and the Holy Spirit by trusting on Christ? These false teachers certainly were never born again; the description which we have of them is the proof of it. The last verse of this chapter gives the conclusive evidence. Believers, true Christians, are never compared to dogs or swine; they are the sheep of His flock. A sheep cannot be transformed into a dog or a swine, nor will a sheep do what a dog or a swine does. They were therefore never true children of God. They had escaped the outward pollutions of the world, which is a different thing from the escape of the corruption which is in the world by lust; the latter stands for the inward deliverance by the new birth, the former for an outward reformation which had taken place when they professed the knowledge of the Lord and Saviour Jesus Christ, when for a time forsaking their evil ways so that they escaped the pollutions. But not having a new nature they became entangled therein and overcome, so that it was worse with them than in the beginning, before they had made a profession. They had known the way of righteousness as made known in the Gospel of Christ, but the life which is offered in that way of righteousness, with the fruits of righteousness which follow, they had never accepted by a living faith. And this seems to be the case with the vast majority of the false teachers of today, the destructive critics, and those who deny the Deity of our Lord. They were never born again; they never had a true experience of real salvation, hence they are but natural men, not having the Spirit.

III. THE FUTURE OF THE EARTH. THE CONCLUSION

CHAPTER III.

1. Mocking at the Lord's Coming. 1-7.
2. The Future of the Earth. 8-10.
3. Exhortation and Conclusion. 11-18.

1. Mocking at the Lord's Coming: Verses 1-7. The opening statement shows conclusively that Peter is the author and that this second Epistle was sent to the same believers to whom the first Epistle was addressed. The critics claim that this chapter marks a separate Epistle in itself and that it was combined by mistake with the preceding two chapters. Like so much else the critics put forth this is a foolish speculation wholly unwarranted.

Peter states the reason for this second Epistle "to stir up their pure minds by way of remembrance." He had already used a similar statement in the first chapter (i:12), but now exhorts them to be mindful of the words which were spoken before by the holy prophets and the commandment of the Lord and Saviour through the apostles. The evil had been prophetically pictured by Peter and now he charges them to use the Word of God in the coming days of peril and apostasy, and remember especially its prophetic forecast. The apostle Paul did the same after he had given the warning of the coming of grievous wolves and false teachers (Acts xx:30). Such is the resource of the true church today, and in the degree, as we remember the words spoken by the prophets and by the apostles, give heed to them, we shall be kept in the perilous times. Both the prophets and the apostles warned of the evil to come as each age closes with apostasy and judgment; so did the Lord Himself when He predicted the future of the age and the conditions which precede His physical and glorious return. All have given the warning. Enoch was a prophet, as we learn from Jude; he prophesied about the coming of the Lord to execute judgment. There were apostates in his day who ridiculed his testimony and who spoke against him (Jude, verse 15).

Noah was a preacher of righteousness; he built the ark and sounded the warning, but no one paid any attention to him, and "as it was in the days of Noah so shall it be when the Son of Man cometh," said our Lord. The prophets warned of the judgment in store for Jerusalem; the warning was not heeded, and such a great one as Jeremiah was not believed, and cast into the dungeon. The prophet Amos speaks of those who "put far off the evil day." There were mockers and unbelievers each time an age ended. As already shown, the combined testimony of the apostles is on the same lines. Peter then writes: "Knowing this first, that in the last days mockers shall come with mockery, walking after their own lusts, and saying, Where is the promise of His coming? for, from the day the fathers fell asleep, all things continue as they were from the beginning of the creation."

While before Peter had shown the quality of the false teachers, he now points out by the revelation given unto him, that there would be unbelief and outright mockery touching the visible return of the Lord Jesus Christ. In both Epistles this great coming event, the coming of the Lord in the clouds of heaven, has a prominent place. The false teachers, whose doom will be sealed when Christ comes again, also ridicule and scoff at the idea that He will ever show Himself again. And why do they mock and sneer? It has its source in unbelief. These men are infidels. Every destructive critic is an infidel. The records of the past embodied in the Holy Scriptures are denied to be authentic and reliable. The prophets of God were Jewish patriots who dreamt of a great Jewish future. The magnificent prophecies as to the coming kingdom and the rule of the King of kings are classed with the apocalyptic ramblings of the "Sibyline writings." The Lord Jesus Christ is even impeached as to His knowledge and is regarded as being under the ignorant prejudice of the times in which He lived. It all emanates from the rejection of the Bible as the inerrant revelation of God.

Never before has this prophecy been so literally fulfilled

as now. The Holy Spirit has revived the study of prophecy. The midnight cry has gone forth. The blessed hope has been restored to the church, and the forgotten prayer, "Even so, Come, Lord Jesus," is being prayed by the members of the body of Christ as never before. There is more preaching and teaching going on today on prophecy than ever before in the history of the church. It is one of the signs that the end of the age is very near. But the revival of prophecy has resulted in the activity of Satan. He both perverts and ridicules the coming of the Lord, and as that blessed event draws near, there will be increasing ridicule and mockery from the side of the apostates.* They dream of human progress, for they are "evolutionists." Their pet law, "the survival of the fittest," must work on till the last vestige of the beastly in man has worked itself out by a natural process, for they deny the need as well as the power of redemption. They call a belief in the coming of the Lord "pessimism," and have even attempted to brand those who believe in a catastrophic ending of this present evil age "enemies of civilization and human progress." What God hath spoken, what the mouth of all His holy prophets have declared, that the hope of the world is the coming and the enthronement of the Lord Jesus Christ, is extremely distasteful to them, for it conflicts with the program they have invented, a program which has no scriptural support whatever. They take the ground of an assumed unchangeableness of the world, that a sort of cycle governs nature, and thus they deny the positive statements of the Word of God and exclude God from His own creation.

---

*Of late certain presses of "evangelical denominations" have turned out tons of literature warning against the pre-millennial teachings. The Methodist church of Canada circulated a series of 5 pamphlets which attacked the blessed hope. They were the production of an infidel. The Chicago University and similar institutions also fight prophecy. Sneers and ridicule about His Coming, the end of the age, the increase of evil and the coming judgments are constantly multiplying. It is all a fulfillment of what Peter has written.

Science, meant to be a helpmeet to faith, is used by them to uphold their infidelity. They constantly speak of science contradicting revelation, which is not true. The deluge which Peter mentions as an evidence of a past catastrophe, when the world was overflowed with water, they wilfully forget or, as it is now generally done, class it with the myths of other nations, though science has abundantly proven that there happened such a judgment. But they do not want to believe that there can be a supernatural interference with the world. They believe in things continuing as they are and steadily improving. Up to the very time when the predicted sudden destruction shall come upon them, they say "Peace and safety" (1 Thess. v). It was so, no doubt, when the deluge swept the unbelieving and secure generation of that time to eternal doom.*

2. The Future of the Earth: Verses 8-10. A great revelation follows. The heavens that are now, and the earth by the same word have been stored up, reserved for fire against a day of judgment and destruction of ungodly men. Then in verse 10, "But the day of the Lord will come as a thief; in which the heavens shall pass away with a great noise, and the elements shall be dissolved with fervent heat, and the earth and the works that are therein shall be burned up." As the earth was once judged by water so shall it be judged by fire in the future, and not the earth only but also the heavens, that is the heavens surrounding the earth. Years ago infidels used to ridicule the statement of Peter that the earth and the surrounding heavens would be consumed by fire. They spoke of it as

*Some apply the words relating to a past judgment to the judgment which passed over the original earth on account of Satan's fall. That there was such a judgment the second verse of the Bible teaches and geologic facts confirm that the earth passed through a pre-historic destruction. But the reference is to the deluge. Almost every nation on earth has traditions of the deluge, though often in a perverted form. While the apostates and sneerers make everything of historical evidence and tradition, they ignore the universality of traditions concerning the flood.

an impossibility that the earth with its rivers, lakes and oceans could ever pass through such a conflagration, so that all is consumed. Well informed infidels no longer ridicule this statement, for astronomy with the help of the spectroscope has revealed the fact that other bodies in the heavens have passed through great conflagrations, that other globes have been burned up, and not a few astronomers have advanced the theory that this will be the fate of the earth on which we live. Peter had no telescope, nor did he know anything about astronomy. How did he find out that the earth would be destroyed by fire? It was the Spirit of God who revealed it to him.

The question arises what event is it of which Peter speaks here? He speaks of "the day of the Lord." What phase of that coming day is it? It certainly is not the coming of the Lord for His Saints as revealed in 1 Thess. iv. Nor is it the day of the Lord in its beginning, when the Lord appears in power and great glory. Now it is still "man's day," and when He appears the Day of the Lord begins. One day, Peter tells us, with the Lord is as a thousand years, and a thousand years as one day. From Revelation we learn that Christ will reign over the earth with His Saints for a thousand years and that is "the Day of the Lord." The beginning of it will be as a thief, and it will bring fiery judgments, for He will be revealed "in flaming fire." But what Peter speaks of is not so much the beginning of that day of the Lord as it is the end, when the thousand years have expired. When the thousand-year reign of Christ as King is over there follows a little season during which Satan is loosed from his prison; the revolt of which Revelations xx:8 speaks is followed by fire falling down from God out of heaven, and after that we see the great white throne, the judgment of the wicked dead. "And I saw a great white throne, and Him that sat on it, from whose face the earth and the heavens fled away, and there was found no place for them" (Rev. xx:11). It is this of which Peter writes, when the day of the Lord is ended, the earth and the surrounding heaven will pass away; it will be through a mighty conflagration from beneath and from above.* When Peter writes in verse 13 of new heavens and a new earth, he states what John beheld in his vision of chapter xxi:1. "And I saw a new heaven and a new earth; for the first heaven and the first earth were passed away and there was no more sea."

Some of these Jewish believers were evidently thinking that the Lord was slack about the fulfillment of the promise concerning that day. The apostle tells them that the Lord's slackness is His long-suffering, "He is not willing that any should perish, but all should come unto repentance."

3. Exhortation and Conclusion: Verses 11-18. In view of such a future the apostle exhorts once more to holy living and godliness, "waiting for and earnestly desiring the coming of the day of God." The thought which is often expressed in the words "hastening the coming of the day of God," that we might act and serve, sending the Gospel to the heathen, and do other things, thus hastening the coming of the Lord, is not warranted by the text, nor is it true. God cannot be hastened by the creature, nor can He be delayed in the execution of His eternal purposes.

As stated in the preceding annotations, the fiery ending of the Day of the Lord, and with it the Day of God, the eternal Age, when God is all in all, is what Peter teaches. "But we, according to His promise, wait for new heavens and a new earth, wherein dwelleth righteousness." The promise is found in Isaiah lxv:17, "For, behold, I create new heavens and a new earth; and the former shall not be remembered, nor come to mind." This is not the millennium, which in this chapter of Isaiah is described in verses 18-25, but that

*It will be observed, that the Spirit does not speak here of the coming of Christ, except to say that it will be scoffed at in the last days. He speaks of the day of God, in contrast with the trust of unbelievers in the stability of the material things of creation, which depends, as the apostle shows, on the word of God. And in that day everything on which unbelievers rested and will rest shall be dissolved and pass away. This will not be at the commencement of the day, but at its close; and here we are free to reckon this day, according to the apostle's word as a thousand years, or whatever length of period the Lord shall see fit.

——Synopis of the Bible—J. N. Darby.

which comes into existence after the earth and the surrounding heavens have passed through the great conflagration. Once more Isaiah speaks of the earth and heavens which will remain forever. (See chapter lxvi:22.) This new earth and the new heavens will be the glorious and eternal dwelling-place of the redeemed, for the New Jerusalem comes finally out of the highest heaven to find its eternal resting place there (Rev. xxi). "Wherefore, beloved, seeing that ye wait for these things, be diligent to be found in Him in peace without spot and blameless."

In conclusion, Peter refers to Paul as "our beloved brother Paul." The Epistle to the Galatians was then in circulation and everybody could read there of Peter's failure in Antioch. (Gal. ii:12-16). The loving remark by Peter shows that he had readily seen his mistake and that there was no clash between the two servants of the Lord Jesus Christ. The Epistle which Paul had written to the same Jewish Christians to whom Peter wrote is without question the Epistle to the Hebrews. (See Introduction to Hebrews.)

The second Epistle of Peter ends with another warning, so well suited for our times, "Beware, lest, being carried away with the error of the wicked (destructive critics and deniers of Christ), ye fall from your own steadfastness." And the safeguard is "Grow in grace and in the knowledge of our Lord and Saviour Jesus Christ."

"To Him be Glory both now and forever, Amen."

THE FIRST EPISTLE OF JOHN

The First Epistle of John

Introduction.

This Epistle is not addressed to any one church nor does it mention, like the other New Testament Epistles, the author of the document; it is anonymous. We are not left in doubt who penned this Epistle in spite of its anonymous character. There can be no question that the author of the Fourth Gospel is also the author of this Epistle. Its opening statement is linked with the opening of the Gospel and throughout it is written in the thought and language of the Fourth Gospel. Inasmuch, then, as that Gospel is indisputably the work of John the Apostle, this Epistle is also the work of his inspired pen. "The internal testimony furnished by this Epistle to its author being the same with the author of the Fourth Gospel is, it may well be thought, incontrovertible. To maintain a diversity of authorship would betray the very perverseness and exaggeration of that school of criticism which refuses to believe, be evidence never so strong" (Alford).

Historical Evidence.

While the internal testimony confirms conclusively the Johannine authorship of the Epistle there is also a mass of historical evidence which attributes the Epistle to the beloved disciple. The oldest testimony is that of Polycarp, who was personally acquainted with the Apostle John. We refer to the introduction of the Gospel of John where we give fuller information on Polycarp and his testimony to the Fourth Gospel. He makes, in one of his writings, a direct reference to 1 John iv:3, in fact, he quotes this verse almost verbatim. It is, therefore, a testimony to the genuineness and the authorship of this Epistle. Irenaeus, the disciple of Polycarp, frequently quotes the Epistle of John and states that it is John's. Notable is the reference in his work against heresies as quoted by Eusebius. He cites John xx:31 and connects it with 1 John ii:18 and iv:1-3 and 1 John v:1. After these two witnesses, Polycarp, who knew John, and Irenaeus, the disciple of Polycarp, every authority among the church fathers mentions this Epistle as being the work of John the Apostle. It is not necessary to quote all these references—by Clement of Alexandria, Tertullian, Cyprian, Origen, Dionysius of Alexandria, Eusebius, Jerome, and many others. We mention but one more of the ancient testimonies, that which is found in the Muratorian fragment. This old and very reliable source of the second century has in it the following paragraph: "What wonder is it, then, that John brings forward each detail with so much emphasis, even in this Epistle, saying of himself, "What we have seen with our eyes, and heard with our ears, and our hands have handled, these things have we written to you. For so he professes that he was not only an eye-witness, but a hearer, and, moreover, a historian of all the wonderful works of the Lord in order. In harmony with this evidence is the testimony of the oldest fourth century Greek manuscripts, which give the title of the Epistle as "*Joannou-A*"—that is—"John 1." Its rejection by the Gnostic Marcion is of no importance, for he excluded from the Scriptures all the writings of the Apostle because they deal a death-blow to his anti-Christian inventions. Lücke, one of the great scholars of bygone days, states that the Gospel of John and the Epistles of John are the genuine works of the Apostle, and he adds, "Incontestably, then, our Epistle must be numbered among those canonical books which are most strongly upheld by ecclesiastical tradition."

It is, therefore, not necessary in face of such internal and external evidences to state the objections of destructive critics like Scaliger, S. G. Lange, Bretschneider and the Tübingen school. As it is with other portions of Scripture they have no case at all in attacking the authorship of this Epistle.

When and Where It Was Written.

The Epistle itself gives no definite answer to these questions. Some have attempted to fix the date as being before the destruction of Jerusalem in the year 70 A. D. They base their assumption on Chapter ii:18 and claim that "the last time" means the closing days for Jerusalem, which is incorrect. The term, "the last time," has in this Epistle the same meaning as in 1 Timothy iv:1 and 2 Timothy iii:1, and therefore does not mean the last days before the City of Jerusalem was destroyed. But it is clear that John wrote the Fourth Gospel record first and his Epistle was written after the Gospel, so that the Epistle was written probably about the year 90, preceding the Revelation, which was written about the year 96.

Irenaeus states that the Gospel was written by John in Ephesus; an ancient tradition states that the Epistle was written from the same place.

To Whom was it Written.

The fact that this Epistle starts, unlike the other Epistles, without any address, introductory greeting or closing salutation, has led some to call it a treatise and not an Epistle. But the personal address and appeal, the style throughout fully sustains the Epistolar character. Others, again, have termed the Epistle a second part of the Gospel (Michaelis), while others speak of it as an introduction to the Gospel. That the Epistle is closely related to the Gospel is very true, but that does not necessitate a closer external relationship.

Dr. Bullinger, in the *Companion Bible*, suggests that this Epistle also was originally addressed to believing Hebrews in the dispersion. This view was held by others before him (Benson and others); but there is nothing whatever in the Epistle to warrant such a conclusion. On account of a remark by Augustinus on 1 John iii:2 that John wrote "to the Parthians," many commentators have adopted this view, which is, however, without any foundation whatever. The Epistle was evidently not addressed to any one church but to believers in a number of assemblies. John was acquainted with these believers, who seemed to have been mostly Gentile converts. (See Chapter v:21.) If the tradition is true that the Epistle was written in Ephesus, it is not improbable that it was sent to the seven churches in the province of Asia, Ephesus, Smyrna, Pergamos, Thyatira, Sardis, Philadelphia and Laodicea, the churches to whom the Lord sent the messages a few years later when John was in Patmos.

The Purpose of the Epistle.

The purpose of the Epistle is stated by the writer in two places; "These things write we unto you that your joy may be full" (i:4). "These things have I written unto you that believe on the name of the Son of God; that ye may know that ye have eternal life, and that ye may believe on the name of the Son of God" (v:13). According to the Gospel of John Chapter xx:31, this also is the purpose of the Gospel. He writes to those who believe on the Son of God and who have that eternal life which was manifested in the Lord Jesus, and which is imparted to all who believe on the Son of God and which establishes fellowship with the Father and the Son. The Epistle has been rightly called a family letter, that is, believers are viewed as the family of God, hence the repeated use of word *teknia*, children. The Gospel of John was written on account of the false teachings concerning the Person of Christ, which began in the second half of the first century.* The Epistle of John is very outspoken against those errors touching the Deity of the Lord Jesus Christ and His sacrificial work. They flourished later under the name of Gnosticism, Docetism, Montanism and others. Marcion, a Gnostic leader, when Polycarp, the disciple of John met him, was addressed by Polycarp with these words, "I know thee, thou firstborn of Satan." While these evil doctrines and denials were not yet fully developed in John's

*See Introduction to John's Gospel.

day, they existed and increased, hence the warnings in Chapter ii:18-25 and iv-1:6. What antichristianity is will be learned from these passages. All the evil systems of today, which are sweeping with increasing force through Christendom towards their divinely appointed and revealed doom are exposed in this Epistle in their true character. Christian Science, falsely so called; the liberal theology, which denies that Christ is the Virgin-born Son of God, the modern religion, the destructive criticism and other systems and cults are all branded by John as antichrists. These many antichrists are finally to be merged into a personal antichrist, the man of sin. Our annotations will enlarge upon all this.

The Message of the Epistle.

The Epistle has a deep spiritual message for the children of God. As already stated, the Epistle, like the Gospel of John, witnesses to Christ as the Son of God and the eternal life which He is Himself and which He imparts to the believer. Thus the Epistle opens, "That which was from the beginning, which we have heard, which we have seen with our eyes, which we have looked upon and our hands have handled, of the Word of life. (And the life was manifested, and we have seen it, and bear witness, and shew unto you that eternal life, which was with the Father, and was manifested unto us.) That which we have seen and heard declare we unto you, that ye also may have fellowship with us; and truly our fellowship is with the Father and with his Son Jesus Christ." The great truth which is developed by the Holy Spirit is not so much the life which the believer has in Christ, that is, the eternal life imparted unto him, but it is that life which is in the believer, and the manifestation of that life, a manifestation of the same characteristics as manifested by the Lord Jesus Christ in His blessed life. As born of God, believers have God as their Father, they are children of God. God is Light and God is Love and, therefore, those who are born of God, in whom there is eternal life, must also manifest light and love, walk in righteousness and in love. This is the message of the First Epistle of John. All the blessed things which cluster around it we shall discover in our analysis and annotations.

The Divisions of The Epistle

The divisions of the first Epistle of John have always been considered a difficulty, so that leading expositors of the past have expressed the belief that there is no contextual connection at all in the Epistle. Calvin shares this belief as well as others. Bengel in his great work "the Gnomen" maintained that there is a logical and contextual arrangement. He divided the Epistle in three parts, naming them in Latin as follows: **I. Exordium**—Introduction i:1-4. **II. Tractatio**—Treatment and discussion i:5-v:12. **III. Conclusio**—Conclusion v:13-21. The Numerical Bible gives also a three-fold division. I. God as Light and in the light, and the light in us. i-ii:11. II. Growth by the Truth, which is nothing else but the light manifested. ii:12-27. III. The Manifestation of the children of God by the fruit found. ii:28-v. This is a helpful arrangement. The "Scofield Bible" gives two main divisions. I. The Family with the Father. i-iii:24. II. The Family and the world. iv-v.

We divide the Epistle into six sections, as follows:

I. THE LIFE MANIFESTED. Chapter i:1-4.

II. LIGHT AND DARKNESS. THE TESTS. Chapter i:5-ii:17.

III. ERROR AND TRUTH. Chapter ii:18-27.

IV. RIGHTEOUSNESS AND LOVE AS MANIFESTED BY THE CHILDREN OF GOD. Chapter ii:28-iii:18.

V. HEREBY WE KNOW. Chapter iii:19-v:12.

VI. THE CONCLUSION. Chapter v:13-21.

Analysis and Annotations

I. THE LIFE MANIFESTED Chapter i:1-4.

The opening verses of this Epistle are very precious and are the key to the whole Epistle. Three Scriptures speak of what was in the beginning. "In the beginning God created the heavens and the earth" (Gen. i:1). This is the beginning of all things which God called into existence out of nothing "In the beginning was the Word, and the Word was with God, and the Word was God" (John i:1). This takes us beyond the first verse of the Bible. It reveals Him, by whom and for whom God created all things, in His eternal existence with God and as God. The third Scripture is the first verse of John's Epistle. "That which was from the beginning, which we have heard, which we have seen with our eyes, which we have looked upon, and our hands have handled, of the Word of life." This is a different beginning from the beginning in Genesis i:1 and John i:1; it means the manifestation of the Son of God in incarnation among men. He, who is the true God and the eternal life, the life and light, was manifested as man here below. This truth is stated by John in his Gospel in the 14th verse of the first chapter: "And the Word was made flesh and tabernacled among us (and we beheld His glory, the glory as of the Only Begotten of the Father), full of grace and truth." To this John refers in the first statement of his Epistle. John and his fellow-disciples had walked with Him and talked with Him. It must be noted that the Apostle speaks of Him as "the Word of Life;" he does not say therefore "who was from the beginning" but, which was from the beginning. First he mentions what they had heard; but one may hear a person and not be near to that person. But they were closer to the Word of Life, he writes, "which we have seen with our eyes;" yet one may have seen a person without being close to that person; but they had more than a passing vision "which we have contemplated" which is more than a mere seeing, it denotes gazing with a purpose, with a desire and with admiration. A statement of still greater nearness follows, "our hands have handled"—John and the other disciples had known Him, the Word of Life, intimately.

"And the Life was manifested, and we have seen it, and bear witness, and shew unto you that eternal life which was with the Father, and hath been manifested unto us." He whom they heard, with whom they were in touch, whom they knew and gazed upon is the eternal Life which was with the Father. It is more than that He spoke of eternal Life and promised eternal Life; He Himself is the eternal Life. He was with the Father and came into the world, to manifest what that Life is. While He manifested the Father, as He witnessed "whosoever seeth Me seeth the Father," He also displayed as man what eternal life is in His blessed and perfect life He lived on earth. And this eternal life is communicated to all who believe on the Son of God. This life which was with the Father, manifested in the Lord Jesus on earth, is the life which is in us.* To know then what life we possess as believers, we must not look in ourselves, or to other believers, but to Christ and the life He manifested on earth. As another has said, "When I turn my eyes to Jesus, when I contemplate all His obedience, His purity, His Grace, His tenderness, His patience, His devotedness, His holiness, His love, His entire freedom from all self-seeking, I can say, that is *my* life. It may be that it is obscured in me; but it is none the less true, that it is my life."

"That which we have seen and heard declare we unto you, that ye also may have fellowship with us, and truly our fellowship is with the Father, and with His Son Jesus Christ.

---

*"The life has been manifested. Therefore we have no longer to seek for it, to grope after it in the darkness, to explore at random the indefinite, or the obscurity of our own hearts, in order to find it, to labor fruitlessly under the law, in order to obtain it. We behold it: it is revealed, it is here, in Jesus Christ. He who possesses Christ possesses that life."

And these things write we unto you, that your joy may be full."

What they had seen and heard they have declared unto others, to those who also believe on Him, so that they too might share in the same fellowship, the fellowship of the Father and His Son Jesus Christ. The life which believers possess, the eternal life given through grace, the life He manifested on earth and which is in us, fits us for fellowship with both the Father and the Son. What such a fellowship demands and the tests of it is developed subsequently. To have such fellowship, bestowed through grace, is the blessed calling of all the saints of God. Such fellowship is eternal life and there is nothing beyond that in heaven itself, while we enjoy it here the fullness of it will be enjoyed in glory. But what is fellowship with the Father and with His Son Jesus Christ? It is but little understood in its real meaning. Fellowship means having things in common. The Father's delight is in Him who pleased Him so perfectly. For the Father His blessed Son is the One altogether lovely. Believers knowing the Son also find their delight in Him; He is for our hearts the One altogether lovely. As we then delight ourselves in Him, in His obedience, in what He is in love and devotion to the Father, we share the same feelings and thoughts with the Father, which is fellowship with the Father. Whenever the believer praises and thanks the Father for His Son, tells the Father of his deep appreciation of Him, how he loves Him, longs to be more like Him, walk even as He walked, then he is in fellowship with the Father. And the Son has given to us the knowledge of the Father. "No man knoweth the Son, but the Father; neither knoweth any man the Father, save the Son, and to whomsoever the Son will reveal Him" (Matt. xi:27). It is in the Gospel of John where the blessed words of the Son concerning the Father are recorded. He manifested unto His own the name of the Father. In the five chapters in the Gospel of John, beginning with the feet-washing and ending with the great intercessory prayer of our Lord (chapters xiii-xvii) the word "Father" occurs fifty times. It is in this part of the Gospel the Son makes known the Father. Through the Son we have the knowledge of the Father and the knowledge of the Father's love. His delight was to glorify the Father in a life of devotion and obedience. And as the believer delights Himself in the Father, honors Him and yields obedience to Him, he has fellowship with the Son, has the same thing in common with the Son. Fellowship with the Father and with the Son is therefore not a feeling or some extraordinary experience.

"All this flows, whether in the one or the other point of view, from the Person of the Son. Herein our joy is full. What can we have more than the Father and the Son? What more perfect happiness than community of thoughts, feelings, joys and communion with the Father and the Son, deriving all our joy from themselves? And if it seem difficult to believe, let us remember that, in truth, it cannot be otherwise; for, in the life of Christ, the Holy Ghost is the source of my thoughts, feelings, communion, and He cannot give thoughts different from those of the Father and the Son. They must be in their nature the same. To say that they are adoring thoughts is in the very nature of things, and only makes them more precious. To say that they are feeble and often hindered, while the Father and the Son are divine and perfect, is, if true, to say the Father and the Son are God, are divine, and we feeble creatures. That surely none will deny. But if the blessed Spirit be the source, they must be the same as to nature and fact.

This is our Christian position then, here below in time, through the knowledge of the Son of God; as the apostle says, "These things write we unto you, that your joy may be full."*

II. LIGHT AND DARKNESS. THE TESTS.

Chapter i:5—ii:17.

1. God is Light. Walking in Darkness and in Light. i:5–7.
2. What the Light manifests. 8–10.
3. The Advocacy of Christ to maintain the Fellowship. ii:1–2.
4. The Tests of Fellowship. 4–17.

---

*J. N. Darby.

I. God is Light. Walking in Darkness and in the Light: i:5-7. The message they had heard of Him and which they declared to others is, that God is light and in Him is no darkness at all. Light, perfect, pure light is God's nature; He is absolutely holy, with no darkness in Him at all. That God is light was manifested in the life of the Lord Jesus, for He was and is holy. Fellowship with the Father and the Son means, therefore, to have fellowship with light, and that excludes a walk in darkness. "If we say that we have fellowship with Him and walk in darkness we lie and do not the truth." If one professes to have fellowship with God and walks in darkness, he lies, for darkness can have no fellowship with light. "But if we walk in the light as He is in the light, we have fellowship one with another, and the blood of Jesus Christ His Son cleanseth us from all sin." But what is this walk in the light? It is not the same thing as walking according to the light. It does not mean to live a perfect and sinless life. Walking in the light is not the question of *how* we walk, but *where* we walk, and the place where the believer walks is the light. It means to walk daily in His presence, with our will and conscience in the light and presence of God, judging everything that does not answer to that light. Whatever is not right is brought at once in His presence, exposed to the light, confessed, judged and put away. Such is the walk in the light which fellowship with God demands. The result of such a walk in the light is mutual fellowship among believers, because each has the same nature of God and the same Spirit, the same Christ as the object before the heart and the same Father. It cannot be otherwise. Then there is another thing stated, "The blood of Jesus Christ His Son cleanseth us from all sin." Walking in the light shows us what we are and we cannot say that we have no sin. But we have no consciousness of sin resting upon us before a holy God, though we know that sin is in us, but we have the assurance of being cleansed from it by His precious blood. Such is the blessed position of a true Christian. Fellowship with the Father and with His Son, walking in the light as He is in the light, fellowship one with another and the cleansing power of the blood.

2. What the Light Manifests: Verses 8-10. The light makes known that sin is in us. If the believer, the child of God, says that he has no sin, the light contradicts him. If we say we have no sin, we deceive ourselves, and the truth is not in us. The denial of sin within is a delusion. This evil teaching that the old Adamic nature is eradicated in the believer is widespread in our day among Holiness, Pentecostal and other sects. True spirituality is to confess daily, walking in the light, that in our flesh there dwelleth no good thing. And if sin is committed it needs confession. He is faithful and just to forgive us our sins and to cleanse us from all unrighteousness.

The light also manifests another evil, the claim of a sinless perfection. If we say that we have not sinned, we make Him a liar and His Word is not in us. Some have applied this verse to the unsaved; it has nothing to do with the sinner, but relates to a true believer, who in presumption makes the claim that he lives without sinning. And the reason why children of God make such unscriptural claims is inattention to His Word, for the Word makes manifest what sin is, and the Apostle says "If we say that we have not sinned . . . His word is not in us."

3. The Advocacy of Christ to Maintain the Fellowship: ii:1-2. For the first time John uses the endearing term "my little children," meaning the born ones of God, who are born into the family of God by having believed on the Son of God. One might conclude inasmuch as belief in the eradication of the old nature and sinless perfection is a delusion, that the child of God must sin. But, while sin is within, and a sinless perfection is beyond our reach, it does not mean that the believer should continue in sin. He had written these things that they might not sin. But if any man sin a gracious provision has been made. Let it be noticed that the application, as it is often done, to the sinner who is outside, who knows not Christ at all, is totally wrong. It means the little children, the members of the family of God. If any true child of God sins we have an advocate with the Father (not God, it is the matter of the family), Jesus Christ the righteous. The advocacy of Christ restores the sinning believer to the communion with the Father and the Son which sin interrupted. He does not wait till we come repenting and confessing, but in the very moment we have sinned He exercises His blessed office as our Advocate with the Father and His intercession produces in us repentance, confession and self-judgment. Thus we are maintained by Himself in the fellowship into which the grace of God has called and brought us. When the believer sins it does not mean that he has lost his salvation. Many a child of God has been harassed through ignorance, and imagined that he committed the unpardonable sin. The sin of a believer does not make him unsaved or lost, but it makes fellowship with the Father and the Son impossible till the sin is judged and confessed. This is accomplished by His advocacy.

"The Lord Jesus as much lives to take up the failure of His own, as He died to put away their sins by His blood. This, too, is founded on propitiation; but there is besides the blessed fact that He is the righteousness of the believer in the presence of God. His one expiatory sacrifice avails in abiding value; His place is before God as our righteousness; and there for the failing He carries on His living active advocacy with the Father."

4. The Tests: Verses 4-17. John now writes of the characteristics of the life which the believer has received, the eternal life, and applies certain tests. The profession of a Christian is that He knows God. But how do we know that we know Him? The answer is, "If we keep His commandments." This is not legality in the least which puts the believer back under the law. John knows nothing of that. Obedience is the leading trait of the imparted life. It is set on doing the will of God. Christ walked on earth in obedience; His meat and drink was to do the will of Him that sent Him. Inasmuch as His life is in us as believers, it must manifest itself in obedience to the will of God.

It is the same which we find in 1 Peter i:2, sanctified, or set apart, unto the obedience of Jesus Christ. It is not a sinless obedience as it was in Him; while the believer has his heart set on obeying the Lord and doing His will, he often fails and stumbles, but he continues to aim at doing the will of God, for that is the nature of the new life. "He that saith, I know Him, and keepeth not His commandments, is a liar and the truth is not in him. But whoso keepeth His Word, in him verily is the love of God perfected; hereby know we that we are in Him."

One who professes to know God and does not manifest obedience is no Christian at all, but he is a liar, and the truth in the knowledge of the Lord is lacking in such a one. He is a mere professing Christian, one who has the outward form of godliness but does not know the power of it, because he has not the life in him, which is His life and in which he delights to obey. The first great test of the reality of the divine life in the believer is obedience.

Then follows a second test: "He that saith he abideth in Him ought himself also so to walk, even as He walked." In His prayer our Lord told the Father, "They are not of the world even as I am not of the world;" and again, "As Thou hast sent me into the world so have I sent them into the world" (John xvii:16, 18). Believers are not of the world as He is not of the world, because they are born again and have His life in them. They are in Him, abiding in Him, and therefore they must walk as He walked, which does not mean to be what He was, for He was without sin, but it is a walk after His own pattern, the reproduction of His character and life through the power of the Holy Spirit. In the next two verses we read of the old commandment and of the new commandment (Verses 7 and 8). The old commandment is explained as the word which they had heard from the beginning, that is, the same beginning as mentioned in Chapter i:1, the manifestation of Christ on earth. But what is the commandment of which he speaks next? It is something new now, for the life which was in Him on earth is in believers now. Therefore, it is true in Him and in us because the darkness is passing away and the true light already shineth. Christ is life and light and as His life is in us we share it in Him; this is that which is new. It was true of Him first, and now it is true of us, too. This is followed by another test. "He that saith he is in the light, and hateth his brother is in darkness even until now." The life must manifest itself in love. Light and love go together; both are manifested in Christ, He was light and love. If He is, therefore, in the believer, and he possesses that life, and professes to be in the light, and with such a profession hateth his brother, he shows thereby that he is in the darkness until now. Love cannot be separated from that life and light which was in Him and which is in us as believers. He that abideth in the light loveth his brother and because he does there is no occasion of stumbling in him. In him who loves there is neither darkness nor occasion of stumbling; in him who does not love there is both darkness and stumbling. He who hates his brother is a stumbling block to himself and stumbles against everything. Not loving the brethren and manifesting hatred against them is the sure sign of being in darkness and walking in darkness. Such are the tests of Christian profession; light and love, obedience and loving the brethren; where there is no life from God there is absence of love for the brethren and a walk in darkness and not in the light. It seems that many in John's day were in that deplorable condition, while today such is almost universally the case.

Verses 12-17 contain a message to those who are in the light, who possess that life and in whom it is manifested in obedience and in love. He addresses the fathers and the young men. Before he does this he mentions that which all believers, even the most feeble, possess. "I write unto you little children (the term of endearment which means the whole family of God) because your sins are forgiven you for His name's sake." This is blessedly true of every child of God. Each has "redemption through His blood, the forgiveness of sins." It is the thing which is settled for time and eternity for all those who are in Christ.

Then different grades are mentioned: fathers, young men

and little children. The meaning is in the spiritual sense, fathers in Christ, young men in Christ and babes in Christ. The word "children" used in verses 13 and 18 is a different word from the one used in verse 12. In this chapter in verses 1, 12 and 28 the little children are all the family of God, but in verses 13 and 18 it means young converts.

The maturity of the fathers consists in knowing Him that was from the beginning, that is, the Lord Jesus Christ. Spiritual progress and maturity is a deep knowledge and appreciation of Christ. The Apostle Paul illustrates what real Christian maturity is. He had but one desire to know Him; not I but Christ; Christ is all. The Fathers have Christ for their fullest portion and walking in Him have learned the depths of His Grace and the glory of His person. They are occupied not with their experience but with Himself. It has been well said, "All true experience ends with forgetting self and thinking of Christ." To know Him, to know Him still better, to be entirely dependent on Him, to have none other but Him, never losing sight of Him—that is the highest attainment of a Christian.

He speaks next of the young men, who have advanced in their Christian life. They had gone forward in undaunted faith and courage and overcame the difficulties; they overcame by faith the wicked one. The strength of the new life, that is, Christ, was manifested in them in conflict. The "babes" come next, the young converts, who have not much experience in conflict. To them he writes, "Ye have known the Father." Every newborn babe in Christ cries, enabled by the Spirit of adoption, "Abba, Father." To know God as Father is the blessed birthright of every newborn soul.

Once more he writes the same to the fathers. He can add nothing to it for the highest attainment is to know Him, as the fathers know Him. But he has more to say to the young men. He tells them that they are strong, because the Word of God was abiding in them, which is the source of power and strength of every believer and because the Word of God abided in them they overcame the wicked one. Then follows the exhortation and warning not to love the world, the world of which John speaks later, "which lieth in the wicked one."

This world-system in every aspect, whether we call it the social world, the political world, the commercial world, the scientific world, the religious world—all is not of the Father. All its glory is not of the Father. The love of the world is, therefore, inconsistent with the love of the Father. The controlling principles in it are the lust of the flesh, the lust of the eyes and the pride of life. May we remember once more that our Lord speaks concerning His own, "They are not of the world even as I am not of the world." Grace has taken us out of this old world, with its corruption which is there by lust and has put us into another world, so to speak, in which Christ is the center and the attraction. That new sphere is our place. The only way to escape this world with its beguiling influences is by separation from it. And that separation becomes real when we know Him, as the fathers know him, and find our joy and our satisfaction in Christ. "And the world passeth away, and the lust thereof; but he that doeth the will of God abideth forever." But if this exhortation was needed in John's day, how much more is it needed in our days, when, as never before, the god of this age blinds the eyes of them that believe not, when this world system, in its godless and seductive character, develops a power and attraction unknown before, and when on all sides professing Christians are "lovers of pleasure more than lovers of God."

III. Truth and Error. Verses 18-27.

This section contains a warning which is addressed to the babes, the little children, young believers. Truth and error, are contrasted. Seducers were trying to lead them astray, for we read in verse 26: "These things have I written unto you concerning them that seduce you." He reminds them that it is "the last time," a striking expression, for since it was written centuries have come and gone, and what was true then is true now, that it is the last time; only the Lord is still patiently waiting, not willing that any should perish.

Christ was manifested, the truth revealed in Him and the world rejected Him and His truth. Satan became the god of this age, with the mystery of iniquity working in it from the very beginning. Antichristianity is not a new thing of our times; it was here from the very beginning. John writes, "Even now there are many antichrists, whereby we know it is the last time." And the last time has its "last days" which are now upon us. Antichristianity is increasing on all sides till *the* antichrist, the man of sin, will be revealed (2 Thess. ii). An antichrist is not a vicious lawbreaker, an out and out immoral man. An antichrist is one who rejects Christ, who does not allow His claims; who denies that Jesus is the Son of God. It is of great significance that John speaks of the antichrists in his day as having gone out from among the professing body of Christians (verse 19). They were not true believers but only professed belief; they had left the flock and gone into apostasy, "that they might be made manifest that they were not all of us."

In verses 22 and 23 we have a picture of the antichrists of John's day and a prophecy of antichristianity down to the end of the age when the great opposer will appear in a person, the personal antichrist. "Who is a liar but he that denieth that Jesus is the Christ? He is antichrist that denieth the Father and the Son. Whosoever denieth the Son hath not the Father. He who confesseth the Son hath the Father also." Antichristianity is the denial that Jesus is the Christ. It includes every denial of the Person of the Lord Jesus, the denial that He is the Son of God come into the flesh, His Virgin birth and that He was sent by the Father. Such denials were prominent in John's lifetime. Gnosticism was troubling the Church. They denied the Messiahship and Deity of the Lord Jesus Christ. Other systems were present in embryo, known later by the name of Arianism, etc. Denying the Son they denied the Father also. These are important statements for our own days, the last days of the present age. What began in the days when the Holy Spirit penned this Epistle is now full-grown in the world. It is all about us in various forms throughout the professing

Church, only with this difference, the apostates in the beginning were more honest than the apostates in our times. They were in the professing Church and when they began their denials they went out, separated themselves from the true Church. The apostates of today remain in the professing Church and maintain outwardly a Christian profession, so that it becomes the solemn duty of true believers to separate themselves from these enemies of the Cross of Christ. They deny both the Jewish Hope, which centers in the promises of the Messiah, and the Christian Hope, which is the Father and the Son. They reject the truths of the Old and the New Testament. They speak of the God of Abraham, who promised the seed to come from Abraham, as a tribal god. They make common cause with the Jewish apostates in denying that there are predictions concerning the Messiah in the Old Testament. We give but one illustration of this fact. Jews deny that the fifty-third chapter of Isaiah is a Messianic prophecy; the servant of Jehovah is explained to mean the nation Israel and not the Christ of God. This infidel view is held today by many preachers and teachers in various evangelical denominations, in spite of the fact that the New Testament tells us that it is Christ of whom Isaiah spoke. Rejecting Isaiah vii:14, the prophecy concerning the Virgin birth, they reject the Virgin birth itself, and brazenly utter the greatest blasphemy which human lips can utter, that Christ was born like any other man. They speak of Him as a great leader and teacher, as having divinity in Himself, in a degree higher than found in the rest of the race. His absolute Deity is not believed; that He is the propitiation for sins is sneered at, that He will ever appear again in His glorified humanity in a second visible and glorious manifestation is ridiculed. Thus antichristianity is present with us in the camp of Christendom in such a marked and universal way as unknown before.* With denying Christ they deny the Father. All

---

*Many college professors and presidents of institutions lean towards this side. We mention Shailer Mathews, of Chicago; President King, of

that we have seen in this Epistle concerning Him, the true God and the eternal life, fellowship with the Father and with His Son, walking in the light, the advocacy of Christ and loving the brethren, is denied by them. They speak of "love;" they speak of toleration and the "Christ-spirit." But those who are the brethren, who contend for the faith once and for all delivered unto the Saints, who believe on the Son of God, in His sacrificial work on the Cross, are denounced by them, belittled and branded as fanatics. And the end is not yet. Let them continue in their evil ways under the guidance of the lying spirit of darkness and they may yet stoop to actual persecution of those who constitute the body of Christ. The conditions in Christendom today are the most solemn the true Church of Jesus Christ has faced. The heading up in "*the* Antichrist" cannot be far distant. As John writes these Christ-deniers, these blasphemers, who make the Holy Son of God the offspring of—we dare not finish the sentence!—may speak of "the Father," but they have not the Father, because only those who confess the Son of God, Christ come in the flesh, have the Father.

John writes all this to the babes, young believers, warning them against the lie. He useth the word "liar," for such the apostates are. In using this word repeatedly, he reveals his character as "Boanerges"—the son of thunder. Then he tells these babes how they may be guarded and kept. He reminds them that they have the anointing of the Holy One, that is, the Holy Spirit dwelling in their hearts and with Him they have the capacity to know and judge all these things. If they follow His guidance in and through the Word they would be kept in the Truth and guarded from accepting the lie. Let us again remember it is not the fathers, or the young men John addresses, but the babes. Here is a strong argument against the teaching so widespread among true believers, that the Holy Spirit is not given to a believer in regeneration, but that the gift of the Spirit

---

Oberlin; Harry E. Fosdick, of Union Seminary; President Hibben, of Princeton; Dr. Faunce, of Brown University; Professor Charles F. Kent, of Yale; and scores of other rationalists.

must be sought in a definite experience after conversion. This is a serious error which opens the door to the most subtle delusions as found in certain Holiness sects and Pentecostalism. Verse 24 gives another instruction and exhortation. It is the truth concerning Christ, which they had heard from the beginning, which abiding in them will keep them. And besides "the anointing which ye have received of Him abideth in you, and ye need not that any man teach you, but as the same anointing teacheth you of all things, and is truth, and is no lie, and even as it hath taught you, ye shall abide in Him." The teachers in this instance who tried to seduce them (verse 26) were not gifts of Christ to His body, but false teachers, who came with a lying message. They did not need these teachers; the Holy Spirit was their teacher and infallible guide, but never apart from the written Word. All false teaching they were to repulse and fall back upon Him who guides in all truth. They were safe against all error as they abided in that.

IV. Righteousness and Love as Manifested by the Children of God.

Chapter ii:28—iii:18.

1. **The Children of God and Their Coming Manifestation. ii:28; iii:3.**
2. **Sin and the New Nature. 4–9.**
3. **Righteousness and Love. 10–18.**

1. The Children of God and Their Coming Manifestation: Verses ii:28—iii:3. The address to the babes in Christ ended with the 27th verse, and now once more he speaks of the *teknia*, the little children, by which all believers are meant. The exhortation has been much misunderstood. It does not mean that by abiding in Him the believer may have confidence at His appearing. John speaks of himself and other servants of Christ, who minister the Gospel and the Truth of God. He urges the little children to abide in Him, "that when He shall appear *we* may have confidence and not be ashamed before Him at His coming." He wants them to walk carefully, to be faithful in all things, so that John and the other servants may not be left ashamed in that coming day. It is the same truth which Paul mentions in 1 Thess. ii:19-20.

Verse 29 mentions the test of righteousness. It is an acid test. "If ye know that He is righteous, ye know that every one that doeth righteousness is born of Him." But the purpose of it is not to question the reality of their salvation as born again, to make them doubt, but the test is given so that they might be enabled to reject a spurious profession. Before he proceeds with the truth expressed in this verse, he mentions the fact that as born of God they are the children of God and what they shall be.

In verses 1 and 2 the words "sons of God" must be changed to "*children of God.* John never speaks of "sons of God" in his message. It is in the writings of Paul the Holy Spirit speaks of believers as "sons and heirs." But John unfolds the truth that believers are in the family of God by the new birth, hence the use of the word "children" to denote the community of nature as born of God. As children of God we are partakers of the divine nature. It is the love of the Father which has bestowed this upon all who believe. And most emphatically the Spirit of God assures us through the pen of John, "Now are we the children of God." There can be no doubt about it, it is our present and known position, because having believed on Him we are born again and are in possession of eternal life. That which we shall be has not yet been manifested, but while it is not yet manifested we, nevertheless, know what we shall be. But how do we know? We know it because the Holy Spirit has revealed it in the Word of God. "But we know that when He shall appear, we shall be like Him; for we shall see Him as He is." This is our blessed assurance! To this God has called us; it is "the Hope of His calling" (Ephesians i:18). It is that to which we are predestined, to see Him as He is and then infinitely more than that "to be like Him." We see Him now by faith in His Word and are changed into the same image from glory to glory; when we shall see Him in that soon coming day, when He comes for His Saints, we shall see Him bodily and then our bodies will be fashioned like unto His glorious body. Of all this the world knows nothing. It knew Him not, knew not His life, nor His glory; it does not know the life which is in the children of God and what glory awaits them. And this hope is a purifying hope. We see that John speaks of the blessed Hope as Peter and James, addressing Jewish believers, do not.

2. Sin and the New Nature: Verses 4-9. He makes a contrast between sin and the new nature and shows the marks of one who abides in Christ and one who hath not seen Him neither knows Him. "Every one that practiseth sin, practiseth lawlessness; for sin is lawlessness," this is the correct rendering. The definition of sin as "transgression of the law" is misleading and incorrect. Before there ever was a law, sin was in the world (Romans v:12, etc.); how then can sin be the transgression of the law? It is not *sins* of which John speaks, but *sin*, the evil nature of man. Here the Apostle regards man as doing nothing else but his own, natural will; he lives as a natural man. He acts independently of God, and, as far as he is concerned, never does anything but his own will. John is, therefore, not speaking of positive overt acts, but of the natural man's habitual bent and character, his life and nature. The sinner, then, sins, and in this merely shows in it his state and the moral root of his nature as a sinner, which is lawlessness. But the born one, the child of God, is in a different position. He knows that Christ was manifested to take away our sins and that in Him there was no sin. If one knows Him and abideth in Him, that one sinneth not. If the believer sins it is because he has lost sight of Christ and does not act in the new life imparted unto him. Another object usurps the place of Christ, and then acting in self-will he is readily exposed to the wiles of the devil using his old nature and the world to lead him astray. If a man lives habitually in sin, according to his old nature, he hath not seen Him nor known Him. A child of God may sin but he is no longer living in sin; if a professing believer lives constantly in sin it is the evidence that he has not known Him at all. There were such who tried to deceive them. Their teaching was evidently a denial of holiness, that there was no need of righteousness. But the demand is for righteousness, while those who practise sin, live habitually in it, are of the devil. No true believer lives thus, for he knows the One whose life he possesses was manifested that He might destroy the works of the devil.

"Whosoever is begotten of God doth not practise sin, because his seed abideth in him, and he cannot sin, because he is begotten of God." This verse has puzzled many Christians, but it is quite simple. Every creature lives according to its nature. The fish has the nature of a fish and lives its nature in the water; a bird has its own nature and lives it in the air, and not under the water as the fish. Our Lord said to Nicodemus, "that which is born of the flesh is flesh." Man has a fallen nature, the nature of sin, and that nature can do nothing but sin. That is why He said, "Ye must be born again." In the new birth the divine nature is imparted. This nature is He Himself, Christ, the eternal life. Christ could not sin for He is God, and God cannot sin. The new nature believers possess cannot sin, for it is His nature. But why do new-born ones sin? Because the Christian has two natures, the old nature and the new nature. The old nature is not eradicated; a believer when he sins does so because he has given way to that old nature, has acted in the flesh. But the new nature followed will never lead to sin, for it is a holy nature, and for that nature it is impossible to sin. Some have suggested out of ignorance that the translation ought to be instead of cannot sin "ought not to sin," or "should not sin." The Greek text does not permit such a translation, anything different from "cannot sin" is an unscriptural paraphrase.

3. Righteousness and Love: Verses 10-18. The test as to the children of God and the children of the devil follows in this section. Whosoever doeth not righteousness is not of God, neither he that loveth not his brother. The message from the beginning, that is the same beginning as in chapter i:1—is that we should love one another. This was the commandment given by the Lord, "This is my commandment, That ye love one another, as I have loved you" (John xv:12). There is natural affection in the world, even in the animal creation. The natural man also can make himself amiable and speak of love and toleration. In fact an amiable character, a loving disposition through self-improvement is urged and practised among the antichristian cults, such as New Thought, Christian Science and the Liberalists, the advocates of the new theology. But the love of which John speaks is exclusively of God and unknown to the natural heart of man. Yet all these antichrists go to the Epistle of John and quote him to confirm their evil doctrine of "the brotherhood of man and the universal fatherhood of God." John does not speak of loving man as such, but loving the brethren, the other born ones in the family of God, and that is a divine love. It is the great test of the divine nature, "We know that we have passed from death unto life, because we love the brethren." The world not only knows nothing of that divine love, but the world hates those who are born of God. "Marvel not, my brethren, if the world hate you." This fact is illustrated by Cain. He was of the devil. He slew his brother because Cain's works were evil, he was an unbeliever, and his brother's were righteous, Abel believed and that was counted to him for righteousness. And so the world hates the brethren, the children of God on the same ground and for the same reason. Then again he tests profession: "He who loveth not his brother abideth in death. . . . Whosoever hateth his brother is a murderer." Hating the brother is the evidence that the professing Christian is in the state of death and linked with the murderer from the beginning.

The better rendering of verse 16 is, "Hereby we know love, because He laid down His life for us." Such love must be manifested in a practical way towards the brethren.*

---

*"But 'we know that we have passed from death unto life, because we love the brethren.' Not because we love *certain* of the brethren.

V. Hereby We Know.

Chapters iii:10—v:13.

1. Hereby we know that we are of the Truth. Verses 19-24.
2. Hereby know ye the Spirit of God. iv:1-4.
3. Hereby know we the Spirit of Truth and of Error. 5-6.
4. The Love manifested toward us. 7-19.
5. The final Tests as to the Possession of Eternal Life. iv:20; v:13.

1. Hereby we know that we are of the Truth: Verses 19-24. If the love of God dwells in the heart of the child of God it must be manifested in a practical way. Love must be expressed in deed and in truth, which is the fruit of true faith. If the believer does this he knows that he is of the truth. If it is lacking he is but an empty professing believer. But if we know that we are of the truth, by bearing such fruit of faith, we can assure our hearts before Him, and we can draw nigh with confidence. As our hearts do not condemn us, knowing that we are of the truth, we have confidence toward God and whatsoever we ask, we receive of Him, because we keep His commandments, and do those things that are pleasing in His sight. Where there is not a good conscience and the Holy Spirit is grieved real nearness to

---

let us remember. We may love even the children of God for some other reason than *as* His children. We may love them, perhaps, in gratitude to them for services that we may be receiving from them. Further than this, we may mistake for brotherly love that which is merely self-love in a subtler form. Men minister to our comfort, please us, and we think we love them; and in the true child of God there may be yet, after all, as to much that he counts love to the brethren, a similar mistake. A love to the children of God, as such, must find its objects wherever these children are, however little may be, so to speak, our gain from them; however, little they may fit to our tastes. The true love of the children of God must be far other than sociality, and cannot be sectarian. It is, as the Apostle says, 'without partiality, and without hypocrisy.' This does not, of course, deny that there may be differences that still obtain. He in whom God is most seen should naturally attract the heart of one who knows God according to the Apostle's reasoning here. It is God seen in men whom we recognize in the love borne to them; but, then, God is in all His own, as the Apostle is everywhere arguing; and, therefore, there is nothing self-contradictory in what has just been said."—F. W. Grant.

God and the effectual prayer which availeth much are impossible. It is the same blessed truth our Lord spoke in connection with the parable of the vine. "If ye abide in me, and my words abide in you ye shall ask what ye will, and it shall be done unto you" (John xv:7).

But what is His commandment? Strange that some expositors have read into it the ten commandments. The context answers the question: "And this is His commandment, that we should believe on the name of His Son Jesus Christ, and love one another, as He gave us commandment. And He that keepeth His commandment dwelleth in Him, and He in him. And hereby we know that He abideth in us, by the Spirit He hath given to us."

2. Hereby know ye the Spirit of God: iv:1-4. The last sentence of the preceding chapter gives the assurance that the believer has the Holy Spirit. There is no such thing as a true child of God without the Holy Spirit. The indwelling Spirit is the proof that He Himself dwells in us. But how do we know that it is the Spirit of God? How can a test be made? The sphere of the Spirit is the territory in which the spirit of error and darkness operates and where the liar from the beginning counterfeits. Many false prophets inspired by the spirit of darkness had gone out into the world and the Apostle gives a warning not to believe every spirit but to try the spirits.* The true test is the Person of the Lord Jesus Christ. Every spirit that confesseth that Jesus Christ is come in the flesh is of God. But this means more

*"The false prophets are certainly no fewer in number at the present time than when the Apostle spoke; yet, in general, we may say they assume less divine authority. We have sunk down so far into the wisdom of the world that man is credited with a place which God has lost. Inspiration is the inspiration of genius, rather than of God. We are more and more getting to lose the reality of the last, just as we are coming more and more to believe in the former. We believe in brilliancy, in eloquence, in intellect, in whatever you please in this way, but the assumption of speaking in any direct way by the Spirit of God no more exists, for the mass, except as one may say that the Spirit of God is as liberal as men are, and speaks in very diverse fashion—in poets, philosophers, and all the acknowledged leaders among men." —Numerical Bible.

than a mere confession with the lips, it means to own the Person and Lordship of Jesus Christ our Saviour. The demons know how to confess Him and yet they are demons (Matthew viii:29). The spirit of antichrist denies Him, does not confess that Jesus Christ is come in the flesh. This spirit which is not the Spirit of God manifests itself in the most subtle forms. It is called "true Christian charity" in our days to make common cause in what is called "social service" with those who do not confess Christ, who do not own Him as Saviour and Lord. These many antichrists speak of Him as man, they go so far as to call Christ a manifestation of God in human form, but they deny that He is very God come in the flesh. As stated before the most prominent form of it is today the denial of His Virgin birth. Anything which denies the full glory of the Lord Jesus Christ which in any way detracts from His glory, is the spirit of antichrist. About a hundred years ago a movement was in existence which claimed to be another Pentecost, just as there are movements today which claim the same unscriptural thing. The leader of that movement, Edward Irving, put great stress upon the incarnation, that Jesus came in the flesh. But after a while the demons which stood behind the movement brought forth the horrible doctrine of the peccability of Christ, that He had a corrupt nature like any other man. Such is the subtlety of Satan, the old serpent. He always strikes at Christ and His glory.

3. Hereby know we the Spirit of Truth and the Spirit of Error: Verses 5-6. The fifth verse has a good description of these antichrists and their following. These men, with their boasted learning and scholarship, their great swelling words, called eloquence, their natural amiability and cultured, courteous manners are of the world. They were never born again. If they had ever seen themselves lost and undone, and found in Christ their peace with God, they would yield complete obedience to Him and not deny His glory. When they speak they speak of the world. They speak of world conditions, and how they may be improved, of a better human society. Quite true they are even religious, but what they speak is not that which is of the Spirit, but what concerns the world system. The crowds want to hear that for it pleases the flesh and thus the devil brings his audience to hear them. Such antichrists in cap and gown have multiplied by the thousands; they are found in the leading pulpits of all denominations.

The test as to the Spirit of Truth and the spirit of error is stated in these words: "We are of God; He that knoweth God heareth us; he that is not of God heareth us not. Hereby know we the Spirit of Truth and of error." The test is the Apostle's doctrine. The Epistles are the full revelation of the doctrine of Christ, they contain the "many things" which the Lord spoke of when on earth, and which should be revealed when the Holy Spirit came. He has come and has made known the blessed things which eye hath not seen, nor ear heard, the things which God has prepared for them that love Him, but which are now revealed by His Spirit, the Spirit of Truth (1 Corinthians ii:9-10). The spirit of error denies these doctrines. In our day the enemy has invested a most subtle slogan, "Back to Christ." It sounds well but behind it stands the father of lies. These men who speak of going back to Christ charge our beloved brother Paul with having a theological system of his own, which they claim Christ, on earth, never taught. They reject the great redemption truths made known by the Lord through the Apostle to the Gentiles. Their cry "Back to Christ" is the spirit of antichrist.

4. The Love Manifested Towards Us: Verses 7-19. These blessed words are addressed to the beloved, true believers. The great center of this passage is "God is Love." Love is of God. But how do we know that God is Love? Such an antichristian system as "Christian Science" babbles about the Love of God, but that which alone expresses the Love of God, and by which it is known that God is Love, they reject completely. The question, how do we know that God is Love? is answered in verses 9 and 10. "In this was manifested the Love of God toward us, because that God sent His only begotten Son into the world, that we might live through Him. Herein is love, not that we loved God, but that He loved us, and sent His Son to be the propitiation for our sins." Apart from this there is no knowledge of the love of God. He who is born again knows that love, for in believing it (John iii:16) he receives eternal life, and that love was perfect in Him when we had no love for Him—not that we loved God, but that He loved us. In His great love He has met every need. This love, the nature of God, is in those who are born again. Every one that loveth is born of God and knoweth God. He that loveth not knoweth not God. "Beloved, if God so loved us, we ought to love one another. If we love one another, God dwelleth in us, and His love is perfected in us." Love therefore is the very essence of the new nature and must be manifested towards all who are the objects of the love of God and are in the family of God by having believed that love. "His presence, Himself, dwelling in us rises in the excellency of His nature above all the barriers of circumstances, and attaches us to those who are His. It is God in the power of His nature which is the source of thought and feeling and diffuses itself among them in whom it is. One can understand this. How is it that I love strangers from another land, persons of different habits, whom I have never known, more intimately than members of my own family after the flesh? How is it that I have thoughts in common, objects infinitely loved in common, affections powerfully engaged, a stronger bond with persons whom I have never seen, than with the otherwise dear companions of my childhood? It is because there is in them and in me a source of thoughts and affections which is not human. God is in it. God dwells in us. What happiness! What a bond! Does He not communicate Himself to the soul? Does He not render it conscious of His presence in love? Assuredly, yes. And if He is thus in us, the blessed source of our thoughts, can there be fear, or distance, or uncertainty, with regard to what He is? None at all. His love is perfect in us."*

---

*J. N. Darby.

His love is perfected in us by loving one another. Once more he uses the phrase "Hereby we know." "Hereby we know that we dwell in Him, and He in us, because He hath given us of His Spirit." "The Love of God is shed abroad in our hearts by the indwelling Spirit." He proceeds: "We have seen and testify that the Father sent the Son to be the Saviour of the world." Whosoever shall confess that Jesus is the Son of God, God dwelleth in Him and he in God." What wonderful words these are! Can there be anything greater and more wonderful than dwelling in God and God dwelling in us! And this is true of every believer. If we confess that Jesus Christ is the Son of God, if we rest in His finished work as well, knowing the Father sent Him to be the Saviour, and our Saviour therefore, then the Holy Spirit dwells in us and as a result God dwelleth in us and we in God. There can be no question about it for God says so. The enjoyment of it is a different matter. If it is not real to us and if we do not enjoy it there is something which hinders it in ourselves. If a great king should pay us a visit in our home and dwell there and we do not recognize the fact of the honor and privilege bestowed upon us, and if we do not trouble about it and show our appreciation of it, we would have no enjoyment in such a visit. To have the reality of it and enjoy the wonderful truth that God dwells in us and we in Him we must practise what our Lord said in John xiv:23, "If a man love me he will keep my words, and my Father will love him, and we will come unto him, and make our abode in him." We must dwell in love, the very nature of God, and that love is manifested towards Him and towards the brethren. Verses 12 and 16 make this clear. "And we have known and believed the love that God hath to us. God is love; and he that dwelleth in love dwelleth in God and God in him."

Another important fact is stated in the verses which follow: "Herein hath love been perfected with us, that we have boldness in the day of judgment, because as He is, even so are we in this world. There is no fear in love but perfect love casteth out fear, because fear has torment; and he that feareth is not perfected in love." It has nothing to do with *our* love, as some take it nor with seeking an experience of being "perfect in love." It is His love which casteth out fear, believing that love and dwelling in it. If we believe and know what God has made us in His infinite grace what Christ is, that as He is so are we, how can we fear anything! The coming day of judgment we await not only without any fear, but with boldness, for the day will only bring the full display of what Christ is and what we are in Him and with Him. The knowledge of His perfect love, the love which has reached down to us and lifted us so high, casteth out all fear.*

5. The Final Tests as to Eternal Life; Verses iv:20—v:13. Once more brotherly love is applied as the test. "If a man say, I love God, and hateth his brother, he is a liar." God is in the believer, he is the object of God's love, if therefore the brother is not loved, but hated, it is an evidence that God does not dwell in such a heart and again the beloved disciple brands such an one as a liar.

"Whosoever believeth that Jesus is the Christ is born of God and every one that loveth Him that begat, loveth him also that is begotten of Him." This is very logical. Then he gives a counter test to show it is genuine. "By this we know, that we love the children of God, when we love God and keep His commandments." If we love God and keep His commandments, we can rest assured that we love

*"It is a blessed love that Christ came into the world for such sinners as we are. But then there is the day of judgment. When I think of the love, I am all happy; but when I think of the day of judgment, my conscience is not quite easy. Though the heart may have tasted the love, the conscience not being quite clear, when I think of judgment I am not quite happy. This is what is provided for here. 'As He is so are we in this world.' The love was shown in visiting us when we were sinners; it is enjoyed in communion: but it is completed in this, that I am in Christ, and that Christ must condemn Himself in the day of judgment, if He condemns me, because as He is, so am I in the world. I am glorified before I get there. He changes this vile body and makes it like to His glorious body. When I am before the judgment seat, I am in this changed and glorified body; I am like my judge."—Synopsis.

the children of God also. If the soul goes out to Him in love, and it is shown by unreserved fidelity to His will, then love for those begotten of Him, the other members of the family of God, will be the result. "For this is the love of God that we keep His commandments, and His commandments are not grievous." It is a different thing from the law which is called elsewhere a yoke which no one was able to bear (Acts xv:10). Keeping His commandments means to be obedient to His Word, being subject unto Him in all things, for love to God is the spirit of obedience. But the children of God are in the world, though no longer of it. There are hindrances all about in the world which knew Him not and which knows not the children of God. All in this world is opposition to God and hinders true obedience. But that which is born of God overcometh the world. Our faith is the victory which overcometh the world. What faith is it? It is the faith which is occupied with the Son of God, which yields obedience to Him, does His will. Such a faith is the victory that overcomes the world and its attractions. This is stated in verse 5.

"And He, the Son of God, even Jesus Christ, came by water and blood—not by water only, but by water and blood." "And it is the Spirit that beareth witness, because the Spirit is Truth" (Verse 6). How beautiful is this passage and what divine perfection it reveals! Only John in his Gospel gives the account of the opened side of our adorable Saviour and that water and blood came forth out of the pierced side. "And he that saw it (John) bare record and his record is true and he knoweth that he saith true that ye might believe" (John xix:35). What the sinner needs is cleansing, a cleansing morally and a cleansing from guilt. The water is for cleansing, the blood telling of expiation cleanses from guilt. To make here of the water baptism, and of the blood the Lord's supper, is as false as it is ridiculous. It is purification and propitiation as accomplished and provided for in the death of Christ for the believer. As a result of the Holy Spirit is here on earth. Note the Apostle John does not put forward his own testimony here as given in the above passage, but the Holy Spirit Himself beareth witness to it. He is on earth for this purpose to bear witness to Christ and the work of Christ. How awful the rejection of that witness appears in the light of these words—that rejection which is so widespread and pronounced in antichristian modernism! The seventh verse has no business in our Bibles. It must be stricken out. It is an interpolation and all the historical evidences are against it. The oldest manuscripts do not contain these words which we read in verse 7. Leaving out this inserted verse we notice the connection which exists between verse 6 and 8. "And there are three that bear witness on earth, the Spirit, and the water, and the blood; and these three are one." The Spirit is the abiding witness of accomplished redemption, and He dwells in the believer.

Verses 9-13 need no further detailed annotations. They are so plain and simple that only one wilfully blind can misunderstand them. God's witness is concerning His Son. The believer who believes on the Son of God hath the witness in himself, that is, by the indwelling Spirit, and by the salvation he possesses, the new nature, the eternal life. Any man who does not believe God's witness concerning His Son hath made Him a liar. Think of it, dear reader, the creature of the dust makes God, who cannot lie, a liar! This is the heinous sin of the great religious world. The record we have is, that God hath given to us eternal life, that this life is in His Son, that if we have the Son we have life, if we have not the Son we have not life. Verse 13 concludes the argument and teaching of the Epistle concerning eternal life.

VI. Conclusion.

Chapter v:14-21.

The conclusion of this great Epistle mentions first the practical confidence which a believer may have, the outcome of that relationship and fellowship with the Father and His Son, which the doctrinal part so blessedly unfolds. We can come in prayer to Him with boldness and whatever we ask "according to His will He heareth us; and if we know that

He heareth us, whatsoever we ask, we know that we have the petitions which we have asked of Him." As a loving Father He listens to the cry of His children and He answers if it is according to His will, and the child of God would not have it differently, and desire anything to be granted him which is contrary to the will of God. Our unanswered prayers we joyfully recognize as being not according to His will. It is not true faith when fanatics, like faith curists, say that God *must* do certain things. That is not faith but presumption.

But what is the sin unto death (Verse 16)? God chastises the sinning believer often through sickness. And the chastisement may lead to the physical death of the child of God. Such was the case in Corinth (1 Corinth. xi:31). It is the same case as James v:14, 15. If the sin is not unto physical death as a chastisement, we can pray for the brother and he will be restored. But there is a sin unto death. Ananias and Sapphira committed such a sin. No prayer in such a case does avail anything. God in His governmental dealings takes the offender away as to his life on earth. It does not affect the salvation of the soul, as those teach who think that one who has believed, has eternal life, and is a member of the family of God, can be lost again.

The conclusion of the Epistle consists in three statements that "we know": "We *know* that whosoever is born of God sinneth not; but he that is begotten of God keepeth Himself and that wicked one toucheth him not." Sin is the touch of the wicked one. If the believer guards himself, by living in the fellowship with the Father and the Son, walking in the Light, the wicked one cannot reach him; he lives according to his new nature and sinneth not. "*We know* that we are of God and the whole world lieth in the wicked one." Hence God's children should be separated from the world. If a believer is not he moves on the very territory of the wicked one and the author of sin finds occasion to touch him and lead him to sin. "*We know* that the Son of God is come, and hath given us an understanding, that we may know Him that is true, and we are in

Him that is true, even in His Son Jesus Christ. This is the true God and eternal life."

The final exhortation is "Little children (*teknia*—all God's children), keep yourselves from idols. Amen." What is an idol? Anything and everything that draws the affection and devotion of heart and soul from the Lord Jesus Christ. May He, through the power of His Spirit, keep us all from idols. And we shall be kept if we give in our hearts and lives the pre-eminence to our Lord and walk in the light as He is in the light.

SECOND AND THIRD EPISTLES OF JOHN

Second and Third Epistles of John

Introduction.

We treat these small documents together. No intelligent person can doubt that both Epistles were written by the same person. We do not need to investigate the objections and inventions of rationalists like Bretschneider, those of the so-called Tuebingen school and the modern critics, who deny the Johannine authorship and teach that the fictitious "John the Presbyter of Ephesus" wrote these two letters.

But all these modern conceptions are answered by the ancient authorities which ascribe both Epistles to the writer of the First Epistle, that is, the Apostle John. Irenaeus, who as a boy had listened to Polycarp, who knew John personally, bears witness to the genuineness of the Second Epistle, so does Clement of Alexandria, the Muratorian fragment, Dionysius of Alexandria, and others. Both Epistles seem to have been accepted from the very beginning as the inspired testimony of John.

The internal evidence is conclusive. Both Epistles are in tone, style and vocabulary like the Gospel of John and the First Epistle of John. The great characteristic words of the other writings of John (the Gospel and John I) "Love," "Truth," "World," etc., are found in these two Epistles. They are, indeed, complementary to the First Epistle and give some of the truths contained in the First Epistle in a practical way. The warning contained in the Second Epistle concerning receiving one who does not bring the doctrine of Christ, that is an Antichrist, connects closely with the instructions of 1 John iv. There is no question but both Epistles are appendices to the First Epistle.

The Second Epistle.

The Second Epistle is addressed by the Elder unto the

elect lady and her children. The word elder has the same meaning as it has in 1 Peter v. Some take it that the elect lady means an assembly, and her children the members of the assembly. But that is a very strained application.

The word "Kyria" (lady) excludes this meaning, besides other reasons which we do not follow here. She was a Chrision woman of note, generally known and beloved, having children, whom the Apostle had found walking in the Truth. She had also a sister with children, who seems to have been in the same place where the Apostle was, probably in Ephesus. This is indicated by the last verse of the Epistle, "The children of thy elect sister greet thee." The keynote of this message to the elect lady, unknown by name, is the Word "Truth." The Apostle lets them know that he loves them, as well as all other believers in the truth. That is the ground of real love; every child of God—man, woman or child—is best beloved for the sake of the truth, the blessed truth so abundantly poured forth in the First Epistle, the truth which is Christ Himself. And that truth "dwelleth in us, and shall be with us forever." Thus the truth known binds together in closest fellowship all who know Him. Then follows a blessed greeting, "Grace, mercy and peace shall be with you, from the Father, and from the Lord Jesus Christ, the Son of the Father, in truth and love." The statement, "the Son of the Father" is unique; it is not found elsewhere in the New Testament and is in full keeping with the object of this little Epistle, for the denial of Christ coming in the flesh, and the warning against these deceivers, is the chief message of the Epistle. The great joy of the Apostle was that he found them walking in the truth, that the children of the elect lady walked according to the commandment received from the Father (1 John iii:24). Having the truth necessitates walking in the truth. One who claims to have the truth and does not walk in it, shows that he does not know the truth in his heart. But walking in the truth is the result of having and knowing the truth.

What we have stated before, that these two Epistles are

appendices of the First Epistle, is seen by the fifth verse (1 John iii:23-24). It is the old and the new commandment. It was old because it was manifested in Christ Himself; new because it is just as true in us as in Him. Divine love flows from love, and reproduces itself in all who know the truth, that is, who know Christ. And this is love that we walk after His commandments. It means obedience to Him, and what else is obedience but love in exercise?

But why does he write all this? With the seventh verse he gives the reason and it is a very solemn one, indeed. Well may we look to these words in our own days for they have a great meaning for the children of God living in these closing days, as they had a meaning in the beginning of the dispensation. "For many deceivers are entered into the world, who confess not that Jesus Christ is come into the flesh. This is a deceiver and an Antichrist." This was true in the beginning of the age, and all through the present age the old serpent has made its many attempts to attack Christ and foster the lies concerning His Person and Glory, but never before has this been so evident as in our own days. The reason is that the age is about to end. Denying that Jesus Christ is come in the flesh was mentioned by John in his First Epistle (Chapter iv). It includes all phases of evil doctrines concerning Christ, the Son of the Father. It is a denial of His essential Deity, His true humanity, His Virgin birth, His infallibility, His holy character, His physical resurrection, and His bodily presence in Glory. We need not mention again how many such antichrists are about in these days. And John brands them in plain words as deceivers. No matter what names they have, what scholarship and honors they claim, what beautiful characters they have assumed as natural men, if they deny anything about Christ, they are deceivers. He calls, therefore, to look diligently whether some of this awful leaven is not affecting them. If in any way they were contaminated with it they, John and the fellow teachers, might lose the full reward. (See 1 John ii:28). Then follows the instructions in verses 9-11.

"Whosoever transgresseth and abideth not in the doctrine of Christ hath not God. He that abideth in the doctrine of Christ, he hath both the Father and the Son." Even the smallest error about the Person of Christ is a transgression of the doctrine of Christ and if followed will lead to a complete rejection of the truth, as it has been so often seen in cases of apostates. Such deniers have not God, while he who abideth in the doctrine of Christ hath both the Father and the Son. After this declaration comes a divine command which is just as binding as any other command in the Word of God. "If there come any unto you, and bring not this doctrine, receive him not in your house, neither bid him Godspeed; for he that biddeth him Godspeed is partaker of his evil deeds." This is strong language and yet not too strong when we remember what is at stake. Any one who brings not the doctrine of Christ, the doctrine as unfolded in the previous Epistle, concerning Christ the Son of God come in the flesh, dying for sinners and all that clusters around it, is an antichrist. Furthermore he makes God a liar and in denying the doctrine of Christ robs God of His glory and man of his salvation. And every man who denies the Virgin Birth, or teaches the peccability of Christ, or denies His physical resurrection is such a one. He must be shunned. Fellowship with him is an impossibility. He is not to be welcomed to any Christian home, nor is he to be given the common greeting. If met anywhere there is to be no acknowledgment whatever, not even a "Good Morning" or "Good Night." This is the meaning of the expression "Godspeed." But is not this intolerant? Yes, the intolerance of divine love. If such deceivers are welcomed and fellowship is had with them even in the slightest degree, the believer puts his sanction on a denier of Christ. God will hold all responsible who fellowship any man, any set of men, any institution or anything else, which deny His Son and His Glory. This is unpalatable to many. Nowadays it is called "Christian charity and broadmindedness" to mingle with Unitarians, Critics and baptized infidels of various descriptions. His honor and glory is in the background. Happy are we if we stand firm and refuse such fellowship, practising this divinely given injunction by the Apostle of Love. God will be our rewarder.

"Having many things to write unto you, I would not write with paper and ink, but I trust to come unto you, and speak face to face, that our joy may be full. The children of the elect sister greet thee. Amen." Thus ends the Second Epistle.

The Third Epistle

The Third Epistle is addressed by the elder, the aged Apostle John, to a brother by name of Gaius. A Gaius is mentioned in Acts xix:29; xx:4; Romans xvi:23 and 1 Corinthians i:14. It is impossible to say whether this is the same. John calls him well-beloved, whom he loved in the truth. Thus he emphasizes the truth once more as he had done before. He wishes that he might prosper in his body, in health, as even his soul prospered. He had heard from the brethren who testified of the truth in him and that he walked in the truth. He rejoiced in this and declares "I have no greater joy than to hear that my children walk in truth." And this is not only the aged Apostle's joy, but it is the joy of the Lord. How He must rejoice when His beloved children in whom He dwells walk in truth! Gaius had been very gracious and hospitable. Perhaps the brethren who gave such a good report to John were the recipients of Gaius's kindness. They had witnessed before the assembly how faithful he was in entertaining them, helping them on their journey in every way possible. He had done this not only with the brethren in his locality, but with brethren who were strangers, ministering servants of the Lord Jesus Christ, who went forth for His Name's sake, taking nothing of the Gentiles. In going forth in ministering the Word they depended on the Lord. The evil of today, even among those who preach the truth, of demanding so much money for so much service was unknown in the Church. Nowhere do we read in the New Testament of a "salaried" ministry. The evils of going to the world for support of the Lord's work, or using the methods of the world are widespread and detrimental to true faith and a true testimony to the truth. The work of the Lord and the servants of Christ are to be supported only by the Lord's people and not by the unsaved. Such, then, who go forth for His Name's sake, taking nothing from the Gentiles (those who are outside) are to be received and those who receive them, help them on their journey as Gaius did, are fellow helpers to the truth. They are going to share in that coming day in the fruit of their labors. This is the true fellowship in the truth, as Paul expressed it in Galatians, "Let him that is taught in the Word communicate unto him that teaches in all good things" (Galatians vi:6). It is in contrast from what the Second Epistle demanded—withdrawal from those who bring not the doctrine of Christ, a complete separation from them; but here it is identification with those who know the truth and teach the truth.

This is a bright picture presented in Gaius. Alas! there is another side in this Third Epistle. There was one by name of Diotrephes. His name means "Nourished of God." Of him John writes as follows: "I wrote unto the church, but Diotrephes, who loveth to have the pre-eminence among them, received us not. Wherefore, if I come, I will remember his deeds which he doeth, prating against us with malicious words; and not content therewith, neither doth he himself receive the brethren, and casteth them out of the church." We let another speak on this. "We have another evil designated very clearly here. Diotrephes is the Scriptural example of the clerical tribe, as contra-distinguished from the ministry of Christ. There is no service, because there is no love. He is the representative of the spirit which opposes the free action of the Holy Spirit, setting itself even against apostolical authority in order to gain or maintain his own individual pre-eminence. Self-importance, jealousy of those over us, impatience of others equally called to serve, scorn of the assembly, yet sometimes humoring the least worthy for its own ends—such are the characteristics of clericalism. I do not mean in clergymen only; for there are men of God incomparably better than their position tends to make them; as on the other hand this evil thing is nowhere so offensive as where the truth that is owned, wholly condemns it."* Diotrephes wanted to be the leader of the assembly, a kind of a pope in embryo. He loved the pre-eminence and this self-love and seeking to maintain his position led him to act so outrageously that he excommunicated the brethren and dared to rise up against the Apostle himself. What harm such jealousies, self-seeking, self-glorification and ecclesiastical bossism have worked and are working in the body of Christ! and nowhere so much as in circles where the full truth is known and confessed. But why did Diotrephes love to have the pre-eminence? Because, unlike the Apostle and the beloved Gaius, he did not give the Lord Jesus Christ the pre-eminence in all things; he did not walk in the truth. When the Lord comes, before His judgment-seat, all these things will be brought to light and dealt with by Him.

John does not leave us with the sad picture of Diotrephes. 'Beloved, follow not that which is evil, but that which is good. He that doeth good is of God; but he that doeth evil hath not seen God." It is another one of the tests as we found them in the First Epistle. Doing good is the active service of love. God does not do evil, but He does good, hence if we do good as believers in the truth, we are of God. Then he mentions Demetrius. Perhaps he was one of the servants who went about doing good, preaching the truth, and whom Diotrephes would not receive. How blessed that the Holy Spirit through John's letter endorses and recommends him. "Demetrius hath good report of all, and of the truth itself; yea, and we also bear record, and ye know that our record is true." Such is the comfort of all true servants who walk in the truth, that the Lord knoweth. "I have many things to write, but I will not with ink and pen write unto thee. But I trust I shall shortly see thee,

---

*William Kelly on Third John.

and we shall speak face to face. Peace be to thee. Our friends salute thee. Greet the friends by name." Both Epistles end, with a coming face to face meeting. Let us remember there is to be some blessed day a "face to face" meeting, when the Saints of God will meet together for eternal fellowship, but above all when we shall be face to face with Him. How soon it may be! But while we wait for that meeting may we walk in the light and in the fullest enjoyment of our fellowship with the Father and with His Son, our blessed Lord. To Him be glory and dominion for ever. Amen.

THE EPISTLE OF JUDE

The Epistle of Jude

Introduction

The Epistle of Jude is the last epistle preceding the great final book with which the Holy Scriptures conclude, the book of Revelation. We believe the place given to this epistle is the right one, for, as we shall see, it reveals the conditions, religiously and morally, which prevail on earth before the great coming event takes place, of which Revelation has so much to say. Some have called it "the preface to the Revelation."

The Author

We are not left in doubt who the writer is, for he mentions himself in the beginning of it. It is Jude, the servant of Jesus Christ and brother of James. But who is this Jude or Judas? Among the disciples were two by the name of Judas. There was Judas Iscariot, who ended his miserable career, after he had become the instrument of the devil, by hanging. In John xiv:22 we read, "Judas saith unto Him, not Iscariot, Lord, how is it that Thou wilt manifest Thyself unto us, and not unto the world?" The Spirit of God makes it plain that Judas Iscariot did not address Jesus by the name Lord, which expresses faith in His Deity, but that there was another Judas in the apostolate who speaks here. When we turn to the names of the twelve in Matthew x:2-4, we find the name of Judas but once; it is the name of him who betrayed the Lord. The Judas whose words are recorded in the above passage in the Gospel of John, is called in Matthew x:3 "Lebbaeus whose surname was Thaddaeus." In Luke vi:16 and Acts i:13, his name is given as Judas of James; it must be noticed that the words in the authorized version "the brother" are in italics, which means that they are supplied by the translators. It is not so in the first verse of this epistle; here the writer calls himself "brother of James." But there is still another Judas found in the Gospels. His name is recorded in

Matthew xiii:55. "Is not this the carpenter's son? is not His mother called Mary? and his brethren, James, and Joses, and Simon, and Judas?" The James, the brother of the Lord mentioned in this passage, is the author of the Epistle of James. (See introduction to the epistle of James). The question then arises, Is the writer of the epistle before us, the Apostle Judas of James, also called Lebbaeus, surnamed Thaddaeus, or is it Judas, the one who is called one of the Lord's brethren, and therefore the natural brother of James, the writer of the Epistle of James? Some maintain that Jude is the Apostle Judas, while others see in Jude the brother of James, as given in Matthew xiii:55. We endorse the latter view. We give the reasons why the writer of this epistle cannot be the Apostle Judas.

1. He does not speak of Himself as an Apostle. He designates himself as a servant of Jesus Christ. Whenever an Apostle calls himself a servant of Jesus Christ, he adds his apostleship, as we learn from Romans i:1; Titus i:1; 2 Peter i:1. The only exception is the epistle to the Philippians, in which Paul associates with himself in the address Timothy, and then speaks of himself and Timothy as servants of Jesus Christ.

2. If he were the Apostle Judas, the brother of the Apostle James, the sons of Alphaeus, we have to face great difficulties, as Dean Alford states, involving the wholly unjustifiable hypothesis, that those who are called in Scripture the brethren of our Lord were not His brethren, but His cousins, sons of Alphaeus (Cleopas).

But why does the writer of this epistle not speak of himself as "the brother of the Lord?" it has been asked. James does not do so in his epistle either. He is silent about this relationship and so is his brother Jude. "The question, Why does not Jude mention his earthly relationship to the Lord? shows great ignorance of the true spirit of the writers of the New Testament. It would be the last thing I should expect, to find one of the brethren of the Lord asserting this relationship as a ground of reception for an epistle. Almost all agree that the writer of the epistle of James was the person known as the brother of the Lord. Yet there we have no designation. It would have been in fact altogether inconsistent with the true spirit of Christ (Luke xx:27, 28), and in harmony with those later susperstitious feelings with which the next and following generations regarded His earthly relatives. Had such a designation as "*Adelphos tou Kyriou*" (brother of the Lord) been found in the address of an epistle, it would have formed a strong à priori objection to its authenticity."*

Jude is therefore the one mentioned in Matthew xiii:55. Apart from this epistle we know nothing more of him. The date of the epistle is about the year 65.

Its Authenticity

It is authenticated by different ancient sources. The Muratorian fragment mentions it as Jude's Epistle. Clement of Alexandria cites it as Scripture, as well as Tertullian and others. The theories of some objecting critics need not to be considered.

To whom the epistle was originally addressed is not stated. Some have surmised that like James and the Petrine Epistles Jude addressed originally Jewish believers. This may be true, for Jude mentions, prominently, like Peter, Old Testament facts, besides some Jewish traditional matters, which thereby are confirmed as facts. Concerning the apocryphal writings, especially the Book of Enoch, which Jude is charged with having used in the composition of his epistle, we shall have more to say in the annotations.

Jude and 2 Peter Chapter II

As stated in the introduction to the second Epistle of Peter, Jude's testimony is very much like the testimony of the Apostle Peter in the second chapter of his second epistle. Hence there has been a long controversy whether

*Prolegomena

Jude copied from Peter or Peter copied from Jude. We have stated before that if Jude had copied from Peter, his epistle could not be an inspired epistle, and so if Peter copied from Jude. Jude may have known Peter's Epistle, but that does not mean that he used Peter's Epistle, but the Holy Spirit gives a similar testimony through Jude, which is, after a closer examination, somewhat different from Peter's epistle. This is pointed out in the annotations.

The Message of Jude

It seems about the time when Jude wrote his letter a departure from the faith set in among believers. This is confirmed by the fact that other epistles written about the same time give warnings of the same nature as those given by Jude. The message of Jude may be called a prophetic history of the apostasy of Christendom from its beginning in apostolic days down to the end of the age, when the complete apostasy will be dealt with and completely destroyed by the coming of the Lord. It is the darkest forecast of the end of the age which the Spirit of God has given in the epistles. While apostasy and antichristianity have held sway all through the history of Christendom, there is coming in the end of this age a consummation, the evils of which are pictured by the Holy Spirit through the pen of Jude. We know that we are living right in the midst of the fulfillment of Jude's message. The epistle is, therefore, of great importance for our times.

Analysis and Annotations

I. The Introduction: Verses 1-2. Jude in his brief introduction speaks of the Christian believers, whom he addresses, as called ones, sanctified by God the Father, and preserved in Jesus Christ. The latter statement may also be translated "kept for Jesus Christ." What was true of the believers in Jude's day is true of all believers. Especially comforting is the fact, that, no matter how dark the days may be, however strong the current of evil, those who are "the beloved of God called Saints" will be preserved in Jesus Christ and kept for Him as the members of His body, till He comes. He keeps His own. It is the blessed assurance that the believer's keeping rests in His own hands. In the Revelation we see in the glory vision that Christ holds seven stars in His right hand, which is the symbol of the hand of His power with which He keeps His own. Then there is the prayer that "mercy, and peace, and love may be multiplied."

11. The Purpose and Occasion of the Epistle: Verses 3-4. "Beloved, giving all diligence to write unto you of our common salvation, I was constrained to write unto you exhorting you to earnestly contend for the faith which was once delivered unto the saints."

It had evidently been upon the heart of Jude to write an epistle to the Christians whom he knew. He gave all diligence to carry out his intention. This must mean that he prayed and thought over this matter. He then decided to write about the common salvation. This is the Gospel.

It is the nearest and the dearest object to every believer, for it is the matchless story of God's love. It reveals the Son of God, our Lord, who died for our sins, who was buried and rose again the third day. There are blessed depths and heights in this Gospel, the salvation which believers have in common, which have never yet been measured. Jude thought to make this the theme of his epistle. Then something happened. The power which was to guide his pen constrained him to write about something else. The Holy Spirit constrained him to exhort Christians to contend earnestly for the faith once and for all delivered unto the saints. Here is a very fine illustration at the close of the New Testament of how the Word of God was given. Jude had a desire to write about the common salvation; but the Holy Spirit wanted him to write about something else and He constrained him to do so, not in his own words but in words given by God.

What faith is meant? Not a creed or confession of faith as formulated by a denomination, sect or party, but *the* faith, which has been delivered once for all unto the saints. It is the same faith concerning which our Lord asked the question, "Nevertheless when the Son of Man cometh, shall He find the faith on the earth?" (Luke xviii:8). It is the faith revealed in the Word of God. The heart of that faith is the Son of God, our Lord Jesus Christ, and the Apostles' doctrine made known by the Holy Spirit; it is therefore the whole body of revealed truth. This faith is given by revelation, a different thing from what is being taught today, as if this faith were the product of a process of evolution through the religious experiences of the race for thousands of years. The truths which man needs cannot be found by searching. This faith is "once for all delivered unto the saints." It is permanent, irrevocable and like Him who has revealed it, unchanging. Nor is this faith delivered to the world, but to the Saints, that is to the body of Christ, the church.

That faith was being corrupted when Jude received the commission to exhort Christians to contend earnestly for it. They were ungodly men, having taken on the Christian profession without possessing the reality of it. The evil they introduced was twofold. They turned the grace of God into lasciviousness and they denied the rights of Christ to be Lord and Master. They professed to believe in grace, but abused it so that they might indulge in their own lusts;

they knew nothing of the power of godliness manifested in holy living and therefore they denied the authority of the Lord Jesus Christ.

III. Examples from the Past: Verses 5-10. The Spirit of God reminds them of certain apostasies in past history and how God in judgment dealt with it. If we compare this section of Jude's Epistle with 2 Peter ii:4-8 we shall see at once how both documents differ from each other. Peter speaks first of the angels that sinned; then of Noah and the flood and finally of Sodom and Gomorrha and the deliverance of Lot. Jude on the other hand does not mention Noah at all, nor Lot. He speaks first of the Israelites who had come out of Egypt and were destroyed in the wilderness because they believed not. This is followed by the angels who kept not their first estate; then comes Sodom and Gomorrha and the judgment which fell upon these cities, and finally Jude adds something which is not found elsewhere in the Word of God, the incident about Michael contending with the devil about the body of Moses. It is far fetched with this different testimony which Jude gives to charge him with having copied Peter, or Peter having used Jude.

When we examine these examples of the past, we discover that they are not chronologically arranged. If they were reported according to the time when they happened, Jude, like Peter, should have mentioned first the angels that sinned; after which Sodom and Gomorrha would be in order, followed by the Israelites who fell in the wilderness and after that Michael contending with the devil. Why this unchronological arrangement in this Epistle? There must be a purpose in it. We believe the arrangement is made in the manner as it is to teach us the starting point and the goal of apostasy. It starts with unbelief. The people had been saved out of Egypt, but they believed not and were destroyed in the wilderness, except those mentioned in the Word who believed. Thus all apostasy starts with unbelief in what God has spoken. The angels which kept not their first estate, who left their own habitation, and who are now chained, are the same angels of whom Peter speaks, those who brought in the corruption described in the opening verses of Genesis vi. They gave up the place assigned to them. This is the next step in the progress of apostasy. Unbelief leads to rebellion against God. Sodom and Gomorrha come next. Here we find the grossest immoralities and going after strange flesh. These vicious things are still in the world, and why are they so prominent in our days? On account of unbelief. Then follows the statement, that these apostates are filthy dreamers who defile the flesh, despise dominion, and speak evil of dignities. This is lawlessness. This is the goal of all apostasy. The predicted lawlessness with which this age ends is the fruitage of infidelity. Such is the development of apostasy. Unbelief, rebellion against God and his revealed truth, immorality and anarchy. These steps may be traced in our own times.

To show that Michael the archangel would not rail against the fallen angel-prince, now the devil, as these apostates despise dominions, the incident concerning Michael contending against the devil about the body of Moses is introduced. He durst not bring a railing accusation against the former Lucifer, the son of the morning, for Michael still recognized in him the once great and glorious creature. It is stated by some of the early church fathers that this episode was recorded in a Jewish apocryphal book "Assumption of Moses." This book is no longer in existence. Another Jewish tradition has it that Michael had been given the custody of the grave of Moses. Jude does not quote from tradition, nor does he quote from a source now no longer available, or, as others surmise, used one of Zechariah's visions (chapter iii), but the Holy Spirit revealed unto him what actually took place when Moses had died. It seems that Michael the archangel was commissioned by the Lord to conduct the funeral of Moses (Deut. xxxiv:5-6). Then the devil appeared upon the scene claiming the body of the servant of the Lord, for what purpose is not revealed.*

*See Annotation, Vol. I. Deut. xxxiv: 5-6.

And Michael durst not bring against him a railing accusation but said, The Lord rebuke thee. But it is different with these apostates. They are compared with irrational animals, following their natural inclinations.

IV. A further description of the apostates: Verses 11-13. The Spirit of God pronounces a woe upon them. The eleventh verse is of much importance. At the close of the New Testament we are reminded of Cain, the first murderer of the human race. Some expositors claim that his name is introduced here because he is a representative of all bad men; others think that he is mentioned because these apostates hated those who are of the truth, as Cain hated Abel. The way of Cain was the way of unbelief. He did not believe what God had spoken, while Abel believed. He had not faith like Abel, who offered unto God a more excellent sacrifice than Cain, by which he obtained witness that he was righteous. Cain was a religious man nevertheless, but his religion may be termed a "blood-less religion." He brought the labor of his hands, that which he had gathered from the land upon which the curse rested. The apostates go in the same way of self-will and in that way they reject the record of God concerning His Son. They have no use for the blood of redemption; the salvation they preach is the salvation of "Do," by character. They rush also greedily after the error of Balaam. Money is the chief object with them. They teach error for reward, knowing all along that their teaching is contrary to the revelation of God. Money, honor and glory from men, self-exaltation and self-gratification are the leading motives of these men. The third characteristic is the sin of Core (Korah). The sin of Korah was open rebellion and opposition against the authority of God and the priesthood He had instituted. These apostates of the last days manifest the same spirit of rebellion and defiance. They have no use for the Lord Jesus Christ as the appointed mediator, priest and advocate. The perdition of Korah will overtake them likewise.

Not Jude, but the Holy Spirit, denounces them in the strongest language. (See annotations 2 Peter ii). They are doubly dead, first in their own fallen nature, and in the second place by turning their ears from the truth and going into apostasy. They are like trees which give the promise of fruit in an imposing bloom, but which withers away; they do not yield any fruit whatever. They are plucked up by the roots without any hope of a revival. They are like the wild waves of the sea, foaming out their own shame (Isaiah lvii:20-21); wandering stars to whom is reserved the blackness of darkness forever. The wandering stars in the universe belonged once to some great solar system. They detached themselves and began their wanderings. As they left their center they wandered further and further away, deeper and deeper into the immense space of cold and darkness. So these apostates left the center and became eccentric rushing, like these wandering stars of the heavens, into the outer darkness.

V. The testimony of Enoch: Verses 14-16. The Holy Spirit introduces quite abruptly Enoch, the seventh from Adam. There is a deep spiritual significance in this. Enoch lived as an age was about to close. Before the evil days of Noah, with universal violence, corruption and wickedness, had come, Enoch walked with God and bore a prophetic testimony of what was to come in the future. He suffered on account of the testimony he bore to that generation. The ungodly spoke against him, but he kept on in his walk with God and in his testimony, till the day came when he was suddenly removed from the earth. "By faith Enoch was translated that he should not see death; and was not found, because God had translated him, for before his translation he had this testimony, that he pleased God" (Hebrews xi:5). Enoch represents prophetically the true church living at the close of the age, bearing witness to the coming of the Lord, and waiting in faith for the promised translation. The Spirit of God mentions Enoch for this purpose and for our encouragement.

Much has been made by critics and rationalists about this reference to Enoch. What Jude writes about Enoch is found in a Jewish Apocryphal book by the name of "The

Book of Enoch." The book consists of supposed revelations which were given to Enoch and to Moses. Its object seems to be a vindication of the ways of providence and to set forth the coming and terrible retribution for sinners. The book was known to the early church fathers who refer to it often in their writings. For centuries it seems to have been lost. About the close of the 18th Century an Ethiopian translation was discovered in Abyssinia and translated into English and German. Critics claim that this book of Enoch was used by Jude, inasmuch as he inserted this reference to Enoch, which is almost verbatim found in that book. But according to these critics the book of Enoch was written in the second century and from this they reason that Jude did not write this epistle in the year 65 A. D. But there are other scholars who have ascertained that the Book of Enoch was in existence before Christ. Even if the critics were correct that this book was written in the second century of our era, it is no evidence that Jude could not have written his epistle in the year as stated above. The writers of the book of Enoch might have used Jude's statements about Enoch. The fact that Jude in giving by the Holy Spirit this paragraph concerning Enoch proves the record, whether it was handed down by tradition or written in the book of Enoch, to be true.

VI. The Exhortations: Verses 17-23. These exhortations are for the people of God, whose lot is cast in these predicted evil days. The first exhortation is to remember the words which were spoken before of the apostles of our Lord Jesus Christ. To hold fast these words and remember them is the great need in the days of apostasy. Peter bears the same witness (2 Peter iii:1-3). Building yourselves up on your most holy faith is the next exhortation. Nothing else is worth while building up for believers living in the last days. Prayer is needed. But it is not prayer *for* the Holy Spirit, for another Pentecost, which is nowhere promised, nor for another baptism with the Spirit, but it is prayer *in* the Spirit. The exhortation "Keep yourselves in the love of God" means to keep oneself in the consciousness in that fellowship with the Father and with the Son of which John speaks in his first epistle, that is enjoying the love of God in Christ Jesus our Lord. Looking for the mercy of our Lord Jesus Christ unto eternal life, which means, looking for Himself, for His coming. The final exhortations give instructions as to the believer's attitude towards those who have been led away.

VII. The Conclusion: Verses 24-25. "Now unto Him that is able to keep you from stumbling, and to present you faultless before the presence of His glory with exceeding joy, to the only wise God our Saviour, be glory and majesty, dominion and power, both now and ever. Amen."

Beautiful doxology with which this epistle ends! His own are being kept in the evil days with which the age closes. They are the preserved in Jesus Christ kept for Him. And while we wait for Him, He is able to keep us not only from falling, but from stumbling. And then comes that day in which He will present His own, His beloved people, whom He bought by His own precious blood. He will present them faultless before the presence of His glory with exceeding joy. And what a day of joy and gladness, as well as of glory, it will be, when He shall see the travail of His soul and will be satisfied, the day in which He will present to Himself a glorious church, not having spot or wrinkle, or any such thing; but that it should be holy and without blame! (Ephes. v:27).

THE REVELATION

The Revelation

Introduction

This great final Book of the Word of God may well be called the capstone of the entire Bible. A pyramid becomes a pyramid by the great capstone, and the Bible becomes the full and complete revelation of God through this document "The Revelation of Jesus Christ." If this book were not in the Bible, the Bible would be an unfinished book; the issues raised in the preceding documents would be forever unsolved.

This disposes at once of the miserable attempts which have been made by critics and others to eliminate the book of Revelation from the canon of the New Testament. Revelation is a necessity. "A book which offers in some way or other to open up those secrets of God which yet lie hidden in the future, seems wholly in place in our sacred Scriptures. It is towards some such book that our thoughts have been moving as we travelled through the Gospels, the Acts and the Epistles; for all alike point forward to a consummation of all things, to a time when the Kingdom of God shall be finally and completely established, when all creation shall cease to groan and travail, when the inheritance of which we have received the first fruits shall be wholly ours. It is, moreover, towards some such book that our hearts seem to yearn as we travel through the earlier volumes of experience, discovering the contradictions between what should be and what is, accumulating impressions of the Protean forms and tremendous power of wickedness, and craving for the manifestation of triumphant righteousness. Thus both the Christian Bible and the Christian consciousness seem to demand a book of revelation for their completion or satisfaction."*

---

*C. Anderson Scott.

The Authorship

The title of the Book as we find it in the King James Version is "The Revelation of St. John the Divine"; the better title would be to take the opening words of the Book and call it "The Revelation of Jesus Christ." But the above title tells us that John is the author. This is confirmed by the book itself, for we read twice in the first chapter that the writer says "John to the seven churches," and again, "I, John, who also am your brother" (i:4, 9). Furthermore, at the close of the book he names himself again: "And I, John, saw these things" (xxii:8). The church down to the middle of the third century has but one testimony as to the authorship of this book, and that is, the Johannine, that John the beloved disciple, the son of Zebedee, wrote this book in the isle of Patmos when banished there. The only exceptions were the Alogians, a heretical sect which also rejected the Gospel of John, and a controversialist by name of Caius.

As it is of much interest to be acquainted with the testimony of the many early witnesses in refutation of the destructive critics, who attack this great book, we give a brief summary of these historical evidences.

The first witness is *Justin Martyr*, who wrote about the year 140 in the Dialogue, "that a certain man, whose name was John, one of the Apostles of Christ, prophesied in an apocalypse (revelation) which came to him that believers should reign a thousand years in Jerusalem." *Melito*, Bishop of Sardis, according to the historian Eusebius, wrote treatises on "the devil and on the Apocalypse of John." This was about the year 170. Then follow the testimonies of *Theophilus*, Bishop of Antioch (180); and *Apollonius*. A greater witness still is Irenaeus. We remind the reader of our introduction to the Gospel of John, and call to mind the fact that Irenaeus was in his youth acquainted with Polycarp, who was a disciple of the Apostle John. A number of times Irenaeus speaks of "Ioannes Domini disciplus"—John the disciple of the Lord—and that he had written the Apocalypse. *Tertullian* (about 200 A.D.) refers in his writings four times to the Revelation as being the work of the Apostle John. The so-called *Muratorian* fragments quote from the Revelation, and it can be shown by the context of the passage that the Apostle John was believed to be author. *Clement* of Alexandria (about 200 A.D.) mentions also John, the beloved disciple as the writer of the book. A scholar of Clement was *Origen* (233 A.D.). He made careful research about the canonicity and genuineness of the books of the New Testament. While he reported carefully any doubts or disputes about different books, he has nothing to say about the Revelation and its author. He quotes from the book frequently, and it proves that in his time no question was raised about John being the author. *Hippolytus*, Bishop of Ostia (240 A.D.) quotes John's words many times and does not leave us in doubt that he means the son of Zebedee. Then follow a host of witnesses. The first commentator, as far as we know, of the Revelation was Bishop *Victorinus*. He states positively that the Apostle John wrote the Revelation (about 303 A.D.). *Ephrem Syrus* (about 378), the greatest scholar in the Syrian church, repeatedly in his numerous writings, cites the Revelation as canonical and ascribes it to the Apostle John. The Syrian translation of the Bible, the Peshito, probably made in the second century, does not contain the Book of Revelation, yet Ephrem Syrus possessed the Syrian translation. Scholars who have examined this question say that the Peshito in its original version had the Book of Revelation, and that it was later detached, while others advanced the theory that the Peshito translation may have been made in the first century when the Apocalypse was not yet generally known.

After citing many more witnesses, including Athanasius, Gregory of Nyssa, Ambrose, Augustine and others, Dean Alford says: "The Apostolic authorship rests on the firmest ground. We have it assured to us by one who had companied with men who had known St. John himself; we have it held in continuous succession by Fathers in all parts of the church. Nowhere, in primitive times, does there appear any counter-tradition on the subject."

The First Critic

This unquestionable historical evidence of the Johannine authorship of the Apocalypse was first attacked by Dionysius, the disciple of Origen and Bishop of Alexandria. In the second half of the third century this scholar raised his voice against the solid traditional view, declaring that not the same man could have written the fourth Gospel, the Epistles of John and the Revelation. He also pointed out the contrast between the language, the grammar, and the diction of the Apocalypse and the other writings of the Apostle John. He suggested another man by name of John, a Presbyter of Ephesus, as the author of the Revelation. He spoke of two tombs in Ephesus, one in which the body of the Apostle was buried and in the other John the Presbyter. But Dionysius spoke of this John the Presbyter, yet he was entirely unknown to him. It was a new idea he invented to back up his contention, for such a person was wholly unknown to the ecclesiastical tradition in the church of Alexandria in the middle of the third century. Nor does it appear that his opinion on the authorship of the Revelation made any permanent impression on the Alexandrine church. That this "John the Presbyter" is a fictitious person, who never existed, is fully demonstrated by the entire, the complete disappearance of John the Presbyter from the memory of the church of the second century.

But modern critics like Bleek, Duesterdieck, Ewald and others have seized upon this man of straw and followed the invention of Dionysius about the two Johns. Other critics have gone a step further and reject wholly the tradition that the Apostle John lived and died in Ephesus, thus making the other John the sole outstanding bearer of the name in that community, ascribing to him not only the Book of Revelation but also the Fourth Gospel. Modern critics reject the Johannine authorship of the Revelation. They hold that a work of small compass, by somebody, nobody knows who wrote it, was worked over by somebody else, then expanded by somebody else, passing through three or four redactions till it took on the form of the book we call "The Revelation." They also claim that at best the Revelation is "a Christian redaction of a Jewish Apocalypse."

The Book also received a strange treatment from the different Reformers. Luther for a time treated the Revelation with suspicion and questioned its inspiration; later he greatly modified this opinion. Zwingli followed the theory of Dionysius and attributed it to another John; he excluded it from the Bible. Calvin, however, believed in its canonicity and upheld the apostolic authorship. Melanchthon did the same.

All the criticism has not affected in the least the truth that John, the Apostle, the author of the Gospel of John and the Epistles, is the author also of the Book of Revelation. The fact is, the Holy Spirit seems to have taken special care to preserve such historical evidences for the Revelation of Jesus Christ, which makes the true authorship and date unimpeachable.

"The Apostolic authorship and canonicity of the Apocalypse were generally accepted, and went unchallenged, until toward the third century. Then contrary views began to make their appearance. But when the evidence, direct and indirect, on either side is weighed in respect of its date, its quantity, its quality, its freedom from bias, the external evidence in favor of the Johannine authorship, outweighs the other at every point."

The Date of the Book

It is interesting to find that modern critics have done the opposite with the date of the Book of Revelation from what they have done with other Bible books. They generally fix the date of a book later than the traditional view holds; but they assign to the Apocalypse an earlier date than that which the church has held in the past. Some have dated it during the reign of Nero. They do so on account of some particular interpretation of certain historical allusions. Of late some of the critics have adopted the later date, the year 96 A.D., that is, the traditional view held from the beginning. Irenaeus, the friend of Polycarp, who knew John, stated about the year 180 that "the Revelation was seen at Patmos at the end of Domitian's reign." Domitian reigned from 81 to 96 A.D. Then Clement of Alexandria left the testimony behind that John returned from his exile to the island of Patmos on the death of the emperor, which was Emperor Domitian, in the year 96. This is the correct date.

The Message and Interpretation

Revelation is marked out in the beginning as a Book of Prophecy (i:3). Of this we have more to say in the Preface and Key to Revelation, which follows this introduction. Furthermore, the Book is in greater part written in symbolical language, which is a very important fact to be remembered in the interpretation. The message is prophetic, and this message is clothed in symbols, which are not difficult to interpret. Our analysis will show that the accusation brought against this Book, as being disjointed, a veritable chaos, is wholly unfounded. Like all the other Books of the Word of God it has a perfect arrangement.

There are three modes of interpreting this Book, with its prophecies and symbols. The *historical* interpretation claims that the Book covers the entire history of the church and pictures the antagonism of the forces of evil in the world against the church. This method was in vogue during the Reformation period and for several centuries down to the nineteenth, especially during the Napoleonic upheavals, it was the acknowledged method of interpretation. It still has supporters. The Reformators saw in the Antichrist, the beast, the pope and the Romish church. Luther was very strong on that. On the other side, the Catholic exegetes, who also employed the same method, branded Protestantism as the Antichrist, and discovered that the mysterious 666 was contained in the name of Dr. Martin Luther. Then Napoleon was seen by believers living toward the end of the eighteenth and the beginning of the nineteenth centuries as fulfilling the thirteenth chapter in Revelation. Many predictions were made and the different numbers, the three years and a half, etc., applied to the stirring history of that time, just the same as men today are trying to figure out the duration of the "Times of the Gentiles," and when certain events must occur.

The *Preterist* School of interpretation teaches that the greater part of the prophecies of this Book have been fulfilled in the past in the struggles of the past, especially with the struggle of the church with the Roman Empire, and that the victory of the church as foretold in the Book is accomplished. The third school is the so-called *Futurist.* This method of interpretation is the only satisfying one and in full harmony with the entire Prophetic Word. We follow this method in our annotations. Nothing beyond the third chapter of this Book is fulfilled; all is still future, this is the claim of the Futurist school. The two chapters in which the word "church" is exclusively found in Revelation (chapters ii and iii) contain the prophecy concerning the church on earth. This divinely given history of the church is about finished and the predicted events from chapter iv to the end of Revelation are yet to be accomplished. Chapters vi-xix contain the specific prophecy of the end of the age, the last seven years, the unfulfilled 70th week of Daniel's great prophecy. The scripturalness of this interpretation will be readily discovered by reading the "Preface and Key to Revelation."

There are other theories of interpretation. One of them is the Judaizing interpretation of the late Dr. Bullinger, who taught that nothing is fulfilled in the Apocalypse, that the seven churches in Asia are yet to come into existence. We request our readers and students of the Word to study carefully the article which follows this introduction and the analysis of the Book.

PREFACE AND KEY TO THE REVELATION

"The Revelation of Jesus Christ, which God gave unto Him." This is the first sentence with which this last book in God's Word begins. The best title therefore is, "The Revelation of Jesus Christ." Our Lord received, according to this opening statement, a revelation from God. This must be understood in connection with Himself as the Son of Man. As the Only Begotten He had no need of a revelation; in His Deity He is acquainted with all the eternal purposes. One with God He knows the end from the beginning. But He, who is very God, took on in incarnation the form of a servant, and thus being in fashion as a man, He humbled Himself (Phil. ii:7-8). And as the Man who had passed through death, whom God raised from the dead, and exalted at His own right hand, God gave Him this revelation concerning the judgment of the earth and the glory of Himself. "God raised Him from the dead and gave Him glory" (1 Peter i:21). What this Glory is which He received from God is fully and blessedly revealed in this book. It is the revelation of His acquired Glory and how this Glory is to be manifested in connection with the earth. And this revelation He makes known to His servants, because His own are sharers with Him in all He received from God.

Pre-eminently His Revelation

The Revelation is pre-eminently His revelation; the revelation of His Person and His Glory. "In the volume of the book it is written of Me . . ." (Heb. x:7). Martin Luther asked, "What Book and what Person?" and answered, "There is only one Book—the Bible; and only one Person—Jesus Christ." The whole Book, the Word of God, bears witness of Him, Who is the living Word. He is the center, the sum total and the substance of the Holy Scriptures. The prayerful reader of the Bible will never read in vain if he approaches the blessed Book with the one desire to know Christ and His Glory. His blessed face is seen on every page and the infallible Guide, the Holy Spirit, never fails to satisfy the longing of the believer's heart to know more of Christ. Inasmuch as this last Bible book is the Revelation of Jesus Christ, an "Unveiling" of Himself, we find in it the completest revelation of His Person and His Glory.

It is here where many expositions of Revelation have missed the mark. Occupied chiefly with the symbols of the Book, the mysteries, the judgments and the promised consummation, they have neglected to emphasize sufficiently Him, who throughout this Book is pre-eminently the center of everything. The reader of Revelation does well to read first of all through the entire Book with this object in mind, to see what is said of our Lord, of His Person, His present and His future Glory.

We shall find all the features of His Person and His Work mentioned. He is the Alpha and Omega, the first and the last (i:11); the Ancient of Days (i:14 compare with Daniel vii:9); the "I Am," that is, Jehovah, "I am He that liveth" (i:18); the Son of God (ii:18). These terms speak of His Deity. His earthly life in humiliation is touched upon in the statement, "the faithful Witness" (i:5). His death on the cross is likewise mentioned—"He hath washed us from our sins in His blood" (i:5); "He was dead" (i:18); "the Lamb as it had been slain" (v:6); "worthy is the Lamb that was slain" (v:12). He is mentioned twenty-eight times as the Lamb in Revelation and each time it reminds us of the cross and the great work accomplished there. His resurrection is seen, for He is called, "the First begotten from the dead" (i:5), and He speaks of Himself as, "He that was dead, and, behold, I am alive forevermore" (i:18); and again, "these things saith the first and the last, who was dead and is alive" (ii:8).

Then we behold Him "in the midst" in glory, seen face to face by all the redeemed and worshipped by them, as well as by the heavenly hosts and ultimately by every creature, the fulfillment of Phil. ii:10-11, "that at the name of Jesus every knee should bow, of things in heaven, and things on earth and things under the earth, and that every tongue should confess that Jesus Christ is Lord, to the glory of God the Father" (Rev. v:13-14). After the fifth chapter we have His revelation as the executor of the decreed judgments. He opens the seals; He sends forth the seven angels with the judgment trumpets and the seven angels with the judgment vials, in which the wrath of God is completed. "The Father judgeth no man, but has committed all judgment unto the Son" (John v:22). Then He is seen in the glorious union with the Bride (xix:7-10) and as the victorious Christ who passeth out of heaven followed by the armies of heaven (xix:11-21), conquering the opposing forces of evil, executing the wrath of Almighty God, appearing as King of kings and Lord of lords. The twentieth chapter reveals Him as the reigning Christ. He and His Saints with Him will reign over the earth for a thousand years. And all which follows reveals Him and His Glory as well as the blessed and eternal results of His work.

A Book of Prophecy

Aside from the title of the Book, which indicates that it deals with things future, there is a direct statement which determines its prophetic character. In the first beatitude of the seven which are found in the Book, we read that it is a Book of Prophecy—"Blessed is he that readeth, and they that hear the words of this Prophecy" (i:3). It is known to every intelligent student of the Bible that a good part of it is Prophecy. The great prophecies concerning the people Israel and the nations of the world are found in the Old Testament Scriptures. In the New Testament there is but one Book of Prophecy, the Revelation. As it is the capstone of the entire revelation of God, without which the Bible would be an unfinished book, we find in its pages the consummation of the great Prophecies which were given by the Prophets of God in Old Testament times.

For the study of this New Testament Prophetic Book, the knowledge of the chief content of the Old Testament Prophetic Word is therefore an absolute necessity. For instance, to a Christian who does not have a fair grasp of Daniel's great Prophecies, or is ignorant of the place which the people Israel hold in the purposes of God, the Book of Revelation is a sealed book, without any possible meaning. This is one of the chief reasons why this Book has suffered so much both from the critics and from the hands of commentators. The Apostle Peter saith, "Knowing this first, that no prophecy of the Scripture is of any private interpretation. For the prophecy came not in old time by the will of man, but holy men of God spake as they were moved by the Holy Spirit" (2 Peter i:20-21). The better translation for "private interpretation" is, "its own interpretation." It means that the interpretation of prophecy must be done by comparing Scripture with Scripture. The holy men of God, the prophets, were the instruments of the Holy Spirit and made known God's purposes in a progressive way. To understand any prophecy is only possible by taking the entire Prophetic Word into consideration. That there is a wonderful harmony in the great body of prophetic dispensational truths as found in the Bible we have demonstrated in another volume.* This principle finds its strongest application in the interpretation of the Revelation.

The Three Classes

In 1 Corinthians x:32 the Apostle Paul speaks of three classes into which the human race is divided: the Jews, the Gentiles, and the Church of God. In the Old Testament there was no Church of God, for the Church is a New Testament institution. As the Revelation is the book of consummation these three classes must be seen in the contents of this Book. Many expositors have seen nothing but the struggles of the Church in her history in this Book. This is true of the so-called Preterist school and also of the Historical school of interpretation. The Preterist school teaches a fulfillment of all the apocalyptic visions in the struggles of the Church in the past. The Historical school

*"Harmony of the Prophetic Word"—a volume which has been used under God's blessing to open the minds of many to the meaning of Prophecy.

also teaches that the visions concern mostly the Church. These schools of interpretation leave out the Jews and what is written concerning them and their final history during the end of the age, preceding the glorious appearing of our Lord. Of late another school of interpreters has come into existence. They teach that the entire Book of Revelation concerns the Jewish people and that there is nothing about the Church in this last Book of the Bible. Any interpretation of Revelation which ignores the Jews, the people Israel and the fulfillment of Old Testament predictions concerning them is wrong. And any interpretation which teaches that there is nothing about the Church in Revelation is equally wrong. The Church and her destiny on earth, the destiny of the true Church and the destiny of the apostate Church, or Christendom, is found in the Book. The Jews and what concerns them in the end of the age, the Gentiles, the nations of the earth, and the judgments in store for them, as well as the future of the earth, a future of glory and blessing: all this is recorded in our New Testament Book of Prophecy.

The True Interpretation

There is a true interpretation of Revelation which is in harmony with all previous prophecies and which opens the Book to our understanding. But how are we to find this true interpretation? We answer, the Book itself furnishes it. This is an important fact, both convincing and conclusive. It is therefore of no profit to examine the different theories and schools of interpretation. We shall avoid the terms Preterist, Historical and Futurist, and not try, as it has been attempted, to reconcile these different modes of interpretation. There must be one true interpretation, and we claim that this is given to us by the Lord Himself in this Book.

The Key Which Fits

It has often been truthfully said, every Book in the Bible contains a key which unlocks the Book. The Revelation is no exception. John the beloved disciple was in banishment in the isle of Patmos, as Daniel the man greatly beloved, was a captive in Babylon. The Lord called these two great servants to behold the panorama of the future. Both wrote down their visions. While in the Book of Daniel we find no direct command to write, we find such a command in the first chapter of Revelation. John received divine instruction how to write the Revelation. We find this in the nineteenth verse, "Write therefore what thou hast seen, and the things that are, and the things that are about to be after these."* John, guided by the Holy Spirit then wrote the Revelation according to the divine direction. In examining this command to write we find that three things are mentioned. He is to write first the things he had seen, then the things which are, and finally the things that are about to be after these. When John received these instructions he had already seen something, and the vision he had he was instructed to write down. Then present things, the things which are, and future things, to be after present things have passed away, must be located in this book. So we have the past, the present and the future in this key verse.

Three Divisions—Where are They

It is then clear that the Book of Revelation must be divided into three main divisions. How are we to locate these divisions? They are marked, so that we are not left in doubt about it. In the beginning of the fourth chapter we find a significant statement which shows where the third division begins. After these things, that is after the contents of the opening three chapters were past, John heard the same voice speaking to him once more. He sees a door opened in heaven and is told, "Come up hither, and I will shew thee the things which must take place after these things" (iv:1). There can then be no doubt at all that with the fourth chapter the seer beheld the things which take place after the preceding things which are, have passed away. The third

*This is the correct translation of this important verse.

division of Revelation begins with the fourth chapter. John beholds future things from heaven into which he had been taken "in the Spirit." The things he had seen and the things which are, are therefore contained in the first three chapters of the Book.

The first chapter contains the things he had seen. "What thou seest write in a book" was the first instruction John received (verse 11). In the nineteenth verse he is told, "Write therefore what thou hast seen." Between verse 11 and verse 19 he saw a vision, which he was to write, and this vision constitutes the first section or division of the Book. The second and third chapters form the second division, the things which are. The beginning of the fourth chapter to the end of the Book is the final, the third division. There is no better and more logical key. And this key given in the Book determines the true interpretation.

The Patmos Vision

"The thing thou hast seen"—the first section of Revelation is the great Patmos vision, chapter i:12-18. It is the vision of the glorified Son of Man in the midst of the seven golden candlesticks (or lampstands).

The Things Which Are

The things which are, the present things, begin the prophetic section of the Revelation. The second and third chapters of Revelation, the things which are, contain the messages of our Lord addressed to the seven churches of Asia Minor. These messages contain the first great Prophecy of Revelation. The prophecy concerns the Church on earth. We shall show in our comment on these two chapters that we have in them a divine history of the Church on earth. It is one of the most remarkable sections of the Prophetic Word. What this present age is to be religiously and how it will end is made known in other parts of the

New Testament. Our Lord in some of His Kingdom parables (Matthew xiii) reveals the characteristics of this age. The parables of the sower, the evil seed sown into the field, the mustard seed parable and the parable of the leaven are prophetic and teach, in part at least, what the church messages reveal. The Holy Spirit in the Epistolar testimony also reveals the religious and moral characteristics of the age, and depicts its departure from the truth, and its end. The destiny of the true Church is heavenly. She has a "blessed hope," which is to be with the Lord in Glory. She is the Body of Christ, and He is the "Head of the Body." The Church is also the Bride of Christ and He is the Bridegroom. The Body is united to the Head in Glory; the Bride will be joined to the Bridegroom. 1 Thessalonians iv:13-18 is the Scripture which reveals this end for the true Church on earth. The professing Church, Christendom, which rejects the doctrine of Christ and goes into apostasy has a far different destiny. The Lord will disown that which has denied His Name, and judgment and wrath is to be poured out upon apostate Christendom (2 Thess. i:7-9). These predictions concerning the Church on earth are contained in the seven Church messages. When we come to the close of the third chapter we find a significant promise, and equally significant threat. "I also will keep thee from the hour of temptation (trial) which shall come upon all the world to try them that dwell upon the earth" (iii:10). This is the promise. It tells of the removal of the true Church, composed of all true believers, from this earthly scene. "I will spue thee out of my mouth" (iii:16). This is the threat to the apostate Church. Both the promise and the threat will be fulfilled. After the third chapter the word church does not occur again in Revelation. The reason for this is obvious. The history of the Church on earth terminates with the close of the third chapter. Because the true Church is no longer here but has been taken up into Glory, and that which professes to be the Church is disowned by the Lord, therefore no more mention of the Church is made in Revelation.

The Things Which Are After These

The future things, things after the removal of the true Church from the earth, occupy the greater part of this Book. It is of the greatest importance to see that nothing whatever after the third chapter of Revelation has yet taken place. Some speak of a past and partial fulfillment of some of the visions found in this section. In view of the scope of the Book this is impossible. The open door in heaven, the voice which calls the Seer to pass through that open door into heaven, is symbolical of the great coming event, the realization of the blessed Hope of the coming of the Lord for His Saints. That this open door is mentioned immediately after the third chapter and John is suddenly in the spirit in the presence of the throne in heaven is very significant. It proves that the entire situation is now changed. And the first great vision is a vision of the Saints in Glory occupying thrones and worshipping God and the Lamb. With the sixth chapter the great judgment visions of this Book begin. These great punitive dealings with the earth are executed from above. All transpires after the Lord has taken His Saints into Glory. No seal can be broken as long as this event has not been. But after the Rapture, the Seals of the Book, which the Lamb received, are broken by Him, the trumpet and the vial judgments fall upon the earth. All this takes place after the home-going of the true Church and before the glorious appearing of our Lord Jesus Christ (xix:11, etc.).

Now this portion of Revelation from chapter vi to xix contains the events which transpire during the end of the age. It is the unfulfilled seventieth week of the great prophecy in the Book of Daniel (Dan. ix:24-27). This "end of the age" will last twice 1260 days, that is seven years. It is absolutely necessary to understand the scope of the seventy-week prophecy in Daniel in order to understand the greater part of these chapters in the Revelation.* We are led back

*"The Prophetic Daniel," by A. C. G. contains a very simple exegesis of Daniel's prophecies.

upon Jewish ground. Events in connection with the Jewish people and Jerusalem are before us. The times of the Gentiles have taken on their final form of ten kingdoms which Daniel saw on the fourth beast as ten horns, and Nebuchadnezzar on the image as ten toes. The empire in which these ten Kingdoms come into existence is the Roman empire. It will have a revival and come into existence again. Then a wicked leader will take the headship of that resurrected Roman empire, and another Beast, the false prophet, the Antichrist will domineer over the Jewish people and persecute their saints, the remnant of Israel, while the earth and the dwellers upon the earth experience the great judgments. The last half of these seven years is called the great tribulation. We must also remember that our Lord left behind a great Prophecy concerning the end of the age. This Prophecy is contained in the Olivet Discourse, the first part of which (Matt. xxiv:4-44) harmonizes in a striking manner with the events in Revelation vi-xix. Our Lord calls special attention to Daniel and likewise speaks of the great tribulation. In our brief annotations we shall point out some of the interesting and convincing details.

The glorious climax is the visible manifestation of the Lord out of heaven, crowned with many crowns,* the defeat and overthrow of the Beast and the kings of the earth and their armies, the binding of Satan, and the reign of Christ with His saints for a thousand years. After that follows the great white throne judgment, which is the judgment of the wicked dead, the glories of the new Jerusalem, the eternal destiny of the redeemed and the eternal destiny of the lost.

If this last great Book of the Bible is studied in this divinely given order it will no longer be, as is so often said, a sealed book. All fanciful interpretations and applications of these great visions to past or present history can no longer be maintained as soon as we reckon with the fact that these

*Compare Revelation xix:11-21 with Daniel vii:11-14 and Matthew xxiv:27-31.

visions are not yet fulfilled, and are going to be fulfilled after the true Church is no longer on the earth.

The Promised Blessing

"Blessed is he that readeth, and they that hear the words of this Prophecy, and keep those things which are written therein, for the time is at hand" (verse 3). A blessing is promised to him who readeth, and who hears and keeps. It does not say that a blessing is for him who understands and knows everything which is in this Book. If such were the condition the writer and the reader would have no claim on this promised blessing. The Bible-teacher, or any other man, who says he knows and understands everything found in this great finale of God's Word is very much mistaken. We cannot be sure about everything in some of these visions and the full meaning of some may not be understood till the world sees the fulfillment. The blessing is promised to all His people who give attention to the Revelation of Jesus Christ. What is the blessing we may expect through the reading and prayerful study of the words of this Prophecy?

First of all we receive through this Book a wonderful vision of our Saviour and Lord. This is what we need as His people above everything else, and it is this which brings blessing into our lives. As stated before, this Book is pre-eminently His revelation, a blessed unveiling of His person and Glory. But we also get another blessing. In reading through this Book we see what is in store for this age, what judgments will overtake the world, and how Satan's power will be manifested to the full upon those who rejected His grace. Judgment, tribulation and wrath are swiftly coming upon this age. Out of all this our gracious Lord has delivered us. There is no judgment, no wrath for us who know Him as our sin-bearer and our hiding-place. Praise must fill our hearts when we read the words of this Prophecy and remember the grace which has saved us from all which is coming upon this age. Another blessing is the assurance of ultimate victory and glory. Dark is the age, and becoming darker, but in Revelation we behold the glory which is coming for His Saints first of all and after the judgment clouds are gone, for Jerusalem, the nations and the earth. Reading Revelation fills the heart with the assurance and certainty of the outcome of all. It is a solemn atmosphere which fills the whole Book of Revelation. As we continue to read and continue to breathe this heavenly and solemn atmosphere it will result in a closer walk with God, a more spiritual worship and a greater and more unselfish service for Him "Who loveth us and hath washed us from our sins in His own blood, and hath made us priests and kings unto God His Father."

The Divisions of the Revelation

Title: The Revelation of Jesus Christ

I. THE PATMOS VISION OF THE GLORIFIED SON OF MAN. Chapter i.

CHAPTER I.

1. The Introduction. Verses 1-3.
2. Greeting and Benediction. Verses 4-5.
3. The Praise. Verses 6-7.
4. The Testimony of the Almighty. Verse 8.
5. John in Patmos. Verses 9-11.
6. The Great Vision of Christ in Glory. Verses 12-16.
7. The Commission. Verses 17-21.

II. THE THINGS WHICH ARE. THE SEVEN CHURCH MESSAGES REVEALING THE HISTORY OF THE CHURCH ON EARTH. Chapters ii-iii.

CHAPTER II.

1. Ephesus, the Post-Apostolic Period. Verses 1-7.
2. Smyrna, the Period of Persecution. Verses 8-11.
3. Pergamos, the Period of Corruption. Verses 12-17.
4. Thyatira, the Romish Corruption. Verses 18-29.

CHAPTER III.

5. Sardis, the Reformation Period. Verses 1-6.
6. Philadelphia, the Faithful Remnant. Verses 7-13.
7. Laodicea, the Indifferent and Apostate Church. Verses 14-22.

III. THE THINGS WHICH ARE AFTER THESE, THE END OF THE AGE, THE CONSUMMATION AND THE FINAL MESSAGES. Chapters iv-xxii.

First Division: The Heavenly Scene. Before the Throne. Chapters iv-v.

CHAPTER IV.

1. The Open Door and the Vision of the Throne. Verses 1-3.
2. The Twenty-four Elders. Verse 4.
3. The Description of the Throne. Verse 5.
4. The Four Living Creatures and the Great Praise and Worship. Verses 6-11.

CHAPTER V.

1. Who is Worthy to open the Book? Verses 1-3.
2. The Answer. Verses 4-5.
3. The Vision of the Lamb. Verses 6-7.
4. The Worship of the Living Creatures and the Elders. Verses 8-10.
5. The Worthiness of the Lamb Acclaimed by all Beings. Verses 11-14.

Second Division: The Opening of the Seven Seals. Chapters vi:viii:5.

CHAPTER VI.

1. The First Seal. The White Horse; the Conquering Rider. Verses 1-2.
2. The Second Seal. The Red Horse; the Rider with the great Sword. Verses 3-4.
3. The Third Seal. The Black Horse; the Rider with the Balance. Verses 5-6.
4. The Fourth Seal. The Pale Horse; the Rider Followed by Hades. Verses 7-8.
5. The Fifth Seal. The Cry of the Souls Under the Altar. Verses 9-11.
6. The Sixth Seal. The Shaking of all Things. The Anticipation of the End. Verses 12-17.

Between the Sixth and Seventh Seal. A Parenthetical Vision. (Chapter vii.)

CHAPTER VII.

1. The Remnant of Israel Called and Sealed. Verses 1-8.
2. The Saved Multitude of Gentiles Coming out of the Great Tribulation. Verses 9-17.

End of the Parenthesis.

3. The Seventh Seal. Verses 1-5.

CHAPTER VIII:1-5.

Third Division: The Sounding of the Seven Trumpets. Chapters viii:6-xi:18.

CHAPTER VIII:6-13.

1. The First Trumpet. Verses 6-7.
2. The Second Trumpet. Verses 8-9.
3. The Third Trumpet. Verses 10-11.
4. The Fourth Trumpet. Verses 12-13.

CHAPTER IX.

5. The Fifth Trumpet. The First Woe. Verses 1-12.
6. The Sixth Trumpet. The Second Woe. Verses 13-21.

Between the Sixth and Seventh Trumpets. Parenthetical Visions. (Chapters x-xi:14.)

CHAPTER X.

1. The Descending Angel. Verses 1-7.
2. The Little Book. Verses 8-11.

CHAPTER XI.

3. The Temple, Altar and Jewish Worshippers. Verses 1-2.
4. The Two Witnesses. Verses 3-6.
5. The Beast and the Witnesses. Verse 7.
6. The Treatment of the Slain Witnesses. Verses 8-10.
7. Their Public Vindication. Verses 11-12.
8. The Great Earthquake. Verses 13-14.

End of the Parenthesis.

9. The Seventh Trumpet. Verses 15-18.

Fourth Division: Satan's Power and Satan's Masterpieces. Chapter xi:19-xiii.

CHAPTER XI:19.

1. The Vision of the Opened Temple. Verse 19.

CHAPTER XII.

2. The Great Sign. Verses 1-5.
3. The Escape of the Woman. Verse 6.
4. War in Heaven, and Satan cast out of Heaven. Verses 7-12.
5. The Dragon Persecuting the Woman. Verses 13-17.

CHAPTER XIII.

6. The Beast out of the Sea. Verses 1-10.
7. The Beast out of the Earth. Verses 11-18.

Fifth Division: The Power of God in Intervention. Grace and Judgment Manifested. Chapter xiv.

CHAPTER XIV.

1. The Lamb upon Zion and the 144,000. Verses 1-5.
2. The Proclamation of the Everlasting Gospel. Verses 6-7.
3. Babylon has Fallen! Verse 8.
4. The Eternal Wrath for the Worshippers of the Beast. Verses 9-11.

5. The Blessed Dead who Die in the Lord. Verses 12-13.
6. The Harvest and the Vintage. Verses 14-20.

Sixth Division: The Seven Angels Having Seven Plagues; the Vials of Wrath. Chapters xv-xvi.

CHAPTER XV.

1. The Seven Angels with the Seven Plagues. Verse 1.
2. Another Scene of Worship. Verses 2-4.
3. The Seven Angels Proceeding out of the Temple. Verses 5-8.

CHAPTER XVI.

4. The First Vial. Verses 1-2.
5. The Second Vial. Verse 3.
6. The Third Vial. Verses 4-7.
7. The Fourth Vial. Verses 8-9.
8. The Fifth Vial. Verses 10-11.
9. The Sixth Vial. Verse 12.

Between the Sixth and Seventh Vial, Parenthetical Vision. Verses 13-16.

10. The Seventh Vial. Verses 17-21.

Seventh Division: The Great Harlot, Babylon, and her Judgment. Chapters xvii-xviii.

CHAPTER XVII.

1. The Description of the Woman. Verses 1-6.
2. The Interpretation by the Angel. Verses 7-15.
3. The Destruction of the Harlot. Verses 16-18.

CHAPTER XVIII.

4. The Angelic Announcement. Verses 1-3.
5. The Call to Separate. Verses 4-5.
6. Her Pride and Righteous Destruction. Verses 6-8.
7. The Universal Lamentation over Her. Verses 9-19.
8. The Rejoicing Heavens. Verse 20.
9. Her Utter and Everlasting Destruction. Verses 21-23.
10. The Blood of the Saints found in Her. Verse 24.

Eighth Division: The Manifestation of the King and the Millennium. Chapters xix-xx:6.

CHAPTER XIX.

1. The Four Hallelujahs in Heaven. The Marriage of the Lamb. Verses 1-10.
2. Heaven Opened. The Coming of the King. Verses 11-16.

3. The Battle of Armageddon and the Execution of Wrath. Verses 17-21.

CHAPTER XX:1-6.

4. The Binding of Satan. Verses 1-4.
5. The Reign of Christ and His Saints for a Thousand Years. Verses 5-6.

Ninth Division: After the Thousand Years. The Vision of the New Jerusalem. Chapters xx:7-xxii:5.

CHAPTER XX:7-15.

1. Satan Loosed. The Last Revolt. Verses 7-9.
2. Satan's Eternal Doom. Verse 10.
3. The Great White Throne Judgment. Verses 11-15.

CHAPTER XXI.

4. The Eternal State. Verses 1-8.
5. The Vision of the Holy City of Jerusalem. Verses 9-27.

CHAPTER XXII:1-5.

6. The River and the Tree of Life. Verses 1-2.
7. The Seven Glories of the Redeemed. Verses 3-5.

Tenth Division: The Final Messages. Chapter xxii:6-21.

CHAPTER XXII:6-21.

1. The Angel's Message. Verses 6-11.
2. The Message of the Lord. Verses 12-13.
3. The Two Classes. Verses 14-15.
4. The Final Testimony of Christ Concerning Himself. Verse 16.
5. The Answer of the Spirit and the Bride. Verse 17.
6. The Final Warning. Verses 18-19.
7. The Final Message; the Final Prayer; the Final Benediction. Verses 20-21.

Analysis and Annotations

I. THE PATMOS VISION OF THE GLORIFIED SON OF MAN.

CHAPTER I.

1. The Introduction. 1-3.
2. Greeting and Benediction. 4-5.
3. The Praise. 6-7.
4. The Testimony of the Almighty. 8.
5. John in Patmos. 9-11.
6. The Vision of Christ in Glory. 12-16.
7. The Commission. 17-21.

1. The Introduction: Verses 1-3. The book does not contain "revelations" but it is one great revelation, "The Revelation of Jesus Christ." The third verse is of much importance. It pronounces a blessing upon all who read and hear the words of this prophecy and who keep the things that are written therein. Here, as already stated, we read that the Revelation is a great prophecy.

2. Greeting and Benediction: Verses 4-5. The churches addressed were in the Province of Asia. (See Acts xvi:6; xix:10.) The words of greeting "Grace and peace unto you" tell of the two great possessions of the church. Though the professing church may fail in her testimony, grace and peace, even in the dark days of apostasy, will never fail. In the greeting here Jehovah-God, the great "I am"—Who is, Who was and Who is to come—stands first. Then follows the Holy Spirit in His own completeness and His diverse activities, spoken of as "the seven Spirits." And finally the name of our Lord. "He is the faithful witness," who lived as such in holiness and perfect obedience on earth. "Tho First-Begotten from the dead"; He died that shameful death on the Cross and God raised Him from the dead. "The Prince of the kings of the earth." This is His future title and glory.

3. The Praise: Verses 6-7. This is the true Glory-song.

It contains the blessed Gospel of Grace. What He has done for us; what He has made us; and what we shall be with Him. It is the first doxology in this Book. See the swelling praise and worship two-fold, three-fold, four-fold and seven-fold in Chapters iv:11; v:13; vii:12. And then for the first time in this Book His personal, visible and glorious coming is announced.

4. The Testimony of the Almighty: Verse 8. God, so to speak, puts His seal upon it. The words of the preceding verse "Even so, Amen" must be read with this verse. The speaker is Jehovah, the Almighty.

5. John in Patmos: Verses 9-11. John was in banishment in the Isle of Patmos. Patmos is a small rocky isle, and about ten miles long and six wide. According to ancient tradition this island was used as a place of exile for offenders who belonged to the better classes. John was exiled on account of his faithful witness to the Word of God and the testimony of Jesus. He came to be in the Spirit on the Lord's day. Does this mean "the day of the Lord," that is, the day of His visible manifestation, or does it mean He was in the Spirit on the Lord's day, the first day of the week? Dr. Bullinger teaches that the Lord's day means "the Day of the Lord" (Isa. ii:12), and says: "John was not in a state of spiritual exaltation on any particular Sunday at Patmos, as the result of which he saw visions and dreamed dreams. But as we are told he found himself by the Spirit in the day of the Lord." But this view is not correct. It is not the prophetic day of the Lord, but the Lord's day, the day which the early church from the beginning celebrated as the day of His resurrection. In Corinthians we read of "the Lord's supper" in the same way as "the Lord's day" is used here. Nor could John have been projected to the day of the Lord when his first message given to him by the glorified Christ concerned the church and her history on earth.

6. The Vision of Christ in Glory: Verses 12-16. A voice had spoken, as of a trumpet telling him to write in a book what he was about to see and to send the message to the seven churches. And as he turned he beheld the greatest vision human eyes has ever seen. He saw seven golden candlesticks (lampstands); these represent the seven churches (verse 20) and are symbolical of the whole church. "In the midst," John saw one "like unto a Son of Man." But He is more than Man, He is the Ancient of Days as well as Son of Man, the Alpha and the Omega, in His humiliation and in His exaltation. He was the Son of Man on earth; He is Son of Man in Glory. When He comes back to earth and receives the Kingdom, He will receive it as Son of Man to judge the earth in righteousness. Here we behold Him in His judicial character. The robe down to His feet expresses His dignity as the King-Priest, who is about to enter upon His future work. The golden girdle is symbolical of His divine righteousness. His white head and hair identify Him with the Person whom Daniel saw sitting in judgment (Dan. vii:9-12). The flaming eyes, the fiery burning feet, the voice like the sound of many waters, the two-edged sword, all are symbolical of His glory and character.

There is one feature of the vision which needs an explanation. What do the seven stars mean, which are in the right hand of the Son of Man? Verse 20 gives the answer. They are the seven angels of the seven churches. Angels and stars are symbolical figures. The application of these terms to church-officers or bishops and pastors is incorrect. Stars are used in scripture to typify true believers. Stars are heavenly bodies which shine during the night; so are true believers in a heavenly position with the responsibility to shine in the night. The lampstands represent the visible, professing church; the stars represent the true believing element in the Church. They are in the right hand of Himself, held securely there. Furthermore, only true believers have an ear to hear what the Spirit saith. The stars are called angels, because an angel is a messenger and true believers are likewise that.

7. The Commission: Verses 17-20. John fell at His feet as dead. Compare with Daniel x:4-11. The vision was overpowering. But graciously His hand rests upon His prostrated disciple, the same who once leaned upon His bosom, and he hears the blessed words His people know and love so well, "Fear not!" Once more He bears witness as to Himself. He is "He that liveth," the Jehovah, the Self-existing One; He was dead; He died the sinner's death and won the victory. He is alive forevermore; as the risen One He has the key of Hades and of Death. Then follows the Commission which the reader finds fully explained in the Preface and Key to Revelation.

II. THE THINGS WHICH ARE. THE SEVEN CHURCH MESSAGES AND THEIR PROPHETIC MEANING

CHAPTER II.

1. Ephesus. The Post Apostolic Period. 1-7.
2. Smyrna. The Period of Persecution. 8-11.
3. Pergamos. The Corruption Period. 12-17.
4. Thyatira. The Romish Corruption. 18-29.

The two chapters which follow the introductory chapter contain seven messages to seven local churches which were in existence in the province of Asia in the days when the Apostle John was prisoner in the Isle of Patmos. The view held by the late Dr. Bullinger and a few of his followers that these churches are yet to come into existence in connection with believing Jews during the great tribulation with which the age closes, must be rejected as extremely fanciful. The omniscient Lord on the throne detected in each of these local assemblies certain traits which at different periods of His church on earth would become the leading features. We have therefore, in these seven messages the history of the entire church in embryo. This assertion is fully confirmed by a closer study of these messages.

1. Ephesus. The Post-Apostolic Period: Verses 1-7. Ephesus was the church characterized by the greatest purity in doctrine and in walk. To the Ephesians, as "the faithful brethren in Christ," was addressed the most wonderful revelation God has given to man. It stands therefore for the model church in the apostolic age. But when Paul said farewell to the elders he predicted not smooth things, but the incoming failure (Acts xx). Ephesus means "desired" and that corresponds with her original holy character. He reveals Himself afresh as being in the midst and holding His own in His blessed pierced hands, so true of believers at all times. The descriptions of Ephesus suit the apostolic church, and immediately after the apostles had passed away, except John. But He finds fault with it. His omniscient eyes look to the heart and there He finds declension. "I have against thee that thou leavest thy first love." He, the one altogether lovely was no longer the all absorbing object before their hearts. Paul manifests the full meaning of first love. His constant cry was: "Not I but Christ"—"That I may know him;" for him to live was Christ. Declension began in the church not with less service, less suffering or anything else, but with a decreasing heart-devotion to the Person of our Lord. That is where all backsliding begins. He calls to repentance, a return to Himself. The Nicolaitanes, whose works the church then hated, are mentioned again in the third message, where we shall define the word and the teaching of the Nicolaitanes. A promise to the overcomer follows.

2. Smyrna. The Period of Persecution: Verses 8-11. Smyrna means "bitterness" and is a form of myrrh which was largely used for the embalming of the dead. When the wise men brought myrrh to the child, the new-born king of the Jews, the meaning of it was that the King would have to die. Smyrna was a suffering church, many of its members had to seal their faith by dying the martyr's death. Corresponding with this characteristic, the Lord speaks of Himself as "The First and the Last, who was dead and is alive." That is His comfort for the church passing through the horrors of persecution and intense sufferings. In connection with this message to Smyrna the synagogue of Satan is mentioned. It means the Judaistic faction of the church, who, while they claimed to be Christians, also claimed to be Jews, observing the law, the Sabbath day and other parts of the legal system of Judaism. This synagogue of Satan helped in the afflictions of Smyrna. Nor is the same "synagogue of Satan" missing today in the professing sphere of Christendom.

He announces that the devil would cast some of them into prison, that they should have tribulation for ten days, and that it would require faithfulness unto death to gain the crown of life. The Apostolic age was followed by the martyr age, which lasted up to the beginning of the Fourth Century. Pagan emperors under the inspiration of Satan, the roaring lion, persecuted the church. No one knows how many hundreds of thousands died the martyr's death, flayed and burned alive, cast before wild animals and cruelly tortured; thus they were faithful unto death and gained the crown of life. It is also significant that the address to Smyrna contains the number ten; church history records ten great persecutions.

3. Pergamos. The Corruption Period: Verses 12-17. After the devil had played the roaring lion for several centuries, trying to exterminate the church of Jesus Christ, he discovered that "the blood of the martyrs is the seed of the church." He then stopped the persecutions suddenly and began to corrupt the church. This is the meaning of the message to Pergamos, which means "twice married," a typical name for the professing church which claims to be the bride of Christ, but is married to the world. Pergamos is dwelling where Satan has his throne. Milton described Satan being in hell.

> "High on a throne of royal state,
> That far outshone the wealth of Ormuz or of Ind,
> Satan exalted sat."

But that is not Scripture. Satan will be in hell, in his final abode "the lake of fire," but he is not there now. He is the god of this world (age); his throne is right here on earth. And Pergamos had been married to the world. This is also indicated by the mention of Balaam, who cast a stumbling block before the children of Israel, by inducing them to take the daughters of the heathen and thus give up their God-demanded separation. The church then gave up her pilgrim character, settled down in the world, became a world institution, as revealed by our Lord in the parable of the mustard seed. What happened in the beginning of the Fourth Century church-historians have proclaimed as the "triumph of Christianity." It was rather "the defeat of Christianity," for that happened which corrupted the church of Christ.

The instrument of the devil used to bring about this was the Emperor Constantine. He had a rival by name of Maxentius, whom he faced in battle. Constantine claimed that the night before he had a vision of Christ bearing a cross with the words: "*In hoc signo vinces* (In this sign thou shalt conquer). He had the next morning a beautiful banner made, which was called *the Labarum*, and went forth to battle, in which Maxentius was defeated as well as another competitor by name of Licinus. Constantine then became emperor and nominally a Christian and head of the church, while retaining his heathen title as *Pontifex Maximus*, the high-priest. Then the corruption of the church resulted. The church became a political world institution, like the mustard seed, rooting itself in the field (the world) became a great tree, opening its branches to the fowls of the air to defile (Matt. xiii; see annotations there). Heathen priests became Christian priests. Heathen temples were changed into Christian churches; he demanded all children to be "christened," that is, made Christians by putting water upon their heads; heathen days of feasting and drinking were made into Christian days, like our "Christmas" and nearly all the other saints' days.

Here again the Nicolaitanes are mentioned, but, while the Ephesians hated the deeds of the Nicolaitanes, here in Pergamos we find the doctrine of the Nicolaitanes, and the Lord says: "which thing I hate." What is it, then? Some say that there was a certain Bishop Nicol who taught bad doctrines and his followers were called "the Nicolaitanes." But this Bishop Nicol is a fictitious person; he cannot be historically located.

Nicolaitanes is Greek; it is a compound. *Nikao* is a verb

and means to have the upper hand, to domineer; *laos* means the people (our English "laity"). Nicolaitanes signifies "the domineerers of the people." A priestly class had sprung up in the church, domineering over the rest of the people, the so-called laity. And this domineering class claimed a superior place in the body of Christ and a priesthood which rightly belongs to the Lord Jesus Christ. This evil was rejected in Ephesus, but is fully sanctioned and tolerated in Pergamos. Priestly assumption became then, and ever since has been, the corruption of Christianity. This is what our Lord hates and what He hates we must hate with Him.

4. Thyatira, the Period of the Romish Corruption: Verses 18-29. The corruption which set in like a great flood with the fourth century increased till the depths of Satan (verse 24) were reached. Thyatira brings us into the period of the Papacy and its wickedness, ecclesiastical and otherwise. Here our Lord reveals Himself as "the Son of God." Rome speaks more of Him as the son of the virgin, the son of Mary, than as the Son of God. The Roman Catholic apostasy has put a woman in the place of the Son of God. Her corruption is fully revealed in verse 20. Jezebel, who called herself a prophetess, was permitted to teach and seduce God's servants to commit fornication and to eat things sacrificed unto idols. Jezebel the wicked woman represents the Papacy. Jezebel was a heathenish woman married to an Israelitish King. She was a queen and an idolatress and persecuted the true prophets of God (1 Kings xviii-xxi). Apply all this to the Romish church with her spiritual fornication and idolatry. The church, or, rather, the papacy, assumes the place of teacher and dictator and Christ is rejected. The name Jezebel has a twofold meaning. It means "a chaste one"; the other name is "dunghill." Rome claims to be the Bride of Christ; in reality she is a harlot, and called so in chapter xvii, and therefore a dunghill of all vileness and corruption. In verse 21 we find another important hint. It is said, "she repents not." Rome does not change. She is the same today in every respect as she was 500 years ago. She will continue in her perverted state of impenitence till her predicted doom will overtake her (compare verse 22 with chapter xvii.) She is the woman of which our Lord spoke in the fourth kingdom parable in Matthew xiii (see annotations there) which took leaven (corruption) and put it into the three measures of meal (symbolical of the doctrine of Christ). It is noteworthy that beginning with the message to Thyatira the Lord announces His coming, that is, His second visible coming. Every following message speaks of it. This shows that the three preceding church periods and conditions are passed and the conditions pictured in Thyatira, Sardis, Philadelphia and Laodicea will continue till He comes. The Apostolic age cannot be brought back; nor will there be again a persecution by Roman emperors; nor will the church again become corrupted as in Pergamos. The Romish conditions continue to the end of the age.

CHAPTER III.

1. Sardis. The Reformation Period. 1-6.
2. Philadelphia. The Faithful Remnant. 7-13.
3. Laodicea. The Indifferent and Apostate Church. 14-22.

1. Sardis. The Period of the Reformation: Verses 1-6. We have traced briefly the decline during the 1450-1500 years of Church history. The climax is reached in Thyatira, prophetically the Roman abomination and apostasy. In Sardis we see the progress of evil stayed. Roman Catholicism, as already mentioned, is a fixed and unchanging religious system. Rome will yet have for a brief season a startling revival and get back her place as the mistress of the nations. But in Sardis we see a reaction. Sardis means "those escaping." It is the reformation period, the movement which produced Protestantism. The reformation itself was of God and the great men who were used were the most mighty instruments of the Holy Spirit. It was the greatest work, up to that time, since the days of the apostles. But out of it came the human systems which go by the name of Protestantism. The reformation began well, but soon developed in the different Protestant systems into a dead, lifeless thing.

They have a name to live but are dead. This is the verdict of our Lord upon the churches which sprung out of the reformation: "Thou hast a name that thou livest and art dead."

2. Philadelphia. The Faithful Remnant: Verses 7-13. Philadelphia means "brotherly love." As Sardis came out of Thyatira, a protest against it, so Philadelphia comes out of Sardis and is a protest against the dead, lifeless, Spiritless condition prevailing in Protestantism. Out of the deadness of the state churches over and over again came forth companies of believers, energized by the Holy Spirit. Philadelphia has been variously applied to early Methodism,the evangelical movements, missionary efforts and to the revivals of the nineteenth century. But it is more than that. It is a complete return to the first principles. The message makes this clear. It is the one message (besides Smyrna) in which the Lord does not say, "I have against thee," it is that which pleases Him and which He commends. It is a revival and turning back to the first love. The Lord Jesus Christ is once more as the all absorbing object before the heart; Philadelphia repudiates all that dishonors Him and owns alone that worthy, ineffable Name. It is a faithful remnant gathering around His Name as there was a faithful remnant in the closing days of the Old Testament (Mal. iii:16-17). All human pretensions are rejected. The truth of the unity of all believers is owned and manifested in brotherly love towards all the Saints. They walk in the path of separation, in self-judgment, in lowliness of mind; they have a little strength, which means weakness; they are a feeble few. Twice the Lord speaks of obedience to His Word. "Thou hast kept my Word"—"Thou hast kept the Word of my patience." And the Philadelphian does not deny His Name. These are the two chief characteristics of this phase of Christianity during the closing days of the professing Church on earth: Obedience to His Word and faithfulness and devotion to His Name. The Word and the Name are denied in the last days. The apostasy of Christendom consists in the rejection of the written Word and the living

Word. And turning their backs upon a dead profession, going on in confessed weakness are such paralyzed in their service? Far from it! The Lord promises to open the door for service which no man can shut. Every child of God may test this. True and continued service is the result of true and continued faithfulness to the Lord. Especially is this service to be blessed to those who hold to a perverted Judaism (verse 9). And there is the great promise, which they believe and hope for, the coming of Himself to keep them out of the great tribulation (verse 10). In Philadelphia there is a revival of prophetic truth, an earnest waiting for the coming of the Lord. Philadelphia is not a defined church-period, but rather a description of a loyal remnant called out by the Spirit of God and bearing the final testimony to the whole counsel of God by word and deed. If the reader desires to please the Lord, then study the details of the message to Philadelphia and walk accordingly.

3. Laodicea. The Indifferent and Apostate Church: Verses 14-22. Loadicea means "The judging or rights of the People." It is opposite of Nicolaitanism. The domineerers of the people still go on in Rome, but in Protestantism the people (the laity) arise and claim their rights and do the judging. This condition was also foreseen by the Apostle Paul. "For the time will come when they (the laity) will not endure sound doctrine; but after their own lusts shall they heap to themselves teachers, having itching ears" (2 Tim. iv:3). We see in Laodicea the final religious and apostate conditions of protestant Christendom and the complete rejection of the professing body. "I will spue thee out of my mouth." He Himself is seen standing outside, which shows that He is rejected. But infinite Grace! He knocks and is still willing to come in and bestow the riches of His Grace. And the Philadelphian-Christian, who is separated from the Laodicean state, whose heart is filled with the Love of Christ can learn a lesson here. If our Lord stands outside and yet knocks and waits in patience, we too with Him outside of the camp where He is disowned, can try to gain admittance to Laodicean hearts. Epaphras did this (Col. iv:12-13). Laodicea consists in a proudly boasting spirit with total indifference to the Lord Jesus Christ and to His Name. It is religiousness without any truth nor the power of the Holy Spirit. Lukewarmness expresses it all. "Lukewarmness, a perfect jumble of sacred and worldly matters. The word does not point chiefly to half-heartedness. But as lukewarmness is produced by pouring of hot and cold water together into the same vessel, so in the Laodicean state, intense worldliness will be varnished over by plausible and humanitarian and religious pretences." Great reformation movements for the advancement of religion and the betterment of the world, the rejection of the Gospel as the power of God unto salvation, are characteristic features of this final phase of Christendom. It will continue and wax worse and worse till His patience is exhausted. Then the true church will be caught up with the departed Saints to meet Him in the air, and Laodicea will be spued out of His mouth. It is important to notice that Thyatira (Rome), Sardis (Protestantism) and the two phases of Protestantism represented by Philadelphia and Laodicea co-exist. They go on together. This is seen by the fact that in each our Lord speaks of His second coming (ii:25; iii:3, 10-11, 16). The Lord takes His own to Himself. Rome and an apostate Protestant Christendom continue on earth during the period of judgment, preceding the visible coming of the Lord.

III. THE THINGS WHICH ARE AFTER THESE. THE END OF THE AGE. THE CONSUMMATION AND FINAL MESSAGES

Chapters iv-xxii

1. THE HEAVENLY SCENE
CHAPTERS IV-V.

1. The Open Door and the Vision of the Throne. **1-3.**
2. The Twenty-four Elders. The Throne. 4-5.
3. The Four Living Creatures and the Worship. **6-11.**
4. Who is Worthy to Open the Book? v:1-3.
5. The Answer. **4-5.**
6. The Vision of the Lamb. **6-7.**
7. Worship and Praise. **8-14.**

1. The Open Door and the Vision of the Throne: Verses 1-3. The scene changes suddenly. We are no longer on earth but are transported into heaven. The true church is gone and the apostate Church, while still on earth to pass into the judgments of the great tribulation, is no longer owned by the Lord and, therefore, not mentioned. That is why the word "church" disappears entirely from the book after the third chapter. The open door and the voice which calls "come up hither" and John's presence in glory in the spirit, clearly indicate symbolically the fulfilment of 1 Thess. iv:15-17. That for which the faithful remnant waited, the blessed hope of the Church, has suddenly come to pass. The departure of the true Church from the earth will be as sudden as its beginning (Acts ii:1-2).

John's first vision in heaven is the established throne, the sign and symbol of the universal government of God. While thrones on earth begin to totter and to fall and man's day closes in the predicted upheavals, there is a throne which cannot be affected nor disturbed. Yea, He who sitteth there and looks down upon earth and sees man's rebellion and madness laughs at them and holds them in derision (Psalm ii:4). The occupant of the throne was to look upon like a Jasper (rather the diamond) and a sardine stone. Our Lord and the glory of His Person are symbolically represented in these stones. His glory in the brilliant stone, His redemption work in the blood-red Sardine. The rainbow in emerald-green tells us that in the judgments about to come upon the earth mercy will be also remembered. It is the covenant sign. Though judgments come, yet mercy is in store for Israel and the earth.

2. The Twenty-four Elders. The Throne: Verses 4-5. Who is represented by these twenty-four elders? They cannot be angels. Angels are never seen seated upon thrones (not seats, as in the authorized version), nor are they crowned, nor can they sing redemption's song as the Elders do. There is only one possible meaning. They represent the redeemed, the saints in glory. They are Priests (clothed in white) and they are Kings (crowned); they are the royal priesthood in the presence of the throne. And why twenty-four? It points us back to the work David did for the temple. He appointed twenty-four courses of the priests (1 Chron. xxiv). Twice twelve would suggest the saints of the Old and New Testaments.

There were lightnings and voices and thunderings. This is repeatedly stated. See viii:5, xi:19, xvi:18. It is the symbol of God's throne in its judicial aspect.

3. The Four Living Creatures and Worship: Verses 6-11. The sea of glass is a reminder of the great laver in Solomon's temple in which the priests had to wash. Now it is solidified because no more water is needed for the cleansing of the saints. The word "beast" should be changed to "living creatures" or "living ones." They are not symbolical of the church, or a special class of saints, but they are the same supernatural beings seen in the Old Testament and always in connection with the throne and the presence of Jehovah. They are the cherubim of Ezekiel's great vision, chapters i and x. Their constant cry, "Holy, Holy," reminds us of the seraphim also (Isa. vi). The worship here is the worship of Him who is the Creator.

4. Who Is Worthy to Open the Book: Chapter v:1-3. Much has been written about the meaning of the book written within and sealed with seven seals. What the book contains is no secret whatever. Beginning with the sixth chapter the seals are opened and after they are all broken the contents of the book are made known. The book contains the judgments for this earth preceding His coming in power and glory and the beginning of His reign. It is, therefore, the book of the righteous judgments of God, preceding the glorious manifestation of the King of kings.

5. The Answer: Verses 4-5. John receives the answer to the question the strong angel had proclaimed. One of the Elders told him, "Behold the lion of the tribe of Judah, the Root of David, has prevailed to open the book, and the seven seals thereof." No further comment is needed; the Lord Jesus Christ is the Lion of Judah and the Root of David. "The King's wrath is as a roaring lion" (Prov.

xix:12). He is now to be revealed in mighty power and strength to execute judgment. (See Gen. xlix:9.) And He is also the Root of David.

6. The Vision of the Lamb: Verses 6-7. And now He is seen who alone is worthy to open the book. He does not appear as a Lion in majesty, but He is seen by John as a Lamb standing, as having been slain. The Lamb slain is the Lion. His victory was gained by dying, and, therefore, He must have as the Lion the victory over all His enemies. Thrice the number seven is repeated revealing His perfection. Notice especially three descriptions. He is "in the midst." He is the center of God's government and of heaven itself, as He is for His people the center of all their thoughts and affections. He is seen "as a Lamb standing." Now He is seated at the right hand of God, but when the time comes when His enemies are about to be made His footstool, He will arise to act. He will arise and have mercy upon Zion (Psa. cii:12). And He is seen as "the Lamb slain." The Greek word here suggests "slain in sacrifice."

7. Worship and Praise: Verses 8-14. A great worship scene follows at once. The four living Creatures join in with the Elders, but the latter alone have harps and golden bowls full of incense, which are the prayers of the saints. The harps express their great joy and praise and the bowls full of incense denote the priestly ministry of the redeemed. Such is part of our glorious future, an endless praise of deepest joy, and perfect ministry. The prayers of the saints are not the prayers of the past, but the prayers of Jewish saints, so beautifully rewritten in the Psalms, when the time of Jacob's trouble is on the earth. And then the new song! This is redemption's song, the song of redeeming love; the old song was the praise of God as the Creator in His glory (Job xxxviii:7). Redemption is now accomplished for the saints in glory; they look forward to the glorious manifestation with Himself and the great new song bursts forth. The praise of Him becomes universe-wide. The innumerable company of angels joins in it. "The number of them was myriads of myriads and thousands of thousands."* And the praise described here leads us on to the time when God will be all in all. It is the never-ending praise, the Hallelujah-chorus of redeemed Creation! The four living creatures say "Amen"; the Elders worship. Omit "Him that liveth forever and ever," as these words do not belong here.

2. THE OPENING OF THE SEVEN SEALS CHAPTERS VI-VIII:5.

1. The First Seal. 1-2.
2. The Second Seal. 3-4.
3. The Third Seal. 5-6.
4. The Fourth Seal. 7-8.
5. The Fifth Seal. 9-11.
6. The Sixth Seal. 12-17.
7. **Parenthesis.** The Remnant of Israel. vii:1-8.
8. The Saved Multitude. 9-17.
9. The Seventh Seal. viii:1-5.

1. The First Seal: Verses 1-2. The Lamb, invested with all the authority to execute judgment, having received His commission from God, begins now to open the seals of the book which is in His hands, the hands which were once nailed to the cross. It is evident that the breaking of the seals does not begin till His Saints are gathered around the throne in glory. Until then it is still the day of grace. When the first seal is opened one of the living creatures said in voice of thunder, "Come." The words "and see" must be omitted here and in verses 3, 5 and 7. A rider upon a white horse appears; his is a bloodless conquest. He has a bow, but no arrow. He receives a crown and goes forth to conquer. Many expositors make this rider the Lord Jesus or some power which represents Him. It is positively incorrect. The rider here is a great counterfeit leader, not the personal Antichrist, but the little horn which Daniel saw coming out of the ten-horned beast (Dan. vii). This coming leader of the revived Roman empire will go forth to conquer and become its political head. He is Satan's man as we shall see later.

---

*This is according to the Greek.

2. The Second Seal: Verses 3-4. The second seal reveals a rider upon a red horse. He takes away the false peace, which the rider upon the white horse as a divine judgment act established. The universal peace of which the world dreams without the presence of the Prince of Peace, will be of short duration. Another awful war follows. It will not be war alone between nation and nation, but it will be a world-wide reign of terror and bloodshed, a carnage unknown before in the history of the world. See in Matthew xxiv how our Lord mentions the great conflict of nation against nation and kingdom against kingdom.

3. The Third Seal: Verses 5-6. The black horse rider brings famine, exactly what our Lord mentions next in Matthew xxiv: "There shall be famines." Famine follows war and inasmuch as the second seal brings the greatest war, the third seal will bring the greatest famine. The judgments of God fall then on the earth. Our Lord also mentions famines.

4. The Fourth Seal: Verses 7-8. The next rider under the fourth seal is named death. And Hades, the region of the unseen (not hell), is populated. Sword, hunger, death, that is pestilences and the beasts of the earth, claim an awful harvest (Ezek. xiv:21). And so our Lord spoke of "pestilences." These four seal judgments are hardening judgments.

5. The Fifth Seal: Verses 9-11. The four living Creatures have uttered their four-fold "Come." They are thus seen in connection with the providential government of the world. Under the fifth seal the scene changes completely. John saw under the altar the souls of them that had been slain. And they cry, "How long, O Lord!" Who are they? Not the martyrs of past ages. They are risen from the dead and are in glory with redeemed bodies. The words of the Lord in the Olivet Discourse give us the key. Speaking to His Jewish disciples He said: "Then shall they deliver you up, and shall kill you and ye shall be hated of all nations for my Name's sake" (Matt. xxiv:9). The Lord speaks of another company of Jewish disciples who will bear a witness during the end of the age, after the rapture of the Church. He will not leave Himself without a witness. He calls a remnant of His people Israel and they bear a witness to the coming of the Messiah, their coming deliverer and King. Many of them suffer martyrdom. Their cry, "How long?" is the well-known prayer of Jewish saints; and their prayer to have their blood avenged is equally a Jewish prayer. Christians are not supplicating for vengeance on their foes. The prayer for vengeance refers us to the imprecatory psalms prewritten by the Holy Spirit in anticipation of the final persecution of Jewish believers. And the fellow-servants and their brethren, who are yet to be killed (verse 11), are the martyrs of that remnant during the final three and one-half years, which is the great tribulation.

6. The Sixth Seal: Verses 12-17. Are the things mentioned under this seal to be taken in a literal sense or symbolically? Most of it is symbolical, yet at the same time great physical phenomena are also involved. The earthquake possibly means a literal earthquake. "Earthquakes in diverse places" our Lord predicted. And they increase as the age draws to its close. But the language is symbolical. Everything is being shaken in this poor world. The civil and governmental powers on earth all go to pieces; every class from kings to slaves is affected by it and terrorized. The political and ecclesiastical world is going to pieces. And when these shaking times have come, when thrones fall and anarchy reigns, when the great collapse of civilization and human society has come with signs on earth and in heaven, the earth-dwellers will see in anticipation the approaching day of wrath. Terror fills every breast and those who sneered at prayer, as the Christ-rejectors do now, will gather for a prayer-meeting to appeal to the rocks to cover them. Read the following Old Testament passages in connection with this seal: Isaiah xxiv, xxxiv:2-4; Joel ii:30-31; Zephaniah i; Haggai ii:6-7.

7. Parenthesis. The Remnant of Israel: Chapter vii:1-8. This is the first parenthesis. It must not be taken chronologically. The six-seal judgments extend over the entire period of the ending age. The rider upon the white horse will be on the scene to the end, wars will continue to the end, and culminate in the battle of Armageddon, and so do the famines and pestilences. And the sixth seal brings the end in view. We shall see the correspondence with the seventh trumpet and seventh vial later. The trumpet and vial judgments are more intense and more terrible than the seal judgments. In a certain sense they are parallel; the effect of each is continuously felt. The parenthetical vision of the seventh chapter also covers the entire period of the last seven years and brings before us even the vision of what will be after the great tribulation.

How much confusion would have been avoided if expositors and Christians in searching for the meaning of this vision, had not lost sight of two great facts: 1. This chapter can have no application to the Church on earth, nor to the Church in glory, for the simple reason that the Church is already complete and translated to glory. 2. The vision states clearly that the sealed company is "of all the tribes of the children of Israel."

The sealed company is of Israel. After the Church is removed to glory, when the fulness of the Gentiles is come in (Rom. xi:26) the Lord will turn in mercy to Israel and call, before the judgments fall, a remnant which will also be sealed (See Ezek. ix). This remnant is frequently seen on the pages of Old Testament prophecy. This sealed company also bears a great testimony. They are the preachers of the Gospel of the Kingdom, as a witness to all nations before the end comes (Matt. xxiv:14). Therefore, during the time when the judgments are executed from above there will be a world-wide preaching of the Gospel of the Kingdom, proclaiming the coming of the King, calling to repentance and faith in His Name, and offering mercy still.

8. The Saved Multitude: Verses 9-17. The application of this passage of Scripture to the redeemed Church in glory is wrong. This Scripture does not apply to the Church in glory, but to saved Gentiles on earth. It is a company which comes "out of the great tribulation." The church enters the glory before that great tribulation begins. The great multitude represents those Gentiles who will hear the final testimony and believe. They will have turned in repentance to Him and will be washed in His precious Blood. Our Lord speaks of them in the great judgment of the nations as sheep, who stand at His right hand and inherit the Kingdom (Matt. xxv:31, etc.). The brethren of our Lord mentioned in Matthew are the remnant of Israel. For a complete exposition see "The Gospel of Matthew," by the author of this volume. This great company, therefore, does not stand before a heavenly throne, but before the millennial throne on earth. It is a millennial scene after the tribulation is passed.

9. The Seventh Seal: Chapter viii:1-5. The silence in heaven when the seventh seal is opened is indicative of the solemn things which are now to come. The scroll is now fully opened and there is an ominous hush as the seven angels prepare to sound their trumpets of judgment. John beholds these seven angels, but before they begin to sound "another angel" is seen standing at the altar. This angel is not a creature, but like *the* angel of Jehovah in the Old Testament, is our Lord Himself. He is seen as the Priest in behalf of the praying, suffering saints on earth. No angel can offer the prayers of the saints, but He, who is the one Intercessor, alone can do that. And for what do they pray on earth? For mercy for those who persecute the remnant of Israel? No! They pray for divine intervention, for the fire of judgment as Elijah did.

3. THE SOUNDING OF THE SEVEN TRUMPETS

CHAPTERS VIII:6-XI:18.

1. The First Trumpet. 6-7.
2. The Second Trumpet. 8-9.
3. The Third Trumpet. 10-11.
4. The Fourth Trumpet. 12-13.
5. The Fifth Trumpet. ix:1-12.
6. The Sixth Trumpet. 13-21.
7. **Parenthesis.** The Angel and the Little Book. **x:1-11.**

8. The Temple. xi:1-2.
9. The Two Witnesses. 3-12.
10. The Earthquake and the Seventh Trumpet. 13-18.

1. The First Trumpet: Chapter viii:6-7. The judgments which follow can hardly be fully interpreted at this time. It would be folly to dogmatize about them. The historical application we reject, because the scope of the book makes it clear that these judgments have not yet taken place. What many of these things mean may perhaps never be fully understood till they are actually in fulfillment. The first four trumpet judgments evidently stand by themselves. The fire the Lord cast down is doing its work. The first trumpet manifests the same evidences of divine wrath as came upon Egypt, when Israel suffered there, under the seventh plague (Exodus ix:23). Hail (heat withdrawn), fire and blood are all the symbols of divine wrath. The trees and the green grass were burned up. The green things are symbols of agricultural and commercial prosperity.

2. The Second Trumpet: Verses 8-9. That this is not a literal mountain is obvious. A mountain in Scripture language represents a Kingdom (Isaiah ii:2; Zech. iv:7; Psalm xlvi:2; and especially Jerem. li:25). The sea is typical of nations. Some kingdom, internally on fire, signifying probably revolution, will be precipitated into the restless sea of nations, and the result will be a still greater destruction of life and commerce, which is represented by the ships.

The Third Trumpet: Verses 10-11. In the preceding trumpet-judgments things were cast upon the earth, but here is a star which falls. It is some person who claimed authority and who becomes an apostate, whose fall produces the awful results given here. It may be the final Antichrist who first may have claimed to be for Israel a great teacher with divine authority and then takes the awful plunge. Worm-wood is his name and the waters became worm-wood and bitter.

4. The Fourth Trumpet: Verses 12-13. The sun, the moon and the stars are now affected. The sun is the symbol of the highest authority; the moon, who has not her own light, is symbolical of derived authority; and the stars are symbolical of subordinate authority. The symbolical meaning of this trumpet judgment is that all authority within the revived Roman empire will be smitten by the hand of one above and as a result there will be the most awful moral darkness. These four-trumpet judgments tell of prosperity taken first from the earth; a great power burning with the fires of revolution affecting the nations; a great leader will fall and become worm-wood; and authority disowned and smitten will fill the territory of the Roman empire (Europe) with the densest darkness.

5. The Fifth Trumpet: Chapter ix:1-12. The remaining three trumpets have a "woe" attached to each. This is announced in the last verse of the preceding chapter, where the word angel should be "eagle." An eagle, the bird of prey, proclaims the three-fold woe. He acts thus as a herald of great judgments (Matt. xxiv:28, Rev. xix:17-18). The fifth trumpet is a special judgment upon apostate Israel: because those who suffer are they "which have not the seal of God on their foreheads" (verse 4). The great tribulation in the second half of the week, comes now into prominence. If we turn to chapter xii:12 we read something similar to the eagle's message of woe. "Woe unto the inhabiters of the earth and of the sea! for the devil is come down unto you, having great wrath, because he knoweth that he hath but a short time." Preceding the sounding of the fifth trumpet the eagle proclaimed the woe upon the inhabiters of the earth. The star which is seen fallen from heaven with the key of the pit of the abyss is Satan himself cast out of heaven. The details of this event we learn in the twelfth chapter. He has the key to the pit of the abyss, the same word "deep," used in Luke viii:31. "And they (the demons) besought Him that He would not command them to go out into the deep (abyss)." He unlocks the prison house of the fallen angels and the most awful satanic agencies come forth to begin their "dread" work of torment. The smoke first, symbolical of darkening;

the locusts next, symbolical of these demon powers. Awful darkness prevails and the most diabolical delusions, producing fearful torments among apostate Israel and the inhabiters of the earth. It is the time of the strong delusion (2 Thess. ii:4-11) which has come. And over them is a King. His name is given in Greek and Hebrew, showing that it is both Jew and Gentile that come under His power. Both names mean distinction.

6. The Sixth Trumpet: Verses 13-21. The sixth angel is commanded by a voice from the horns of the golden altar to loose the four angels who are bound at Euphrates, and as a result an innumerable company of horsemen is released.* They are prepared for a specific time to do their work. Euphrates is once more mentioned under the pouring out of the sixth vial. We believe the sixth vial judgment gives the key to these horsemen here. Euphrates does not mean the Turkish empire, as we shall more fully show when we come to the sixth vial. This river was both the boundary line of the old Roman empire and the land of Israel. Restraining influences held back the tide of nations on the other side of the river; this restraint is now removed and therefore a great invasion takes place. As the land of Israel is nearest it will suffer first, but the revived Roman empire will be the objective of these invading hordes. The "third part" stands for the Roman empire, the coming European confederacy. This invasion is under the King of the North. It is seen in its beginning here and is consummated under the sixth vial. There the "Kings of the Sunrise" are included. And under the sixth vial they are more specifically gathered for the great day of God Almighty.

7. Parenthesis. The Angel and the Little Book: Chapter x:1-11. The proclamation of the mighty angel is the first recorded event in this parenthesis. Who is this angel? It is Christ Himself. We saw our Lord in angel's form before the opening of the seventh seal and then He appeared

---

*Greek: twice ten thousand times ten thousand, that is, 200 million. The number would indicate the immense, uncountable hordes.

in priestly dignity. Here before the sounding of the seventh trumpet he appears again in the same form, but He is called a mighty angel and we behold Him in royal dignity. The cloud, the rainbow, the face like the sun, His right foot upon the sea, the left on the earth, the voice like a lion and the seven thunders, all declare this to be correct. The hour is rapidly approaching when the kingdoms of this earth are to become His Kingdom. This is seen under the seventh trumpet. And, therefore, He is seen now in this attitude of royal dignity. The words which He speaks (verses 6 and 7) bear out this interpretation. "There shall be no longer delay." Man's day is about to close. The mystery of God is now to be finished, "as He hath declared to His servants, the prophets;" or in better rendering "the mystery of God also shall be completed according to the good tidings which He declared by His own servants, the prophets." How great has been that mystery! Evil had apparently triumphed; the heavens for so long had been silent. Satan had been permitted to be the god of this age, deceiving the nations. And Israel, too, is included in this mystery. And now the time has come when the mystery of God will be completed, when the glorious messages, the good tidings of the prophets concerning Israel's blessing and the kingdom, will be fulfilled.

But what is the little book which the angel holds in His right hand? It is not a sealed book, but open. It stands for the prophecies in the Old Testament relating especially to Israel during the time of the great tribulation, which is yet to come upon the earth, culminating in the personal and glorious appearing of the Lord to begin His millennial reign.

8. The Temple: Chapter xi:1-2. We see at once how Jewish things come now into view. To apply these verses to the Church and make the temple the Church is absolutely wrong. The temple and the altar are Jewish; the holy city is Jerusalem. After the Church has left the earth the Jewish people will be fully restored to their own land, and their land restored to them. They will possess Jerusalem once more. When the Jews are once more masters in their own promised land they will erect another temple and then restore the Levitical worship as far as it is possible. Such a temple must be in Jerusalem (see Isaiah lxvi:1-4). In that temple the personal Antichrist, the beast out of the land of whom we shall read in chapter xiii, will appear and claim divine worship. (See 2 Thess. ii:3-4.) Apostate Israel in corrupt alliance with equally apostate Gentiles is seen in the opening verses of this eleventh chapter, as the court without the temple. But in the midst of this corrupt mass, which will follow the delusion of the Antichrist and accept Satan's man as their Messiah, there will be the God-fearing remnant. This remnant is here divinely recognized as worshippers. Therefore that coming is called "the temple of God," because the Lord owns the true worshippers found in the midst of the unbelieving mass.

9. The Two Witnesses: Verses 3-12. Much has been written on these two witnesses who will appear in Jerusalem. It is clear they are still future and their work will be in that city. Some make them Enoch and Elijah and others think they will be Moses and Elijah returned in person. Some have claimed to be a re-incarnation of Elijah. Such claims are fanatical. No second coming of Moses is anywhere promised in the Word. Something, however, is said about the work of Elijah in the future (Mal. iv:5-6). But the words of our Lord in Matt. xi:14, speaking of John the Baptist, and Matt. xvii:12, seem to make it clear that no literal coming of the same Elijah, who went into glory, without dying, is meant. Yet the deeds of these two witnesses clearly link them with the work of Moses and Elijah. They each do both the things that Moses and Elijah did separately. We take it then that these two witnesses represent the great testimony to be given in Jerusalem during the 1,260 days of the great tribulation. Perhaps the leaders will be two great instruments, manifesting the spirit of Moses and Elijah, endowed with supernatural power, but a large number of witnesses is unquestionably in view here. They maintain in the midst of the Satanic scenes a powerful testimony for God.

The period of the great tribulation was mentioned in verse 2. Here for the first time the beast is mentioned. This Beast coming out of the pit of the abyss, the deep, is the revived Roman empire under the little horn, seen by Daniel on the four-horned beast (Dan. vii:8). While he dominates over the Gentiles, he will turn in fury against these Jewish saints, and the two witnesses will be slain. He makes war with the godly remnant (Dan. vii:21). A part of that remnant will be killed. The vileness of these coming days of Satan's rule on earth is seen in the treatment of the bodies of Jehovah's servants. The wicked are so elated over the silencing of the testimony that they refuse to permit their burial so that they may feast their eyes upon the sickening spectacle. They rejoice and make it a festive occasion, because torment had come to their consciences through the testimony of the slain. Gentiles, who side with apostate Israel are mentioned, but especially a class which is called "they that dwell on the earth" rejoices over the end of the witnesses. The same class is mentioned several times. Study the passages where they are mentioned: Chapter iii:10, vi:9, 10; viii:13; xi:9, 10; xii:8; xiv:6, 7; xvii:8. They are the apostate, nominal Christians who are utterly blinded and hardened. Phil. iii:18-19 gives their character and destiny. They claim possession of the earth as belonging to them, but God is not only the God of heaven, He is also "the God of the earth" (Rev. xi:4). God's power is manifested in the physical resurrection and the visible translation of the two witnesses. Their enemies see a great miracle. The apostates who ridicule even now a physical resurrection, who sneer at the blessed Hope of a coming translation of the saints, will witness these two great facts. No wonder that a great fear fell upon them. The raised witnesses belong to the first resurrection (xx:4).

10. The Earthquake and the Seventh Trumpet: Verses 13-18. The terror becomes still greater when the whole city is shaken by a mighty earthquake. This is not a symbolical earthquake but a convulsion of nature by which the fourth part of the city falls and 7,000 men are killed. It marks the end of the second woe. Then those who escaped the visitation gave glory unto the God of heaven. It is only inspired by fear. They do not turn in repentance unto God. Here ends the parenthetical vision.

The seventh trumpet brings us to the very end of the tribulation and to the beginning of the millennial reign. It is Jerusalem's deliverance. He who alone is worthy receives the Kingdom. How clear this ought to make the fact that our Lord has no earthly Kingdom now, but He receives the promised Kingdom on the earth at the end of these things. See Dan. vii:14. Heaven worships too; they celebrate the fact that He has taken His great power. It is a review of all that takes place and what follows when He appears out of heaven. The nations were full of wrath (Ps. ii; xlvi:6); His wrath is come; resurrection will follow; this points to the time after the kingdom (chapter xx:12). And His servants, the prophets and the saints, receive their reward, to reign with Him.

4. SATAN'S POWER AND MASTERPIECE.

CHAPTERS XI:19-XIII.

1. The Vision of the Opened Temple. xi:19.
2. The Woman With Child. xii:1-5.
3. The Escape of the Woman. 6.
4. War in Heaven. 7-12.
5. The Dragon Persecuting the Woman. 13-17.
6. The Beast out of the Sea. xiii:1-10.
7. The Beast out of the Earth. 11-18.

1. The Vision of the Opened Temple: Chapter xi:19. What follows now brings the great tribulation, the 1,260 days, into prominence. As we have seen the seventh trumpet takes us right to the end. But now we are led back.

Verse 19 of chapter xi belongs properly to the twelfth chapter. The Ark contains the covenant made with Israel. This is now to be remembered and connected with it are the manifestations of coming wrath for those who oppress His people.

2. The Woman with Child: Chapter xii:1-5. Who is represented by the Sun-clothed woman? Romanists have made out of her the Virgin Mary. Many expositors claim it is the Church which is represented by this woman. Some claim the woman is the professing Church and the man-child represents, according to their view, a class of overcomers who will escape the tribulation. This is a favored interpretation of some of the so-called "holiness people."

In the light of the scope of this book the woman cannot possibly have anything to do with the Church. Again, Christian Science has made the most absurd claim that this woman represents that instrument of Satan, the deluded woman, whom they worship as the founder of their cult. A hundred years ago another sect existed in England under the leadership of a woman, who also claimed to be the one of this vision. We do not need to seek long for the true meaning of the woman seen by John. She represents Israel. Everything in the symbolical statements bears this out, especially the crown with the twelve stars (Gen. xxxvii:9).

"Thus she is seen clothed with the glory of the sun—that is, of Christ Himself as He will presently appear in supreme power as Sun of Righteousness (Mal. iv:2); for the sun is the ruler of the day. As a consequence, her glory of old, before the day-dawn, the reflected light of her typical system, is like the moon under her feet. Upon her head the crown of twelve stars speaks naturally of her twelve tribes, planets now around the central sun."

It is Israel, what she is in the purposes of God. And the child, the nation brought forth, is the Messiah, Christ. Even so Paul writes of Israel, "of whom as according to the flesh Christ came, who is over all, God blessed forever" (Rom. ix:5). The identity of the child is established beyond controversy by the fact that the child is caught up unto God and His throne, destined to rule all nations with a rod of iron (Psa. ii:9; Rev. ii:27). The great red Dragon, the enemy of the woman and the child, is Satan. Seven crowns are symbolical of his authority as the god of this age and the ten horns symbolical of his power. These historical facts are seen first through this vision. But this is done for the one purpose of bringing into view what is yet in store for Israel during the end time. Christ ascended upon high, took His place at the right hand of God, is waiting till His enemies are made His footstool. Then the present Christian age began. It is not recorded in this vision at all. He who came from Israel and who was rejected by His own, is nevertheless Israel's Messiah, the Hope of Israel. In Him and through Him alone the promises made to Israel can be fulfilled. The fulfillment of these promises is preceded by great sorrows and tribulation, the travail pains which come upon Israel during the great tribulation, before He, whom Israel once disowned, is revealed as Deliverer and King. And the red Dragon will do His most awful work during that period of tribulation, a work of hatred against the faithful seed of the woman.

3. The Escape of the Woman: Verse 6. The flight of the woman, Israel, has been taken by some to mean the dispersion of that nation during this age and Israel's miraculous preservation. But that is incorrect. It is true Israel has been miraculously preserved and Satan's hatred, too, has been against that nation. But here we have a special period mentioned, the 1,260 days, the last three and one-half years of Daniel's seventieth week. It means, therefore, that when the Dragon rises in all his furious power to exterminate the nation, God will preserve her. However, before we are told the details of that preservation and Satan's hatred, we read of the war in heaven. Satan is cast out of heaven, down upon the earth. Verses 15-17 and the entire chapter xiii will tell us what he will do on the earth.

4. War in Heaven: Verses 7-12. This great scene takes place before the great tribulation begins. Satan's place is not in hell at this time. As we saw in the message to Pergamos his throne is on earth, he is the god of this age. His dominion is in the air, he is the Prince of the power of the air (Eph. ii:2). Our present conflict as believers is "against principalities, against authorities, against the rulers of the darkness of this world, against the wicked spirits in the heavenlies"

(Eph. vi:12). Satan as the accuser of the brethren has access even into the presence of God. His accusations are ended. All the redeemed are gathered before the throne. All the malice and power of Satan could not frustrate the purpose of God. His grace and power have been victorious. Thus when the saints come into the heavenly possession Satan's dominion there is at an end. The purchased possession, the region above, will be redeemed by the power of God (Eph. i:13). Michael and his angels will begin their short and decisive war against Satan and his angels. Michael is the one archangel mentioned in Scripture. It is not the first time he met Satan face to face (Jude 9). And Daniel speaks of Michael, "And at that time shall Michael stand up, the great prince which standeth for the children of thy people; and there shall be a time of trouble, such as never was since there was a nation even to that same time; and at that time thy people shall be delivered, every one that shall be found written in the book" (Dan. xii:1). From this we learn that Michael will not only cause the expulsion of Satan out of heaven, but he will also stand up for the believing portion of Israel.

Satan is then cast out into the earth and his angels are cast out with him. It is identical with what we have seen already under the fifth trumpet, the star fallen out of heaven, opening the pit of the abyss with the darkening smoke and the locust swarms coming forth. Then there is joy in heaven because the accuser is cast down and his accusations are forever silenced. And the "woe" is pronounced upon those who dwell on the earth.

5. The Dragon Persecuting the Woman: Verses 13-17. He turns in fury against the woman which brought forth the man-child. Satan realizes now that his time is short. His expulsion from heaven will soon be followed by his arrest and imprisonment in the pit for a thousand years, and after that there is prepared for him his eternal home of misery, the lake of fire. As he knows that Israel is mostly concerned in the final drama, and the believing portion of that nation will inherit the kingdom, he turns in wrath against them.

Verse 6 should be connected with verse 14. It is symbolical language again we have here. The wilderness is a place of isolation, and the place prepared, speaks of God's care for them. But it is not the entire nation. The apostate part sides with Satan and with Satan's man, the Antichrist. But there is another part, which is preserved. This part is in the place of isolation among the nations. The water cast out by Satan is symbolical of the hatred which Satan stirs up against the people amongst the nations. But there will be other agencies in the earth by which this Satanic attempt to wipe from the face of the earth this faithful part of the nation will be frustrated.

6. The Beast Out of the Sea: Chapter xiii:1-10. This chapter brings now fully into view the Satanic powers operating during the great tribulation—the forty-two months. Satan's masterpieces are on the earth; energized by him and endued with his powers they work together to stamp out all that is left of the truth on earth. Their combined efforts are directed against the godly remnant of Jews and against those Gentiles who accepted the message of the Gospel of the Kingdom.

And John sees this first beast having ten horns with crowns and seven heads and these heads had names of blasphemy. Daniel had seen Babylonia, Medo-Persia and Greco-Macedonia under the emblem of the lion, the bear and the leopard. John sees this beast here like a leopard, with bear's feet and lion's mouth. This revived Roman empire is an amalgamation of parts of the previous world empires. The preceding ones are absorbed by the last, the Roman empire. Therefore the revived Roman empire will contain the different elements in one great monster. This Roman empire will be revived in the first part of the final seven years. We saw this under the first seal. Here is the beginning of the period for which the Dragon gives to him his power, and his throne and great authority. It becomes now fully possessed by Satan. The ten horns are the ten kingdoms which will exist in that empire. We are told later that these ten kings "have one mind and shall give their power and strength unto the beast" (xvii:13). In the same chapter the beast is also seen coming out of the abyss (xvii:8) denoting its Satanic origin. The heads represent the seven forms of government which have characterized the empire in the past, the seventh becomes the eighth. One of the heads is especially mentioned; later we read "he is the eighth, and is of the seven, and goeth into perdition" (xvii:11). He was as it were wounded to death, and his deadly wound was healed, and all the world wondered after the beast. This head denotes the imperial form of government, which had died, and now is revived in the person of the leader, the Prince of Daniel ix:27, the little horn, which Daniel saw in the midst of the ten horns. This will be Satan's man, one of his masterpieces. The whole earth will wonder after that beast and its Satan-possessed head.

7. The Beast Out of the Earth: Verses 11-18. The second Beast is not an empire with a great leader, but a person. The first Beast is out of the sea; the second out of the earth (land). The first has ten horns; the second has two. The Beast out of the sea comes first; the other Beast follows him. The first Beast is a political power; the second is a religious leader. The first is a Gentile power and its head a Gentile; the second is a Jew. The first Beast has Satanic power; so has the second Beast. The second Beast induced the worship of the first Beast whose dominion is over the entire Roman world and after whom the whole earth wonders; the sphere of the second Beast is Palestine. The first Beast through its head makes in the beginning of the seven years a covenant with many of the Jews, but in the middle of the week he breaks that covenant (Dan. ix:27). That covenant will probably be the permission given to the Jews to build a temple and to resume their sacrificial worship. The first and the second Beast make a covenant, which marks the beginning of the seventieth week of Daniel. But when the little horn, the first Beast, becomes energized by Satan, he breaks that covenant. Then the second Beast demands the worship of the first Beast as well as the worship of himself. This second Beast is the final, personal Antichrist. He has two horns like a lamb, and speaks like a dragon. He is a counterfeit lamb and his two horns are an imitation of the priestly and kingly authority of Christ. He is the one of whose coming our Lord spoke (John v:43). He is the man of sin, the son of perdition described by Paul in 2 Thess. ii. He must be a Jew or his claim of being Israel's true Messiah would not be accepted by the Jews.

Daniel also gives an interesting prophetic picture which bears out his Jewish character and his wicked, satanic ways. See Daniel xi:36-39. This second Beast is also called the false Prophet (xvi:13; xix:20; xx:10). He does lying wonders. He reigns as the false king in Jerusalem and sits as god in the temple. He will be the religious head of apostate Judaism and apostate Christendom. It is the strong delusion of the second chapter of Second Thessalonians. He also demands the worship of the first Beast. He makes an image of the first Beast and gives breath to it, so that it can speak. Whoever has not the mark of the Beast on hand and forehead cannot buy nor sell, and whosoever does not worship the Beast will be killed. And those who worship the Beast and receive the mark are lost souls. Great will be the number of martyrs at that time. To find out what the mark is and some of the other details would only be guesswork. No one can imagine the horrors of that time when Satan rules for a short time on earth and produces the great tribulation, such as was not before on earth, nor ever can be again.

But what does the number 666 mean? If we were to state all the different views on this number and the different applications we would have to fill many pages and then we would not know what is right and wrong. Seven is the complete perfect number; six is incomplete and is man's number. Here we have three times six. It is humanity fallen, filled with pride, defying God. The number 666 signifies man's day and man's defiance of God under Satan's power in its culmination.

5. GRACE AND JUDGMENT

CHAPTER XIV.

1. The Lamb and the 144,000. 1-5.
2. The Everlasting Gospel. 6-7.
3. Fall of Babylon Anticipated. 8.
4. Wrath for the Worshippers of the Beast. 9-11.
5. The Blessed Dead. 12-13.
6. The Harvest and the Vintage. 14-20.

1. The Lamb and the 144,000: Verses 1-5. A series of visions follow the dark scenes in chapter xiii. The conditions under the domineering power of the two Beasts are going to be changed. The Lord will answer the prayers of the persecuted Jewish people and deliver them by His personal coming out of the opened heaven. This glorious manifestation is fully revealed in the nineteenth chapter. Here it is anticipated. There is much said about this intervention in behalf of the suffering godly remnant in the Old Testament. As an illustration we call attention to Psalms xliv and xlv. In the forty-fourth Psalm we find a description of their suffering and the cry to heaven: "Arise for our help, and redeem us for thy mercies' sake." In the forty-fifth Psalm the answer to this prayer is recorded. The King riding in majesty, dealing with His enemies, surrounded by redeemed companies, is beheld in that Psalm. The entire Book of Psalms should be studied from the viewpoint of prophecy; it will shed much light upon these events of this portion of Revelation. But who are the 144,000 standing with the Lamb upon Mount Zion, having His Name and His Father's Name written on their foreheads? In the previous chapter we saw a company on earth who have the mark of the Beast on their foreheads; but here is a company who have His Name and the Father's Name on the forehead. A good many have made of this company a portion of the Church, a first-fruits, who, according to this theory, have lived separated lives and are caught up into heaven, while the other believers, who did not live as near to God as they did, will have to suffer in the great tribulation. The reader who has followed the unfolding of this book will see at once that such an interpretation is impossible. These 144,000 have nothing to do whatever with the Church. And the 144,000 learn to sing this new song. Who then are the harpers? They are the martyred company seen in connection with the fifth seal and they also include now their brethren which were slain during the great tribulation. The characteristics of the 144,000 are next given. Verse 4 must not be interpreted in a literal sense. Those who apply it to a first-fruits of the church have done so, and it has led to much confusion and even worse things. Literal impurity is not in view. If it had a literal meaning this company would consist of men only. The woman, the great harlot Bablyon and her daughters, the God-less and Christ-less religious world-systems (chapter xvii) are then on earth. They did not defile themselves with the corruptions and idolatries prevalent on the earth. They kept themselves from spiritual fornication. They are the first-fruits and the earnest of the blessings soon in store for the earth. They were devoted to the Lamb and no lie (not guile) was in their mouth. The lie and delusion of the end-time were utterly repudiated by them.

2. The Everlasting Gospel: Verses 6-7. This has nothing to do with the preaching of the Gospel during this church-age. The Angel must not be taken as a literal angel. The preaching of any Gospel to those who dwell on earth is never committed to angels, but to men. This is true of the Gospel of Grace which redeemed sinners are privileged to proclaim during this age, and of the everlasting Gospel during the end of the age. The Gospel preached is the Gospel of the Kingdom and the preachers are this faithful remnant of God's earthly people. Nothing of this preaching was said in chapter vii, though the result, the gathered multitude coming out of the great tribulation is seen there. But here, where the moral and spiritual characteristics of the remnant of Israel are seen, their testimony also comes into view. What this everlasting Gospel is we need not explain, for verse 7 gives us the information. It is everlasting because it concerns the Creator as the only object of worship. And it will sound the loudest and go forth in no uncertain sound at the time when pandemonium reigns on earth, and heaven is about to open to manifest the King of Glory. How great is God's mercy! And the nations who hear and turn to God will enter the coming Kingdom. Read in connection with verses 6 and 7 Psalm xcvi. It will give you a great deal of light on this portion of Revelation.

3. The Fall of Babylon anticipated: Verses 8. This is an anticipative announcement of what will also happen as the great tribulation nears its close. The particulars are not given here. These and what Babylon is and how Babylon the great (city must be omitted in this verse) falls, we shall find in chapters xvii and xviii. God's intervention in judgment upon the great whore is simply mentioned here.

4. Wrath for the Worshipers of the Beast: Verses 9-11. Here we have a third angelic announcement. It concerns the worshipers of the Beast. They drink of the wrath of God. It is "without mixture," that is, no mercy is found in the cup of His indignation. It serves as a solemn warning. Babylon falls prior to the glorious appearing of the King, and the Beast will afterward manifest his power as never before. Therefore, the warning concerning the inevitable fate of those who worship the Beast and take its mark.

5. The Blessed Dead: Verses 12-13. It is a voice which proclaims this. It refers especially to those who are martyrs at that time. Certainly all our loved ones who fall asleep in Jesus are blessed. They are absent from the body and consciously present with the Lord. But here is the comfort for those who faithfully resist the worship of the Beast, who refuse to take the mark. They become martyrs. The Book of Revelation will be read and studied during the great tribulation. Satan through the Beasts, will try to annihilate it and the rest of the Bible. But it will be a failure as all former attempts to get the Bible out of the world have failed. Here then, is first the warning. If they worship the Beast they will be lost forever. Then there is the alternative to resist the Beast and be killed as to the body, but die in the Lord. "From henceforth" means during the tribulation when the great persecution goes on.

6. The Harvest and the Vintage: Verses 14-20. This brings now the coming of the Son of Man with judgment power into view. The harvest and the vintage have come. The sickle is put in. The reapers used will be angels (Matt. xiii:41). The day of vengeance has come. Read Isaiah lxiii:1-6; Joel iii; Zechariah xii-xiv. This will greatly help to a better understanding of the harvest and the vintage. The nations and their armies will be in the land; the Assyrian from the North, foreshadowed by the wicked work of Antiochus Epiphanes (Dan. viii) will do his awful work; the false prophet, the second Beast is in Jerusalem. But then the judgment clouds break. The battle of Armageddon comes into view for the first time in verse 20. How we ought to praise Him, for His infinite grace which has separated us from these awful judgments of vengeance and wrath. His people will be at home when these things come to pass.

6. THE SEVEN VIALS

CHAPTERS XV-XVI.

1. The Victors' Song and Worship. xv:1-4.
2. The Seven Angels Leave the Temple. 5-8.
3. The First Vial. xvi:1-2.
4. The Second Vial. 3.
5. The Third Vial. 4-7.
6. The Fourth Vial. 8-9.
7. The Fifth Vial. 10-11.
8. The Sixth Vial. 12.
9. **Parenthesis.** The Seventh Vial. 13-21.

1. The Victors' Song and Worship: xv: 1-4. And now the last seven angels appear; seven seal judgments first, followed by seven angels with trumpets and next the last seven angels. With these seven angels who have the seven last plagues for the world, the wrath of God is completed. Before these angels go forth we behold another worship scene. Who are they? Not the twenty-four Elders, but they are the harpers which we saw harping and singing in chapter xiv:2-3. They are the martyred company worshiping in glory. Here we are told of their victory and their song, the song of Moses and of the Lamb. The song of Moses (Exod. xv) is the song of an earthly deliverance and the song of the Lamb concerns a spiritual deliverance. They are redeemed by power and by blood.

2. The Seven Angels Leave the Temple: Verses 5-8. A wonderful sight it is. There is again an ominous silence similar to the silence in connection with the opening of the seventh seal. The silence is not mentioned. But the text shows an impressive scene of silence. Quietly the procession of these ministers of judgment file out of the temple. They are clothed in pure, white linen; this is symbolical of the righteousness which demands the judgment wrath about to be poured out. And the golden girdles with which their breasts are girdled speak still more of divine righteousness. God in His righteousness must judge and now His wrath in completeness is about to be felt on the earth. The angels left the temple empty-handed, but the four living creatures give into their hands the bowls full of the wrath of God. And behind that smoke is the fire of judgment.

3. The First Vial: Chapter xvi:1-2. The great voice commands the seven angels to go on their way and to empty the bowls upon the earth (Ps. lxix:24). And these vials of judgments affect not only the Roman empire, but the entire world, for the whole world is guilty before God. The first vial poured out produces a grievous sore upon the worshipers of the Beast. While it is undoubtedly true that we have symbols also in these vial judgments, it is nevertheless possible that some of these plagues may have, besides the symbolical, also a literal meaning. The sixth plague which came upon Egypt, the first judgment upon the persons of the Egyptians, was also a sore (Exod. ix:10-11). The worshipers of the Beast and of the image will be dreadfully afflicted.

4. The Second Vial: Verse 3. This is poured out into

the sea. The sea represents the Gentiles. These will now experience the wrath of God. See the plague in Egypt (Exod. vii:17-25). That was a literal thing; but not so here. Some apply it to the continued carnage which will be one of the leading features of the final history of the times of the Gentiles. That it presents a state of the most unspeakable corruption and spiritual death is obvious.

5. The Third Vial: Verses 4-7. Another scene in which the blood is prominent. The Apostates denied the blood, sneered at it as the Unitarians and Christian Scientists do in our own days, and now the angel of the waters saith, "Thou hast given them blood to drink, for they are worthy." They have to feel the dreadful results of having rejected the Christ of God and accepted the man of sin. The children of Israel had to taste their own idolatry when Moses put the ashes of the burnt golden calf in the water and made them drink it (Exod. xxxii:20). They have to taste the vileness and bitterness of their apostasy. They reap what they sow. All the joys of life typified by rivers and fountains of water, are poisoned and corrupted. It is a retributive judgment of God falling upon the earth.

6. The Fourth Vial: Verses 8-9. The fourth vial is poured into the sun and men are scorched with great heat. Some also apply this literally, but the symbolical meaning is to be preferred. There can be no doubt that the powers of nature will also bear witness to the wrath of God. Famines, droughts, great floods, volcanic disturbances, great and widespread earthquakes and other physical phenomena will occur throughout these days of tribulation. However, the sun here is not the physical sun, but means, as under the fourth trumpet, the supreme authority governing them (the Roman empire). Under the fourth trumpet great moral darkness came upon all; here it is fearful, fiery agony "scorched with great heat." The government, Satan-ruled as it is, becomes now the source of the most awful torment to those who are under its dominion. God, in judgment and in His wrath, permits those terrible things to come to pass. Everything under these vial judgments will become more aggravated than under the trumpet judgment.

7. The Fifth Vial: Verses 10-11. Under the fifth trumpet we saw the star fallen from heaven. It synchronizes with chapter xii:7-12—Satan cast out of heaven. Then Satan fallen from heaven gave his power and authority to the Beast, the head of the empire. Here the throne (not seat) of the Beast is dealt with. His throne and his kingdom is deluged with wrath. All becomes darkness.

8. The Sixth Vial: Verse 12. Once more the river Euphrates is mentioned. It dries up when the sixth bowl is poured out so that the way of the kings of the East (literal: from the rising of the sun) might be prepared. We have hinted before at the correspondence between the trumpet judgments and the pouring out of the vials. This now becomes very marked, for under the sixth trumpet the river Euphrates is also mentioned. There the forces which keep back hostile powers are removed and here the river is dried up. As already stated the Euphrates was the boundary of the Roman empire and the land of Israel. It is a kind of barrier which separates the West from the East. This barrier symbolized by the river Euphrates is now completely removed, so that the kings from the sunrise can invade the land. This invasion is also seen in connection with the sixth trumpet. The nations must gather from all quarters in and about Palestine. We find much of this revealed in the Old Testament and it would be strange if the revelation were silent on so important an event. Ezekiel describes a great invader, a confederacy of nations (Ezek. xxxviii and xxxix). Gog, Magog, the Prince of Rosh (Russia), Meshech, Tubel, Persia, Cush and Put are mentioned as forming this confederacy. The term "Kings of the sunrise" may even mean the far Eastern Asiatic nations, like China and Japan. The drying up of the Euphrates seems therefore to mean the removal of the barrier, so that the predicted gathering of the nations may take place (Joel iii:2). What began under the sixth trumpet is consummated when the sixth vial is poured out. It is an act of judgment-wrath, while at the same time these opposing nations are gathering for the great day of God Almighty.

9. Parenthesis. The Seventh Vial: Verses 13-21. Just as we had a parenthetical vision between the sixth and seventh seal, and between the sixth and seventh trumpet, so we find here a very brief one between the sixth and seventh vial judgment. Armageddon is not yet, but it now comes in view. Unclean spirits, like frogs, creatures of the slimy, evil-smelling swamps and of the night, now proceed out of the mouth of the trinity of evil. The Dragon is Satan; the Beast, the political head of the empire, and the false Prophet, the Antichrist. Satanic influences, emanating from him and his two master-pieces are then at work; and they are of such a nature that we cannot fully understand them. They are the spirits of demons, working miracles.

The seventh angel pours his vial into the air. This is Satan's sphere. His power and dominion are now dealt with in wrath. While Satan was cast out of heaven, he may still maintain part of the atmosphere immediately above the earth, thus upholding his claim as the prince of the power of the air (Eph. ii:2). A great voice declares "It is done." All that follows shows that the climax is reached. The judgment shown is sweeping everything. A great earthquake as under the sixth seal and the seventh trumpet takes place. The great city Babylon is divided into three parts; the cities of the nations fall. It is the hour of collapse, when the stone from above does its smiting work (Dan. ii). "It is done!" The Lord has come. The nineteenth chapter will furnish us the particulars.

7. BABYLON, THE HARLOT AND HER JUDGMENT CHAPTERS XVII-XVIII.

1. The Description of the Woman. xvii:1-6.
2. The Angel's Interpretation. 7-15.
3. The Desolation of the Whore. 16-18.
4. The Angelic Announcement. xviii:1-3.
5. The Call to Separation. 4-5.
6. Her Pride and Destruction. 6-8.
7. Lamentation and Jubilation. 9-20.
8. Her Utter and Eternal Destruction. 21-24.

1. The Description of the Woman: Chapter xvii:1-6. Babylon was mentioned for the first time in this book in chapter xiv:8; her fall was then anticipated. In two chapters we have a description of her and the details of her overthrow and complete destruction. Babylon is seen as a great, world-wide ecclesiastical, political and commercial system, and her dwelling-place, from where she exercises authority, is a great city, which is the seven-hilled city Rome. There are many who believe that the literal Babylon is in view here in these two chapters. It is claimed that literal Babylon on the banks of the Euphrates is to become once more a large city and the seat of government during the end of this age. Literal Babylon never was a part of the Roman empire, and as the Babylon of Revelation xvii and xviii is seen in closest identification with the empire, and for a time at least is at its center and capital, the Babylon in Asia is ruled out at once. Rome was the great center of the Roman empire and Rome will once more become the seat where the woman pictured in this chapter will exercise her authority.

In the first part of this chapter we have a description of the great harlot Babylon. Who, then, is this woman, branded a harlot, whom one of the seven angels who poured out the vials showed to John? She represents the papal system in its final power and control in the world. We shall see how this assertion is fully confirmed by the words of this chapter. We saw in the church-message to Thyatira, which stands for the papacy and its great corruption, that Rome is pictured as the woman Jezebel, corresponding to the woman in the parable of the leaven. And of Thyatira it is said "she repents not." This shows that Rome will continue in her corrupt ways to the end, till judgment overtakes her. She is to be cast into great tribulation (ii:22). When the true Church is caught up, the papal system, as we call it, the Roman Catholic "church" will see a great revival. For a time she has been stripped of the temporal power she once had, but it will be restored to her. Along with the revival of the Roman empire there will be a revival of papal Rome. But we must look very briefly at some of the descriptions of this woman, the harlot. "She sitteth upon many waters." We find the interpretation in verse 15. "The waters which thou sawest, where the whore sitteth are peoples, and multitudes, and nations and tongues." Rome even now can boast of her children among all nations. She gets her support from the whole world. And when she gets her revival she will have a still greater dominion. The kings of the earth will yield once more to her spiritual fornication. Then John saw the woman upon a scarlet colored beast, full of names of blasphemy, having seven heads and ten horns. Who is the Beast she rides? It is the first Beast of chapter xiii, the revived Roman empire. She becomes identified with that empire. Her attire is purple and scarlet and she is decked with gold, precious stones and pearls. The Pope and his Cardinals wear these colors. Purple and scarlet are the leading colors displayed in great Romish celebrations; gold, precious stones and pearls describe her enormous wealth and dazzling glory, so attractive to the natural man. And in her hand was a golden cup full of abominations and filthiness of her fornication. How clearly this describes papal Rome. Her service, called worship, her rituals, her splendid edifices, etc., all are fair to behold and pleasing to the eye, like a golden cup. But inside we find her filthiness in doctrine and in practices. She encourages sin by her indulgences. With the celibacy there is also filth connected. And then the vileness and abomination of the confessional. Her shameless character is written upon her forehead. The true Church is to have His name upon the forehead and the great harlot-system bears an inscription.

2. The Angel's Interpretation: Verses 7-15. The interpreting angel told John who the Beast is, the Beast, that was, and is not, and yet is (verse 8). It is the Roman empire as stated before. It was, in an imperial form in John's day. In the fifth century, A. D., it ceased existing as imperial Rome; it is not. But it is to be again, a revival which is here described as coming out of the pit of the abyss (chapter xiii). Verse 9 shows Rome (seven mountains), where the woman sitteth. Therefore, Rome speaks of "the See of the Papacy," and "See" is derived from the Latin *Sedes*, which means seat or throne.

The seven kings or heads in verse 10, mean different forms of government of the Roman empire. Five are fallen; these were Kings, Consuls, Dictators, Decemvirs and Military Tribunes. These are past forms of government. But in John's day the empire had the imperial form of government. This is the meaning of "one is." The other and final form of the Roman empire "is not yet come." That is in John's day it had not yet come. It is the Satanic revival and control of the empire as we saw it in chapter xiii. And the eighth head, which goeth into perdition, is the man who heads the empire, the little horn, which Daniel saw on the ten-horned Beast. The ten horns in verses 12-13 are the kings. They correspond to the ten toes on Nebuchadnezzar's image and the ten horns on the fourth Beast which Daniel saw coming out of the sea. And these ten kings yield their power and strength unto the Beast. In verse 14, their awful future is seen. We shall see this more fully in chapter xix:11-21. They are going to make war with the Lamb, and the Lamb, who is Lord of lords and King of kings, will overcome them. With Him are the called, the chosen and the faithful, that is the redeemed, who come with Him and are manifested when He appears.

3. The Desolution of the Whore: Verses 16-18. The woman rides the Beast for a short time only. She will not be long successful in her regained power. The ten horns, the ten kingdoms, and the Beast* hate her and turn against the whore. First they were all for her and now they unite in making her desolate and naked and burn her with fire. But more than that "and shall eat her flesh," just as Jezebel was eaten by the dogs. It is God in His righteous judgment who decreed her desolation in this way.

4. The Angelic Announcement: Chapter xviii:1-3. Babylon

---

*"And the Beast" is not in the authorized version; it is added in the Revised Version and belongs rightfully in the text.

is now seen under another aspect. In the former chapter we have the religious center of Rome and her wicked idolatries, in the present chapter it includes also the whole system of apostate Christendom in its social and commercial aspect, the so-called "Christian civilization" in its final apostate condition and doom. Papal Rome in her short revival becomes the head of apostate Christendom and controls everything till her appointed doom comes upon her. While we saw in the preceding chapter the desolation of the whore by the ten kings and the Beast, here we see how God views her and that He dethrones this system in His judgment. A strong angel comes down to announce her doom and to lay bare her inner and most awful corruption. A strong descending Angel* whose glory lightened the earth, shows what the boasting thing, she, who bore the blessed name of Christ, has become. She is seen to be the habitation of demons. Even now behind all the denials of the doctrine of Christ and the false doctrines which mark the onward march of the predicted apostasy, demons are the leaders (1 Tim. iv:1).

And the nations drank eagerly her cup and the kings committed fornication with her. These kings are not the ten kings of the Empire for they are used in the judgment of the whore, while the kings mentioned here bewail her destruction (verse 9). And with the system there was connected great commerce; merchants through her became rich.

5. The Call to Separation: Verses 4-5. God always calls out His true children from that which is evil. His own must be a separate people. Saints in past centuries have heard this call and left behind the Romish abominations and thousands sealed their testimony with their blood. And in these days in which our lot is cast, days

---

*This angel may represent the Lord Himself. If this is correct we have the third manifestation of our Lord in the garb of an angel: viii:3 in His priestly dignity; x:1 in His royal dignity and here as the herald and executor of the vengeance of God upon Babylon.

of increasing signs, heralding as never before the approaching end and the homecall of His people to meet Hin in the air, in these days God demands the separation of His true children. Christendom is becoming daily more and more the religious camp of apostasy. And, therefore, He calls: "Let us go forth unto Him without the camp bearing His reproach" (Heb. xiii:13). He who remains in that which denies His Name, is partaker of her sins (verse 4; compare with 2 John, verses 10-11). As all drifts back to Rome and the coming political and religious confederacy, this final Babylon looms up; God's people must hear that call. To whom is this call addressed? Undoubtedly to the remnant of God's ancient people, the believing remnant and also to that large number of Gentiles who hear the final message, the Gospel of the Kingdom.

6. Her Pride and Destruction: Verses 6-8. Like ancient Babylon, the whole apostate system, Rome and all her offspring, was filled with pride. She was lifted up in all her earthly glory and now God breaks her completely. "She shall be utterly burned with fire." As her smoke is to arise forever and ever (xix:3) it is possible that the proud city, Rome, the center of the system of apostasy and commerce, will be destroyed by volcanic action, and where the seven-hilled city once stood there may be instead an immense crater, testifying throughout the millennium of God's righteous retribution. In view of the volcanic conditions on the Italian peninsula this is more than possible.

7. Lamentation and Jubilation: Verses 9-20. And now follows the great and universal lamentation over the destruction of the great world-system. There is weeping and wailing when at last this anti-christian civilization, all Christendom united with Rome, and for a time controlling the commerce of the world, is wiped out by the hand of God. The kings, the merchants, the shipmasters, the company in ships and sailors, all are seen mourning, weeping and wailing. The destruction of the system and of its proud city affects them all. They bewail their great loss. Notice twenty-eight things are mentioned by them. The first is gold and the last the souls of men. How this describes Rome! She is the trafficker in souls and the destroyer of souls as well. And in studying the articles of the commerce of apostate Christendom we notice that these are nearly all articles of luxury. The greatest panic has then come and there will be no recovery of the market. The rich men will weep and howl for their misery is come upon them (James v:1). See also Zeph. i:11, 18.

Heaven is called to rejoice over her, and three classes are mentioned (Revised Version), saints, apostles and prophets. "For God hath judged your judgment of her." This is the better rendering. The judgment which the saints pronounced on her is now executed. The next chapter shows us more fully the rejoicing heavens.

8. Her Utter and Eternal Destruction: Verses 21-24. In Jeremiah li:60-64 we read that Seraiah was commissioned by Jeremiah to attach a stone to the book containing the prophet's words and to cast it into the Euphrates. "And thou shalt say, thus shall Babylon sink and shall not rise from the evil that I will bring upon her and they shall be weary." Here an angel took up a millstone and cast it into the sea, showing by this action the complete and final destruction of the wicked system and the equally wicked city. And what revelation there is in the statement, "for by thy sorceries were all nations deceived." In chapter xx we read that the old Serpent deceives the nations. Sorceries, wicked spirits, demon-powers blinded the eyes of the nations to follow Rome's seductive lure. And thus it is with a lifeless, spiritless Protestantism and its bloodless Gospel. The sorceries of Rome, the demons underneath it all, attract apostate Christendom so that all will be united in the great, final Babylon.

So that we may not question that both chapters refer to Rome, though the entire Apostate Christendom is also in view, her blood-guiltiness is mentioned once more.

8. THE MANIFESTATION OF THE KING AND THE MILLENNIUM

CHAPTER XIX-XX:6.

1. Heavenly Hallelujahs and the Marriage of the Lamb. 1-10.
2. Heaven Opened. His Visible Manifestation. 11-16.
3. The Battle of Armageddon. 17-21.
4. The Binding of Satan. xx:1-3.
5. The Thousand-Year Reign. 4-6.

1. Heavenly Hallelujahs and The Marriage of the Lamb: Verses 1-10. Once more we find the significant phrase "after these things" (chapter iv:1; vii:1; xviii:1). "After these things"—the things which are described in chapters xvii and xviii, the fall of Babylon and the complete destruction of the whore and the system over which she presided and domineered, after these things, voices in heaven are heard again. We were first introduced to the heavens in this book in the fourth chapter.

In chapter xviii:20 we heard the words addressed to heaven, "Rejoice over her, thou heaven, and ye holy apostles and prophets, for God hath avenged you on her." And now we see heaven rejoicing. "I heard as it were a great voice of a great multitude in heaven saying, "Hallelujah." Hallelujah means "Praise ye Jehovah." This Hebrew word is not found elsewhere in the New Testament. Four times this word of praise is found in the beginning of this chapter; the Hallelujah times for heaven and earth are imminent. The Book of Psalms closes with many Hallelujahs; the blessed time which the Psalms so often anticipate, when the earth is judged in righteousness and the glory of the Lord is manifested, is now at hand. The praise here is on account of the righteousness of God exhibited in the judgment of the great whore "which did corrupt the earth with her fornication" and because the blood of God's servants shed by her is now avenged. The great multitude whose Hallelujah is heard first must be the company of martyrs who died during the tribulation. The souls under the altar and their brethren which were slain later utter this praise now. They are seen as a distinct company from the twenty-four Elders. A second Hallelujah is uttered by them, while the smoke of the destroyed city goes up forever and ever.

The whole redeemed company, Old and New Testament Saints, add their Amen and Hallelujah to the outburst of praise on account of the execution of the righteous judgment. And they worship God, for it is His righteousness which accomplished the destruction of the great whore. In the midst of this wonderful and impressive worship-scene the throne begins to be heard. A voice from the throne said: "Give Praise unto God all ye His servants and ye that fear Him both small and great." And the command is at once obeyed. John hears the fourth Hallelujah and it is the greatest, the most magnificent. It is the great Hallelujah-chorus of heaven. Like the voice of many roaring waters, like the voice of mighty thunderings, a great multitude saith, "Hallelujah for the Lord our God Omnipotent reigneth." Who is this great multitude? In the first verse we heard the Hallelujah of the martyred companies. The twenty-four Elders and four living Creatures did not join in this first Hallelujah. Their Hallelujah followed. And now the great outburst of a great multitude. This multitude includes all the redeemed in glory. And they rejoice and give glory for an additional reason which is made known for the first time in this book. The marriage of the Lamb is about to be consummated. "Let us be glad and rejoice, and give honor to Him, for the marriage of the Lamb is come and His wife has made herself ready." The harlot, which claimed to be the bride, being judged, the true bride of Christ is seen in glory. And it is the marriage of the Lamb. His joy is now filled full for He receives her, who is bone of His bone and flesh of His flesh. The second Man, the last Adam, is joined to her who is to rule and reign with Him. But who is the bride about to become the Lamb's wife? Some teach that it is Israel to be united with the Lord in the closest bonds. But these expositors forget that the scene is a heavenly one. This marriage does not take place on earth where the faithful remnant looks up expecting Him to appear for their deliverance, but this marriage is in glory. It is true such relationship is declared to be Israel's in the Old Testament. She was married to Jehovah in a legal covenant and on account of her faithless condition, because Jerusalem played the harlot (Ezek. xvi:35), she was put away. For a time Israel was the wife of Jehovah (Is. liv:1) and then on account of her wickedness became divorced. She will be taken back in the day of her national repentance when the Lord comes. But as one who had been divorced she cannot be a bride again. The bride of Christ to become the Lamb's wife is the Church of the New Testament.

All who accepted Christ as Saviour and Lord since the day of Pentecost constitute the bride of Christ. The Church began on Pentecost and her completion will be the translation to glory (1 Thess. iv:17). She is both the body of Christ and the bride of Christ, as Eve was of the body of Adam and also his bride. The Church is the nearest and the most beloved object of His loving heart.

But how has she made herself ready? And what does it mean, "And to her was granted that she should be arrayed in fine linen, clean and white for the linen is the righteousness of the saints"? The grace of God has supplied the robe and the precious blood is her title to glory. In this respect she was ready. But the words here refer us to the judgment seat of Christ, that award seat before which we must appear. Then the hidden things are brought to light and the wood and the hay and stubble are burned (1 Cor. iii: 12-15). Then "every man shall have praise of God" (1 Cor. iv:5) and what grace accomplished in each one and through each will be manifested. And the clean white linen "is the righteousness of the saints." The word "righteousness" is in the plural. It means more than the righteousness which we are in Christ or the faith in Him which is counted for righteousness (Rom. iv:3). It includes all the blessed results in life and service produced by the Holy Spirit, the practical righteousness of the saints. And yet even these need the washing in that precious blood without which all is unclean and unholy. And so it is grace after all, as indicated by the word "given" (Revised Version); "it was given to her to be clothed in fine linen, bright and pure." He Himself has made her ready and removed every spot, every wrinkle and every blemish. God grant that we His people may daily meditate on this coming glorious event, the marriage of the Lamb, and walk worthy of such a Lord and such a calling. Once more John is commissioned to write: "Write, Blessed are they which are bidden to the marriage supper of the Lamb." And who can estimate the blessedness of being in His ever blessed Presence, at His table, at the marriage supper of the Lamb!

2. Heaven Opened His Visible Manifestation: Verses 11-16. And now we reach the great event so often mentioned in the Old Testament, the event for which this world is waiting, the visible manifestation of Him, whom the heavens received, who returns to judge the earth, to receive the promised Kingdom and rule over the earth for a thousand years. We have reached the great climax in the Revelation. His own words are now to be fulfilled. "Immediately after the tribulation of those days shall the sun be darkened, and the moon shall not give her light, and the stars shall fall from heaven, and the powers of the heavens shall be shaken. And then shall appear the sign of the Son of Man in heaven, and then shall the tribes of the earth mourn, and they shall see the Son of Man coming in the clouds of heaven with power and great glory" (Matt. xxiv:29-30).

Impressive words—"And I saw heaven opened." Heaven was opened unto Him when He came out of Jordan at His baptism. While His baptism foreshadowed His death in the sinner's place, His resurrection and ascension are foreshadowed in coming out of the waters and the open heaven. In heaven at the right hand of God He has been ever since, unseen by human eyes. At last the time has come when God is to make His enemies as the footstool of His feet. Heaven is opened so that He might be revealed in His glorious majesty. And out of the opened heavens He comes forth. He comes as the mighty Victor to judge in righteousness and to make war. "And behold a white horse; and He that sat thereon was called Faithful and True and in righteousness He doth judge and make war." The white horse is symbolical of victorious warfare and glorious conquest. When, seven years before the first seal had been opened (vi:1), a rider appeared upon a white horse achieving great conquest, it was the false king who was then seen in vision. He is as the Beast on earth with the King and their armies to make war with the coming King who comes out of the opened heaven. Glorious sight! He is coming to conquer and to claim His inheritance. The appointed day has come in which God "will judge the world in righteousness by that man, whom He hath ordained; whereof He hath given assurance unto all men, in that He hath raised Him from the dead" (Acts xvii:31). Upon His head are many diadems. The saints wear crowns, but He to whom belongs all power in heaven and on earth wears many diadems, encircling His head in dazzling splendor.

"And He had a name written, that no man knew but Himself." And again it is written, "His Name is called the Word of God." And on His vesture and on His thigh there is a name written, "King of kings and Lord of lords." The unknown Name is the name of His essential Deity. No human name can express what He is in Himself. "No man knoweth the Son but the Father." His Name "the Word of God" refers us to the Gospel of John. As the Word He is the express image of God, that is He makes God visible. He is the expression of God in His character, His thoughts and counsels. And the third name mentioned, "King of kings and Lord of lords," expresses what He is in relation to the earth.

"And he was clothed with a vesture dipped in blood"—"And out of His mouth goeth a sharp sword, that with it He should smite the nations, and He shall rule them with a rod of iron, and He treadeth the winepress of the fierceness and wrath of Almighty God." The blood-dipped vesture has nothing to do with His work on the cross. He is described in Isaiah lxiii:1-4 as the One who has the day of vengeance in His heart, and this passage in Isaiah is here being fulfilled. The two-edged sword refers us to Isaiah xi:4: "He shall smite the earth with the rod of His mouth and with the breath of His lips shall He slay the wicked."

But He is not alone. The armies of heaven follow the great King. They are, like Him, upon white horses and are clothed in fine linen, white and clean. These armies are not angels. It is true, angels will be with Him as He comes, for it is written, then He shall be revealed with His holy angels. Angels will be the reapers in the judgment (Matt. xiii:41) when the age ends and they will be used in the regathering of Israel. (Matt. xxiv:31). But the armies here are not angels. They are the glorified saints; the fine linen, white and clean, identifies them fully. In faith and blessed assurance, you, dear reader, and the writer can say, we shall be in that company with Himself as leader. The Son brings His many sons unto glory (Heb. ii:10). What a sight that will be for the earth-dwellers! Each in that company bears His own image; each reflects His own Glory.

3. The Battle of Armageddon: Verses 17-21. And what a sublime vision comes next! An angel is beheld by the Seer standing in the sun, and with a loud voice he summons the birds that fly in mid-heaven to gather themselves to the great supper of God to eat the flesh of the slain. The birds of prey are summoned in anticipation of the battle of Armageddon which is then imminent. And now the hour of judgment has come. An angel, standing in the sun, the place of supreme authority, gives the invitation to the birds of prey to be ready for the feast which a holy and righteous God will have for them. The day of wrath has come. The slain of the Lord shall be many (Isaiah lxvi:16).

And down on earth there is the greatest gathering of armies the world has ever seen. The Beast, the head of the revived Roman empire, is the commander-in-chief. The kings of the earth are with him. Vast armies camp on all sides. The great valley on the plains of Esdraelon is filled with soldiers. The hills and mountains swarm with armed men. Satan's power has gathered and blinded this vast multitude to the utmost. The unclean spirits, the demons working miracles, have brought them together to the battle of that day. And the hordes from the North, under the Prince of Rosh are coming later. These vast multitudes from the North and beyond Euphrates are described in Ezekiel xxxviii-xxxix. And in that Old Testament prophecy we find a statement which reminds us of the great supper of God in Revelation. "Speak unto every feathered fowl, and to every beast of the field, assemble yourselves and come; gather yourselves on every side to my sacrifice that I do sacrifice for you, even a great sacrifice upon the mountains of Israel, that ye may eat flesh, and drink blood" (Ezek. xxxix:17). "Thus shall ye be filled at my table with horses and chariots, with mighty men, and with all men of war, saith the Lord God" (verse 20).

Zechariah xiv:2 is now being fulfilled. While the vast armies are covering valleys and hills, the objective will be Jerusalem. All nations are gathered against her. "For I will gather all nations against Jerusalem to battle; and the city shall be taken, and the houses rifled, and the women ravished; and half of the city shall go forth into captivity, and the residue of the people shall not be cut off from the city." And now as these armies are massed together the great battle of Armageddon takes place. They are ready to make war against Him, who comes through heaven's portals. "Then shall the Lord go forth, and fight against those nations." (Zech. xiv:3). The battle does not consume much time. Sennacherib's army was suddenly smitten and they all perished, and here are armies in comparison with which Sennacherib's forces were insignificant. One mighty blow from above, one flash of glory and all their strength and power is gone. The stone has fallen (Dan. ii). With one blow the dominion and misrule of the Gentiles is at an end. The Kings of the present day might profitably listen to Nebuchadnezzar's letter in Daniel iv. He began at the times of the Gentiles, and has left this letter to be read by his successors. The words our Lord spoke while on earth "on whom this stone falls it shall grind him to powder" have been fulfilled (Matt. xxi:44). Such is the awful fate which "Christian civilization (?)" and "Kultur (!)" and a Christless christendom is rapidly approaching. And while the armies perish as to the body and God's wrath sweeps the earth clean of the mass of apostates, taking vengeance on them that know not God and that obey not the Gospel, the Beast (the head of the empire) and the false Prophet (the second Beast of chapter xiii), that is the false Messiah, the Antichrist, are cast alive into a lake of fire burning with brimstone. They were not annihilated, for a thousand years later we still find them there (xx:10); and still they are in existence and will ever be as individuals in that place of eternal punishment. And those that were slain as to the body will be raised after the millennium and also share the place with the two, whom they followed and worshipped.

4. The Binding of Satan: Chapter xx:1-3. And now Satan, who was cast out of heaven three and one-half years before the visible and glorious coming of the Lord, and who has been on earth in person, though not beheld by human eyes, is seized to be put into his prison for a thousand years. And the demons, who were liberated by Satan (chapter ix) are likewise shut up in the bottomless pit, though this is not mentioned because it is self-evident. The terms "key" and "great chain" are of course figurative. He is mentioned in all his infamous titles. He is called dragon on account of his horrible cruelty and vileness, the old serpent on account of his maliciousness, guile and deception; he is thc devil, the arch-tempter of man, and Satan because he is the accuser of the brethren, the one who opposed Christ and His people. He is now dethroned as the god of this age, completely stripped of his power; and his dethronement means the complete enthronement of our Lord Jesus Christ. And here is the important statement that this being, the once glorious Lucifer, the Son of the morning and light-bearer, who fell through pride, has been the deceiver of the nations.

5. The Thousand Year Reign of Christ: Verses 4-6. Thrones are seen next by the Seer. "And I saw thrones, and they sat upon them and judgment was given unto them." Daniel also saw thrones in connection with the judgment of the Beast, but nothing is said of those occupying the thrones in Daniel's vision. Here we have the complete revelation, and several times the blessed statement is made that Christ and His saints shall reign with Him for a thousand years. The new age in which all things are put in subjection under His feet, the personal reign of Christ, in which all His redeemed people have a share, begins. It will last a thousand years. Six times we read of the thousand years in this chapter. Because this coming age will last a thousand years it has been called by the Latin word "millennium"; not a few have made the astonishing declaration that such a period of time during which Christ and His Saints reign over the earth has but little foundation in the Scripture. It is quite true that the only place in which the duration of such an age is given is this great final Book of Revelation. And that should be sufficient for any Christian to believe in such an age of a thousand years. However, this age of unspeakable blessing and glory for this earth is revealed throughout the entire Bible. The Old Testament contains hundreds of unfulfilled promises of blessing for Israel, the nations of the earth and even for all creation, which have never seen even a partial fulfillment. Isaiah is full of such promises. In the New Testament there are also passages which clearly teach and point to such an age of glory for this earth. Read Matt. xix:28; Acts iii:19-21; Romans viii:19-23; Eph. 1:10; Col. i:20; Phil. ii:9-11. What awfully disheartening pessimism it would be of we had to believe that the terrible conditions prevailing on the earth now, conditions which have steadily become worse, were to continue and that man's work is to remedy them and produce something better. This earth has a bright and glorious future. Nations will some day no longer turn, as they do now their plowshares into swords, but change their swords into plowshares. Righteousness and peace will surely kiss each other and creation's curse and travail pains will end. Mercy and truth meet together.

But when? Never as long as the great unfoldings of this book, which we have briefly followed, have not come to pass. There can be no better day for the earth as long as He is absent and not on the throne which belongs to Him. But when He comes, when He has appeared in glory and in majesty, then the earth will find her rest and groaning creation will be delivered. As we do not write on the great blessings and glories to come when He comes, we must refrain from following these things. Here in our book the revelation is given that Christ shall reign for a thousand years and His Saints shall reign with Him. Let us notice briefly the different classes mentioned who are associated with Christ in His personal reign. The entire company of the redeemed, as we saw them under the symbolical figure of the twenty-four Elders, occupying thrones and wearing crowns, are undoubtedly meant by the first statement,"they sat upon them and judgment was given unto them." They judge with Him. This is the raptured company whom we saw first in glory in chapters iv and v; and we, dear fellow-believer, belong to this company. Then follow the martyrs, whom we saw under the fifth seal (vi:9-11): "And I saw the souls of them that had been beheaded on account of the testimony of Jesus and for the Word of God." Then we have a third company. "And I saw those who had not worshiped the Beast, nor his image, and had not received his mark on their forehead, or in their hands." These are the other martyrs who were slain during the great tribulation, when the Beast set up the image and demanded its worship (xiii). They lived and reigned with Christ a thousand years. The first resurrection is passed and all who have part in it reign with Christ, are priests of God and of Christ and shall reign with Him a thousand years. Oh! wonderful grace which has saved us! Grace which has saved us in Christ and through His ever precious blood delivered us from eternal perdition! Grace which saved us from Satan's power, from sin and all its curse! Grace which has lifted into such heights of glory and has made us the sons of God and the joint-heirs of the Lord Jesus Christ! And how little after all we enter into all these things, which ought to be our daily joy and delight. How little we know of the power of the coming glory of being with Christ and reigning with Him!

9. AFTER THE THOUSAND YEARS. THE NEW JERUSALEM CHAPTERS XX:7-XXII:5.

1. Satan's Last Revolt. 7-10.
2. The Great White Throne. 11-15.
3. The Eternal State. xxi:1-8.
4. The Vision of the Holy City. 9-27.
5. The Glories of the Redeemed. xxii:1-5.

1. Satan's Last Revolt: Verses 7-9. Satan who was put into the abyss a thousand years before, is now loosed out of his prison. God permits him to come forth once more. Who could have ever thought of such a thing! The arch-enemy who had done his vile and wicked work among the human race, for a thousand years put at last into the place of perfect restraint, and now loosed once more to continue, for a brief season, his work! And he finds nations ready for his deception, not a few, but a number "as the sand of the sea." God permits Satan to come out of his prison, so that the absolute corruption of man might be demonstrated. Man has been tried and tested under every possible condition. He has failed in every age. He failed under the law and he failed even more in the grace-dispensation; and now, under the most glorious conditions, during the millennium, when the Lord Himself is known in all the earth and reigns in righteousness, when want and nearly all the sorrows of a ruined creation are banished, when there is peace on earth, man also fails and does not fully respond to a gracious Lord. But here is a difficulty which many have. Many a sincere post-Millennialist, who has studied the pre-millennial coming of our Lord, has asked this question, "If the whole world is converted during the millennium, how is it then that Satan finds nations ready to side with him after the thousand-year reign of Christ and then leads them on to destruction?" The difficulty is far from being as great as it is generally made. In fact it is easily explained. As far as Israel is concerned, the all Israel living, when He comes, the trusting remnant of Israel, they will constitute the blessed nation in possession of all her promised blessings. They are not mentioned as siding with Satan. No more back-sliding for that nation. Isaiah lix:20-21 vouches for this.

And the Gentile nations in the beginning of the millennium will also be converted. However, the human conditions of the earth will continue. The nations are not in a glorified state. Marriage will continue. Children will be born during the millennium. Indeed the earth will be populated as never before. Billions of human beings can be sustained upon our planet and they will come into existence by natural generation during the golden age of glory. Wars will be unknown. No longer will the flower of manhood be cruelly murdered by human passion in that legalized horrible thing called war. Earthquakes will no longer sweep thousands upon thousands into an untimely grave, nor can famines and pestilences claim their millions. Nor will there be the great infant mortality. Physical death will no longer be the universal rule, but rather an exception (See Isaiah lxv:20). Now every child born during the millennium of the converted nations comes into the world the same as the children in the present age, it is still true, conceived and born in sin. And it is equally true, they must be born again. And as many children of pious, godly parents in this age are Gospel hardened and live on in sin, though they hear the Gospel and see its power, so in the millennium, an enormous multitude will see the glory, live under the best and most glorious conditions the earth has seen since the fall of man, and yet they will be Glory hardened and only submit to the righteousness of that age and yield obedience through fear, for disobedience to the governing laws of the kingdom on earth, will mean sudden and certain judgment. It is not the obedience produced by a believing, trusting heart, but only a feigned obedience. Three prophetic Psalms which speak of these millennial conditions make this clear, if we consider the marginal reading. "As soon as they hear of Me, they shall obey Me, the strangers shall yield feigned obedience unto Me" (Ps. xviii:44). "Say unto God, How terrible art Thou in Thy works! Through the greatness of Thy power shall Thine enemies yield feigned obedience unto Thee" (Ps. lxvi:3). "The haters of the Lord yield feigned obedience unto Him, *but* their time might have endured forever" (lxxxi:15). Study these Psalms in their millennial bearing. Thus many nations submit while sin is in their heart and in their blindness they long and hope for the day when they may cast off the restraint. And that day comes when Satan is loosed out of the prison to deceive these nations again.

It was the final attempt of the dethroned usurper to regain his lost dominion. For thousands of years, in the all-wise purposes of God, he was permitted to be the prince of the power of the air and the god of this age. We have followed his history in this book and seen how he was cast out of heaven upon the earth where he caused the great tribulation. Then we beheld him stripped of all his power. The kingdoms of the world became the kingdom of Christ and the old serpent was cast unto the abyss where he remained a thousand years. Loosed for a little season he tried once more to become earth's master. And fire out of heaven devoured the nations who had revolted. The devil receives his final doom. He is cast unto the lake of fire and brimstone. He goes to a fixed place, a locality where unspeakable and eternal torment is his portion. This place is prepared for the devil and his angels (Matt. xxv:41). And all the wicked will share that place. And he finds others there. The first beings who were cast into this final abode were the Beast (the emperor of the Roman empire, the little horn of Dan. vii), and the false prophet (the personal Antichrist, the second Beast of chapter xiii). They were put there a thousand years before, and as they are there as persons it shows they were not annihilated.

And they shall be tormented day and night for ever and ever—for the ages of ages—never ending—for all eternity. What a solemn truth this is! Yet men meddle with it and deny future, conscious and eternal punishment. Besides these three persons, the nations who were judged and condemned in the beginning of the millennium, when the Son of Man sat upon the throne of His glory (Matt. xxv:31), are also in the Lake of Fire.

3. The Great White Throne: Verses 11-15. And now we reach the last great judgment scene of God's holy Word. Much confusion prevails among Christians about this judgment. There is no such thing in the Word of God as a universal judgment, nor is there a universal resurrection. Every human being that has died will be raised at some time. Our Lord spoke (John v:28) of two resurrections, a resurrection unto life and a resurrection unto judgment. The Revelation speaks of the first resurrection. "This is the first resurrection" (xx:5). And previously the Apostle wrote of a resurrection from among the dead (Phil. iii:11). The first resurrection was finished in the beginning of the millennium. "But the rest of the dead lived not again until the thousand years were finished." The rest of the dead come now into view and they are of necessity the wicked dead, who died in their sins, and whose is the resurrection unto judgment. Some, like "Pastor" Russell, who echoes the evil teachings of others, have invented a third resurrection, a resurrection of the unsaved for a second chance. In the light of this final Bible book there is no room whatever for such a resurrection, which would give the lost another opportunity. Nor does the rest of the Bible mention such a third resurrection. And this great judgment is not a universal judgment. It is taught that the entire human race, the living and the dead, will appear before this great throne. But this is incorrect, for it saith "I saw the dead, small and great, stand before God." No living people are there at all. Again the judgment-scene in Matthew xxv:31, etc., is spoken of as being the universal judgment and identical with the judgment here in Revelation. But this is another error. In the judgment of Matthew xxv the dead are not there, but living nations are judged in the beginning of the millennium. And these nations are judged on account of the treatment of the Jewish preachers of the Gospel of the Kingdom heralded by them during the last seven years of the age. They did not accept the last offer of mercy and that is why they treated the messengers as they did. Furthermore, the throne which the Son of Man occupies in Matthew xxv is upon the earth; the throne in Revelation xx:11 comes into view after earth and heaven fled away. The church and the Saints of God are not concerned at all in the judgment of Matthew xxv, nor in the great white throne judgment. They are at that time in His own presence glorified. Every Christian should have these things clearly defined and know that for him, as in Christ, there is no more judgment or condemnation (John v:24; Rom. viii:1). The judgment seat of Christ before which believers have to appear (2 Cor. v:10) does not concern their eternal salvation, but their works and rewards.

Who is the occupant of this great White Throne? Not God the Father, but God the Son. "The Father judgeth no man but hath committed all judgment unto the Son" (John v:22). The earth and heaven fled from His face. Sin-stained and defiled as they were they flee away from the face of the holy One. The great conflagration of 2 Peter iii:7-12* takes place. Fire of judgment swept the earth before the millennium, the day of the Lord, began; but the all consuming fire comes after the millennium. Out of that great conflagration there arises a new heaven and a new earth (xxi:1).

But what about the millions of saved Israelites and Gentiles who are on the millennial earth? Where are they during this great conflagration? What becomes of them? That they share the eternal blessings and glories in the eternal state is certain. But their abode between the burn-

---

*See Annotations 2 Peter iii.

ing of the earth and the calling into existence of the new heaven and the new earth is unrevealed. Speculation on it would be wrong. We should accept the silences of Scripture as much in faith as we accept the promises of God.

And John sees the dead standing before the Throne. Books were opened and another book was opened, the book of life. "And the dead were judged out of the things which were written in the books, according to their works." The books are symbolical; conscience and memory will speak loudly. Twice we read that they are judged according to their works. And in the "Book of Life" none of their names were written, or they would not have been in that company. "All this would seem to show that, though a millennium has passed since the first resurrection, yet no *righteous* dead can stand among this throng. The suggestion of the "Book of Life" has seemed to many to imply that there are such; but it is not said that there are, and the words "whosoever was not found written in the Book of Life was cast into the lake of fire" may be simply a solemn declaration (now affirmed by the result) that grace is man's only possible escape from the judgment."*

The second resurrection takes place. The sea gives up the dead and death and hades give up the dead. Hades gives up the souls, and Death, used here for the grave, gives up the bodies. Death and Hades were cast into the lake of fire. Both had come into existence because man had sinned, and, therefore, they are cast into the place where all belongs which is contrary to the holiness and righteousness of God. And then that solemn word! "And whosoever was not found written in the Book of Life was cast into the lake of fire." It corresponds to that other solemn statement in John iii:36. "He that believeth on the Son hath everlasting life; and he that believeth not the Son shall not see life, but the wrath of God abideth upon him." To be written in the "Book of Life' means to have life in Christ. Not our works, not our character, not our religiousness, not

---

*Numerical Bible.

our tears, our prayers or our service can put our names in the "Book of Life." Grace alone can do it, and grace does it, as we believe on the Lord Jesus Christ. Reader! is *your* name written there?

The saints of God are in eternal glory; the wicked dead, the lost, are in an eternal lake of fire and suffer conscious, eternal punishment. And how man, blind, presumptuous man, yea, even such who know God, rise up against this solemn truth, the eternal punishment of the wicked. They accuse God of injustice, as if the judge of all the earth would not do right. That the suffering of the lost differs is obvious. It is eternal, because the evil condition remains unchanged. There is no repentance, no faith, no new birth in hell. As there are different rewards for the faithful service of the saints, so are there different degrees of punishment for the unsaved (Luke xii:47-48). This is the second death, not blotting out of existence, but endless in separation from God.

3. The Eternal State: Chapter xxi:18. And now the eternal state comes into view. "And I saw a new heaven and a new earth; for the first heaven and the first earth were passed away and the sea is no more." This is the revelation concerning the final and eternal state of the earth. "Thou hast established the earth and it abideth" (Ps. cxix:90); "But the earth abideth forever" (Eccl.i:4). These divine statements are now fulfilled. Many Christians have a very vague conception of the eternal state of the earth and the abode of the redeemed. They think of it as a spiritual state destitute of any locality. But it is not so. The earth and the heaven abide as definite places throughout all eternity. What a marvellous fact this is! In chapter xx:11 we read that the earth and the heaven fled away and there was found no place. We saw that at that time the great conflagration of which Peter speaks took place, when "the heavens shall pass away with a great noise, and the elements, shall be dissolved with fervent heat, the earth also, and the works that are therein shall be burned up" (2 Peter iii:10). But we read in the same chapter "nevertheless we, according to His promise look for new heavens and a new earth, wherein dwelleth righteousness" (verse 13). During the millennium righteousness reigns upon the earth, but now a state comes for the earth when righteousness shall dwell there. The great burning up meant not an annihilation of the earth and the heavens; God does not annihilate anything, nor does Scripture teach an annihilation of material things and much less the annihilation of human beings, as false teachers claim. The conflagration of the earth and the heaven means their complete purification. The heaven mentioned cannot be the entire heavens; for there is a heaven which cannot be touched by these fires of purification. The heaven is that which surrounds the earth and which was once the peculiar sphere of the great usurper, the prince of the power in the air. And when Peter writes that all this is according to His promise, he has a well-known prophetic statement in Isaiah in mind. "For as the new heaven and the new earth, which I will make, shall remain before me, saith the Lord, so shall your seed and your name remain" (Isaiah lxvi:22). See also lxv:17). From this statement we get definite information that the redeemed Israel established upon the new earth will throughout the eternal state be distinct from the saved nations. They will throughout all eternity bear witness of God's faithfulness as the covenant keeping God. The new heaven and the new earth are therefore the abodes of the redeemed. The new earth, the eternal glory spot of redeemed Israel and the redeemed nations. And the new Jerusalem will come out of heaven to fill the new earth and the new heaven as well. "And I, John, saw the holy city, new Jerusalem, coming down from God out of heaven, prepared as a bride adorned for her husband."

The new Jerusalem, the holy city, comes into view. During the millennium the city of Jerusalem was known as the place of glory for the earth. Numerous Old Testament predictions were fulfilled. In chapter xx:9, she is called "the beloved city." But in Revelation iii:12 we have another Jerusalem mentioned, the same city which John sees coming down out of heaven, the place of the highest glory. It is the abode of the church in all her glory; the statement "prepared as a bride adorned for her husband" establishes this beyond controversy. She is called "holy" for all is holy; and a "city" because the Saints are in blessed communion and fellowship there. In the highest glory she had her abode. But now she is being revealed in all her eternal glory and beauty. During the millennial reign this wonderful city was above the earth and from there Christ reigned and His saints with Him. But here she comes down out of heaven. A thousand years before the marriage of the lamb had taken place (xix:7-8), and now after a thousand years of unspeakable glory, she is still seen "as a bride adorned for her husband." And yet all these things are given in figurative language. What will be the reality! The masterwork of God is at last fully manifested; what He accomplished through Him, who left the Glory to die on the Cross, is made known. The eternal, never ending riches, purchased by Him who was rich and became poor for our sakes, are beginning to be displayed in all their unfading splendor. Then the saints of God will learn to know the full meaning of Eph. ii:7, "that in the ages to come He might display the surpassing riches of His grace in kindness towards us through Christ Jesus." "And I heard a loud voice out of heaven, saying, Behold the tabernacle of God is with men, and He will dwell with them, and they shall be His people, and God Himself shall be with them, and be their God." This is the glorious consummation. It is the goal of a holy, loving God. In Eden He visited man unfallen, walked and talked with Him. Then sin severed this fellowship. He dwelt in the midst of Israel in the holiest of the tabernacle. In this age the church is His habitation by the Spirit, but the blessed consummation in the eternal state will result in God dwelling with His redeemed Creatures. What holy, glorious, never-ending intimacy that will be! It is the time when God is all in all (1 Cor. xv:28). When that time has come all the former things are passed away. "And God shall wipe away every tear from their eyes, and there shall be no more death, nor sorrow, nor crying, neither shall there be any more pain; for the former things are passed away." Tears, death, sorrow, crying, pain and suffering, these came into existence through sin. And all these things, the effects of sin, are now gone. What relief and what joy!

And next comes the eternal state of those who have rejected the Gospel, who lived in their sins and died in their sins, unsaved, unregenerated. "But the fearful, and unbelieving, and abominable, and murderers, and fornicators, and sorcerers, and idolaters, and all liars shall have their part in the lake which burneth with fire and brimstone, which is the second death." God still speaks. How many false teachers are meddling to-day with the solemn Scripture doctrine on the endless punishment of the wicked.

5. The Vision of the Holy City: Verses 9-27. With the ninth verse we are brought back once more to the millennial state. What was briefly stated in chapter xx:4-6 is now more fully revealed and we have a description of the Bride, the Lamb's wife, in her millennial glory, in relation to Israel and to the nations on the earth. One of the angels which had the seven vials appears on the scene to show something to the Seer. We had a similar scene in chapter xvii:1-3. There one of these angelic bearers of the vials showed to John the harlot woman and her judgment; but now he is to see the Bride, the Lamb's wife. "And he carried me away in the Spirit, and set me on a great, high mountain and showed me the holy City, Jerusalem, coming down out of heaven from God." She is seen coming down out of heaven. This coming down precedes the one mentioned in verses 2-3 by a thousand years. Her coming down does not mean here that she actually comes down upon the earth, to dwell on earth during the millennium. Her coming out of heaven in verses 2-3 is undoubtedly to the new earth. But here she comes down to be over the earth.

For a fuller exposition of the symbolical language we refer the reader to the larger exposition of Revelation by the author. We mention briefly that the foundations of the heavenly Jerusalem are twelve precious stones.

The Jasper again stands first; the wall itself is of Jasper, while the first foundation stone mentioned is also Jasper. It stands for the Glory of God. Then the stones follow in their order. The Sapphire (blue); the Chalcedony (a combination of grey, blue and yellow); the Emerald (green); the Sardonyx (a pale blue); the Sardius (blood red); Chrysolite (purple and green); the Beryl (bluish green); the Topaz (pale green or golden); the Chrysoprasus (mixed blue, green and yellow); the Jacinth (combination of red, violet and yellow), and the Amethyst (purple). And what must be the deeper meaning of all these precious stones! What varied aspects of the Glory of God they must represent! And the redeemed in their heavenly city shall know, understand and enjoy it all. What wonderful, unspeakable glory is ahead of us! May we look forward to it every day and willingly serve and suffer the little while down here.

The city itself was seen by John as of pure gold. Gold typifies the righteousness of God in His nature and such the holy city is, composed of the saints who were made through grace the partakers of the divine nature. "And the twelve gates were twelve pearls, each one of the several gates was of one pearl; and the street of the city was pure gold as it were transparent glass." How suitable the pearl to form each gate, the entrance to the city divine. The Pearl is a type of the Church. She is the one pearl of great price for which the Lord gave all He had (Matt. xiii:45-46). And the golden street like unto pure glass shows that all the ways and walks in that city are according to righteousness and that defilement is eternally impossible.

And there was no temple in that city; the Lord God Almighty and the Lamb are the temple of it. There is no need any longer of a certain access into the presence of God, as it was on earth, but there is a free and unhindered fellowship with God and with His ever-blessed Son, the Lamb. Precious it is to hear Him again mentioned as the Lamb. His blessed work which He accomplished can never be forgotten by the Saints in Glory. And the light is not created light, but the light is the Glory of God and the lamp thereof is the Lamb. The Glory of God and Christ, the Lamb of God, will be the light and supersede all created light.

"And the nations shall walk by its light and the kings of the earth bring their glory and honor unto it*; and the gates of it shall not be shut at all by day for there shall be no night there. And they shall bring the glory and honor of the nations unto it." From this we learn that the glory light which shines eternally and undiminished in the holy city is the light in which the saved millennial nations on the earth walk. And the kings of the earth bring their glory and honor unto it; not "into" as it is rendered in the Authorized Version. The heavens then rule, for Christ and His co-heirs are in that holy city, and the government and rule over the earth proceeds from there. The kings bring their glory and honor unto it, they bow in homage in the presence of the holy city. Heaven is acknowledged as the source of all light, glory and blessing. When the nations and the kings of the earth go up to Jerusalem to worship the Lord of Hosts during the millennial age (Psal. lxxii:8-11; Is. lx:1-3; Zech. xiv:16) we doubt not, they will turn their faces upward. Mount Zion in Israel's land will have resting upon it the glory and above it the vision of the City in which the Glory dwells and from which the Glory emanates. And unto it they bring honor and glory. The open gates, never closed, denote security and suggest also communication and intercourse with the earth. "There shall be no night there"; the night of sin and sorrow is forever gone for the dwellers in the holy city. "And there shall in no wise enter into it anything that defileth, neither whatsoever worketh abomination, or maketh a lie, but they which are written in the Lamb's book of life."

5. The Glories of the Redeemed: Chapter xxii: 1-5. After the coming, Jerusalem and her blessings are once more revealed. In the opening verses of this chapter we find the glories of the Redeemed.

Unspeakably beautiful and glorious are the concluding

---

*This is the better rendering.

statements of this glory-section of the Revelation. Seven glories of the Redeemed are enumerated. 1. There will be no more curse. It means a perfect sinlessness; perfect holiness. 2. The throne of God and of the Lamb is there and the redeemed are forever linked with that throne. It is a perfect and blessed government which can never be disturbed by disorder. 3. His servant shall serve Him. Heaven will not consist in idleness. The holy city knows of service. And the service the saints will render to God in glory will be a perfect service. What will it be? We do not know what service it will be. God will have many surprises for His saints in glory. 4. There is also an eternal vision. "And they shall see His face." Oh! joy of all the joys in glory to see Him as He is and never lose sight of Him in all eternity. 5. His name shall be in their foreheads. It tells of eternal ownership and eternal possession. His name and the Glory connected with it will be ours in eternal ages. 6. An eternal day. No more night; no need of any light. He is the light for all eternity. 7. An eternal reign. And they shall reign forever and ever. What glory and blessedness all this means. Such are the coming glories of the Redeemed.

10. THE FINAL MESSAGES

CHAPTER XXII:6-21.

1. The Angel's Message. 6-11.
2. The Message of the Lord. 12-13.
3. The Two Classes. 14-15.
4. His Final Testimony. 16.
5. The Answer of the Spirit and the Bride. 17.
6. The Final Warning. 18-19.
7. The Final Word—the Final Prayer. 20-21.

1. The Angel's Message: Verses 6-11. Here it is an angel who speaks. "And the Lord God of the holy Prophets (literal: of the spirits of the Prophets) sent his angel to show unto His servants the things which must shortly be done." This reminds us of the beginning of the book, where we find a similar announcement. Suddenly some day these things will come to pass. The Lord will call His people to glory in a moment, in the twinkling of an eye, and then these things John had beheld will shortly come to pass. And then His own voice breaks in: "Behold I come quickly; Blessed is He that keepeth the sayings of the prophecy of this Book." Three times we find this announcement in the last chapter (verses 7, 12 and 20). Here it is connected with the walk of the believer. Just as in the beginning of the book a blessing is pronounced upon them that read the words of this prophecy (i:3), so we have at the close of Revelation a similar beatitude. And keeping these blessed words means more than believing in them; their power is to shape our conduct and walk. What godly lives God's people would live on earth, what unselfish and sacrificing lives, if they remembered constantly Him who thus testifies three times in the last chapter of the Bible, "Behold I come quickly." Note the awful results in Christendom to-day for not having kept the sayings of the Prophecy of this Book.

Then the Seer is told not to seal the sayings of this prophecy. Daniel was told to do the opposite (Dan.xii:4). Old Testament prophecy reveals prophetic events in the far distance. They could then not be fully comprehended. But after Christ came and the full revelation of things to come is given, no sealing is needed; the events are at hand, yet grace has delayed and delays still the fulfillment. And the heavenly messenger announces also the fixed state of the two classes into which all humanity is divided. The unjust and filthy, the unsaved, continue to exist in the nature which they possess, and the fact that the desires of that corrupt nature can no longer be gratified must constitute in itself an unspeakable torment. The righteous and holy, those saved by grace, partakers of the divine nature, will always be righteous and holy.

2. The Message of the Lord: Verses 12-13. And now the Lord speaks again. For the second time He announces His coming. Here it is in connection with rewards. "My reward is with Me." He Himself will receive His reward which is due Him as the sin-bearer. He will see the travail of His soul and be satisfied. And with His coming, His own people will receive their rewards. What a stimulating power His soon coming is to service! And the coming One is the Alpha and Omega, the first and the last, the beginning and the end.

3. The Two Classes: Verses 14-15. Once more the two classes come into view. This is in fullest keeping with the end of the Book and the end of the Bible. The Authorized Version here is faulty. Instead of "Blessed are they that do His commandments" the correct reading is "Blessed are they that wash their robes." The former is an interpolation; the latter is the divine statement.* Eternal life and eternal glory cannot be obtained by keeping commandments, by the works of the law. The blood of the Lamb alone is the title to glory. And then the other class. The one who rejects Christ, and thereby denies his lost condition and need of a Saviour, loveth and maketh a lie. He lives according to the old nature and the fruits of the flesh are there.

4. His Final Testimony: Verse 16. How He speaks in this last Bible book! In the beginning of Revelation we find His self-witness in the church-message and once more we hear His voice, bearing testimony to Himself. How majestic: I, Jesus! He reveals Himself once more by the name of humiliation. What comfort it must have been to John! What comfort it is to us! Then He speaks of Himself as the Root and Offspring of David. He is David's Lord and David's son (Psalm cx:1). He is the Hope of Israel and in Him the promises made to David will all be realized. This will be the case when He comes to reign in power and great glory. But He also speaks of Himself as "the bright and morning-star." His coming in power and glory is the sunrise for Israel and the Gentiles, the breaking of the millennial day. But for His Church He comes first as the morning-star, as the morning-star in the eastern sky precedes the rising of the sun in all its glory. The Lord will come as the morning-star some time in the interval between the 69th and 70th week of Daniel and

---

*All leading scholars like Alford, Darby, etc., make the change. Even the Vulgate has it "Beati, qui lavant stolas suas in sanguinem Agni."

as the Sun of Righteousness after that week has come to an end.

5. The Answer of the Spirit and the Bride: Verse 17. As soon as He mentions Himself as the morning-star, there is an answer from the earth. The Spirit now down here, for He came down from heaven on Pentecost, and the Bride, the Church, say, "Come." It is addressed to the Lord. They both long for His coming. And each individual believer who heareth is asked to join with this "Come." Surely in these days of darkness and world-confusion, the Spirit saith, "Come!" And never before were there so many individual believers on earth who say "Come," who wait for His coming. And the Come—from loving hearts—will increase and become a loud and pleading cry, till one blessed day He will answer and come to take His waiting people home. Here also is the final Gospel message of the Bible. He that will, let him take the water of life freely. Once more a loving God makes it clear that the water of life is free to all who want it. It is the last "Whosoever" in the Bible.

6. The Final Warning: Verses 18-19. And what a solemn warning is given! In a larger sense the warning applies to the entire Word of God. Higher criticism, which takes away, and false teachers, who add unto it, find written here their deserved judgment. But the Revelation is specially in view. Whosoever meddles with His Revelation must fall under the severest divine displeasure. Beware! oh ye critics! Beware! ye who call this Book uninspired and warn against the study of it!

7. The Final Word—the Final Prayer: Verses 20-21. We reach the final statements of this great Book. For the third time He announces His coming. "He that testifieth these things saith, surely I come quickly." It is the last time our Lord speaks from heaven. The next time His voice will be heard will be on that day when He descends out of heaven with a shout. While the two former announcements of His coming found in this chapter are preceded by the word, "Behold," this last one affirms the absolute certainty of the event. And there is the answer, the blessed response. "Amen. Even so, come, Lord Jesus." It is the Church which answers His positive and certain announcement. It is the last word recorded in the Bible coming from the lips of man. The first word we hear man address to the Lord in the Bible is the solemn word "I heard thy voice in the garden, and I was afraid" (Gen. iii:10). The last word addressed to the Lord by redeemed man is "even so, come, Lord Jesus." And between these two utterances in Genesis and Revelation is the story of redemption. Well might this final prayer of the Bible be termed the forgotten prayer. But it is equally true, with the revival of the study of prophecy, more hearts and lips are praying to-day for His Coming, than ever before. And the prayer will be answered. May the reader and the writer pray for His Coming daily and may our lives too bear witness to the fact that we expect Him to answer the petition of His people. The final benediction assures us once more of the Grace of our Lord Jesus Christ. The better rendering is "The Grace of our Lord Jesus Christ be with all the saints."

Appendix

Prominent Names and Their Symbolical Meaning in Revelation

Abaddon. (Chapter ix:11.) Destruction. The King over the Locust army, denoting Satan and his agencies.

Abyss, The. (ix:1; xx:1-3.) The pit of the abyss or the deep. This expression occurs seven times in Revelation. Out of the deep, the lowest pit, there comes the demon and into the pit of the abyss Satan will be cast for 1,000 years. The Lake of Fire is a different place.

Accuser, The. Satan is the accuser of the Brethren. xii:10. His expulsion out of heaven occurs in the middle of the week, followed by the great tribulation on earth.

Alpha. The first letter in the Greek alphabet; Omega is the last letter. Therefore Alpha and Omega is equivalent to an A and Z. Symbolical of the first and the last (i:8; xxi:6; xxii:13).

Amen, The. A name of our Lord. He is the "verily," the truth, and assurance and certainty are expressed by this word (i:18).

Angels. Angels are prominently mentioned throughout Revelation. The exposition shows that the angel mentioned in viii:1-5; x:1 is the Lord Jesus Christ. Angels will be used in the end of the age to carry out the decreed judgments. On the angels of the different churches, the symbolical meaning, see the exposition chapter i:20.

The angels are the messengers who carried the Lord's message to the churches. They needed the power of the Spirit to do it. Hence the churches were to hear what the Spirit said to the churches (Rev. ii:7, etc.).

Antichrist, The. The final and personal Antichrist is mentioned for the first time in Revelation in chapter xiii:11-18. He is also called the false Prophet, because he heads up the ecclesiastical corruption and apostasy of the end of the age. He must not be confounded with the first Beast out of the Sea who is a political head, the emperor of the revived Roman empire, the little horn of Daniel vii, and the Prince that shall come of Dan. ix:26.

Antipas. An unknown faithful martyr in Pergamos, known to Christ ii:13, meaning one against all.

Apollyon. (ix:11.) The Greek name of Abaddon, the King over the Locust army. The name means Destruction or Destroyer.

Ark, The. (Chapter xi:19.) It is seen by John in the temple. It means symbolically the assured presence of Jehovah with His people Israel, the faithful remnant, in the trying times of Jacob's trouble.

Armageddon. Mentioned for the first time in the parenthesis between the sixth and seventh vial. (Chap. xvi:12-16). It means "The hill of slaughter." The battle of Armageddon will be of brief duration. It is the stone of Nebuchadnezzar's dream smiting suddenly the ten toes, the ten kingdoms (Dan. ii). The battle of Armageddon is briefly described in chapter xix:19-20.

Alleluia. "Praise ye the Lord." The four Hallelujahs are found in chapter xix:1-5.

Babylon. On the literal and mystical Babylon see exposition of chapter xvii. The literal Babylon will undoubtedly be restored as a city of influence. But the city mentioned in chapter xvii is not the literal Babylon, but Rome. Not only will the Roman empire be revived, *but* also papal Rome. Babylon the great, the mother of Harlots, will see a great revival. The system in its corruption is described in chapter xviii.

Balaam. The heathen Prophet who could not curse Israel, but put a stumbling-block before the children of Israel. Used in Revelation to describe the corruption in the professing church in giving up the divinely demanded separation from the world (chapter ii:14).

Beast, The. The expression "four Beasts in Rev. iv and v, etc., is faulty. The correct rendering is "the four living creatures" or the "four living ones." The term "Beast" applies to the revived Roman empire and its head, the little horn of Daniel, also called Beast in Daniel's vision. The Antichrist is likewise called a Beast. The work of the two Beasts is seen in chapter xiii.

Birds, unclean and hateful. Symbolical of evil persons outwardly professing to be something but full of corruption. They describe the apostate masses of Christendom. (Rev. xviii:2. Also Matt. xiii:31-32.)

Black Horse. The black horse comes into view with the opening of the third seal. Black is the color of night, darkness and death.

Blood, with Hail and Fire. (Chapter viii:7.) Not literal things, but symbols of divine judgment for this earth.

Bow, The. (Chapter vi:2.) The bow without an arrow as in possession by the rider upon the white horse is the symbol of a bloodless conquest.

Bride, The. (xxi:2.) The Bride of Christ, the Lamb's wife (xix:7); it is not Israel but the church.

Brimstone and Fire. The symbols of divine wrath (Isa. xxx:33).

Candlestick, Golden. Symbolical of that which gives light. Representing the seven assemblies. The church is on earth to give light.

Crowns. The symbols of given glory and also rewards for service. The crowns seen upon the seven heads of the dragon (xii:3) and upon the four horns of the Beast (xiii:1) denote despotic authority.

David, Key of. Symbolical of the right to open and to enter in. See Isa. xxii:22. It is a prediction concerning Christ. The authority of the kingdom of heaven.

David, Root and Offspring. (xxii:16.) Christ is the Root and offspring of David.

Demons. Fallen spirit beings; the wicked spirits over which Satan is the head. They will be worshipped by the apostates during the end of the age. Demon-worship is even now going on to some extent, for the Antichristian cults are produced by demons (1 Tim. iv:1.) See Rev. ix:20-21. The word devils must be changed to demons. There is but one Devil, but legions of demons.

Dwellers on the Earth. This class mentioned repeatedly in Revelation are the large number of professing Christians, who did not receive the love of the truth and rejecting the Gospel follow the strong delusion and are utterly blinded, as well as hardened, during the tribulation.

Eagle. (viii:13.) The word angel must be changed to "eagle." Symbolical of the coming judgment, as an eagle is a bird of prey. Eagle's wings (xii:13-17) are symbolical of swift motion, escape and deliverance.

Earth. The prophetic territory of the Roman empire is mostly described by this form, though the entire earth is also indicated.

Earthquake. Symbolical of the shaking of all political and ecclesiastical institutions. But, as we show in our exposition, literal earthquakes will take place.

Elders, Twenty-four. The twenty-four elders typify all the redeemed in Glory. Old and New Testament Saints are included. After chapter xix this term does not appear again, because the church, the bride of Christ, is then seen separate from the entire company of the redeemed, and takes her exalted position as the Lamb's wife.

Eternal State, The. The eternal state is described in chapter xxi:1-8.

Euphrates. This great river is mentioned twice in Revelation, ix:14 and xvi:12. It is the boundary line of the Roman empire and the land of Israel. See exposition of these passages.

Everlasting Gospel. (xiv:6.) The declaration of the Gospel of the Kingdom during the tribulation, and the proclamation of God as Creator to the heathen nations of the world, to prepare them for the gospel of the kingdom.

Fire. Often mentioned in this book and symbolical of the judgments which will be executed upon the earth as well as the everlasting wrath upon the unsaved.

Fornication. Spiritual wickedness in departing from the Truth of God, followed by the literal lusts of the flesh. The days of Lot will be on the earth before the Son of Man cometh.

Four. This number appears a number of times in Revelation. Four living creatures; four corners of the earth; four horns of the golden altar; four angels; four winds. Four is the number of universality.

Frogs. Mentioned between the sixth and seventh vial. Symbolical of demon influences, denoting filthy and wicked things. Frogs come out of slimy and dark waters; evil doctrines.

Glass, Sea of. (Chapter iv:6.) Compare with Exod. xxx:18-21 and 1 Kings vii:23, etc. Symbolical of fixed lasting holiness. No more water needed for cleansing from sin, for the Saints in Glory are delivered from the presence of sin itself.

God, Supper of. (Chapter xix:17.) Symbolical of God's judgment upon the wicked nations and the earth dwellers.

Gold. Symbolical of divine righteousness.

Grass. (viii:7.) Symbolical of human prosperity (Isa. xl:7 and 1 Peter i:24).

Hades. The region of disembodied spirits; literally "the unknown." Christ has the Keys. Hades with Death, because they came into existence through sin, will be cast into the Lake of fire.

Harvest of the Earth. The harvest is the end of the age. In chapter xiv:14-15 we read of the Lord's judgment dealing with the earth.

Hidden Manna. (ii:17.) Symbolical of the reward those who overcome will receive from the Lord.

Horns. Horn is symbolical of power. Horns mean typically kings, and powers and kingdoms (Dan. vii:24).

Image of the Beast. (xiii:12-15.) Compare with Dan. iii It will be a literal image of the princely leader of the revived Roman empire, the first Beast, which John saw rising out of the sea.

Islands. Mentioned under the sixth seal and the seventh vial. Mountains typify kingdoms and governments; islands are symbolical of smaller and isolated governments. All will be affected. No doubt when the great earthquakes will shake the very foundations of the earth, many islands will also disappear.

Jasper. A precious stone, most likely our diamond. See exposition of chapter iv.

Jerusalem. The earthly and the heavenly Jerusalem are mentioned in the book. During the tribulation the earthly Jerusalem will be the seat of the Antichrist, the false Prophet. Jerusalem is for this reason called "Sodom and Egypt" (xi:8). Then Jerusalem will pass through her worst history. A great siege will take place at the close of the tribulation period and the city will fall (Zech. xiv).

After that Jerusalem will become the capital of the kingdom of Christ and a great temple will be erected, the universal place of worship during the millennium. The heavenly Jerusalem is above the earth. From there the glorious reign of Christ and the Saints will be executed. This glorious city will come down out of heaven at the end of the millennium to find its eternal resting-place on the new earth. (Chapter xxi-xxii.)

Jezebel. Symbolical of the Papacy. The corruptress which claims to be the Bride of Christ, but plays the harlot. See chapters ii and xvii.

Judgment. Judgment falls upon the earth during the seven years, which constitute the end of the age. When the Lord comes in His glory the great judgment of the nations takes place. Chapter xix:11, etc., compare with Matt. xxv:31. After the millennium the second resurrection takes place and the great white throne judgment is the judgment of the wicked dead.

King of the Nations. (xv:2-4.) King of the Saints should be changed (see margin) to King of the nations. Our Lord is the King of the nations, the King of kings.

Lake of Fire. The place which God has prepared for the Devil and his angels. The Beast and the false prophet will be cast there; also the Assyrian, the King of the North, the nations who followed the Beast and all the wicked dead. Death and Hades will likewise be put into that place.

The Lamb. The Lamb (John i:29), our Lord in His sacrificial character, is mentioned twenty-eight times in Revelation. The Lamb is worshipped by all. Thus we find the Song of the Lamb, the Throne of the Lamb and the Marriage of the Lamb, and the Wife of the Lamb (the church) in this book.

Lightning. Symbolical of the divine judgment Wrath.

Locust Army. Symbolical of the host of demons, which come out of the abyss to torment mankind.

Lord's Day, The. Mentioned but once in i:10. It is the first day of the week on which John saw the great Patmos vision.

Man-child. (Chapter xii.) The Man-child is the Lord Jesus Christ.

Mark of the Beast. Some special mark which declares ownership. As the Holy Spirit seals those who trust on Christ, so Antichrist will put his mark upon those who follow him.

Millennium, The. Millennium means "a thousand years." Six times this period of blessing and glory is mentioned in Rev. xx.

Moon as blood. The Moon is symbolical of derived authority. Blood is the symbol of death. Apostate Israel and the apostate church passing through the most severe judgments are symbolized by this figure.

Morning Star, The. Christ in His Coming for the church. (Chapters xxii:16; ii:28).

Mountain. A kingdom.

Mountains, Seven. Rome is the city built upon the seven hills. See exposition of chapter xvii.

Nicolaitanes. Mentioned in the message of Ephesus and Pergamos. They signify the domineering, priestly class which assumed an unscriptural place of authority in the church.

Palms. Emblems of victory.

Rainbow. The symbol of covenant and of mercy. Mentioned twice. Around the Throne (chapter iv) and around His head (chapter x).

Rest of the Dead. (xx:5.) Meaning those who had not part in the First Resurrection, hence the wicked dead.

River of Life. (xxii:1.) Symbolical of the fullness of life, glory and blessing.

Saints. The Saints in Revelation include all the Saints. The Old and New Testament Saints are seen under the figure of the twenty-four elders. The suffering Saints are the Jewish Saints and the remnant of Israel, as well as the multitude of nations, who accept the final message and come out of the great tribulation (Chapter vii).

Satan. The entire book reveals his person, his work and his destiny. His work may be traced in the church-messages. Then we have his work during the tribulation and his final work after the millennium.

Scorpions. Symbolical of the torment caused by the army of demons under the fifth trumpet judgment.

Sea. Symbol of the nations. Also the literal sea, which gives up the dead. Then there will be no more sea. All wickedness and restlessness will cease forever.

Seven. The divine number. No other Book in the Bible contains so many "sevens" as this final Bible-book, the Revelation. There are seven angels, churches, attributes of the Lord, heads, horns, eyes, spirits, lamps, seals, trumpets, vials, plagues, stars, thunders, times and a sevenfold doxology.

Song. The songs of the Redeemed and the Song of Moses and the Lamb are mentioned in the Book.

Stars. See exposition on the meaning of the seven stars in His hand. Stars are also symbolical of lesser authorities, which will all fall during the tribulation period. Lights in the night.

Sun. The symbol of supreme authority.

Synagogue of Satan. Mentioned in the messages to Smyrna and Philadelphia. It means a Judaized Christianity as seen in Ritualistic, professing Christendom.

Temple. The tribulation temple is in view in chapter xi:1-3. The millennial temple is seen in vii:15. Then there is the temple in heaven (chapter xvi:17). In the heavenly Jerusalem there is no temple (xxi:22).

Third Part. Mentioned in connection with men, the sea, the stars of heaven, the Sun and the Moon. It probably refers exclusively to the Roman empire, which in its different aspects and authorities, will be affected during these judgments.

Two horns. The Beast out of the land has two horns like a lamb, but speaks like the dragon. He is the counterfeit Christ.

Waters, Many. Symbolical of peoples and nations over which the Romish whore has authority.

White. Color of righteousness and purity; also denoting victorious conquests. We have in Revelation, white Robes, the white horses, white linen, a white cloud and a white Throne.

Witnesses. See in Rev. xi about the two witnesses.

Wrath. We read of the Wrath of God and the wrath of the Lamb. The wrath of God is completed with the pouring out of the vials. The wrath of the Lamb will be executed when He comes in Glory.

Zion. Mentioned only once in Rev., chapter xiv:1. It means the literal Zion in Palestine. Upon that holy hill of Zion the glory will rest during the millennium. See Psalm cxxxii:13-14.